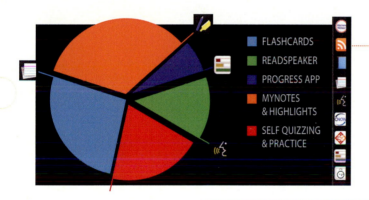
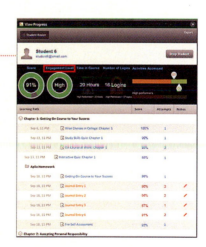

Beginning Essentials in Early Childhood Education

Third Edition

Ann Miles Gordon

Kathryn Williams Browne

Skyline College

CENGAGE

Australia • Brazil • Mexico • Singapore • United Kingdom • United States

*Beginning Essentials in Early Childhood
Education,* Third Edition
**Ann Miles Gordon and Kathryn
Williams Browne**

Product Director: Marta E. Lee-Perriard

Product Manager: Mark Kerr

Associate Content Developer: Naomi Dreyer

Product Assistant: Julia Catalano

Marketing Manager: Chris Sosa

Content Project Manager: Samen Iqbal

Art Director: Marissa Falco

Manufacturing Planner: Doug Bertke

IP Analyst: Jennifer Nonenmacher

IP Project Manager: Brittani Hall

Production Service/Project Manager: Teresa
Christie

Photo Researcher: Sofia Priya Dharshini, Lumina
Datamatics Ltd.

Text Researcher: Kavitha Balasundaram, Lumina
Datamatics Ltd.

Cover and Text Designer: Jeanne Calabrese

Cover Image Credit: © Sunny studio
/Shutterstock.com

Compositor: MPS Limited

For product information and technology assistance, contact us at
**Cengage Customer & Sales Support, 1-800-354-9706
or support.cengage.com.**

For permission to use material from this text or product, submit all
requests online at **www.cengage.com/permissions.**

Library of Congress Control Number: 2014940084

Student Edition:
ISBN-13: 978-1-305-08903-7

Loose-leaf Edition:
ISBN-13: 978-1-305-49691-0

Cengage
20 Channel Street
Boston, MA 02210
USA

Cengage is a leading provider of customized learning solutions with
employees residing in nearly 40 different countries and sales in more than
125 countries around the world. Find your local representative at:
www.cengage.com.

Cengage products are represented in Canada by Nelson Education, Ltd.

To learn more about Cengage platforms and services, register or access your
online learning solution, or purchase materials for your course,
visit **www.cengage.com.**

Printed atCLDPC,USA,02-20

Brief Contents

iii

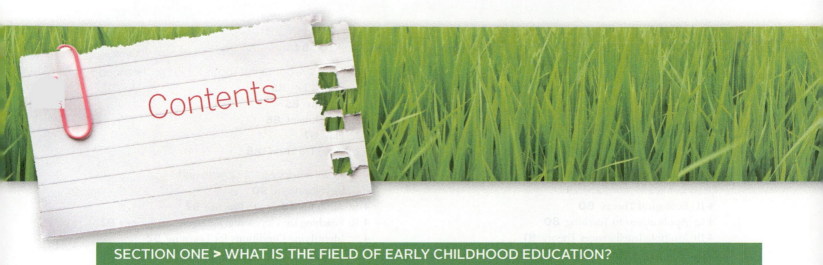

Contents

SECTION THREE > WHO ARE THE TEACHERS?

© iStockphoto.com/Jose Alva

Families and Teachers: An Essential Partnership **158**

SECTION FOUR > WHAT IS BEING TAUGHT?

Creating Environments **172**

Curriculum Essentials **200**

Preface

Our Mission: The Essential Approach

Tomorrow's teachers will confront the challenge of teaching a diverse group of learners differentiated by their abilities, ethnic and cultural backgrounds, family support, values, and beliefs. They will learn to navigate the tension between standards and assessments, and developmentally appropriate principles and practice. New teachers must understand the meaning of professionalism and how their personal development fosters their professional commitment. In order to accomplish this daunting but exciting task, students need a text that is current, comprehensive, and able to connect knowledge and theory to the classroom—one that has eclectic viewpoints and a variety of models that depend on their understanding of themselves as members of a lively and fulfilling profession. *Beginning Essentials in Early Childhood Education* accomplishes that goal.

The purpose of *Beginning Essentials* is to promote the competence and effectiveness of new teachers through the *essentials*: the absolute basic and indispensable elements that create a foundation for teaching young children. These *essentials* include knowledge, skills, attitudes, and philosophies to help form the teaching experience. The authors express a viewpoint about quality early education and what practices ensure excellence. In the area of cultural sensitivity and multicultural relationships, a "both/and" attitude is encouraged, following the National Association for the Education of Young Children (NAEYC) guidelines for developmentally appropriate practices. The value of learning how to use the NAEYC Code of Ethical Conduct is highlighted in each chapter, as is the importance of adapting the NAEYC Standards for Early Childhood Professional Preparation.

Beginning Essentials maintains that every child and family is unique and that they deserve the respect and affirmation of their cultural identity. The text weaves a strong multicultural perspective and consciousness throughout in order to help prospective teachers and caregivers increase their sensitivity to different cultural practices and values.

How Do We Meet the Needs of Today's Learners?

Beginnings Essentials is intended for college students who are interested in young children, beginning teachers who plan to engage in early care and education, practitioners in direct services to children and families, and professionals in the workforce who are enlarging their knowledge base. Throughout our comprehensive chapter coverage and unique pedagogical features, we provide a resource that meets the needs of today's early childhood educators.

Chapter Organization

The book is organized into four sections, each of which asks one of the questions that defines the comprehensive nature of teaching young children: (1) What Is the Field of Early Childhood Education? (2) Who Is the Young Child? (3) Who Are the Teachers? and (4) What Is Being Taught? The book's flexibility allows instructors to begin with any section that seems appropriate to meet the needs of their classes.

Section 1: What Is the Field of Early Childhood Education?

Descriptions of early childhood history, current issues, and the types of programs provide a basis for understanding the complexity of the field.

In Chapter 1, history and current issues are combined to give students a sense of progression and a feel for issues that are challenging today's teachers. The past and the present are woven into a smooth story with four key themes: the importance of childhood, social reform, transmitting values, and professionalism.

Chapter 2 moves the student directly into the variety and depth of early childhood programs and the importance of developmentally appropriate practice (DAP) in creating good programs. The principles of DAP are matched with examples of DAP in action so that students will see a direct correlation between the DAP criteria and classroom application.

Section 2: Who Is the Young Child?

This section begins with a discussion of the young child's growth, followed by an overview of the developmental and learning theories that form the cornerstone of our knowledge about children.

Chapter 3 provides students with an understanding of the nature of the children they will teach and their common characteristics and wide individual differences. Word Pictures, which are age-level descriptions, are a popular feature with students who have used this text, as they enable students to anticipate children's needs and plan appropriate experiences for them.

Chapter 4 gives the student concise descriptions of universal and life-span theories and other developmental topics on which sound teaching principles and practices are based. Play, as a cornerstone of learning, and updated information on brain-based research provide further application of theory to classroom use.

Section 3: Who Are the Teachers?

This section defines the aggregate of influences that teachers in the early childhood setting reflect. Each chapter enlarges the student's view of what makes up a professional teacher.

Chapter 5 describes the roles and responsibilities of an early childhood teacher as "professionalism in action" and introduces students to a broader definition of teaching. Examples of everyday ethical situations provide opportunities for students to discuss their own values and beliefs in response to the NAEYC Code of Ethical Conduct. The chapter also explores team-teaching situations and the importance of teacher evaluations.

Chapter 6 enhances the student's ability to observe, record, and assess the behavior of young children. Along with a comprehensive description of observation tools and effective techniques, there are updated segments about child evaluation, early learning standards, and concerns about testing and screening.

Chapter 7 demonstrates how guidance and behavior are critical factors in the life of a classroom teacher. Problem solving, conflict resolution, and a wide range of guidance techniques give students the necessary tools to guide young children toward their potential.

Chapter 8 offers a perspective on the all-important collaboration of families and teachers in creating the best possible learning environment for young children. Discussions of the definitions of family, today's family structures, and challenges facing families bring a relevancy to students.

Section 4: What Is Being Taught?

This section reflects on what is being taught through the environment and the basic elements of creating curriculum.

Chapter 9 defines the characteristics of high-quality environments that include elements of health, safety, and nutrition, as well as anti-bias and self-help approaches and the inclusion of children with disabilities. The student learns how the deliberate use of the environment serves as a teaching strategy for appropriate behavior and learning.

Chapter 10 is based on the premise that a play-based curriculum is the foundation for early childhood learning, and the chapter provides students with examples of developmentally and culturally appropriate approaches. Students will learn the importance of play, emergent and integrated curricula, projects, and how different learning styles can be applied to curriculum development. A summary of curriculum models and their key characteristics and philosophies demonstrate the application of DAP in the classroom.

Special Features and Pedagogy

We offer numerous learning aids and engaging features to enrich the learning experience of students and to connect theory to practice. These include:

- **Student Learning Outcomes** at the beginning of each chapter are correlated to the main sections in each chapter and show students what they need to know to process and understand the information in the chapter. After completing the chapter, students should be able to demonstrate how they can use and apply their new knowledge and skills.
- **Truth or Fiction Questions** at the beginning of each chapter engage students' curiosity as they find the content and answers highlighted in each chapter.
- **NAEYC Standards** for Early Childhood Professional Preparation at the beginning of each chapter relate to chapter content, stressing the importance of becoming familiar with professional requirements and accountability.
- **Teacher Talks,** found in each chapter, are personal stories by early childhood educators that add a realistic image to the art of being a classroom teacher. Each vignette brings to light an issue or reflection that all teachers face at one time or another.
- **Special Focus Boxes** discuss themes of primary importance. Each chapter will have highlighted feature boxes on *Diversity, DAP* (developmentally appropriate practice), *Professionalism, Standards,* and *Ethics* that emphasize for students the importance of these themes in the early childhood field.
- **Key Terms** are embedded in the margins of each chapter and located where they are introduced to remind the student of the most important concepts.
- **TeachSource Video** features allow students and instructors to relate important chapter content to real-life

scenarios in early child care settings. TeachSource Videos provide students with an opportunity to hear from real educators who are doing the work that they are preparing to do. The TeachSource Videos and other engaging video clips provided on the Education CourseMate website offer critical-thinking questions and give students ample opportunities for reflection and discussion.

- The Word Pictures special section in Chapter 3 describes the major characteristics of children from infancy through 8 years of age. This popular feature helps students become familiar with expected behaviors in young children as a frame of reference for creating programs and planning curriculum that responds to the children's interests as well as their abilities and needs.

- End-of-Chapter Aids provide the student with an overall review of the material within the chapter. The Summary is aligned with the Learning Outcomes at the beginning of the chapter and emphasizes how the key Standards and Learning Outcomes were achieved.

- Correlation Chart to the latest NAEYC Standards for Early Childhood Professional Preparation is found on the inside covers of this book, helping students make connections between what they are learning in the textbook and the standards. The handy chart makes it easy to see where the key standards in the field are addressed in specific chapters and topics throughout the text.

- Culturally Appropriate Practice and DAP continue to be the subtheme of *Beginning Essentials* through the emphasis on an understanding of the child and the **factors affecting a child's growth and development.** We believe it is important that students realize the deep and crucial contributions that children's families, cultures, and languages make to development. NAEYC's years of experience in the definition and application of DAP has given further insights, which are reflected throughout the book.

What's New in This Edition

The third edition of *Beginning Essentials* represents a completely updated work, both in the content and presentation. Some highlights of the new coverage and features include:

- NEW—Teacher Talks, written experiences from classroom teachers, are found in every chapter to bring the reality of the classroom to students. These vignettes enhance the student's understanding of the variety of roles and responsibilities teachers have as well as provide a window to the personal and professional growth of a teacher.

- NEW—Brain Research Says.... is a new feature in each chapter that highlights some of the most important aspects of brain research and development today. The research is linked to classroom use and teacher application through questions that invite students to reflect on how this information relates to their teaching.

- NEW—Teachsource Digital Downloads are downloadable, practical, and professional resources, often customizable, that allow students to immediately implement and apply the textbook's content in the field. The student downloads these tools and keeps them forever, enabling pre-service teachers to being to build their library of practical, professional resources. Look for the TeachSource Digital Downloads label that identifies these items.

- NEW—Special Focus Boxes add greater depth and information in many chapters.

- NEW—Topics such as technology in the classroom, media culture, behavior that is challenging, and intentional and reflective teaching have been added to broaden the students knowledge of early education.

- NEW—The addition of a chart on Developmentally Appropriate Curriculum Models clarifies and defines the differences and similarities of early childhood programs.

- NEW—Updated and revised charts, checklists, and figures support each chapter's content and highlight important information for the student.

- NEW—TeachSource Videos feature footage from the classroom to help students relate key chapter content to real-life scenarios. Critical-thinking questions provide opportunities for in-class or online discussion and reflection.

Accompanying Teaching and Learning Resources

The third edition of *Beginning Essentials* offers many ancillary materials that can support and enhance the text experience and an instructor's presentation of the course. From planning to presentation to testing, materials are available to provide students with an engaging and relevant exposure to the broad scope of topics in early childhood education.

Instructor's Manual and Test Bank

An online Instructor's Manual accompanies this book. The instructor's manual contains information to assist the instructor in designing the course, including teaching tips, chapter outlines, review questions, key terms, additional readings, chapter summaries, and resource lists. For assessment support, the updated test bank includes true/false, multiple-choice, matching, and short answer questions for each chapter.

PowerPoint® Lecture Slides

Helping make your lectures more engaging, these handy Microsoft® PowerPoint® slides outline the chapters of the main text in a classroom-ready presentation, making it easy for instructors to assemble, edit, publish, and present custom lectures.

Cognero

Cengage Learning Testing Powered by Cognero is an online system that allows you to author, edit, and manage test bank content from multiple Cengage Learning solutions; create multiple test versions in an instant; and deliver tests from your LMS, your classroom, or wherever you want.

MindTap™: The Personal Learning Experience

MindTap for Gordon/Browne, *Beginning Essentials* 3e represents a new approach to teaching and learning. A highly personalized, fully customizable learning platform, MindTap helps students to elevate thinking by guiding them to:

- Know, remember, and understand concepts critical to becoming a great teacher;
- Apply concepts, create tools, and demonstrate performance and competency in key areas in the course;
- Prepare artifacts for the portfolio and eventual state licensure, to launch a successful teaching career; and
- Develop the habits to become a reflective practitioner.

As students move through each chapter's Learning Path, they engage in a scaffolded learning experience, designed to move them up Bloom's Taxonomy, from lower- to higher-order thinking skills. The Learning Path enables pre-service students to develop these skills and gain confidence by:

- Engaging them with chapter topics and activating their prior knowledge by watching and answering questions about TeachSource videos of teachers teaching and children learning in real classrooms;
- Checking their comprehension and understanding through *Did You Get It?* assessments, with varied question types that are autograded for instant feedback;
- Applying concepts through mini-case scenarios—students analyze typical teaching and learning situations and create a reasoned response to the issue(s) presented in the scenario; and
- Reflecting about and justifying the choices they made within the teaching scenario problem.

MindTap helps instructors facilitate better outcomes by evaluating how future teachers plan and teach lessons in ways that make content clear and help diverse students learn, assessing the effectiveness of their teaching practice, and adjusting teaching as needed. The Student Progress App makes grades visible in real time so students and instructors always have access to current standings in the class.

MindTap for Gordon/Browne, *Beginning Essentials* 3e helps instructors easily set their course since it integrates into the existing Learning Management System and saves instructors time by allowing them to fully customize any aspect of the Learning Path. Instructors can change the order of the student learning activities, hide activities they don't want for the course, and—most importantly—add any content they do want (e.g., YouTube videos, Google docs, links to state education standards). Learn more at www.cengage.com/mindtap.

MindTap Moves Students Up Bloom's Revised Taxonomy

Create
Evaluate
Analyze
Apply
Understand
Remember & Know

Anderson, L. W., & Krathwohl, D. (Eds.). (2001). *A taxonomy for learning, teaching, and assessing: A revision of Bloom's taxonomy of educational objectives.* New York: Longman.

About the Authors

Ann Miles Gordon has been an early childhood professional for more than 45 years as a teacher of young children, a teacher of parents, and a teacher of college students. She has taught in laboratory schools, church-related centers, and private and public preschool and kindergarten programs. Ann taught at the Bing Nursery School, the laboratory school for Stanford University's Department of Psychology, where she was a head teacher and lecturer in the Psychology Department. Ann also served as an adjunct faculty member in several community colleges, teaching the full gamut of early childhood courses. Ann served as executive director of the National Association of Episcopal Schools for 14 years, where more than 1,100 early childhood programs were a part of her network. Ann is semi-retired and a hands-on grandmother of two, through which she brings an enhanced perspective on center-based care and early elementary grades.

Kathryn Williams Browne has been teaching children, families, and students for more than 40 years. First a teacher of young children—nursery school, parent cooperative, full-day child care, pre-kindergarten, bilingual pre-school, kindergarten and first grade, she moved to Stanford University's lab school, where she served as head teacher and psychology lecturer. Co-authoring with Ann was enhanced by Kate's role as a parent; her consultant and school board experience offered perspectives into public policy and reform. Kate teaches in the California Community College system, directing the ECE/EDU Department and Early Childhood Mentor program, which offer the richness of a diverse student population coupled with the challenges of access and privilege that parallel those in the early education field itself. She is active in faculty both on cam-

pus and statewide, and serves as an advocate on early learning issue, and the special challenges of diversity and professional of early childhood education guide her work.

Ann and Kate are also co-authors of *Early Childhood Field Experience: Learning to Teach Well* (Pearson, 2012); *Guiding Young Children in a Diverse Society*, and *Beginnings and Beyond: Foundations in Early Childhood Education*, 9th edition (Wadsworth/Cengage, 2014).

Acknowledgments

At Cengage Learning, we would like to thank Naomi Dreyer, our development editor, for her skillful guidance, constant encouragement, and gentle nudging to keep us on track, and the entire Cengage team for their professionalism and support.

We owe a great deal to our reviewers whose valuable gift of time and wisdom enhances the book's usefulness. Those whom we wish to thank for their superb insights and suggestions include the following: Alan Weber (Suffolk County Community College), Benita Flores (Del Mar College), Mandy White (Caldwell Community College and Technical Institute), Kathryn Stead (Central Maine Community College), Sara Spruce (Olivet Nazarene University), Marissa Happ (Waubonsee Community College), Christy Cornelius (Jefferson College), and Carol Kessler (Cabrini College).

Classroom teachers who provided Teacher Talks added an important dimension to this edition. We would like to thank Claudia Martin, Daniele Koenig, Teresa Campbell, Tracy Pierce, Michele McLaughlin, and Kathy Wilson, among several who shared their experience and insights.

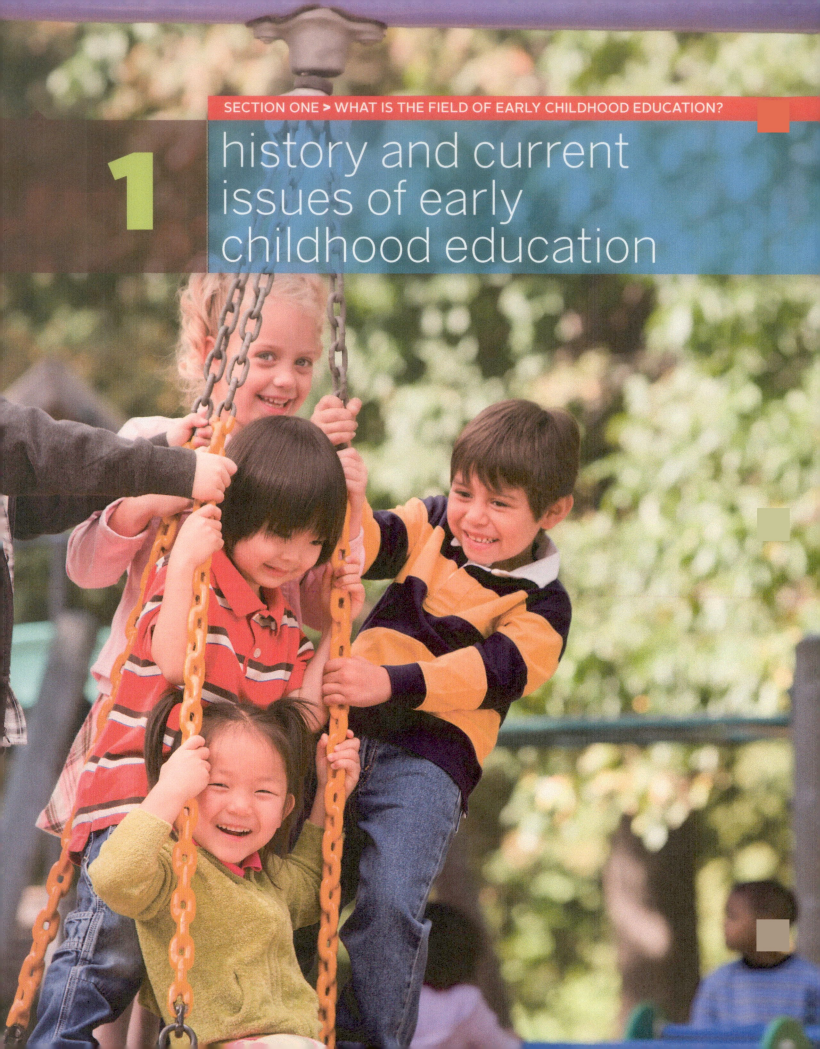

1

history and current issues of early childhood education

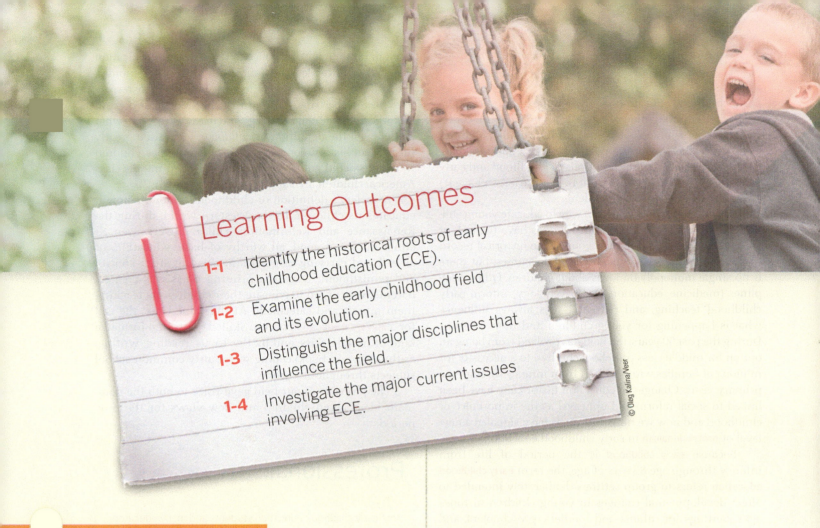

Learning Outcomes

1-1 Identify the historical roots of early childhood education (ECE).

1-2 Examine the early childhood field and its evolution.

1-3 Distinguish the major disciplines that influence the field.

1-4 Investigate the major current issues involving ECE.

© Oleg Kalina/Veer

NAEYC Standards

The following NAEYC Standards For Early Childhood Professional Preparation are addressed in this chapter:

Standard 1: Promoting Child Development and Learning

Standard 2: Building Family and Community Relationships

Standard 6: Becoming a Professional

truth *or* *fiction*

T F The historical roots of early childhood education are primarily from the United States.

T F The core of the early childhood education field is nursery and preschool for young children.

T F The disciplines of Medicine and Psychology have major impacts on the field.

T F Family stressors such as work and poverty are eliminated by sending children to good early education programs.

T F Standards for teacher preparation are universal.

1-1 Historical Roots of Early Childhood Education

Early childhood education is a rich and exciting field. The story of its development is also the chronicle of courageous people who took steps toward improving children's lives. Critical events of the past have had a hand in shaping today's issues. As the conditions of childhood and early education have changed through the centuries, so have its educators adapted to those challenges.

There is more than one right way to educate young children. Every culture has had and still does have the task of socializing and educating their young. The historical record may document several educational philosophies, but there is no single monopoly on ideas about children. Other disciplines (medicine, education, and psychology) inform early childhood teaching, and current issues always influence what is happening for young children and their teachers. During the past 50 years, the field has evolved from being an option for middle-class preschool children to a necessity for millions of families with children from infancy through the primary years. Changes in education historically have been linked to social reform and upheaval as the importance of childhood and how we transmit values have signaled a new level of professionalism in early childhood education.

Because early childhood is the period of life from infancy through age 8 years of age, the term early childhood education refers to group settings deliberately intended to effect developmental changes in young children of those ages. Settings for infants and toddlers, preschoolers, and children kindergarten through grade three (sometimes all elementary grades) all require professionals who build bridges between a child's two worlds: school (or group experience) and home. It is during these years that the foundation for future learning is set; these are the *building-block years,* during which a child learns to walk, talk, establish an identity, make friends, print, and count. In later years, that same child builds on these skills to be able to ride a bike, speak a second language, learn to express and negotiate, write in cursive, and understand multiplication.

1-1a Influences from Abroad

It is impossible to pinpoint the origins of humankind because there are few records from millions of years ago. Some preparation for adult life was done informally, mostly through imitation. As language developed, communication occurred. Children learned dances, rituals, and ceremonies, and both boys and girls were taught skills for their respective roles in the tribe. Ancient historical documents seem to indicate that child-rearing practices were somewhat crude. Even the definition of *childhood* has varied greatly throughout history. For example, in ancient times, children were considered adults by 7 years of age; in middle-class America, children are supported into their early 20s.

A society's definition of childhood influences how it educates its children. In the Western world, during the Renaissance and Reformation, children were seen as either pure and good, all worthy of basic education, or as evil and carrying original sin, needing strict control and punishment. Once the printing press was created, parents were urged to educate their children by teaching them morals and catechism. At the same time, the call for a universal education began. Skilled craftsmen formed a kind of middle class, and by the 1500s, reading, writing, arithmetic, and bookkeeping were fairly common school subjects throughout Europe.

The pioneers of our field gave voice to both the dominant ideas about children and new views for the time period.

Professionalism

Why History?

Most early childhood education students and many educators know little about the origins of their chosen profession. To better inform your teaching practice, link the past to the present so that you will receive the following:

> **Support:** Works of Froebel, Montessori, and Dewey are part of the philosophical foundation on which our educational practices are built. Traditional early childhood practices reflect European values and beliefs. Looking beyond the dominant culture, oral and written records exist describing education in Africa and Asia. Focus on many cultures to broaden everyone's viewpoints.

> **Inspiration:** Knowing our deep roots helps develop professional expression. Ideas of past educators offer you more methods of teaching. An historical overview clarifies how children and learning are viewed based on the religious, political, and economic pressures.

> **Identity and commitment:** Each of us accepts the mission that is central to our field: We are committed to enhancing the education, development, and well-being of young children. We also recognize that it is a reflection of certain cultural norms. Be cautious of theories or opinions claiming to be "universal." For instance, history notes that schools of the past were overwhelmingly created for boys; this gender bias of past practices adds to the underdevelopment of girls and prevails today in parts of the world.

---

professionalism. The competence or skill expected of a professional; in early childhood education, this includes a sense of identity, purpose to engage in developmentally appropriate practices, a commitment to ethical teaching and to child advocacy, and participation in the work as a legitimate livelihood.

early childhood. The period of life from infancy through 8 years of age.

early childhood education. Education in the early years of life; the field of study that deals mainly with the learning and experiences of children from infancy through the primary years (up to approximately 8 years of age).

universal education. Education for all, regardless of race/ethnicity, culture, gender, status, sexual orientation, or religion.

Comenius

John Amos Comenius (1592–1670), a Czech educator, wrote the first picture book for children. Called *Orbis Pictus* (*The World of Pictures,* 1658), it was a guide for teachers that included training of the senses and the study of nature. Comenius believed that "in all the operations of nature, development is from within," so children should be allowed to learn at their own pace and to learn by doing. Teachers should work with children's own inclinations, for "what is natural takes place without compulsion." This idea was later reflected in Montessori's "sensitive periods." Comenius encouraged parents to let their children play with other children of the same age. He also reflected the growing social reform that would educate the poor as well as the rich.

Locke

An English philosopher, John Locke (1632–1714) is considered to be the founder of modern educational philosophy. He based his theory of education on the scientific method and the study of the mind and learning. Locke proposed the concept of tabula rasa, the belief that the child is born

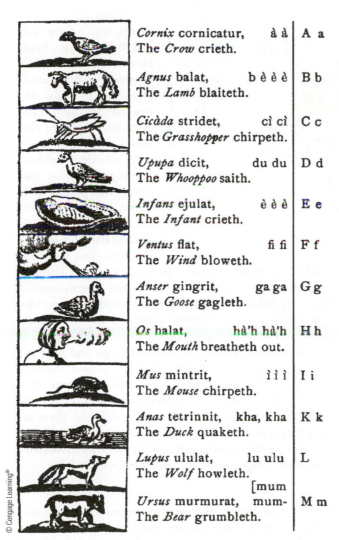

Cornix cornicatur, à à		A a
The *Crow* crieth.		
Agnus balat, b è è è		B b
The *Lamb* blaiteth.		
Cicàda stridet, cì cì		C c
The *Grasshopper* chirpeth.		
Upupa dicit, du du		D d
The *Whooppoo* saith.		
Infans ejulat, è è è		E e
The *Infant* crieth.		
Ventus flat, fi fi		F f
The *Wind* bloweth.		
Anser gingrit, ga ga		G g
The *Goose* gagleth.		
Os halat, hà'h hà'h		H h
The *Mouth* breatheth out.		
Mus mintrit, ì ì ì		I i
The *Mouse* chirpeth.		
Anas tetrinnit, kha, kha		K k
The *Duck* quaketh.		
Lupus ululat, lu ulu		L
The *Wolf* howleth.		
Ursus murmurat, mum- [mum		M m
The *Bear* grumbleth.		

Figure 1-1 *Orbis Pictus,* by John Comenius, is considered the first picture book written for children.

neutral, rather than either good or evil, and is a "clean slate" on which the experiences of parents, society, education, and the world are written. Because Locke believed that the purpose of education is to make man a reasoning creature, a working knowledge of the Bible and a counting ability sufficient to conduct business was fundamental. Locke suggested that instruction should be pleasant, with playful activities as well as drills. He based his theory on the Scientific Method, used extensively in Behaviorist research, and was one of the first European educators to discuss the idea of individual differences gleaned from observing one child rather than simply teaching a group, later reflected in Piaget's work.

Rousseau

Jean Jacques Rousseau (1712–1778), a writer and philosopher, believed that children were not inherently evil, but naturally good. He is best known for his book *Émile* (1761), in which he raised a hypothetical child to adulthood. Rousseau's ideas were revolutionary for the times. They include the following:

> The true object of education should not be primarily vocational.
> Children really learn only from firsthand information.
> Children's view of the external world is quite different from that of adults.
> There are distinct phases of development of a child's mind that should coincide with the various stages of education.

Rousseau thought that the school atmosphere should be very flexible to meet the needs of children and insisted on using concrete teaching materials, leaving the abstract and symbolic for later years. Pestalozzi, Froebel, Montessori, and Dewey were greatly influenced by him, as were the theories of Piaget and Gesell.

Pestalozzi

Johann Heinrich Pestalozzi (1746–1827) was a Swiss educator whose principles focused on how to teach basic skills and the idea of "caring" as well as "educating" the child. Pestalozzi stressed the idea of the integrated curriculum that would develop the whole child; education was to be of the hand, the head, and the heart. He differed from Rousseau in that he proposed teaching children in groups rather than using a tutor with an individual child, blending Rousseau's romantic ideals into a more egalitarian focus on skill building and independence. Pestalozzi's works *How Gertrude Teaches Her Children* and *Book for Mothers* detailed some procedures for mothers to use at home with their children.

tabula rasa. A mind not affected yet by experiences, sensations, and the like. In John Locke's theory, a child was born with this "clean slate" upon which all experiences were written.

integrated curriculum. A set of courses designed to form a whole; coordination of the various areas of study, making for continuous and harmonious learning.

DAP

The Umbrella Unfolds

Developmentally appropriate practice (DAP) defines modern early childhood education. Yet DAP has its roots in history. See both as your read DAP's distinctive focus on the following three components:

> **Age-appropriateness.** What is known about child development and learning informs professionals about age-related characteristics and skills. Rousseau, Montessori, Gesell, and Piaget all ascribed to the notion that the age of the child indicates basic abilities, outlooks, and behaviors.

> **Individual appropriateness.** Every child is unique, with an individual set of personal traits and responses that adults should take into consideration when planning educational experiences for that child. Locke, Montessori, and the schools of Reggio Emilia all celebrate the primacy of the individual.

> **Social and cultural responsiveness.** Children are members of a family, with language and cultural influences that affect who they are and how they might learn best. As children are exposed to a neighborhood, the media, and schooling, they remain rooted in their home values, expectations, and habits. Comenius, Froebel, and Dewey, as well as current best practices, recommend that early educational experiences be meaningful and relevant to children's lives.

Open the three-handled umbrella to ensure that you are "triple-hooked" to what is best for young children.

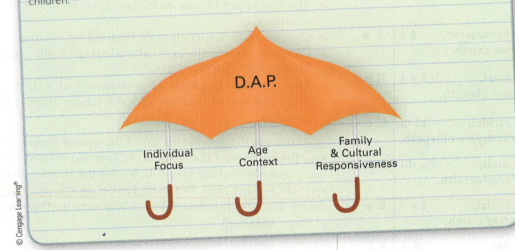

D.A.P.

Individual Focus   Age Context   Family & Cultural Responsiveness

Froebel

Friedrich Wilhelm August Froebel (1782–1852) is known to us as the "father of the kindergarten" (from the German *kinder garten,* "children's garden"). Froebel started his kindergarten in 1836, for children ages about 2 to 6 years, after he had studied with Pestalozzi in Switzerland and had read Comenius. In his book *Education of Man,* he wrote: "Play is the highest phase of child development—the representation of the inner necessity and impulse," so his classroom included blocks, pets, and finger plays. He designed what we now think were the first educational toys, which he

---

developmentally appropriate practices (DAP). That which is suitable or fitting to the development of the child; refers to those teaching practices that are based on the observation and responsiveness to children as learners with developing abilities who differ from one another by rate of growth and individual differences, rather than of differing amounts of abilities. It also refers to learning experiences that are relevant to and respectful of the social and cultural aspects of the children and their families.

---

termed "gifts." These objects demonstrated various attributes (such as color or size), were to be arranged in a special order that would assist the child's development, and were later expanded on by Montessori.

Worldwide, teachers practice the Froebelian belief that a child's first educational experiences should be a garden: full of pleasant discoveries and delightful adventure, where the adults' role is to plant ideas and materials for children to use as they grow at their own pace.

Montessori

At the turn of the 19th and 20th centuries, Maria Montessori (1870–1952) became the first female physician in Italy. She worked in the slums of Rome with poor children and with mentally retarded children. Sensing that what they lacked was proper motivation and environment, she opened a preschool, *Casa di Bambini,* in 1907. Her first class was composed of 50 children from 2 to 5 years of age. The children were at the center all day while their parents worked. They were fed two meals a day, given a bath, and provided medical attention. Montessori designed materials, classrooms, and a teaching procedure that proved her point to the astonishment of people all over Europe and America. After Montessori was introduced in the United States in 1909, her methods received poor reception and were often misunderstood. Today, most Montessori schools are private preschools and child care centers, although there are many that also serve elementary students, and a small (but growing) number of programs are for infants and toddlers. Montessori programs are explained in Chapter 2.

Steiner

Rudolf Steiner (1861–1925) was a German educator whose method is known today as the Waldorf School of Education. This system has influenced mainstream education in Europe, and its international reputation is felt in American

Why were early kindergartens patterned after Froebel's idea that play was the highest form of development? ◄

early childhood programs today. Steiner theorized that childhood is a phase of life important in its own right. It has three periods: that of the "will" (0 to 7 years), the "heart," or feelings (7 to 14 years), and the "head," or a fusion of the spirit and the body (14 years on). Early childhood is the period of the will, and the environment must be carefully planned to protect and nurture the child. Self-discipline emerges from the child's natural willingness to learn and initiate, so adult role-model experiences in early childhood must be carefully selected. For instance, fairy stories help children acquire time-honored wisdom; modern Waldorf followers insist that television be eliminated. The Waldorf program model is described in Chapter 2.

The McMillan Sisters

In the first three decades of the 20th century, the two McMillan sisters pioneered early education in England. Noticing the deplorable conditions in England for children younger than 5 years, Rachel and Margaret McMillan began a crusade for slum children. Health studies of the time showed that although 80% of London children were born in good health, by the time they entered school, only 20% could be classified that way. In 1910, the sisters set up a clinic in Deptford, a London slum area, which became an open-air nursery a year later. The McMillan sisters' regimen for their nursery school children of fresh air, sleep, and bathing proved successful. Although more than

> A child's first educational experiences should be a garden: full of pleasant discoveries and delightful adventure, where the adults' role is to plant ideas and materials for children to use as they grow at their own pace.

700 children between 1 and 5 years of age died of measles in London in about a 6-month period in 1914, there was not one fatal case at Deptford School.

Margaret McMillan invented the name "nursery school." She paid great attention to health: a daily inspection, the outdoor program, play, good food—what she called "nurture." But she saw that an educational problem was also involved and she set to work to establish her own method of education for young children. This was why she called it a "school" (Hymes, 1978–79).

1-1b American Influences

Colonial Days

The American educational system began in the colonies. The one-room schoolhouse was the mainstay of education in colonial New England. Children were sent to school primarily

Diversity

Non-Western Perspectives

Traditional early childhood educational practices reinforce European-American values and beliefs. But there are many ways to care for and educate children and nontraditional perspectives that influenced early childhood education.

> *China and Japan* were influenced by Confucius' writings (551–479 bc), which stressed harmony. Children were seen as good and worthy of respect, a view not held in Europe until later.

> *Native American* writings show close ties and interconnectedness not only among families and within tribes but also between people and nature. Teaching children about relationships and interconnectedness are historical themes of early education among many indigenous peoples.

> *Africans and African Americans* focus on strong **kinship networks**, in which people bond together and pool resources for the common good. These contemporary tendencies may come from ancient roots, historical oppression, modern injustice, or all three.

> *Hispanic and Latino* families model a goal of interdependence and learning to help others. In addition, common patterns of infant care include keeping a baby close and responding to crying quickly, which is an adaptive response to environmental hazards and concern for survival.

We must be careful in our assumptions of what we think is good or right for young children. A wider view of history reveals that there are many "right" ways, and much that is "good" comes from sharing our diverse viewpoints.

kinship networks. Groups formed when people bond together and pool resources for the common good.

for religious reasons. The Bible was used in school, as was the New England Primer and Horn Book. In the South, plantation owners imported tutors from England or opened small private schools to teach just their sons to read and write.

Children in Enslavement

The first African Americans were indentured servants, whose repayment of their debts by servitude would buy them their freedom. By 1620, Africans were being brought to the so-called New World as slaves. Before the Civil War, education was severely limited for African Americans. Formal schools were scarce, and most education came through the establishment of "Sabbath schools." As part of religious instruction, slaves were often provided literary training. However, many plantation owners found these schools threatening and banned them by making laws prohibiting the teaching of slaves. Another facility then developed, that of the "midnight school." Because of its necessary secretive existence, few records are available, although it is reasonable to conclude that the curriculum was similar to that of the prohibited Sabbath schools.

After the Civil War, private and public schools were opened for African Americans. Major colleges and universities were founded by the end of the 1800s. Booker T. Washington, born into slavery, founded the Tuskegee Normal and Industrial Institute in Alabama in 1881 and emphasized practical education and intercultural understanding between the races as a path to liberation. Many former slaves and graduates established schools for younger children.

John Dewey

By the end of the 1800s, a nationwide reform movement had begun. The Progressive Movement (see section later in the chapter) received its direction primarily through one individual, John Dewey (1858–1952). Dewey was the first real native-born influence on education in the United States and had one of the greatest impacts on American education of all time. He believed that children were valuable and that childhood was an important part of their lives. Like Froebel, he felt that education should be integrated with life and should provide a training ground for cooperative living.

As did Pestalozzi and Rousseau, Dewey felt that schools should focus on the nature of the child. Dewey's beliefs about children and learning are summarized in Figure 1-2.

Patty Smith Hill

Patty Smith Hill (1868–1946) of Teacher's College, Columbia University was an outstanding innovator of the time and one of the Progressive Movement's most able leaders. It was she who wrote the song "Happy Birthday" and founded the National Association for Nursery Education, known today as the National Association for the Education of Young Children (NAEYC). Trained originally in the Froebelian tradition, she worked closely with G. Stanley Hall and later with John Dewey. She advocated free choice and a relevant curriculum. She expanded the Froebelian focus on small-motor work to include large-muscle equipment for climbing and construction. She also urged that kindergarten and first grade be merged so that both groups would have independent, creative activity before formal academic instruction.

Lucy Sprague Mitchell

Early childhood education in the United States grew out of Dewey's progressive movement largely because of Lucy

truth or fiction?

T F The historical roots of early childhood education are primarily from the United States.

There are several European influences as well as non-Western perspectives that influence early childhood educational philosophy and practice.

Many graduates of Tuskegee and Hampton Institutes became teachers of African-American children of former slaves. ◄

Library of Congress Prints and Photographs Division Washington, D.C|LC-USZ62-26378|

Dewey's Creed	What It Means Today
1. "I believe that only true education comes through the stimulation of the child's powers by the demands of the social situations in which he finds himself."	Children learn to manage themselves in groups, to make and share friendships, to solve problems, and to cooperate.
2. "The child's own instinct and powers furnish the material and give the starting point for all education."	We need to create a place that is child centered, a place that values the skills and interests of each child and each group.
3. "I believe that education, therefore, is a process of living and not a preparation for future living."	Prepare the child for what is to come by enriching and interpreting the present to him. Find educational implications in everyday experiences.
4. "I believe that . . . the school life should grow gradually out of the home life . . . it is the business of the school to deepen and extend . . . the child's sense of the values bound up in his home life."	Values established and created in the home should be enhanced by teaching in the schools.

© Cengage Learning®

Figure 1-2 John Dewey believed that teachers are engaged in a dignified calling that included more than academic instruction; learning to live a social life was equally important, expressed in *My Pedagogic Creed* (Washington, DC: The Progressive Education Association, 1897). *(With special thanks to Sheila Roper of the MacClintock Photo Collection, Special Collections, Morris Library, Southern Illinois University at Carbondale.)*

Sprague Mitchell (1878–1967) and her contemporaries. Raised in an environment of educational and social reform, Mitchell developed the idea of schools as community centers as well as places for children to learn to think. She gathered together many talented people to build a laboratory

truth*or fiction*?

T F The core of the field is nursery and preschool for young children.

The traditional nursery school (preschool) exemplifies a developmental approach to learning where experiences are organized to meet all needs and serve children 2½ to 5 years of age.

school to implement and experiment with progressive principles, Bank Street College of Education to promote them, and a workshop for writers of children's literature. Mitchell became a major contributor to the idea of educational experiments, teacher-planned curriculum experiences that would then be observed and analyzed for children's reactions.

Abigail Eliot

Abigail Eliot (1892–1992) is generally credited with bringing the nursery school movement to the United States. She had worked with the McMillan sisters in the slums of London. As a social worker in Boston, she had visited many day nurseries and recalled them as places with "dull green walls, no light colors, nothing pretty—spotlessly clean places, with rows of white-faced listless little children sitting, doing nothing" (Hymes, 1978–79). She founded the Ruggles Street Nursery School, teaching children and providing teacher training, and was the first director until it was incorporated into Tufts University to become the Eliot-Pearson Department of Child Study. Eliot became the first woman to receive a doctoral degree from Harvard University's Graduate School of Education, and after retiring from Tufts, she moved to California, where she helped establish Pacific Oaks College.

1-2 The Field and Its Evolution

1-2a Nursery School

The very phrase *nursery school* conjures up images of a child's nursery, a gentle place of play and growing. Coined to describe a place in which children were nurtured by the McMillans and Eliot, the nursery school took Dewey's philosophy to heart. By the 1920s and 1930s, early childhood education had reached a professional status in the United States. Nursery schools and day nurseries went beyond custodial health care, fostering the child's total development. Their schools reflected the principles of a **child-centered approach**, active learning, and social cooperation. The children were enrolled from middle- and upper-class homes as well as from working-class families. However, until the 1960s, nursery schools served few poor families. Nursery schools are considered the core of early childhood education (see "Teacher Talks" in this chapter and Chapter 2).

Nursery schools [are about] fostering the child's total development . . . [and] reflect the principles of a child-centered approach, active learning, and social cooperation.

© iStockphoto.com/dalton00

child-centered approach. The manner of establishing educational experiences that takes into consideration children's ways of perceiving and learning; manner of organizing a classroom, schedule, and teaching methods with an eye toward the child's viewpoint.

Traditional nursery school is often called preschool. The developmental approach is influenced by the many early progressive thinkers in early childhood development, some being Pestalozzi, Froebel, Montessori, Dewey, Piaget and others. The main idea is to provide an environment for children to explore materials of their interest (free play) and have opportunities to develop social competence and emotional well-being. Katherine Read Baker best describes this in her classic book titled *The Nursery School: A Human Relationship Laboratory (1950)*. She developed an educational model that focuses on the child's needs, growth patterns and relationships with others.

This approach encourages young children to express themselves through creativity, physical activity, language and intellectual skill. Typically, nursery/preschools center on the child's social and emotional well-being which is why outdoor play also is a big part of the day. Outdoor play is developmentally appropriate because children are developing both fine and gross motor skills and they need the space to explore and develop these skills. Most have half-day schedules but many have extended days. These schools provide a variety of activities throughout the day including free choice indoors and outside, large and small muscle play, creative arts, social and dramatic play, building and construction with blocks and manipulative toys, and teacher-directed times.

The traditional Nursery school aligns with my values because I remember my nursery school vividly as my most enjoyable educational experience. When I went to elementary and middle school from 1st grade to 7th grade, I remember noticing the big difference in attitude of my teachers. I was much more curious to learn while in an environment that was open and free for hands on activities, but then school became rigid and I felt like I was never good enough; it took away any curiosity to learn and sometimes I felt trapped in jail. When I was looking for a preschool for my children, and then for myself as a newly-educated ECE teacher, I took time to tour many schools. I found an amazing school, and later discovered that it only hires teachers with degrees in Early Child Development. It was remembering what I loved about nursery school when I was a child that helped me get there.

—Claudia

Standards

Spin-Offs from the Core

Nursery schools in the United States have served several purposes for the field of early childhood education. See how these spin-offs promote three key Standards:

> **Standard 1:** Promoting Child Development and Learning. **Laboratory schools** attempted a multidisciplinary approach, blending the voices from psychology and education with those of home economics, nursing, social work, and medicine. Research centers and child development laboratories began in many colleges and universities from about 1915 to 1930. The Child Study Movement of the 1920s to 1960s is discussed later in this chapter. "The purpose was to improve nursery schools, and, therefore, we brought in the people who were studying children, who were learning more about them, so we could do a better job" (Hymes, 1978–79).

> **Standard 2:** Building Family and Community Relationships. **Parent cooperative schools** promoted parent education as a vital function of early childhood programs. The first of these parent participation schools was developed in 1915 at the University of Chicago. Either part- or full-day programs, these are organized and run by parents, usually with a professional head teacher or director (see Chapter 2).

> **Standard 6:** Becoming a Professional. By 1950, when Katherine Read (Baker) first published *The Nursery School: A Human Relationships Laboratory* (in its ninth printing and in seven languages), the emphasis of the nursery school was first on understanding human behavior, then on building programs, guidance techniques, and relationships accordingly. The nursery school was for children to learn as they played and shared experiences with others. It was also where adults could learn about child development and human relationships by observing and participating.

1-2b Kindergarten

The word **kindergarten** is a delightful term, bringing to mind the image of young seedlings on the verge of blossoming. The first kindergarten was a German school started by Froebel in 1837. In 1856, Margarethe Schurz, a student of Froebel's, opened the first kindergarten in the United States and inspired Elizabeth Peabody (1804–1894) of Boston to open the first English-speaking kindergarten there in 1860. In 1873, Susan Blow (1843–1916) opened the first public school kindergarten in the United States.

Looking at the kindergarten in historical perspective, it is interesting to trace its various purposes. During the initial period (1856–1890), Froebel's philosophy was the mainstay of kindergarten education. At the same time, charity kindergartens emerged as instruments of social reform where teachers conducted a morning class for about 15 children and made social (and welfare) calls on families during the afternoon. By early 1900, traditional kindergarten ideas were influenced by a scientific approach to education and by Dewey's notion of school-as-community. In an era of rising social conscience in the 1960s, helping the less fortunate became a "cause," much like the conditions that led to the creation of Head Start. The 1970s saw a focus on intellectual development and a programmatic shift that placed more emphasis on academic goals for the 5-year-old. In the 1990s, the concept of developmentally appropriate practices, or DAP, advocated more holistic, broad planning for kindergarten, as well as cultural and family responsiveness. Currently, standards and teacher-directed instruction are again on the rise; thus, kindergarten is the stage for a clash between developmental play and academic preparation. The kindergarten is found in some form in nearly every country of the world. Although the content of the program and the length of the day vary widely in the United States, kindergarten is available in every one of the states. The program model is described in Chapter 2.

Kindergarten is the stage for a clash between developmental play and academic preparation.

© iStockphoto.com/dalton00

1-2c Programs with a Message

Child Care

Child care is not a modern phenomenon. Some of the first nursery schools in England operated from 8:00 am until 4:00 or 5:00 pm; the McMillan's Deptford School was full-day. By definition, a full-day child care program is a place for children who need care for a greater portion of the day than the traditional nursery school offers. A full-day option is also educational. Much of the curriculum of a good full-day program will echo the quality of the traditional nursery school or preschool.

Although the economic crisis of the Depression and the political turmoil of World War II diverted attention from children's needs, both gave focus to adult needs for work. Out of this necessity came the nurseries run by the Works Progress Administration (WPA) in the 1930s and the Lanham Act nurseries of the 1940s. The most renowned program of mid-century was the Kaiser Child Care Centers. Today, child care is a full-day experience for children from 0 to 5 years (and older as extended care) to help working families, and it is provided either in homes or centers (see Chapter 2).

Equal Rights

In the 1900s, gaining access to high-quality education for poor people and people of color was difficult. As Du Bois (1903 [1995]) wrote, "[T]he majority of Negro children in the United States, from 6 to 18, do not have the opportunity to read and write. . . . [E]ven in the towns and cities of the South, the Negro schools are so crowded and ill-equipped that no thorough teaching is possible." Only a legal challenge to segregation offered new focus, struggle, and ultimately improvement for African American children. The movement for equality came under black leadership, embraced unprecedented numbers of African Americans, and became national in scope. A persistent black initiative forced a reformulation of public policies in education. Finally, the historic case of *Brown v. Board of Education of Topeka* (1954) overturned the concept of "separate but equal." The Civil Rights Act of 1964 continued the struggle for equality of opportunity and education and attempted to address continuing **racist** attitudes and behavior.

Head Start

A small piece of metal made its worldwide debut and jolted American education. Sputnik, the Soviet satellite, was successfully launched in 1957, causing mainstream America to ask: Why weren't we first in space? What is wrong with our schools? The emphasis in education quickly settled on engineering, science, and math in the hope of catching up with Soviet technology.

As the Civil Rights struggle soon followed, it became clear that education was a major stumbling block to equality of all people. It was time to act, and Project Head Start was conceived as education's place in the "war on poverty." Froebelian and Montessori goals formed the basis of Head Start, helping disadvantaged preschool children. This was a revolution in U.S. education, the first large-scale effort by the government to focus on children of poverty.

Project Head Start began in 1965 as a demonstration program aimed at providing educational, social, medical, dental, nutritional, and mental health services to preschool children from a diverse population of low-income families.

---

laboratory schools. Educational settings whose purposes include experimental study; schools for testing and analysis of educational and/or psychological theory and practice, with an opportunity for experimentation, observation, and practice.

parent cooperative schools. An educational setting organized by parents for their young children, often with parental control and/or support in the operation of the program itself.

kindergarten. A school or class for children 4-to 6-years-old; in the United States, kindergarten is either the first year of formal, public school or the year of schooling before first grade.

child care. The care, education, and supervision of another's child, especially in an organized center or home dedicated to the enterprise; usually denotes full-day services.

racist. Attitudes, behavior, or policies that imply either a hatred or intolerance of other race(s) or involving the idea that one's own race is superior and has the right to rule or dominate others.

DAP

Its mission was defined as **compensatory education** with parent involvement and community control. In 1972, it was transformed into a predominantly part-day, full-year program that includes children with special needs, and has been a major part of the U.S. federal commitment to early learning (see Chapter 2).

1-3 Interdisciplinary Influences

Several professions enrich the heritage of early childhood. This relationship has been apparent since the first nursery schools began, drawing from six different professions to create their practice: social work, home economics, nursing, psychology, education, and medicine. Three of the most consistent and influential of those disciplines are medicine, education, and psychology.

1-3a Medicine

The medical field has contributed to the study of child growth through the work of several physicians. These doctors became interested in child development and extended their knowledge to the areas of child rearing and education.

Maria Montessori

Maria Montessori (1870–1952) was the first woman in Italy ever granted a medical degree. She began studying children's diseases; through her work with mentally defective children, she found education more appealing.

Sigmund Freud

Sigmund Freud (1856–1939) made important contributions to all modern thinking. The father of *psychodynamic personality theory*, he drastically changed how we look at childhood. Freud reinforced two specific ideas: (1) people are influenced by their early life in fundamental and dramatic ways, and (2) early experiences shape the way people live and behave as adults. Although he was not involved directly in education, Freud and psychoanalytic theory influenced education greatly (see Chapter 4).

Arnold Gesell

Arnold Gesell (1880–1961) was a physician who was concerned with growth from a medical point of view. Gesell began studying child development when he was a student of G. Stanley Hall, and later established the Clinic of Child Development at Yale University, where the data he collected with his colleagues became the basis of the recognized norms of how children grow and develop. He was also instrumental in encouraging Abigail Eliot to study with the McMillan sisters in England.

Gesell's greatest contribution was in guides from his maturation theory, best known today as "ages & stages" (see Chapters 3 and 4).

Benjamin Spock

Benjamin Spock's book *Baby and Child Care* was a mainstay for parents in the 1940s and 1950s. In a detailed "how-to" format, Dr. Spock (1903–1998) preached a commonsense approach, and the book has sold 50 million copies around the world in 42 languages. Spock saw himself as giving practical application to the theories of Dewey and Freud, particularly the idea that children can learn to

---

compensatory education. Education designed to supply what is thought to be lacking or missing in children's experiences or ordinary environments.

direct themselves, rather than needing to be constantly disciplined. He suggested that parents "child-proof" their homes—a radical thought at the time. Some people associated permissiveness (as it relates to child rearing) with Spock's methods, although Spock himself described his advice as relaxed and sensible while still advocating firm parental leadership.

T. Berry Brazelton

Dr. T. Berry Brazelton (1918–) is a well-known pediatrician who supports and understands the development of infants and toddlers. He developed an evaluation tool called the Neonatal Behavior Assessment Scale (also known as "the Brazelton") to assess newborns. Cofounder of the Children's Hospital Unit in Boston, professor emeritus of pediatrics at Harvard Medical School, and founder of the Brazelton Touchpoints Center, he is well known for his pediatric guides for parents (Touchpoints). His writings speak to the parents' side of child rearing, although he also reminds parents how teachers can help them. Brazelton advocated for a national parental-leave standard, is involved in a federal lobbying group known as Parent Action, and hosted the cable TV series, *What Every Baby Knows.*

1-3b Education

Early childhood is one part of the larger professional field of education, which includes elementary, secondary, and college or postsecondary schools. Along with Dewey, the McMillan Sisters, Steiner, and Eliot, several other influential figures from this field bear attention.

Susan Isaacs

Susan Isaacs (1885–1948) was an educator of the early 20th century whose influence on nursery and progressive schools of the day was substantial. In 1929, she published *The Nursery Years,* interpreting Freudian theory for teachers and providing guidance for how schools could apply this new knowledge of the unconscious to the education of children. She wanted children to have the opportunity for free, unhindered imaginative play not only as a means to discover the world but also as a way to work through wishes, fears, and fantasies. The teacher's role was different from that of a therapist, she asserted, in that teachers were "to attract mainly the forces of love, to be the good but regulating parent, to give opportunity to express aggression but in modified form" (Biber, 1984).

The Progressive Education Movement

As indicated earlier in reference to John Dewey, it was the Progressive Movement of the late 1800s and first half of the 20th century that changed the course of education in both elementary and nursery schools in America. Coinciding with the political progressivism in this country, this philosophy emphasized a child-centered approach that gained advocates from both the scientific viewpoint, such as G. Stanley Hall and John Dewey, and a psychoanalytic bent, such as Susan Isaacs and Patty Smith Hill.

A new kind of school emerged from these ideals. Movable furniture replaced rows of benches. Children's projects, some still under construction, were found everywhere. The curriculum of the school began to focus on all of the basics, not just a few of the academics. If a group of 6-year-olds decided to make a woodworking table, they would first have to learn to read to understand the directions. After calculating the cost, they would purchase the materials. In building the table, geometry, physics, and math were learned along the way. This was a group effort that encouraged children to work together in teams, so school became a society in miniature. Children's social skills were developed along with reading, science, and math. The teacher's role in the process was one of ongoing support, involvement, and encouragement.

The Schools of Reggio Emilia

In the last quarter-century, an educational system in Italy has influenced early childhood thinking. Loris Malaguzzi (1920–1994) developed his theory of early childhood education from his work with infants, toddlers, and preschoolers as the founder and director of early education in the town of Reggio Emilia, Italy. His philosophy includes creating an amiable school that welcomes families and the community and invites relationships among teachers, children, and parents to intensify and deepen in order to strengthen a child's sense of identity. Reggio Emilia has attracted the attention and interest of American educators because of its respect for children's work and creativity, its project approach, and its total community support.

1-3c Psychology

The roots of early childhood education are wonderfully diverse, but one tap root is especially deep: the connection with the field of psychology. In the past 100 years, the study of people and their behavior has been linked with the study of children and their growth.

The Child Study Movement

The Child Study movement of the 1920s and 1930s gave education and psychology a common focus. Besides the Gesell Institute, many research centers and child development laboratories were established at colleges and universities around the country. Early ones include Hampton Institute in 1873; the University of Chicago, founded by John Dewey in 1896; Bank Street School in 1919; and the laboratory nursery school at Columbia Teacher's College in 1921. Bing Nursery School at Stanford University and the Harold Jones Center of the University of California at Berkeley were founded after World War II, joining Pacific Oaks College on the West Coast. Their inception reflected the interest of several disciplines in the growth of the young child.

> Schools of psychology looked for children to observe and study.
> Schools of education sought demonstration schools for their teachers-in-training.

Professionalism

> Schools of home economics wanted their students to have firsthand experiences with children.
> On-campus schools provided early education children of student, staff, and faculty children.

This period of educational experimentation and child study led to an impressive collection of normative data by which we still measure ranges of ordinary development. It was the impetus in the United States that began the search for the most appropriate means of educating young children.

Developmental and Learning Theories

There is no one theory or name that encompasses all of developmental psychology. Many theories have affected how we see young children and early education: psychodynamic, behaviorist, cognitive, maturation, humanist, sociocultural, and multiple intelligences. In the last 25 years, neuroscience and brain-based research has expanded our knowledge of how children grow and learn. New developments give us in-depth understanding of human functioning that has profound implications for children and learning (see Chapter 4).

What Is Neuroscience and Why Should We Care?

Brain Research says

When the field of psychology began to develop in the 1800s, new questions began to surface about the brain and the mind. Freud's ideas about the subconscious mind, Piaget's concepts of the thinking mind, and behaviorists' work on changing thoughts and attitudes via shaping behavior all led to the emergence of cognitive science in the late 1980s. A landmark report by the National Academy of Sciences entitled *From Neurons to Neighborhoods: The Science of Early Childhood Development* (Shonkoff & Phillips, 2000) joined early childhood education with neuroscience. Since then, the development and availability of brain-imaging techniques provide glimpses of brain activity as an individual thinks and feels.

We are now in what might be called the "century of the brain." If the human brain is like the hardware of a computer, the mind may be seen as the software. Further, this software changes as it is used; people assign different meaning to the inputs and outputs of things. Brain structures can now be mapped on a matrix. The work of cognitive neuropsychologists allows us to link specific regions of the brain with specific cognitive processes such as verbal and memory skills, attention, emotional responding, and motor coordination. Experimental techniques used on animals (that could not be ethically used with humans) have revealed the brain regions that connect with psychological processes. Combining computed tomography (CT) and magnetic resonance imaging (MRI) developed during the late 20th century with the more recent functional magnetic resonance imaging (fMRI) and positron emission topography (PET) allows us to determine the location of tumors or lesions as well as study the genetic basis of differences (Byrnes, 2001; Ansari & Coch, 2008).

The new frontier of neuroscience is showing us the remarkable plasticity of the brain, as well as the critical nature of the early years. "Early experiences determine whether a child's developing brain architecture provides a strong or weak foundation for all future learning, behavior and health" (CDC/Harvard, 2007). Neuroscience and education create an ideal partnership in outlining a better understanding of how we learn so we can create more effective teaching methods and curriculum (Carew & Magsamen, 2010; Dubinsky, et al, 2013).

Questions

1. If this is the "century of the brain," what do you think will change in educational practices?
2. What do you think parents should know about brain development in the first five years of a child's life?
3. What would "investing in young children" look like in your community? In your state?

1-4 Issues of Today

The themes of early childhood education continue to influence practices and policies of today. For instance, by the year 2000, 48% of the nation's schoolchildren were children of color (CDF, 2011). Nearly one in 10 ten Americans was born elsewhere; 10% of residents in the United States are immigrants. The terrorist attacks of September 11, 2001, changed the way Americans view the world and in turn are seen by it. Events and circumstances are reflected in the major issues facing early childhood educators today:

1. Ethic of social reform: quality child care, no child left behind legislation, and developmentally appropriate practices
2. Importance of childhood: family pressures and children's health risks
3. Transmission of values: the media culture and social diversity
4. Professionalism: children's programs, standards for teacher preparation, ethics in early care and education, and advocacy

truth or fiction?

T F Medicine and psychology have major impacts on the field.

From Montessori to Brazelton in medicine and from child development to brain-based research in psychology, many ideas have influenced how we understand young children.

1-4a Ethic of Social Reform

This first theme dictates that schooling for young children will lead to social change and improvement. Montessori, the McMillans, Patty Smith Hill, Abigail Eliot, and Head Start all tried to improve children's health and physical well-being by attending first to the physical and social welfare aspects of children's lives. Today, the ethic of social reform refers to an expectation that education has the potential for significant social change and improvement. This is dramatically demonstrated in three current issues: quality child care, No Child Left Behind legislation, and developmentally appropriate practices (DAP).

Quality Child Care

Child care is part of a modern way of life; each day, more than 20 million children spend time in early care and education settings, which constitutes 63.5% of the 3- to 5-year-olds enrolled in center-based or out-of-home care (U.S. Census Bureau, 2010). More than 67% of mothers are in the workforce (CDF, 2011). Without question, the need for child care has been firmly established.

The key word is *quality*—the terms "good quality" and "high quality" identify specific features in early childhood programs. Quality early care and education contribute to the healthy cognitive, social, and emotional development of all children, but particularly those from low-income families. Yet data from the CDF (2011) paint a bleak picture for those who might benefit the most. Child care costs are disproportionately high for poor parents and can equal as much as one third of their income. Good, affordable, accessible child care that will meet the increasing needs of American families is one of today's most crucial issues.

Quality is a function of group size, low teacher-to-child ratios, trained and experienced staff, adequate compensation, and safe and stimulating environments (see Chapter 2).

No Child Left Behind, Race to the Top, & Common Core State Standards

One of the primary functions of the public school system in the United States is to prepare students for productive roles in society. The Elementary and Secondary Education Act (ESEA) of 1965 was authorized to close the achievement gap between disadvantaged/minority students and their middle-class/white peers (U.S. Department of Education, 2001). Since then, a national education problem has been identified and a sense of urgency instilled in the public mind

The No Child Left Behind (NCLB) Act was part of the first wave of reforms in the 1980s.

Virtually every state enacted reform measures of some kind, with a focus on higher standards of student performance through the upgrading of curricula, increased requirements for homework, and firmer disciplinary

Professionalism

A Notable Portrait

Marian Wright Edelman is an outstanding children's advocate. Edelman began her career as a civil rights lawyer (the first African American woman to be admitted to the Mississippi state bar). By the 1960s she had dedicated herself to the battle against poverty, founding a public interest law firm that eventually became the Children's Defense Fund (CDF). "[We] seek to ensure that no child is left behind and that every child has a Healthy Start, a Head Start, a Fair Start, a Safe Start, and a Moral Start in life with the support of caring parents and communities" (CDF, 2008). To find out more about Edelman, go to www.childrensdefense.org.

---

media culture. The term used to describe the behaviors and beliefs characteristic of those who engage regularly with various media such as television, computers, and video games.

quality. A function of group size, low teacher-child ratios, trained and experienced staff, adequate compensation, and safe and stimulating environments.

methods. Most notable was the move to standards-based instruction and the requirement that children be tested twice a year to measure progress. In 1989, "Ready to Learn" was published, which included the provision that all children would have equal access to high-quality and developmentally appropriate preschool programs that help prepare children for school. In 2002, the ESEA was reauthorized with stronger goals, and by 2005, it had become the NCLB Act.

Race to the Top was a competitive grant program created in 2009 by the Obama Administration for states to create and adopt common academic standards for kindergarten through twelfth grade. It included an Early Learning Challenge designed to award funds to those states committed to increase the number of children at risk enrolled in high quality learning programs. The continuing challenge for states was to close the school readiness gap in which at children of poverty, disproportionally children of color, enter kindergarten underprepared to succeed. The larger the gap, the more difficult it is to achieve equality of achievement in later schooling.

Common Core State Standards (CCSS) have been developed in mathematics and language arts and adopted by nearly all 50 states to identify the knowledge and skills students need for college and work. These standards challenge all school districts, particularly those with both a school readiness gap and later achievement disparities. CCSS outlines all developmental domains, focuses attention on how children learn, and requires observations and assessments to measure student proficiency.

Developmentally Appropriate Practices

The first definitive position on developmentally appropriate practices was adopted by the NAEYC in 1986. This was followed by expansions to include specifics for programs serving children from birth through age 8 years, outlining both appropriate and inappropriate practices (Bredekamp, 1987). Several key organizations followed suit: the Association for Childhood Education International (ACEI), the National Association of Elementary School Principals and the National Association of State Boards of Education (NASBE) elaborated on their own standards in 1988–91. *Reaching Potentials: Transforming Early Childhood Curriculum and Assessment* (Bredekamp & Rosegrant) was published in 1995, and *Making Early Learning Standards Come Alive* (Gronlund) in 2006.

Open the DAP Umbrella on page 6 as you contemplate how DAP was being applied and discussed throughout the broader early childhood education community. Derived from the changing knowledge base by way of research and extended conversations among professionals, the first major revision of the NAEYC position statement and guidelines was published in 1997, with the 3rd edition in 2009 (Copple & Bredekamp, Eds). Tune into regular revisions as our knowledge base (such as brain research) and awareness of issues (as in special needs, English language learners) expand. DAP is applied throughout the book and discussed at length in Chapter 2.

1-4b Importance of Childhood

The second theme is the importance and uniqueness of childhood. The child holds a special place in the life span; families and society who value children take responsibility for providing a quality life for them. Two issues of today endanger childhood and demand our attention: family stressors and risks to children's health.

Family Stressors

Families encounter many challenges today. The impact of social changes in the past three decades has been hard felt by children and the adults who are raising them. Family structures vary greatly, but the task remains the same: to provide safety and stability, routine, and new experiences. Three stressors that make this task challenging are divorce, work, and poverty.

DAP

Is It DAP?

Look at the major provisions of the NCLB Act pertaining to early learning and the field's response. Do you think the NCLB Act is DAP?

Provision	Description	ECE Response
Adequate yearly progress	Children will be assessed in reading and math (and a third area by state choice) beginning in third grade.	*The trickle down of inappropriate testing or imbalanced curriculum to younger children is a valid concern of early educators.*
Highly qualified teachers	All teachers in core academic subjects must have a B.A. degree, be fully certified, and be highly qualified (by state definition) in their areas of teaching assignment.	*The early learning field, plagued by high turnover and low pay, cannot meet these standards without significantly more funding.*
Reading/ literacy	There are significantly increased funds aimed at having all children achieve reading proficiency by grade three.	*An early childhood concern is that other critical domains of childhood development will be undervalued or overlooked altogether.*

It remains to be seen how this ambitious plan will fare over the coming years and how it will relate to the national child care crisis. If we want all our children to be ready for school, we must improve the quality of child care experiences available to all.

literacy. The quality or state of being able to read and write.

Divorce. Perhaps no one single change has affected children as much as the divorce rate. Children rate divorce second only to death of a parent as the most stressful event in their lives (DelCampo & DelCampo, 2006), and nearly 50% of marriages end in divorce, with just over 60% of American children living in married-couple households (Casey Foundation, 2008). You will likely notice some of these effects:

Effect	Reactions
Predivorce family	**Children:** Increased impusive /aggressive behavior
Stress	**Parents:** headaches, fatigue, mood swings, depression
Parent Separation	**Children:** strong reaction, crying, fighting, withdrawal
Divorce	**Children:** adrift, clingy to teachers
	Parents: overworked, over-whelmed, preoccupied
Aftermath	**Parents:** mothers drastic drop in income, fathers diminished commitment

"Divorce introduces a massive change into the life of a boy or a girl no matter what the age," (Pickhardt , 2011). Those specializing in divorce for children and adolescents note a cumulative effect over time, and yet see children as amazingly resilient with appropriate support. The age and gender of the children involved seem to have some bearing on their adjustment, both for 2- to 6-year-olds and for boys. The dependent young child may have a short-term reaction of anxiety, with regression and efforts to bring the parent close; clinging at separation and loss of self-help skills are difficult but temporary. The parents' ability to be caring and available makes a difference, as does the parents' relationship with each other and the quality of the children's relationship with both parents.

Work. More than two thirds of children 6 to 12 years of age in the United States have all available parents in the workforce, and the same is true of 65% of children younger than 6 years (CDF, 2010). The implications for families are considerable. For women, the double roles of job/career and family nurturer can be overwhelming, creating great conflict and the stress of chronic fatigue. Many men are learning about greater involvement in child rearing and how to adjust to a new financial role. Yet there are vast differences among the various cultural groups and individual adults about the value of and care for children. For both parents, three issues loom large:

Who make up today's families? Family structures you are likely to encounter in your program include single- and dual-parents, grandparents and teens raising children, and blended families raising children together. ◀

> *Concern for good child care.* In many communities, full- or flexible-time child care is unavailable or unaffordable.
> *Struggle to provide "quality time" with children and as a family unit.*
> European models of family leave give parents several months of unpaid leave from their jobs to be at home and establish a bond and family setting. Once back on the job, working parents are less available for direct participation in a classroom and become less involved in their children's education.
> *Financial burden.* Without parental leave, many parents are forced to return to work during the critical early months of infancy or lose income and even their jobs. In the United States, child tax credits and pretax dependent care credits are government and employer supports.

Ethics

Despite economic downturns, we look toward a future trend of U.S. policies that make it more attractive for working adults to spend time with children.

Poverty. The children who are at risk for academic failure are likely to be those who live in poverty, members of minority groups in racial isolation, children with various physical and mental disabilities, children with limited English proficiency, and children from single-parent families (Casey Foundation, 2008). For every five children

truth or fiction?

T (F) Family stressors such as work and poverty are eliminated by sending children to good early education programs.

Quality early childhood programs can educate children and support families, but they cannot solve all the economic and social problems of society or eliminate all family stressors.

---

child abuse. Violence in the form of physical maltreatment, abusive language, and sexual harassment or misuse of children.

child neglect. The act or situation of parents' or other adults' inattention to a child's basic health needs of adequate food, clothing, shelter, and health care; child neglect may also include not noticing a child or not paying enough attention in general.

---

in the United States, one child is poor (CDF, 2008). Most poor children live in families with working parents whose wages are too low for them to earn their way out of poverty. Children who start out at a disadvantage fall further behind in academic achievement throughout their school years. Too many of them reach adulthood unhealthy, illiterate, and unemployable, with limited participation in the social, political, and economic mainstream of national life. This is a personal tragedy for everyone involved and one that calls for intensive reform efforts.

Children's Health Risks

Challenges to positive child health come in several forms. Child abuse and neglect, childhood obesity, and violence/disaster all put children's basic health at risk.

Child Abuse and Neglect. **Child abuse** and **child neglect** are significant problems in this country. One third of all victims are children younger than four (Children's Defense Fund, 2012), and one third of abused and neglected children eventually victimize their own children, perpetuating the cycle (Childhelp, 2012).

A neglected child may be one whose waking hours are mostly unsupervised by adults, in front of the television or simply unconnected with—and unnoticed by—parents or an important caregiver. Child neglect takes more hazardous forms when the basic needs of adequate food, clothing, shelter, and health are unmet. Because families with children represent more than one third of the homeless population and the foster care system is strained, many children are on the move and under great strain and pressure. More than 70 % of the reported child abuse in the United States is for neglect, 16 % is physical abuse, and 9 % is sexual abuse (CDF, 2010).

> Children who experience abuse and neglect have a 59 percent chance of being arrested as a juvenile and are 25 percent more likely to become pregnant as a teenager.

© iStockphoto.com/Oliver Blonde

Problem Area	Signs and Signals (Childhelp, 2012)
Neglect	Unsuitable clothing for weather, dirty or unbathed, extreme hunger, apparent lack of supervision
Physical abuse	Unexplained burns, cuts, bruises, or welts in the shape of an object; bite marks; antisocial behavior; problems in school; fear of adults
Emotional abuse	Apathy, depression, hostility, lack of concentration, eating disorders
Sexual abuse	Inappropriate interest or knowledge of sexual acts; nightmares and bedwetting; drastic changes in appetite; overcompliance or excessive aggression; fear of a particular adult or family member

Reporting suspected child abuse is mandated by law in all states (see Ethics box). The residual effects of child abuse—which occurs in every socioeconomic, ethnic, religious and educational level—are dramatic. Children who experience abuse and neglect have a 60 % chance of being arrested as juveniles and are 25 % more likely to become pregnant as teenagers (Childhelp, 2012).

Child Obesity. Childhood obesity has increased alarmingly in the past decade. According to the National Center for Health Statistics (NCHS, 2011), the prevalence of childhood obesity among children ages 2 to 4 years has increased from 5% in 1980 to 14% in 2009, and in children 6 to 11, there is an even greater increase to over 19.6% of children and teens deemed overweight or obese. Health risks include heart disease, high blood pressure, diabetes, depression, and low self-esteem. Part of the problem is that children are less active on a daily basis than in previous generations; other factors include inadequate access to nutritious food and poor eating habits. The Obesity Society (2010; see Web Resources) notes:

> In the past 30 years, the occurrence of overweight in children has doubled and it is now estimated that one in five children in the US is overweight. Increases in the prevalence of overweight are also being seen in younger children, including preschoolers. Prevalence of overweight is especially

higher among certain populations such as Hispanic, African American and Native Americans.

Moreover, if one parent is obese, the child is three times more likely to be obese in adulthood; if both parents are obese, the risk is 10 times more likely that the child will be an obese adult. Childhood overweight is regarded as the most common prevalent nutritional disorder of U.S. children and adolescents, underscoring the need for regular exercise in programs for young children. First Lady Michelle Obama's emphasis on nutrition and exercise (www.HealthCare.gov) has highlighted appropriate ways to play, eat, and stay healthy.

Violence and Disaster. Violence and disaster are becoming regular features in young children's lives. The trend of children's increasing exposure to conflict that ends in violence is alarming.

> - Parents report tensions between themselves and their children.
> - Increased violence on television and war toys contribute to a sense of being out of control in limiting or influencing children's behavior.
> - Teachers see problems in children's play, that weapon and war play in classrooms is so single-purpose and intense that it is difficult to redirect.

When a real catastrophe happens, children need help making sense of the calamity, then support in recovery. Shock, confusion, fear, anxiety, grief, anger, guilt, and helplessness are all common emotional responses to trauma. Whether the event is national—as 9/11 was for the United States—or local, children worry.

In both cases, organizations such as Adults and Children Together Against Violence (ACT) and Educators for Social Responsibility, as well as the National Association for Mediation in Education, serve as clearinghouses for information and material and as training institutes for teachers. They suggest the following:

> - *Stop, look, and listen.* See what children are really doing and saying (or not).
> - *Be aware of your own feelings.* Self-awareness helps you balance your responses without avoidance or overreaction.
> - *Ask before you tell.* Open-ended questions welcome children's talking.
> - *Provide structure.* Clear routines and variety keeps interest high and focused.
> - *Work with parents and families.* Everyone needs to pitch in here.

1-4c Transmission of Values

The third recurring theme in our educational heritage is that of transmitting values. Values—whether social, cultural, moral, or religious—have been the essence of education for centuries. Rousseau and Froebel valued childhood, so they created special places for children to express their innate goodness and uniqueness, and Puritan fathers valued

---

Developmentally Appropriate Practices for Preschool Movement Programs

1. Toddlers should participate in at least 30 minutes a day of structured play and one to several hours a day of unstructured physical activity. Preschoolers should participate in at least one hour of daily structured physical activity.

2. Preschoolers should not be sedentary for more than one hour at a time and be engaged in unstructured physical activity whenever possible.

3. Basic movement skills should be the building blocks for more complex movement abilities.

4. Indoor and outdoor environments should exceed recommended safety standards for performing large-muscle, gross-motor activities.

5. Teachers and caregivers should understand the importance of physical activity and integrate movement programs as part of the daily educational program.

6. Teachers serve as facilitators, encouraging children to explore and discover a range of movement possibilities.

Figure 1-3 From *Appropriate practices in movement programs for young children, Ages 3–5.* The Council on Physical Education for Children (Reston, VA: A position statement of the National Association for Sport and Physical Education/NASPE, 2000, pages 8–9, 11, 15, 17) and Sanders, S. W. (2002), *Active for life: Developmentally appropriate movement programs for young children.* (Washington, DC: The National Association for the Education of Young Children).

biblical theology; therefore, schools of their time taught children to read to learn the Bible. Today's anti-bias movement (see Social Diversity section) reflects a priority of personal respect and an appreciation of culture as part of the early childhood curriculum.

"People are so overwhelmed," write Brazelton and Greenspan (2001) "While they're whirling around, they don't have time to stop and think, 'What are my values? Do my children really come first? Am I making time for them in my life?'" Many families today are looking for direction for themselves and their children. Many sources shape children's values and behavior, notably the media culture and social diversity.

The Media Culture
In many homes, the television, computer, and video game sets have replaced adult supervision. Consider these facts and the reality that research firms are "applying the study of the human brain and the nervous system to consumer research, in order to determine a consumer's non-conscious response to brands, products, packaging, in-store marketing, advertising, and entertainment content" (Nielsen Media Research, 2014).

> In the United States, 98% of homes contain at least one television.
> The average set is on for more than 6 hours each day.
> Children spend more time watching television (15,000 hours) than they do in school (11,000 hours).
> Children will likely witness on screen 180,000 murders, rapes, armed robberies, and assaults.

What happens to children when they are this plugged into media? Common Sense Media and the National Institutes of Health (NIH) analyzed 173 studies about the effect of media consumption on children, finding a strong correlation between greater exposure and adverse health outcomes. "Couch potato does, unfortunately, sum it up pretty well," states E. J. Emanuel, chair of bioethics at NIH. "The research is clear that exposure to media has a variety of negative health impacts on children and teens. . . . We found very few studies that had any positive association for children's health" (Common Sense Media, 2008). Too much media violence is hazardous to children in these ways (Gordon & Browne, 2013):

Hazards of Too Much Media Violence

Increased aggressiveness and antisocial behavior

Increased fear of becoming a victim

Increased desensitization to violence and victims of violence

Increased appetite for more violence in entertainment and real life

© Cengage Learning®

multicultural education. The system of teaching and learning that includes the contributions of all ethnic and racial groups.

Managing Media

Strategy	Description	Example
Set limits.	Know how many hours of TV children watch and monitor it.	Keep it to 2 hours or less; keep the TV off unless someone is actively viewing; establish rules, such as "Game-playing is part of my daily 'screen time' allowance."
Plan and participate.	Work together with children to decide what to watch.	Watch shows together, pointing out parts that are prosocial and asking about those parts you dislike; use the "pause," "rewind," and "mute" buttons regularly.
Resist commercials.	Young children do not distinguish easily between the sales pitch commercial and the ordinary show.	Help children become "critical consumers" by pointing out exaggerated claims; ask: "What are they trying to sell us?"
Express your views.	Call a station or write a letter about a show or commercial you find offensive.	Ask the children to help write the letter and provide documentation.

© Cengage Learning®

TeachSource Digital Download

> Increased aggressiveness and antisocial behavior
> Increased fear of becoming a victim
> Increased desensitization to violence and victims of violence
> Increased appetite for more violence in entertainment and real life.

Moreover, Northwestern University's Center on Media and Human Development reported that "children from minority families are more likely to 1) live in homes where the television is always on and 2) eat in front of the television" (Levin, 2013) . Managing media is a critical task for adults who are with young children.

Social Diversity
Multicultural Education. Multicultural education is the system of teaching and learning that includes the contributions of all ethnic and racial groups. A comprehensive educational approach that reflects more minority perspectives, multicultural education provides all children with a fuller, more balanced truth about themselves, their own history, and their culture. When the metaphor of "melting pot" changes to one

Professionalism

English Language Learning

Age of Children	How Taught	Noteworthy
0–5 years	Standard is "English-immersion": taught in English with little extra instruction, with some teacher use of home language vocabulary.	Can acquire native-like mastery of second language; risk for substantial erosion of home language and ability to communicate with family.
5+1 years	Standard is "English immersion," but some subjects may be taught in home language to aid skill-building; school-aged children better at formal teaching of second language.	Children have complex social issues that may interfere; low competence in both languages may occur until mastery is achieved.

© Cengage Learning®

of "mosaic" or "mixed salad," we encourage a new way of thinking that might be termed *cultural pluralism*—the idea that we are all one people, but we do not necessarily divest ourselves of our own ethnic origin. The early childhood program will become multicultural as each child's total personal diversity is respected and the child's family, language, and cultural traditions become part of the class and curriculum. Teachers will need special training in anti-bias curriculum approaches (see Chapter 9) that prepare them to be effective in addressing such topics as prejudice reduction training, bicultural expectations, physical and interpersonal environmental factors, varied teaching strategies, inclusive curriculum, and culturally responsible conduct.

Bilingual Education. Bilingual education is a challenge at all levels of education. There are disagreements about how to define bilingualism, how to determine who needs it, and who is to provide the services. Bilingual education has been part of the American experience since before the Revolutionary War, when school was taught in any one of the more than 18 languages that were spoken by the colonists. Speaking English is only part of bilingual education: at issue are the civil and educational rights of people who speak limited English, the respect or assimilation of their culture, and their participation and acceptance in society.

Bilingual programs are so varied that it is difficult to assess them. Some work to mainstream children into regular classrooms as quickly as possible; others try to maintain the child's native language. The "dual/bilingual immersion" method blends language instruction in both languages. Putting together both English speakers and those with limited English encourages two-way learning.

State bilingual education laws vary, requiring special instruction for children who lack competence in English. For example, a 1998 California law effectively ended publicly funded bilingual programs, to be replaced by shorter-term, intensive English-immersion programs at the elementary and secondary levels.

Immigration. Immigration is another serious challenge for schools. Attempting to immerse new children into an "American way" and to teach basic skills needed to succeed in the new country have been central functions of schools throughout U.S. history. Since 1968, Title VII programs (the Elementary and Secondary Education Act, also known as the Bilingual Education Act) have addressed the needs of students with limited proficiency in English. In the United States, there are more than 2.5 million school-aged immigrants and at least as many immigrant children younger than 5 years (CDF, 2010). Immigrant enrollment in schools varies among the states and can reach as high as 95% in some schools.

The language barrier is the most immediate problem, followed by that of acceptance of the immigrants' native culture. Further, many newcomers arrive from countries racked with war, violence, and poverty. These children and families are under tremendous pressures and need

bilingual education. Varied and difficult to assess, it is a system of teaching and learning in which children who speak limited English are taught in English-speaking classrooms.

Our history provides examples of programs for children of many ethnic groups, as well as examples of exclusion from schooling.

Our present DAP practices offer ways to include and welcome social diversity into ECE programs.

PAST

PRESENT

FUTURE

What is our vision of the future for ALL children?

Figure 1-4 Social diversity: A theme of ECE.

help coping with the overwhelming stress and dislocation. The way schools place and monitor immigrant children—both their educational progress and their general well-being—challenges educators and all American citizens to clarify the responsibilities our society has toward its newcomers.

Inclusive Education. Inclusive education has been recognized since the 1970s when the Americans with Disabilities Act was passed to reasonably accommodate individuals with disabilities in order to integrate them into the program to the extent feasible, given each individual's limitations. Key principles follow:

Individuality (understand the limitations and needs of each individual)

Reasonableness (of the accommodation to the program and the person)

Integration (of the individual with others)

---

least restrictive environment. The IDEA (Individuals with Disabilities Education Act) requirement for placing students with disabilities such that children with disabilities are educated with those who are not disabled.

inclusion. When a child with a disability is a full-time member of a regular classroom with children who are developing normally as well as with children with special needs.

Accommodating a child with special needs is unreasonable only if it puts an undue burden on a program, fundamentally alters the nature of the program, or poses a threat to the health or safety of the other children and staff. With these guidelines in mind, children with special needs will do best in the **least restrictive environment**, with as **full inclusion** as possible.

Still, many children have special needs that remain undiagnosed, and others have difficulty finding appropriate placement, particularly in programs for children younger than 5 years. Early childhood special education is a relatively new area of our profession, and most educators need support in learning about special needs and what it means to be inclusive of children with special needs without altering program quality for all children or overwhelming and exhausting staff.

Diversity

Celebrate Differences or Stay Gender-Neutral?

Begin with yourself. Start with self-awareness and reflection on one's own behavior, responses, and attitudes.

What you say and do can make a difference. Acknowledge positive behaviors and milestones by describing what you see and avoid using gender designations (such as "All boys get your jackets," or "All girls go to the snack tables").

Watch your language. Avoid descriptions of children such as "pretty/handsome" and treat the class as a group ("friends" rather than "boys and girls"); be careful of word choices that reflect gender bias (such as "He is confident/She is full of herself").

Establish rules and conduct for cooperation and gender equity. Everybody may play everywhere with any toy; blocks are not just for boys, and the house corner is not for girls only; no child may be kept from playing because of something she or he cannot change—skin color, disability, or gender.

Be ready to intervene and support. If you hear a "No boys allowed," or "Girls can't do that," be ready to intervene in a supportive way, finding out why children think that, evaluating your thoughts, and pointing out what the class rule is.

Think about how to cope with superheroes and Barbie dolls. Develop strategies for all children, including providing activities that all children may use, that are sex fair and sex affirmative in content, and using strategies such as teacher proximity and structured playtime to involve children in activities they may otherwise avoid.

Ethics

> Having multicultural children's books and materials about gay families

If teachers are relinquishing stereotypes about ethnicity, ability, and gender, they must also consider avoiding the rejection of a family for its choice of lifestyle or criticism of a child on the basis of some notion of 'femininity' or 'masculinity.' Research has failed to find evidence that parental characteristics determine sexual orientation (Berger, 2012). Whether or not the issue is controversial, the more forthright approach is to address the issue honestly.

1-4d Professionalism

If you are thinking about working with young children as a career, you may be wondering whether early childhood education is a profession worthy of a lifetime commitment (see Chapter 5). A challenging, intellectually stimulating, and rewarding future can be found in the overarching issue of standards in children's programs and in professional preparation, as well as a third issue of advocacy.

Gender Issues. Gender issues are part of the educational landscape. There is ample research to confirm the widespread occurrence of gender segregation in childhood (Grossman & Grossman, 1994). Sex differences are less apparent in early childhood than is gender-based behavior (see Chapter 4). Although adults may not always directly contribute to biased development, teachers and parents are indirectly responsible for the inequity between the sexes in their children. Sexist treatment in the classroom encourages the formation of patterns of power and dominance that occur very early, although it is inappropriate to our current culture.

Standards

Why You Should Know This

The economics of child care create a trilemma—quality for children, affordability for parents, and adequate compensation for teachers. Quality is significantly related to staff: how many adults there are compared with the number of children in a class; whether the salaries and benefits provide incentive for teachers to be retained for a number of years; and the level of the staff's education and training and their years of experience. To improve quality, we look for the following:

> Improved working conditions for teachers

> Appropriate licensing for early childhood programs and homes

> Staff training and preparation

> Funding commensurate with per-child levels for elementary school children

National efforts include the NAEYC Standards for Early Childhood Professional Preparation as well as research efforts of groups such as the National Child Care Information and Technical Assistance Center (Sakai & Whitebook, 2004), refer to the six Standards of Professional Preparation on the inside cover as you read the book; each chapter will highlight the relevant standards to prepare you to become a professional early childhood educator. Engage in collaborative learning with others to inform your practice and your knowledge base. In doing so, you help lead the early childhood field in bringing the important issues of the profession to national attention.

sexist. Attitudes or behavior based on the traditional stereotype of sexual roles that includes a devaluation or discrimination based on a person's sex.

trilemma. A child care issue involving quality for children, affordability for parents, and adequate compensation for staff.

standards. The rules and principles used as a basis for judgment of quality and positive models for professional preparation, children's programs, and educational practices.

advocacy. The act of supporting, pleading for, or recommending and espousing a particular action or set of ideas on behalf of early education.

Sexuality. Sexuality is not likely to be among typical early childhood curriculum topics, yet teachers are likely to encounter issues of homosexuality:

> Having gay or lesbian families in children's programs
> Working with gay or lesbian coworkers
> Dealing with femininity and masculinity in children's sex role identity

Standards in Children's Programs

The rich array of programs offered for children in group care from infancy through 8 years of age is so diverse, it is often difficult to define and assess standards of care and education with one set of guidelines. Consider these statistics:

> In 11 states, providers in family child care homes do not need any training to be licensed (NACCRRA, 2010)

> 32 states do not require prior training to teach in child care centers and 39 (and the District of Columbia) do not require training of family child care providers (CDF, 2010)

> In 2012, only 7000 programs were accredited by the NAEYC Academy of Early Childhood Programs (NAEYC, 2012)

The most comprehensive set of standards for programs has evolved from DAP and is discussed at length in Chapter 2.

Standards for Professional Preparation

The quality of care in child development centers is linked to the training and education of the staff. Consequently, it is

teachsource video case

Watch the TeachSource Video Case entitled "Teaching as a Profession: An Early Childhood Teacher's Responsibilities and Development." After you study the video clip, view the artifacts, and read the teacher interviews and text, reflect on the following questions:

1. How does preschool teacher Samantha Brade show her sense of the importance of early childhood education, and what values is she trying to transmit?

2. How does Samantha demonstrate professionalism, and why should this inform one's teaching?

© 2016 Cengage Learning®

imperative that we attract and recruit to the field of early childhood education individuals who not only are dedicated to working with young children but also are skilled and competent. Many states are working on developing career ladders and professional development plans for early childhood staff. Consideration must be given to developing a coordinated system that accomplished the following:

truth or fiction?

T (F) Standards for teacher preparation are universal.

Many states are working on standards and career ladders of their own. In addition, NAEYC has a set of six standards for professional preparation.

> Welcomes people into the field from a variety of points
> Offers clear career pathways with articulated training and credentialing systems
> Provides a variety of incentives to stay in the field (see Chapter 5)

Advocacy

Is this profession a worthwhile one? The early years are a special time of life, and those who work with young children might reflect on the following aspects of professionalism:

Sense of identity. Early childhood education professionals see themselves as caregivers who strive to educate the whole child, taking into consideration the body, the mind, and the heart and soul (see Chapter 3).

Purpose to engage in DAP. Quality care and education call for blending child development and learning the strengths, interests, and needs of each child as well as the social and cultural contexts in which children live (see Chapter 2).

Commitment to ethical teaching and to child advocacy. Being a professional means behaving with a child's best interests in mind, maintaining confidentiality when discussing issues in the classroom and about families, upholding a code of ethics, and taking oneself and one's work seriously (see Chapter 5).

Participation in the work as a legitimate livelihood. The people who provide care and education to young children deserve wages and working conditions that are worthy of their efforts.

Ours is a profession that is constantly growing, branching out in many directions and ready to meet emerging challenges in flexible, innovative ways.

summary

1.1 To identify the historical roots of early childhood education, it is important to recognize that our roots include influences from abroad and from America. European figures include Comenius, Locke, Rousseau, Pestalozzi, Froebel, Montessori, Steiner, and the McMillan Sisters. American influences come from Colonial days and from the slavery experience—Dewey, Hill, Mitchell, and Eliot.

1.2 In examining the early childhood field and its evolution, one notices that the ECE field can be divided into three main components: nursery school and its spin-offs, kindergarten, and programs with a message that deal with child care, equal rights, and Head Start.

1.3 The major disciplines that distinguish the ECE field are the three major interdisciplinary influences of medicine, education, and psychology. Important figures in medicine are Montessori, Freud, Gesell, Spock, and Brazelton. Educational influences came from Isaacs, the Progressive Education Movement with Dewey, and the schools of Reggio Emilia. The child study movement and the many developmental and learning theories from psychology also helped form ECE philosophy and practices, with the most current being neuroscience and brain-based research.

1.4 An investigation of the major current issues involving ECE reveals that issues of today focus on the four major themes in ECE. The *ethic of social reform* involves quality child care, federal efforts of NCLB (no child left behind), Race to the Top & Common Core, as well as DAP (developmentally appropriate practices). The *importance of childhood* surrounds family stressors of divorce, work, and poverty as well as children's health risks such as abuse and neglect, obesity, and violence and disaster. The *transmission of values* includes media culture and several aspects of social diversity, such as multicultural and bilingual education, immigration, inclusion, gender issues, and sexuality. *Professionalism* can be seen in Standards for children's programs and professional preparation as well as Advocacy.

web resources

Annie E. Casey Foundation, KIDS COUNT Data Center **http://www.aecf.org**

Association for Childhood International Education **http://acei.org**

Center for the Study of the Child Care Workforce **http://www.ccw.org**

Childhelp **http://www.childhelp.org**

Children's Defense Fund **http://www.childrensdefense.org**

National Association of Child Care Resources and Referral Agencies **http://www.naccrra.org**

National Association for the Education of Young Children **http://www.naeyc.org**

National Center for Health Statistics **http://www.cdc .gov**

The Obesity Society **http://www.cdc.gov/nchs/**

U.S. Department of Health & Human Services **http://www.hhs.gov**

references

Ansari, D., & Coch, D. (April, 2008). Bridges over troubled waters: education and cognitive neuroscience. In *Trends in Cognitive Science, 10* (4).

Berger, K. S. (2012). *The developing person through the life span, 8e.* New York: Worth Publishers.

Biber, B. (1984). *Early education and psychological development.* New Haven, CT: Yale University Press.

Brazelton, T. B., & Greenspan, S. D. (2001, March). The irreducible needs of children. *Young Children,* 6–13.

Bredekamp, S. (Ed.) (1987). *Developmentally appropriate practices.* Washington, DC: NAEYC.

Bredekamp, S., and Copple, C. (Eds.) (2009). *DAP in early childhood programs serving children from birth through age eight* (3rd ed.). Washington, DC: NAEYC.

Bredekamp, S., & Rosegrant, T. (Eds.) (1995). *Reaching potentials: Transforming early childhood curriculum and assessment* (vols. 1 and 2). Washington, DC: NAEYC.

continued

Byrnes, J. P. (2001) *Minds, brains, and learning.* New York: Guilford Press.

Carew, T. J. & Magsamen, S. H. (2010, September). Neuroscience and education: An ideal partnership for producing evidence-based solutions to guide 21st century learning. In *Neuron, 67*(5, 9), 665–688.

Casey Foundation. (2008). *Kids count data book.* Baltimore, MD: Annie E. Casey Foundation.

Center on the Developing Child at Harvard University (2007). A science-based framework for early childhood policy: Using evidence to improve outcomes in learning, behavior and health for vulnerable children. **http://www.developingchild.harvard.edu.**

Children's Defense Fund. (2010). *The state of America's children: Leave no child behind.* Washington, DC: Author.

Center for Media Literacy. (2008, August). *Literacy for the 21st century: An orientation and overview of media literacy education.* Available at: **http://medialit.org.**

Childhelp (2012). *Signs of child abuse, 2010.* Available at: **http://www.childhelp.org.** Retrieved January, 2012.

Childhelp (2009). *Child abuse in America, 2006.* Available at: **http://www.childhelp.org/resources.** Retrieved March, 2009.

Common Sense Media and Department of Clinical Bioethics, National Institutes of health. (2010, December) *Media + child and adolescent health: a systematic review.* **www.commonsensemedia.org**

Corbett, S. (1993, March). A complicated bias. *Young Children.*

DelCampo, D. S., & DelCampo, R. L. (2006). *Taking sides: Clashing views in childhood and society* (6th ed.). Dubuque, IA: McGraw-Hill.

DeMause, L. (1974). *The history of childhood.* New York: Psychohistory Press.

Derman-Sparks, L., et al. (1989). *Anti-bias curriculum: Tools for empowering young children.* Washington, DC: NAEYC.

Derman-Sparks, L., & Olsen Edwards, J. (2010) *Anti-bias education for young children and ourselves.* Washington, DC: NAEYC.

Dubinsky, J. M., Roehrig, G., & Verma, S. (2013, August/September). Infusing neuroscience into teacher professional development. In *Educational Researcher, 42*(6) 317–329.

Du Bois, W. E. B. (1903). The talented tenth. In F. Schultz (Ed.), *Notable selections in education.* Guilford, CT: Dushkin Publishing Group.

Edelman, M. W. (2008). *The state of America's children.* Washington, DC: Children's Defense Fund.

Gronlund, G. (2006). *Making early learning standards come alive.* Washington, DC: NAEYC & Redleaf Press.

Grossman, H., & Grossman, S. H. (1994). *Gender issues in education.* Boston: Allyn & Bacon.

Hymes, J. L., Jr. (1978–79). *Living history interviews* (Books 1–3). Carmel, CA: Hacienda Press.

Levin, D.E. (2013) *Beyond remote-controlled childhood; Teaching young children in the media age.* Washington, DC: National Association for the Education of Young Children.

McMillan, R. (Deptford School). Available at: **http://www.spartacus.schoolnet.co.uk/WmcmillanR.htm.**

National Association of Child Care Resources and Referral Agencies (NACCRRA) (June, 2010) Child Care in America fact sheet. **http://www.naccrra.org**

National Association for the Education of Young Children. (2005). *Accreditation criteria and procedures of the National Academy of Early Childhood Programs.* Washington, DC: Author.

National Association for the Education of Young Children (2012). Accreditation programs for young children. **http://www.naeyc.org**

National Center for Health Statistics. (2011, Update). *Prevalence of overweight among children and adolescents: United States.* Hyattsville, MD: U.S. Department of Health and Human Services, Centers for Disease Control and Prevention.

Nielsen Media Research (2014). *Nielsen report on television.* New York: Nielsen Media Research.

Osborn, D. K. (1991). *Early childhood education in historical perspective* (3rd ed.). Athens, GA: Education Associates.

Pickhardt, C. (2013). The impact of divorce on young children and adolescents. In *Surviving (your child's) adolescence.* New York: Wiley.

Sakai, L., & Whitebook, M. (2004). *By a thread: How child care centers hold on to teachers, how teachers build lasting careers.* Kalamazoo, MI: WE Upjohn Institute of Employment Research

U.S. Census Bureau (2010). Current population survey. October 1980 through 2009. Washington, DC: Author.

U.S. Department of Education. (2001). *National household education survey.* Washington, DC: Author.

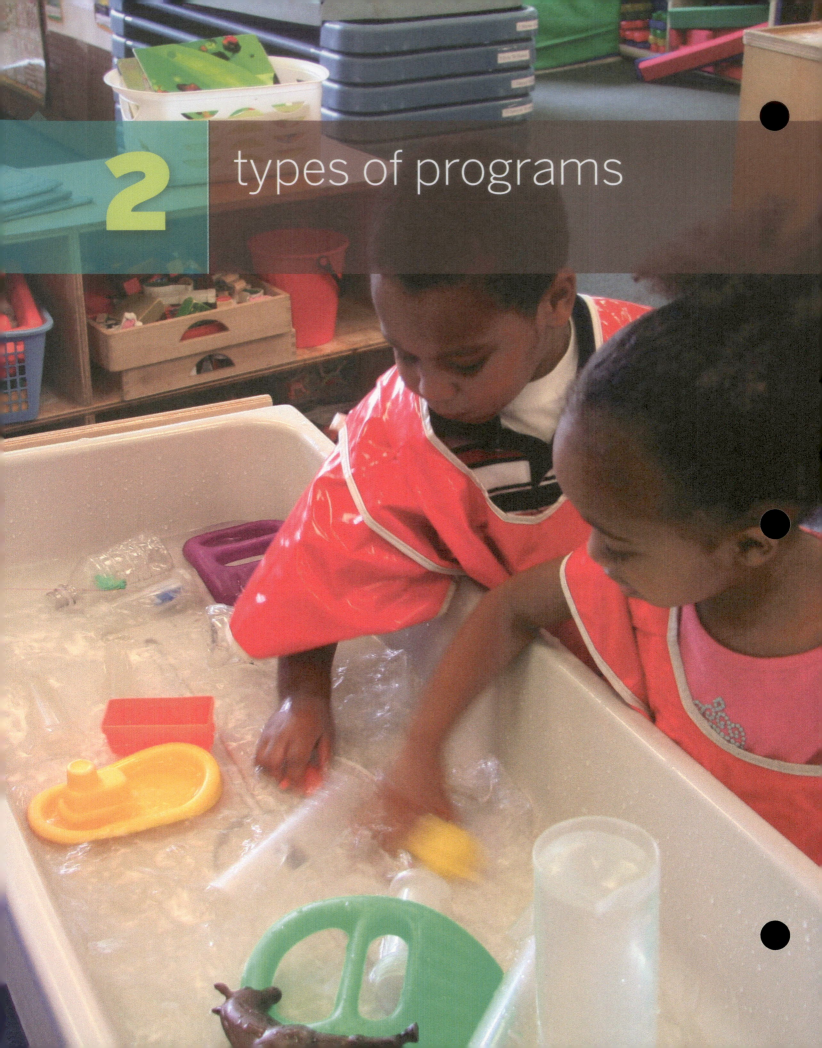

2 types of programs

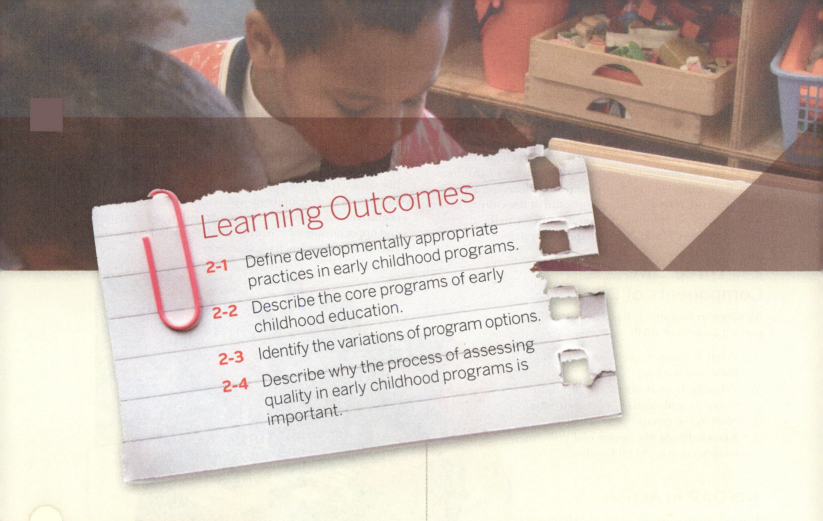

Learning Outcomes

2-1 Define developmentally appropriate practices in early childhood programs.

2-2 Describe the core programs of early childhood education.

2-3 Identify the variations of program options.

2-4 Describe why the process of assessing quality in early childhood programs is important.

© Cengage Learning®

NAEYC Standards

The following NAEYC Standards for Early Childhood Professional Preparation are addressed in this chapter:

Standard 1: Promoting Child Development and Learning

Standard 2: Building Family and Community Relationships

Standard 3: Observing, Documenting, and Assessing to Support Young Children and Families

Standard 4: Using Developmentally Effective Approaches to Connect with Children and Families

Standard 5: Using Current Knowledge to Build Meaningful Curriculum

Standard 6: Becoming a Professional

Standard 7: Field Experience

truth or fiction

T F DAP does not include family involvement.

T F Two programs form the core of early care and education.

T F Infant/toddler programs are adapted versions of good programs for 3-year-olds.

T F The objectives and goals of the program will determine the type of assessment instrument used.

2-1 Developmentally Appropriate Practice in Early Childhood Programs

Throughout this text and whenever quality early childhood principles are discussed, we use the term developmentally appropriate practices (DAP), those teaching practices that are based on the observation and responsiveness to children who have different rates of growth and learning experiences that are relevant to and respectful of the cultural and social aspects of children and families. Refer to the discussion of the DAP Umbrella in Chapter 1 on page 6.

2-1a Three Core Components of DAP

As noted in Chapter 1, there are three important aspects of DAP:

1. What is known about *child development and learning.*
2. What is known about the strengths, interests, and needs of *each individual child* in the group.
3. Knowledge of the *social and cultural contexts* in which children live.

2-1b DAP in Action

A solid grounding in child development knowledge is the core around which the idea of *developmentally appropriate* is built. Programs are designed *for* young children based on what is known *about* young children (Copple & Bredekamp, 2009). To that mix we add what we learn about the individual children and their families. This collective knowledge is applied to each decision that is made about the program:

> What are children like?
> How do they learn?
> What should they learn?
> When should they learn it?
> How should they be taught?
> How do we know they are learning?

What DAP Looks Like

> Programs and curricula respond to the children's interests as well as their needs.
> Children are actively involved in their own learning, choosing from a variety of materials and equipment.
> Play is the primary context in which young children learn and grow.

---

developmentally appropriate practices (DAP). Practices that are suitable or fitting to the development of the child and are relevant and respectful to the social and cultural aspects of children and families.

> Teachers apply what they know about each child and use a variety of strategies, materials, and learning experiences to be responsive to individual children.
> Teachers consider widely held expectations about each age group and temper that with challenging yet achievable learning goals.
> Teachers understand that any activity has the potential for different children to realize different learning from the same experience.
> All aspects of development—physical, social-emotional, cognitive, and language—are integrated in the activities and opportunities of the program. This includes specific attention to dual-language learners.

Active, involved, and interested: that's DAP! ◄

© 2016 Cengage Learning®

How DAP Benefits Children

Developmentally appropriate principles benefit children in many ways, including the following:

1. Allow children to construct their own understanding of what they are learning and encourage learning from instruction by more competent peers and adults
2. Enhance opportunities to see connections across disciplines through integration of curriculum and from opportunities to engage in in-depth study
3. Provide a predictable structure and routine in the learning environment and through the teacher's flexibility and spontaneity in responding to their emerging ideas, needs, and interests
4. Support children making meaningful choices about what they will do
5. Present situations that challenge children to work at the edge of their capacities and ample opportunity to practice newly acquired skills
6. Provide opportunities to collaborate with their peers and acquire a sense of community
7. Assist children in developing a positive sense of their own self-identity and respect for other people, whose perspective and experiences may be different from their own

8. Capitalize on children's enormous curiosity and capacities to learn
9. Promote self-initiated, spontaneous play along with teacher-planned structured activities, projects, and experiences

2-1c Developmentally and Culturally Appropriate Practice

Culturally appropriate practice is the ability to go beyond one's own sociocultural background to ensure equal and fair teaching and learning experiences for all.

The definition of DAP expands to address cultural influences that emphasize the adult's ability to develop a multiethnic outlook (Hyun, 1998), who notes that preparing

Individual attention and warm relationships are essential components of every program. ◄

DAP

How DAP Planning Works

1. *What does child development tell us about toddlers?* Toddlers express their needs to do everything by themselves, usually more than they can actually achieve. They like to feel independent and will learn quickly if given a little help and encouragement.

2. *What do we know about each child as an individual?* Many of these toddlers rely on family members to help feed and dress them and to clean up their toys. Other toddlers are being taught these skills at home. Most of the children come to the teachers for help. One toddler will persist in putting on her coat while another will throw his shoe across the floor if it does not fit at the first attempt.

3. *What do we know about the social and cultural context of each child's life?* Most of the children in this group come from homes in which help is readily available. The group's dominant cultural values and child-rearing practices reinforce dependence and community, although there is a smaller group of families who want their children to become more independent in taking care of their own needs.

These questions become the focus of conversations between home and school to determine the best solutions for all. Decision making is shared among the teachers and the families.

teachers and caregivers for multiculturalism is not just about becoming sensitive to race, language, gender, ethnicity, religion, socioeconomic status, or sexual orientation. It is also related to an understanding of the way individual histories, families of origin, and ethnic family cultures make us similar to and yet different from others. These insights help teachers to respond positively to the individual child's unique life experiences.

Children's growth and development can be understood only within their cultural context.

2-2 Early Childhood Core Programs

From the types available to the numbers of children who attend these schools, the name of the game in early childhood programs is diversity. The range can encompass full-day or half-day care, infant and toddler programs, primary school, before-school and after-school care, and kindergarten. The ages range from infancy through 10 years, and the programs

culturally appropriate practice. Curriculum that helps children understand the way individual histories, families of origins, and ethnic family cultures make us similar to and yet different from others.

kindergarten. A school or class for children 4 to 6 years old; in the United States, kindergarten is either the first year of formal, public school or the year of schooling before first grade.

Diversity

Connecting Cultures between Home and School

Children need a sense of cultural congruency between their home and school in order to maximize their educational experience. Together, families and teachers can support each other by sharing information that enhances a teacher's understanding of the culture of the family.

FirstSchool, a project of the Frank Porter Graham Child Development Institute at the University of North Carolina at Chapel Hill, partners with schools to improve PreK-3rd grade school experiences for African American, Latino, and low income children and their families. In a recent guide, (Gillanders & Gutman, 2013) noted a variety of methods that teachers can use to enhance children's social-emotional, cognitive, academic, and cultural needs:

1. Focus groups that help identify the effectiveness of the home–school partnership.

2. School-wide questionnaire for in-depth knowledge of the family's beliefs and practices.

3. Home visits to learn about family routines and sociocultural practices.

4. Community visits for staff who reside elsewhere to become familiar with the greater community in which the child lives.

5. Classroom questionnaires to find out how parents perceive their child's progress and their satisfaction with the way the school communicates with them.

6. Parent-teacher conferences used to inform parents of their child's progress and to learn the parents' viewpoint about their children's learning.

7. Phone calls, e-mails, and text messages are used as a quick way to touch base, just say "hello," check up on a child's illness, and to send pictures back and forth of children at work and play.

The information from such data gathering can inform curriculum planning, teaching strategies, parent involvement, and ways to respect and reflect the culture of the children's and families within the classroom.

take place in homes, schools, community centers, churches and synagogues, and business work places.

Programs for young children exist to serve a number of needs, which often overlap. Some of these are the following:

Caring for children while parents work (e.g., family child care homes, child care center)

Enrichment programs for children (e.g., half-day nursery school, laboratory school)

Educational programs for parent and child (e.g., parent cooperatives, parent–child public school programs, high school parent classes)

Activity arena for children (e.g., most early childhood programs)

Specialized setting for children with specific disabilities

Academic or readiness instruction (e.g., kindergarten, many early childhood programs)

Culturally or religiously specific programs (e.g., a school setting with a definitive African American focus or a faith-based school that teaches religious dogma)

Philosophy-specific programs (e.g., Montessori, Reggio Emilia, Waldorf schools)

Training grounds for teacher education (provide opportunities for student teachers to learn best practices and observe young children)

NAEYC DAP in Action

DAP in Action—Respect for Cultural Diversity

Using NAEYC's criteria for cultural diversity, these examples demonstrate how DAP supports greater consistency between home and school cultures when you:

> Build a sense of the group as a community, bringing each child's home culture and language into the shared culture of the school so each child feels accepted and gains a sense of belonging

> Provide books, materials, images, and experiences that reflect diverse cultures that children may not likely see, as well as those that represent their family life and cultural group

> Initiate discussions and activities to teach respect and appreciation for similarities and differences among people

> Talk positively about each child's physical characteristics, family, and cultural heritage

> Avoid stereotyping of any group through materials, objects, language

> Invite families' participation in all aspects of the program

> Take trips to museums and cultural resources of the community

> Infuse all curriculum topics with diverse cultural perspectives, avoiding a "tourist" approach

Figure 2-1 All children and their families deserve to be in programs in which their lives are respected and in which they can be proud of their cultural heritage (NAEYC, 1998). (Source: Data from NAEYC, 1998)

---

faith-based school. A school that teaches religious dogma.

teacher talks | Teaching in a Faith-Based Setting

I am a teacher at a large preschool that is part of the local Jewish community. The preschool shares the site with a synagogue, the temple offices, and the religious grade school. I do not happen to be Jewish so I have had much to learn about working in such an environment. When I first came to the school 10 years ago, I was nervous about fitting in. I believed that I would be the only non-Jewish person at the school. As it turned out, I found this community to be very welcoming. In our particular school, about half of the teachers are Jewish. Our students in the preschool are not all Jewish either. The student body is made up of Temple members, children who live in mixed faith families, and children who are not Jewish at all but come to our school for the stellar education they receive here. This diversity is typical of the area in which we live and it's one of the things that makes our school great. We are proud to reflect and serve the surrounding neighborhood.

I have found that no matter what religion is involved, certain principles hold true. These are some of the insights I've gained:

1. My first responsibility is to the children's development. Developmentally appropriate practices can be adapted to any curriculum, including one based on a faith perspective.

2. At their core, religions are moral-and-values based. Issues such as justice, equality, compassion, and service to others are ideals common to many secular early childhood programs and familiar to early childhood teachers. For example, we teach our students about helping others who are less fortunate by collecting *Tzedakah* (charity) coins from the children every Friday. We count the coins at the end of the year and decide as a class how to use this money to help others. Classes have used the money to buy food for our local food bank, to buy books to donate to shelters, and to plant trees in Israel. At my school, we use the Jewish holidays to teach values to young children as well. My favorite holiday to celebrate in pre-school is Tu B'Shevat, the new year of the trees. On this day my class learns how trees grow and why they are important to people and to the earth. Then we all go outside under the trees in our yard to eat treats and have a birthday party for the trees.

3. It is important to make an effort to get to know the values and beliefs you will be representing. I had to learn the blessing that is recited before each meal in Hebrew. The children appreciated that I was learning about their faith along with them.

4. We know that parents are an integral part of a child's school experience. In my setting, many parents are temple members and have an added stake in the school. This can prove to be quite different from teaching in a preschool environment with a yearly turnover. In some schools parents are seen only at pick-up time, at my school parents are welcome to join us for school wide Shabbat Service every Friday. They are present at many holiday functions and if they are Jewish, these same parents may be sending their child to our religious school on our campus for years to come.

I find that having the Jewish teachings and blessing helps the teachers remember to stop and see the wonders of our everyday world and to have reverence for the wonders of the magical time of early childhood.

By Danielle

2-2a Factors that Determine Types of Programs

Programs in early childhood settings are defined by many factors, and each is a part of the mission of the program. Any given program is a combination of those factors, and each has an impact on the quality and type of learning that takes place. Some of those factors are the following:

1. Ages of the children being served
2. Philosophical, theoretical, or theological ideals
3. Goals of the program
4. Purpose for which the program was established
5. Requirements of the sponsoring agency
6. Quality and training of teaching staff
7. Shape, size, and location of the physical environment
8. Cultural, ethnic, languages spoken, economic, and social make-up of the community
9. Financial stability
10. Professionalism of staff

2-2b Special Features

A program usually has a number of goals that may result in special features. One goal may be to encourage children to share their knowledge and skills and to learn from one another, and the program will reflect that goal in several ways.

Mixed-Age Grouping

One way to achieve the goal for cooperative learning is to have **mixed-age groups**, where children of several age levels are in the same classroom. This practice is often referred to

---

mixed-age group. The practice of placing children of several levels, generally one year apart, into the same classroom. Also referred to as family grouping, heterogeneous grouping, multiage grouping, vertical grouping, and ungraded classes.

as *family grouping* or *heterogeneous, vertical,* or *ungraded grouping,* and although not a new idea, it is emerging as an area of considerable interest to early childhood educators. Montessori schools, one-room schoolhouses, and the Reggio Emilia schools have observed this practice for many years.

The age range among children in mixed-age groups is usually more than 1 year. There are a number of developmental advantages when children interact with peers above and below their age level:

1. Each child's own developmental level and pace are accommodated, allowing children to advance as they are ready.
2. Age and competition are de-emphasized as cooperative learning is enhanced.
3. Caring and helping behaviors toward younger children and a sense of responsibility toward one another are fostered.
4. Diverse learning styles and multiple intelligences are appreciated.
5. A variety and number of different models for learning and for friendships are available.

---

looping. The practice of keeping a teacher and a group of children in a class together for two or more years.

traditional nursery school/preschool. The core of early childhood educational theory and practice; program designed for children aged two-and-a-half to five years of age, which may be a part- or an all-day program.

6. Children grow in independence in their work and in socialization.

The risks associated with mixed-age groupings include the following:

1. The potential for older children to take over and overwhelm the younger ones is real, as is the possibility that younger children will pester the older children. This requires monitoring by the teaching staff, and the Reggio Emilia schools offer a good model here. In these Italian programs, older children have the responsibility to work with the younger children, explaining things and helping them find appropriate roles to take in their projects.
2. The academic and social advantages of mixed-age grouping cannot occur without a variety of activities from which children may freely choose and the opportunity for small groups of children to work together.
3. Teachers must be intentional about encouraging children to work with others who have skills and knowledge they do not yet possess.

Mixed-age groupings reflect the principles of Dewey, Piaget, Gardner, and Vygotsky, through the interactions of peers as well as adults. The practice of mixed-age grouping has much to commend it and must be seriously addressed as an issue in programs for young children.

Looping

The practice of keeping a group of children and their teacher together in the same class for at least 2 years is called **looping**.

Like mixed-age grouping, looping is an old idea revisited and is found today in the Waldorf schools and Reggio Emilia programs. Looping is often paired with mixed-age classrooms, which further extends the natural, family-like atmosphere.

The benefits of looping are as follows:

1. Providing stability and emotional security to children
2. Giving teachers a greater opportunity to get to know children and therefore be able to individualize the program for them
3. Fostering better social interactions among children
4. Enhancing a sense of family and community within the classroom

Critics of looping cite the need for experienced teachers who enjoy teaching across the age levels and who can work with the same children over an extended period of time.

2-2c The Core Programs of Early Childhood Education

Two types of programs form the basis for a number of variations that exist in the field today. Traditional nursery schools and child care programs reflect the historical nature of early childhood education.

The Traditional Nursery School/Preschool

The **traditional nursery school/preschool** exemplifies a developmental approach to learning in which children actively explore materials and in which activity or learning centers are organized to meet the developing skills and interests of the child. Most of these programs serve children from 2½ to 5 years of age.

Developmentally, a traditional nursery school focuses on social competence and emotional well-being. The curriculum encourages self-expression through language, creativity, intellectual skill, and physical activity. The basic underlying belief is the importance of interpersonal connections children make with themselves, each other, and adults.

The daily schedule (Fig. 2-2) reflects these beliefs:

> Large blocks of time are devoted to free play, when children are free to initiate their own activities and become deeply involved without interruptions. This not only emphasizes the importance of play but also allows children to learn to make their own choices, select their own playmates, and work on their interests and issues at their own rate.

> There is a balance of activities (indoors and out, free choice, and teacher-directed times) and a wide variety of activities: large- and small-muscle games, intellectual choices, creative arts, and social play opportunities.

> Although nursery schools are often half-day programs, many now offer extended hours through lunch time.

The role of the teacher and methods of teaching are important. Nursery schools assume that young children need individual attention and should have personal, warm relationships with important adults. This philosophy reflects the influence of Dewey, Piaget, Erikson, and others and is reflected in the program in many ways:

> The groups of children are generally small, often fewer than 20 in a class.

> The teacher-to-child ratio is low, as few as 6 to 10 children for each teacher.

Sample Schedule for Traditional Nursery School

9:00	Children arrive at school
9:00–9:45	Free play (indoors)
9:45	Cleanup
10:00	Singing time (large group)
10:15–10:30	Toileting/snack time (small groups)
10:30–11:30	Free play (outdoors)
11:30	Cleanup
11:45	Story time
12:00	Children leave for home

© Cengage Learning®

Figure 2-2 A sample schedule for traditional half-day nursery schools is the core of early childhood education programs.

> Teachers learn about children's development and needs by observation and direct interaction, rather than from formalized testing, individually and in small groups.

> Teachers encourage children to express themselves, their feelings, and their thinking. Such rapport between teacher and pupil fosters self-confidence, security, and belonging. Proponents of the traditional nursery school believe that these feelings promote positive self-image, healthy relationships, and an encouraging learning environment.

Universal Preschools

Increasing numbers of school districts are increasingly funding prekindergarten programs for 4-year-olds, although some include 3-year-olds as well. Depending on their goal, these programs fall somewhere between traditional nursery schools and not quite full-day care. For some, the focus is on school readiness; others give priority to children at risk for school failure, children who come from families in which English is not spoken, or low-income families. In states in which early education has achieved a level of support, all 4-year-olds are eligible for enrollment, regardless of income. The concept for universal preschools will be a continuing issue.

Full-Day Child Care

As noted in Chapter 1, child care is not a modern phenomenon. Some of the first nursery schools in England operated from 8:00 AM until 4:00 or 5:00 PM.

Full-day child care is for children who need care for a large portion of their waking day and includes basic caretaking activities of eating, dressing, and resting as well as play and learning times. A full-day program includes appropriate curriculum, and the schedule is extended to fit the hours of working parents. Child care centers often serve infants and toddlers as well as the 2½- to 5-year-old range. Many offer an after-school option as well. The schedule for full-day care in Figure 2-3 reflects a balance of play, learning, and daily routines.

Most full-day care takes place in centers, such as churches and synagogues, YWCA and YMCAs, community and recreational facilities, corporate business buildings, and hospitals. They are private and public. Most operate year-round. In addition, child care, especially for children younger than 3 years, may be in a home.

Center-Based Child Care

Child care centers serve children from infancy through preschool, and some include kindergarten and before-school and after-school options. A child care center reflects its goals through the daily schedule, as seen in Figure 2-3:

> The morning starts slowly, as children arrive early. As the day draws to a close, children gather together quietly, with less energy and activity.

---

full-day child care. Child care that begins in the morning and goes through the day, often arranged for the hours that parents work.

Child care centers. A place for care of children for a large portion of their waking day; includes basic caretaking activities of eating, dressing, resting, and toileting, as well as playing and learning time.

Sample Full-Day Child Care Schedule

7:00–8:30	Arrival/breakfast; limited indoor play
8:30	Large group meeting
9:45	Cleanup/toileting
8:45–9:45	Free play (inside)
10:00	Snack time (small groups)
10:15–11:30	Free play (outside)
11:30	Cleanup/hand washing
12:00	Lunch
12:30	Tooth brushing/toileting
1:00–2:00	Nap time
2:00–3:00	Free play (outside)
3:00	Group time
3:15	Snack time (small groups)
3:30–5:00	Inside and outside free play/library hour
5:00	Cleanup
5:15–5:30	Departure

© Cengage Learning®

Figure 2-3 A typical full-day care schedule. Most child care programs combine education and caring for basic needs.

> The center may supply breakfast and midmorning and midafternoon snacks, supplementing a lunch from home. Some centers are funded to supply all of the meals and snacks during the day.

> A nap period for 1 to 2 hours for all the children gives a needed rest and balances their active, social day with quiet, solitary time.

> The program may also include experiences outside the school—field trips, library story hour, or swimming lessons—because children spend the major portion of their waking hours on-site.

> Child care parents may require extra effort; they have full-time jobs as well as child-rearing responsibilities draining their energies. Parents' needs also may be greater and require more of the teachers' time.

> The staff in a full-day setting is often called on to deal with the parenting side of teaching. Children in full-day care may need more nurturing and clearer consistency in behavioral limits from adults.

> The teaching staff has staggered schedules, perhaps a morning and an afternoon shift. Caretakers from both shifts must be aware of what happens when they are not on site to run the program consistently.

family child care. Care for children in a small, homelike setting; usually six or fewer children in a family residence.

The most critical issues on child care were noted in Chapter 1. The quality of full-day child care programs is spotty: some are of good quality, with appropriate compensation to maintain staff professionalism and stability; others are of low quality with untrained staff and low salaries. It is worth repeating here that high-quality, affordable child care is an issue that will not go away and deserves the attention of early childhood professionals and legislators.

Family Child Care Homes

Family child care is a type of service reminiscent of an extended family grouping. The home setting, sometimes right within the child's own neighborhood, offers a more intimate, flexible, convenient, and possibly less expensive service for working parents. The children in a family child care home can range from infants to school-aged children who are cared for after regular school hours. The group size can range from 2 to 12, but most homes keep a low adult-to-child ratio, enrolling fewer than 6 children. There are special challenges with family child care:

> Because they often care for infants, preschoolers, and after-schoolers, the developmental ranges that family child care providers must meet may span up to 12 years. That poses a challenge to develop experiences and activities for a mixed-age group of children.

> Family child care providers work and live in the same environment, posing logistical problems of storage, space definition, and activity space.

> Family child care providers are administrators and managers as well as teachers and caregivers, faced with budgets and fee collections.

Family child care has many advantages:

> It is especially good for children who do well in small groups or whose parents prefer them in a family-style setting.

> Family child care homes often schedule flexible hours to meet the needs of parents who work.

> The wide age range gives children a chance to learn from one another.

> Consistency and stability from a single caregiver throughout the child's early years and a family grouping of children provide a homelike atmosphere that is especially appropriate for infants and toddlers.

> Family child care allows child caregivers to work at home while raising their own children.

Family child care has its disadvantages, too. Many homes are unregulated; that is, they are not under any sponsorship or agency that enforces quality care, and many are exempt from state licensing. Many family child care providers lack knowledge of child development and early education, and are not required to take courses. The National Association for Family Child Care, a network of family child care providers, has established a quarterly publication and is making efforts to address the challenges to these programs.

2-3 Variations of Core Programs

There are many variations of the core programs that provide care and education for young children. These programs differ according to the sponsoring agency, the way they serve children and families, their underlying mission, and their profit or nonprofit status.

2-3a Head Start and Early Head Start

Head Start is a federally funded, comprehensive program providing health, education, and social services to children and their families. Since 1965, Head Start has served more than 30 million children and their families (Head Start, 2012). Most Head Start programs are half-day and serve 3- to 4-year-olds. Head Start programs are housed in churches, synagogues, community centers, elementary schools, and office buildings. The success of Head Start can be attributed to its guiding objectives and principles, most notably expressed through the following:

1. *Its comprehensive nature.* The whole child is nurtured; this includes medical, dental, and nutritional needs, as well as intellectual growth. Extensive health, education, and social services are offered to children and their families.
2. *Parent participation and involvement.* Parents serve as active participants and get involved in the program at all levels: in the classroom as teacher aides, on governing boards making decisions about the program, and as bus drivers and cooks.
3. *Services to families.* Many of the comprehensive services offered to children are extended to parents as well. Paid jobs in the program, on-the-job training, continuing education, job training, and health care are some of the support services families receive.
4. *Community collaboration.* Interest and support from the local community helps Head Start respond to the needs of the children and families it served. Public schools, religious institutions, libraries, service clubs, and local industry and businesses foster responsible attitudes toward society and provide opportunities to work with members of the community in solving problems.
5. *Multicultural/multiracial education.* Since its inception, Head Start has provided a curriculum that reflects the culture, language, and values of the children in the program. Head Start efforts in this regard have been the models for other early childhood programs.
6. *Support for the value of dual-language learning for children whose primary language is not English.* Head Start conducts research and provides resources for families and teachers to help them link culture, language, and learning.
7. *Inclusion of children with special needs.* Since 1972, Head Start has pioneered the inclusion of children with disabilities in its classrooms.
8. *Ecology of the family.* Head Start programs look at children within the context of the family in which they lived and view the family in the context of the neighborhood and community.

Routines, such as snacks, provide a balance to an active and busy day at the child care center. <

© Cengage Learning®

truth or *fiction?*

T F Two programs form the core of early care and education.

The traditional nursery school (often called preschool) and full-day child care are the basis for most other early childhood programs.

Head Start. Federally funded comprehensive program for low-income children who are 3, 4, and 5 years old.

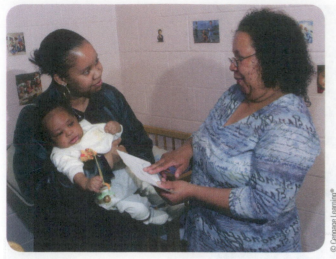

Head Start is a comprehensive program that offers many support services to children and families. ◄

Head Start programs today comply with mandated federal performance standards, a controversial move because these standards of learning focus more heavily on literacy, math, and science. The concern among some early childhood professionals is that the importance of a play-based, developmentally appropriate curriculum will be lost.

Head Start today is challenged by insufficient federal funding, political interference, controversial assessment policies, high numbers of English language learners, and like other programs, staff quality and retention.

Head Start has enrolled nearly 30 million children since 1965.

Early Head Start serves low-income families with infants and toddlers and pregnant women and is based on Head Start's four cornerstones: child development, family development, staff development, and community development. Like Head Start, this program must comply with federally regulated performance standards.

Early Head Start. Federally funded comprehensive program for low-income infants, toddlers, and pregnant women.

educaring. A concept of teaching as both educating and care giving; coined by Magda Gerber in referring to people working with infants and toddlers.

2-3b A Variety of Early Childhood Options

Programs for young children take many forms and allow families to choose the best option to meet their needs. Variations of the core programs are outlined in Figure 2-4.

2-3c Infant/Toddler Programs

Parent relationships are an important part of any program for young children, but especially so when babies

Programs designed for infants help them experiment and explore. ◄

Professionalism

Advocating for Infants

Magda Gerber has been a pioneer in infant care and coined the term **educaring** to describe the relationship between an infant and an adult. Gerber's philosophy is based on a respect for babies and the use of responsive and reciprocal interactions in which baby and caregiver learn about each other. Communicating through caregiving routines (diapering, feeding) in one-to-one intense and focused interactions is a foundation of Gerber's approach to caring for infants and toddlers (Gerber, 1979). Observing, listening, and reading babies' cues are key elements in educaring.

Chart of Variations of Early Childhood Programs

Type	Sponsor	Ages	Schedule	Key Characteristics	Settings
Parent cooperative	School districts, private owners	Preschoolers; often mixed-age groups	Full-day and/or half-day	Parents commit to teaching in the classroom on a regular basis; regular parent education meetings; time-consuming; lower costs	Community centers, privately owned buildings, churches, synagogues
Laboratory schools	College or university	Preschool, infant/toddlers	Full-day and/or half-day	Students and teachers often participate in teacher training and research activities; offer model programs	Located on or near campus
Employer sponsored	Individual business or corporation	Infant/toddlers, preschooler, school age	Full-day and/or half-day	Is an employee benefit option for parents; may be available as a voucher for any child care arrangement	Often on or near job site; hospitals, factories, and government agencies, as well as child care centers and family child care homes
For profit (proprietary)	Corporations and individuals	Infant/toddler, preschool, kindergarten, before-school and after-school ages	Full-day and/or half-day	May be part of a national/regional chain or individually owned; great variety of services and programs offered year-round; major purpose is to make a profit	Individual centers owned by franchise or corporation
Nonprofit centers	Community, churches, synagogues, government agencies	Infant/toddlers, preschool, school age	Full-day and/or half-day	Subsidized by sponsoring organization or government agency, which often provides low or free rent	Community buildings, government office buildings, churches, synagogues
Programs in religious institutions	Religious organization	Infant/toddler, preschool, school age	Full-day and/or half-day	May be a community outreach program where no religious dogma is taught or may be part of the ministry of the sponsor and include religious dogma in the curriculum; tends to be one of the largest providers of child care in the United States; tax exempt as a nonprofit; sharing space with congregational programs may be difficult	Churches, synagogues
Before-school and after-school care	Public schools, community organizations, YMCAs, YWCAs, churches, synagogues	Preschool and elementary school ages	Before and after school hours	Safe place for children during parent's working hours; may provide holiday, vacations, and summer programs	Schools, community centers, YMCAs, YWCAs, child care centers
Nannies	Individual families	Age(s) of children in family, generally preschoolers and elementary ages	According to the family's needs	Very personalized option; nanny may live with the family and may have other household responsibilities; trained in child development	In child's home
Friends and family members	Individuals	Infant/toddler, preschool, school age	Flexible according to parent and caregiver needs; may be full or part time	Can offer stability within a family setting; personal connections; flexibility to meet needs of parents; care for sick children	In friend, family, or child's home

(Continued)

Chart of Variations of Early Childhood Programs—cont'd

Type	Sponsor	Ages	Schedule	Key Characteristics	Settings
Early intervention	Government agencies	Infant/toddler, preschool	Dependent on child's needs	Mandated by the Education of the Handicapped Amendments Act of 1986 for children who are at risk or developmentally delayed; includes comprehensive services; multidisciplinary approach; and Individualized Education Plan (IEP) is created for each child	In homes, centers, schools
Teen parent program	School district	Infant/toddler, preschool	Full-day and/or part-day	Available in high schools as a support service for teens with young children and as education classes for those without children; parents work part-time in the classroom to observe and learn child development and guidance principles	On campus
Home-schooling	Individual family	Ages of children in family	Determined by family	Extreme time commitment because one parent is the teacher; mixed-age grouping; parents often disillusioned with public school and/or want to teach their religious beliefs; lack accountability	
Family Child Care	Individual	Infant to Early Elementary	Flexible; may be full or Part-time	Home setting, wide developmental range, small, family grouping	In caregiver's home

© Cengage Learning®

Figure 2-4 Families have many options to choose from when selecting early childhood programs.

and toddlers are involved. Infant and toddler caregivers support the child's family structure in the following ways:

> Involve the parents in the everyday decisions about the care of their child.
> Provide families with information about the child's day.
> Strengthen the child's sense of belonging to that particular family.

Caregiving routines are at the heart of the infant/toddler program. The caregiver in a quality infant/toddler center understands that feeding, diapering, and playing are, in fact, the curriculum of this age group. The challenge is to find ways to use these daily routines to interact, develop trust and security, and provide educational opportunities. In many cases, the caregiver's role extends to helping parents use these same common occurrences to promote the optimal development of their child.

Infant/Toddler programs differ from those created for 3- and 4-year-olds:

> The mobility of the toddler requires different amounts of space and time in the schedule than are required for infants.

> Common routines such as diapering create the curriculum as caregivers talk with the babies about what they are doing and what is happening to them.
> Routines are the focus of the toddler's day. Mealtimes and toileting provide daily opportunities for toddlers to explore and to express their emerging sense of self. Hand washing—even eating—becomes a time to fill, to taste, to dump, to pick up.
> The curriculum emerges from a developmental need toddlers have of "Me! Mine!" To foster that independence, that wanting to "do it myself," routines that allow for experimentation, mistakes, and messes make a good toddler curriculum.

Good programs for infants and toddlers, then, are distinctly arranged for them and are not simply modified versions of what works well in a program for 3-year-olds.

Kindergarten

The kindergarten year is one of transition from early childhood programs into a more formal school setting. Kindergarten programs are universally available throughout the United States. They are found in elementary public and private schools, churches, and as part of preschool child care centers.

There are three major issues affecting kindergarten today:

1. Whole-day programs. Only a few states fund full-day programs. Too often the arguments regarding the costs of such programs overshadow a more basic question: What are the best and most appropriate kindergarten programs, teaching methods, and curricula, regardless of the length of day?

2. Every state establishes an arbitrary date (e.g., September) by which children must be a certain age to enter kindergarten. In the United States, compulsory age for kindergarten ranges from 5 to 8 years. In recent years, some parents hold children out for 1 year and enroll them when they are 6 years old; teachers retain many children each year in kindergarten; and administrators have created an array of kindergarten-substitute programs called *developmental*, *extra-year*, or *transitional kindergartens*. By the time they finally reach kindergarten, children are now in class with late 4-year-olds as well as 5- and 6-year-olds—a vast developmental span under one roof. Some of the methods used to create more homogeneous kindergarten classrooms, or to raise expectations for kindergarten admittance, are inappropriate uses of screening and readiness tests; discouragement or denial of entrance for eligible children; creation of transitional classes for those who are considered not ready for kindergarten; and an increasing use of retention (NAECS/NAEYC, 2001).

3. Public prekindergartens are often created for children who are from low-income families and/or are at risk due to poverty, language barriers, and literacy skills. These programs focus on helping children improve their skills and become ready for kindergarten.

4. The standards-based movement has changed expectations of what kindergartners will learn. There is a greater emphasis on academics in kindergarten, especially in math, literacy, and science. As a result, there is more testing (starting in third grade) that has implications for what is being taught in kindergartens.

2-3d Early Elementary Grades

Early childhood is defined as children from birth through age 8 years. Often overlooked as part of a comprehensive view of young children are grades one, two, and three,

Redshirting and Readiness

Brain Research says

Neuroscience has established the fact that the brain is constantly changing. This *plasticity* means that the brain is always adapting and reorganizing on a daily basis. New connections are being created by everyday experiences and learning is taking place. Brain plasticity persists into adulthood but is especially pronounced in the early stages of life. At the same time the brain is growing, it is *pruning* itself, getting rid of unused synapses in a "use it or lose it" function. If the brain is rewiring itself so extensively in the preschool and early elementary years, and requires meaningful, positive experiences to grow, it begs the question: "Why is redshirting, or keeping children back one year, still being practiced?" It would appear that redshirting is actually counterproductive because it deprives the child of a challenging and stimulating school environment. The best way to give

children the greatest opportunity to learn is to put them in their age-appropriate classroom setting as soon as possible where their brains are immersed in growing, learning, and changing.

The issue of school readiness has been a hot topic for years. Early childhood professionals agree that children should be able to enter kindergarten when they are of legal age and that schools should be prepared to meet the needs of children where they are in their development. This is supported by recent brain development research that stresses stimulation and challenges as a way to foster brain growth and learning. Instead, schools have developed a variety of methods noted earlier to create more homogeneous classes rather than address the variety of developmental stages of children of kindergarten age. (See further discussion of school readiness in Chapter 15.)

There are many reasons children enter school without the resources and tools to succeed, such as poverty, language and cultural differences, access to high-quality early education programs, and lack of effective early intervention that includes comprehensive services.

Readiness has been defined as ready children, ready families, ready communities, ready early care and education, and ready schools (Rhode Island KIDS COUNT, 2005). All of these are necessary if we want all children to be ready for successful school experiences that use their brain potential to greatest advantage.

Questions

1. When might it be appropriate to delay a child's entry into school?
2. Why do disadvantaged children have the most to lose from delayed entry into school?

Standards

serving children who range from 6 to 8 years old. These grades focus on the basic academic skills of reading, writing, math, science, social studies, art and drama, health and safety, and physical education.

Dramatic changes are taking place in elementary schools. Children this age are developing logic and reasoning skills, and their learning tasks are more difficult than in kindergarten and require greater persistence and effort. As they grow more independent in their learning, elementary school children like choosing their own tasks, working cooperatively in small groups, and participating in planning each day's work. Enhancing the child's

Kindergartners are able to enjoy close friendships.◄

alignment. Coordinated curriculum between various levels of education as well as between curriculum and learning standards.

enthusiasm for learning is a primary task for the teachers of this age group.

Teachers are also challenged by the pressure of local, state, and national standards that dictate what children need to learn at this age and grade level. All states now have these standards for each grade and each subject matter. Using a curriculum that is in **alignment** with the standards is the most effective way to achieve developmentally balanced learning for this age group. This means that the subject matter matches what the standards say children should know, and that instruction and teaching strategies are more developmentally appropriate.

Accountability through learning standards will continue to have a strong impact on the early elementary years.

2-4 Assessing Program Quality

As educators, we are constantly evaluating, judging, and rating:

> *Curriculum:* Will this language game help develop the listening skills of the 3-year-olds?
> *Materials and equipment:* If we order the terrarium, will there be enough money left over for the math lab?
> *Environment:* Will the cubbies create a hazard out in the hallway?
> *Children's behavior:* How can we help Evie and Franco work more cooperatively?
> *Teacher effectiveness:* Yolanda is still having difficulty leading group time. How can we support her?

As a process, assessment is at once a definition, an evaluation, and a plan. A good assessment encourages positive change. A regular assessment keeps the program alive and growing, often bringing renewed dedication and perspectives. Figure 2-5 is a checklist that shows the program areas to include in an evaluation.

2-4a Why Is Program Assessment Important?

To Gain an Overview

Assessing a program gives an overview of how all the various components function together and reveals the entire environment as an integrated whole. These assessments add an awareness of how one area is related to another and how the parts mesh in a particular setting. This includes the following components:

> Children's progress
> Teacher performance
> Curriculum development

The Physical Environment

_____ Are the facilities clean, comfortable, safe?

_____ Are room arrangements orderly and attractive?

_____ Are materials and equipment in good repair and maintained?

_____ Is there a variety of materials, appropriate to age levels?

_____ Are activity areas well-defined?

_____ Are cleanup and room restoration a part of the daily schedule?

_____ Are samples of children's work on display?

_____ Is play space adequate, both inside and out?

_____ Is personal space (e.g., a cubby) provided for each child?

The Staff

_____ Are there enough teachers for the number of children?

_____ How is this determined?

_____ Are the teachers qualified? What criteria are used?

_____ Is the staff evaluated periodically? By whom and how?

_____ Does the school provide/encourage in-service training and continuing education?

_____ Do the teachers encourage the children to be independent and self-sufficient?

_____ Are the teachers genuinely interested in children?

_____ Are teachers aware of children's individual abilities and limitations?

_____ What guidance and disciplinary techniques are used?

_____ Do teachers observe, record, and write reports on children's progress?

_____ Are teachers skilled in working with individual children, small groups, and large groups?

_____ Does the teaching staff give the children a feeling of stability and belonging?

_____ Do teachers provide curriculum that is age-appropriate and challenging?

_____ How would you describe the teachers' relationships with other adults in the setting? Who does this include, and how?

_____ Can the teaching staff articulate good early education principles and relate them to their teaching?

Parent Relationships

_____ How does the classroom include parents?

_____ Are parents welcome to observe, discuss policies, make suggestions, help in the class?

_____ Are different needs of parents taken into account?

_____ Where and how do parents have a voice in the school?

_____ Are parent-teacher conferences scheduled?

_____ Does the school attempt to use community resources and social service agencies in meeting parents' needs?

The Organization and Administration

_____ Does the school maintain and keep records?

_____ Are scholarships or subsidies available?

_____ What socioeconomic, cultural, and religious groups does the school serve?

_____ What is the funding agency, and what role does it play?

_____ Is there a school board, and how is it chosen?

_____ Does the school serve children with special needs or handicaps?

_____ Is the classroom group homo- or heterogeneous?

_____ What hours is the school open?

_____ What age range is served?

_____ Are there both full- and part-day options?

_____ Is after-school care available?

_____ Does the school conduct research or train teachers?

_____ What is the teacher-child ratio?

The Overall Program

_____ Does the school have a written, stated educational philosophy?

_____ Are there developmental goals for the children's physical, social, intellectual, and emotional growth?

_____ Are the children evaluated periodically?

_____ Is the program capable of being individualized to fit the needs of all the children?

_____ Does the program include time for a variety of free, spontaneous activities?

_____ Is the curriculum varied to include music, art, science, nature, math, language, social studies, motor skills, etc.?

_____ Are there ample opportunities to learn through a variety of media and types of equipment and materials?

_____ Is there ample outdoor activity?

_____ Is there a daily provision for routines: eating, sleeping, toileting, play?

_____ Is the major emphasis in activities on concrete experiences?

_____ Are the materials and equipment capable of stimulating and sustaining interest?

_____ Are field trips offered?

_____ Do children have a chance to be alone? In small groups? In large groups?

Cultural Responsiveness

_____ Are multicultural perspectives already incorporated throughout the school, classroom curriculum, and classroom environment?

_____ Do my attitudes (and those of all staff) indicate a willingness to accept and respect cultural diversity? How is this demonstrated?

_____ Do classroom materials recognize the value of cultural diversity, gender, and social class equity?

_____ Do curricular activities and methods provide children opportunities to work and play together cooperatively? In mixed groups of their choice or at teacher direction?

_____ Do schoolwide activities reflect cultural diversity? How is this noticed?

_____ Does the program planning reflect the reality (views and opinions) of families and the community?

_____ Does the curriculum include planning for language diversity? For full inclusion? (Adapted from Baruth and Manning, 1992, and de Melendez and Ostertag, 1997.)

Figure 2-5 Checklist for areas of program evaluation. This checklist can be downloaded from the Education CourseMate website.

Ethics

> Financial structure
> Family involvement
> Community at large
> Governing organization of the school

In program evaluations, each of these is assessed for how it functions alone and how each works in concert with the others.

To Establish Accountability

A program assessment establishes accountability. This refers to a program's being answerable to a controlling group or agency—for instance, the school board or the government office, or parents and the community in which teachers work. These groups want to know how their funds are being spent and how their philosophy is being expressed through the overall program. Accountability among the staff and administrators to each other and the goals and mission of the program are also part of the assessment.

To Make Improvements

Program assessments are an opportunity to take an objective look at how the goals of the school are being met and will support the strengths of the existing program and suggest where changes might improve overall effectiveness. An in-depth assessment increases the likelihood that program goals and visions will be realized, and the assessment helps determine the direction the program may take in the future.

To Acquire Accreditation

Assessments are necessary for schools that wish to be approved for certification or accreditation by various organizations or government agencies. Such groups require that a school meet certain standards before the necessary permits are issued or membership is granted. Agencies, such as a state department of social services or department of education, often license family child care homes, and private schools may need to follow certain criteria to be affiliated with a larger organization (such as the American Montessori Society).

The National Academy of Early Childhood Programs, a division of NAEYC, has established an accreditation system for improving the quality of life for young children and their families. The Academy established standards in 10 component areas, which are defined in Figure 2-6.

2-4b Assessment Essentials

Before beginning a program assessment, consider these essential elements that will help ensure a successful process:

1. *Setting goals.* Without evaluation, goals are meaningless. Evaluation helps shape a goal into a meaningful plan of action. To be useful, an evaluation must include suggestions for improving the performance or behavior. The assessment tool that only describes a situation is an unfinished evaluation; goals for improvement must be established.

2. *Expectations and how they are met.* In every early childhood setting, more than one set of expectations is at work. The director has expectations of all the teachers. Teachers have standards of performance for themselves, the children, and parents. Parents have some expectations about what their children will do in school and about the role of the teachers. Children develop expectations regarding themselves, their parents, teachers, and the school. Be clear about these expectations.

3. A good assessment tool outlines clearly and specifically how expectations will be met in a system of mutual accountability. Assessments also point to where and how improvements can be made, to challenge methods, assumptions, and purposes and to see how expectations are met. Assessments provide information by which to rate performance, define areas of difficulty, look for possible solutions, and plan for the future.

4. *The degree of inclusion.* A good assessment is gender, ability, race, age, and culturally sensitive so that all may participate at their level of achievement.

2-4c How and What to Assess

There are three important steps to take that will ensure a success assessment process. Each is a necessary ingredient for a good assessment, and together they provide a realistic picture of the individual program.

Define the Objectives

Begin with a definition of the program's objectives. With the objectives defined, the choice of an assessment instrument becomes clear. If, for example, a program objective is to provide a healthy environment for children, the evaluation tool used must address the issues of health, safety, and nutrition.

NAEYC Accreditation Standards

These are the ten essential components on which an early childhood program is judged for accreditation through the NAEYC Academy of Early Childhood Programs. They serve as an appropriate outline of what to include in a program evaluation.

Relationships. The program promotes positive relationships among all children and adults to encourage each child's sense of individual worth and belonging as part of a community and to foster each child's ability to contribute as a responsible community member.

Curriculum. The program implements a curriculum that is consistent with its goals for children and promotes learning and development in each of the following areas: social, emotional, physical, language, and cognitive.

Teaching. The program uses developmentally, culturally, and linguistically appropriate and effective teaching approaches that enhance each child's learning and development in the context of the program's curriculum goals.

Assessment of child progress. The program is informed by ongoing systematic, formal, and informal assessment approaches to provide information on children's learning and development. These assessments occur within the context of reciprocal communications with families and with sensitivity to the cultural contexts in which children develop. Assessment results are used to benefit children by informing sounds decisions about children, teaching, and program improvement.

Health and safety. The program promotes the nutrition and health of children and protects children and staff from illness and injury.

Teachers. The program employs and supports a teaching staff that has the educational qualifications, knowledge, and professional commitment necessary to promote children's learning and development and to support families' diverse needs and interests.

Families. The program establishes and maintains collaborative relationships with each child's family to foster children's development in all settings. These relationships are sensitive to family composition, language, and culture.

Community relationships. The program establishes relationships with and uses the resources of the children's communities to support the achievement of program goals.

Physical environment. The program has a safe and healthful environment that provides appropriate and well-maintained indoor and outdoor physical environments. The environment includes facilities, equipment, and materials to facilitate child and staff learning and development.

Leadership and management. The program effectively implements policies, procedures, and systems that support stable staff and strong personnel, fiscal, and program management so all children, families, and staff have high quality experiences.

(Source: Overview of the NAEYC Early Childhood Program Standards, © 2008. http://www.naeyc.org/files/academy/file/OverviewStandards.pdf)

TeachSource Digital Download

Figure 2-6 These 10 NAEYC goals are the standards set to ensure quality programs for young children through the accreditation process.

truth or fiction?

T F The objectives and goals of the program will determine the type of assessment instrument used.

The foundation of an assessment is defined by the program goals and objectives. An appropriate assessment instrument will highlight the relationship between the current practice and the desired outcome.

Choose an Assessment Instrument

Assessment instruments vary with the purpose of the program evaluation. The NAEYC accreditation guidelines are effective (described as 10 essentials for high-quality programs in Fig. 2-6), as are four rating scales developed by the Frank Porter Graham Child Development Institute at the University of North Carolina. Each focuses on a specific early childhood setting:

> Infant/Toddler Environment Rating Scale (ITERS-R) for children from birth to 2+ years of age
> Early Childhood Environment Rating Scale (ECERS-R) for preschool through kindergarten programs serving children 2+ through 5 years of age

An important focus in the assessment process is the relationship between teachers and children. <

> Family Child Care Environment Rating Scale (FCCERS-R) for use in homes that serve infants through school age
> School-Age Care Environment Rating Scale (SACERS) for group care programs for children 5 to 12 years of age

Implement the Findings

The assessment is complete when the results are tabulated and goals are set to meet the assessment recommendation. Program administrators meet with the teaching staff to discuss the challenges the assessment revealed and a process is put in place for addressing them. A calendar is established to create a timeline for improvement, the appropriate staff members are assigned the responsibility for making changes, and the process begins anew.

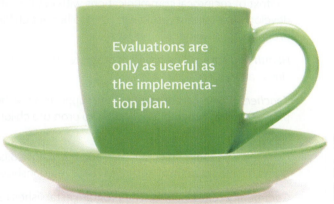

Evaluations are only as useful as the implementation plan.

summary

2.1   High-quality early childhood education settings reflect the three basic elements of developmentally appropriate practice (DAP) by basing their programs on what is known about child development and learning, what is known about each individual child, and what is known about each child's social and cultural context.

2.2   The traditional nursery school and its sister programs of child care center and family child care homes provide the core of early childhood programs.

2.3   The variations on the core programs of early childhood education include college and university laboratory schools, parent cooperatives, religious institutions, government agencies, profit and non-profit groups, public schools, high schools, home-schooling, teen parent programs, nannies, friends and families, and before-school and after-school care.

2.4   A good program assessment provides opportunities to improve the program and make positive changes. Children, families, and staff are analyzed to see how they all work together to meet the goals of the program.

web resources

U.S. Department of Education
    http://www.ed.gov
Families and Work Institute
    http://www.familiesandwork.org
Center for the Child Care Workforce
    http://www.ccw.org

Head Start/Early Head Start
    http://www.acf.hhs.gov/programs/ohs
Children's Defense Fund
    http://www.childrensdefense.org

references

Copple, C., & Bredekamp, S. (2009). *Developmentally appropriate practice in early childhood programs serving children from birth through age 8.* Washington, DC: National Association for the Education of Young Children.

DHHS (U.S. Department of Health and Human Services). *2012 Head Start fact sheet.* Washington, DC: Head Start Bureau, Author.

Gerber, M. (1979). Respecting infants: the Loczy model of infant care. In E. Jones (Ed.), *Supporting the growth of infants, toddlers, and parents.* Pasadena, CA: Pacific Oaks.

Gillanders, C. & Gutman, L. (2013). *Exploring families' beliefs and practices.* Frank Porter Graham Child Development Institute at the University of North Carolina at Chapel Hill.

Hyun, E. (1998). *Making sense of developmentally and culturally appropriate practice (DCAP) in early childhood education.* New York: Peter Lang Publishing.

NAECS/NAEYC (National Association of Early Childhood Specialists in State Departments of Education/National Association of Education for Young Children). (September 2001). Still unacceptable trends in kindergarten entry and placement. *Young Children,* 59–62.

NAEYC. (2005). *NAEYC early childhood program standards accreditation criteria: The mark of quality in early childhood education.* Washington, DC: Author.

NAEYC Professional Preparation Standards (2010). Washington, DC: Author.

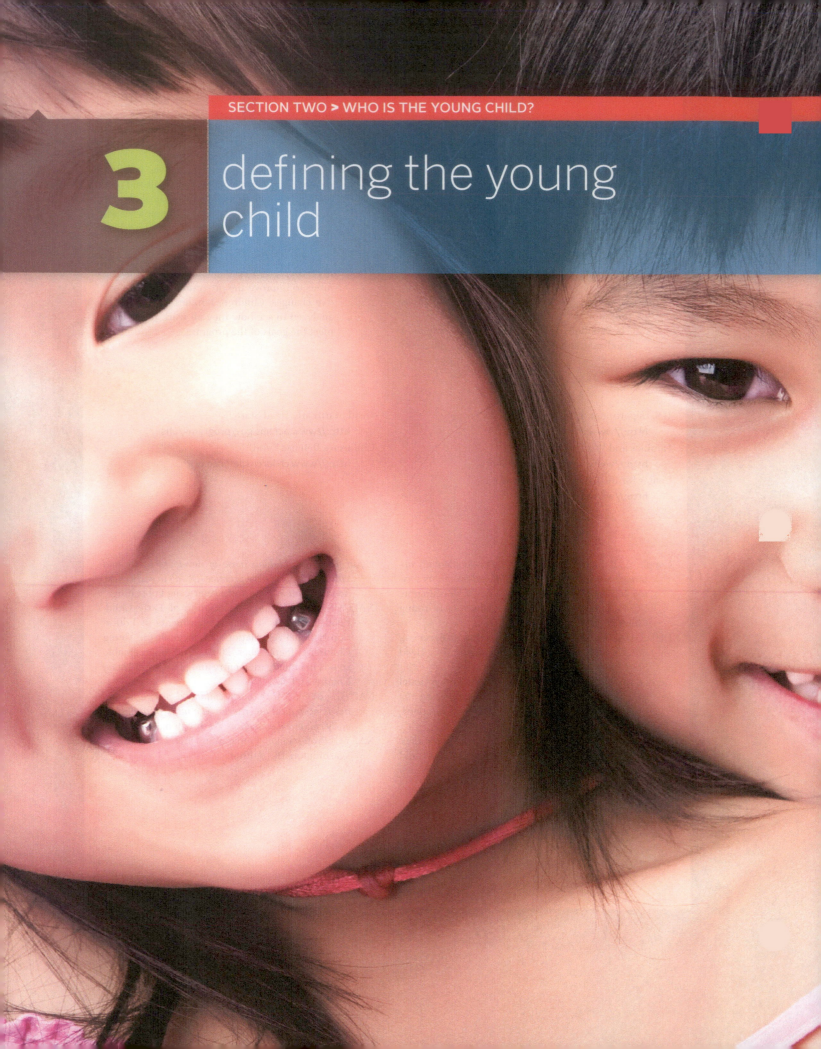

3

defining the young child

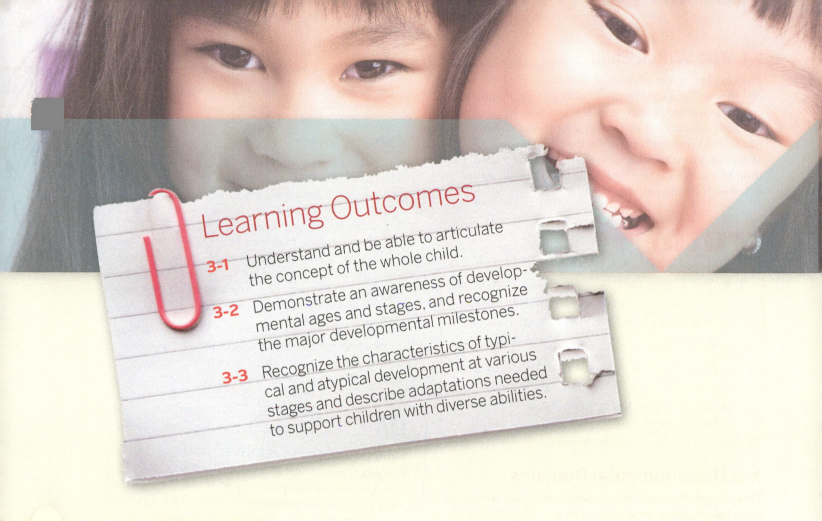

Learning Outcomes

3-1 Understand and be able to articulate the concept of the whole child.

3-2 Demonstrate an awareness of developmental ages and stages, and recognize the major developmental milestones.

3-3 Recognize the characteristics of typical and atypical development at various stages and describe adaptations needed to support children with diverse abilities.

© iStockphoto.com/ChristopherBernard

NAEYC Standards

The following NAEYC Standards for Early Childhood Professional Preparation are addressed in this chapter:

Standard 1: Promoting Child Development and Learning

Standard 2: Building Family and Community Relationships

Standard 3: Observing, Documenting, and Assessing to Support Young Children and Families

Standard 4: Using Developmentally Effective Approaches to Connect with Children and Families

Standard 5: Using Content Knowledge to Building a Meaningful Curriculum

Standard 6: Becoming a Professional

truth or fiction

T F The concept of the whole child suggests that each area of growth is isolated from and does not interact with other areas of growth.

T F Word Pictures are helpful when comparing one child with another.

T F Differences in children can be explained by genetics and environment.

T F There are two types of children with special needs.

3-1 The Whole Child

The concept of the whole child addresses all of the child's developmental domains: physical, cognitive, linguistic, social, and emotional. Each area is taken into account when planning educational experiences for young children. The whole child concept is based on the principle that all areas of human growth and development are interrelated. Each child is a sum total of a multitude of parts and, as such, is different from anyone else.

truth or fiction?

T Ⓕ The concept of the whole child suggests that each area of growth is isolated from and does not interact with other areas of growth.

The concept of the whole child underscores the uniqueness of each child; each child is a combination of the various developmental domains that form the individual child.

3-1a Developmental Domains

Three major developmental domains help to define and express how children grow and develop:

1. *Social-emotional development:* includes a child's relationship with herself and others, self-concept, self-esteem, and the ability to express feelings
2. *Physical-motor development:* includes gross motor, fine motor, and perceptual motor activity
3. *Cognitive-language development:* includes curiosity, the ability to perceive and think, memory, attention span, general knowledge, problem solving, analytical thinking, beginning reading, and computing skills (cognitive development); and children's utterances, pronunciation, vocabulary, sentence length, and the ability to express ideas, needs, and feelings (language development—both receptive and verbal)

whole child. Based on the accepted principle that all areas of human growth and development are interrelated. The concept of the whole child suggests the uniqueness of the person. Although they are often discussed separately, the areas of development (social-emotional, physical, language, cultural awareness, intellectual, and creativity) cannot be isolated from one another.

developmental domains. The classifications of development that broadly define the three major growth areas of body, mind, and spirit that roughly correspond to biology, psychology, and sociology.

Word Pictures. Descriptions of children that depict, in words, norms of development; in this text, these are age-level charts that describe common behaviors and characteristics, particularly those that have implications for teaching children (in groups, for curriculum planning, with discipline and guidance).

Two More Spheres of Influence

Two additional spheres of influence on the growing child are cultural awareness and creative expression, which are outgrowths of both social-emotional development and cognitive-language development.

> *Cultural identity development.* This suggests the interconnections between developmental stages and a growing awareness of one's attitudes toward others. Various cultural milestones appear in each age group which, when appropriately fostered, can increase a child's sensitivity to differences.
> *Creative development.* This includes the usual creative activities such as movement, dance, music, and painting, as well as originality, imagination, divergent thinking, and problem solving.

The Word Pictures, found on pages 53–59, indicate how cultural identity develops throughout the early years. Creative development and cultural identity are highlighted in the Word Pictures as well.

DAP

How Development Is Interrelated

One area of development affects the other. Figure 3-1 helps us to visualize the interrelationship within the whole child. Think about how each developmental area might affect or interact with the others:

> Physical development affects how children feel about themselves. Children who appreciate their body and its power are confident in what they can accomplish (social-emotional domain).
> Cognitive skills interact with language development and creativity. When children have mastered their primary language, they can clarify some of their thought processes.
> The kindergartner who masters the physical task of using scissors is ready to try printing. The fine motor skills enhance the cognitive task for learning to print the alphabet.
> A child with a hearing loss may have difficulty pronouncing words; thus, physical development affects the language domain and possibly the social-emotional area.
> The child who lacks social skills to make friends may exhibit his emotional reactions in the schoolyard by starting a fight and also in the math lesson, where he is unable to focus on the intellectual tasks.
> Observe a classroom during activity time or free play. How many interactions do you see between developmental domains? How do you think this affects a child's ability to learn? As a child, what were your strongest developmental domains?

TeachSource Digital Download

The Architecture of the Brain

Block play is one of the most popular activities in preschool programs. When young children first encounter blocks, they make piles, stack them, or lay them out in a row. As they have more experiences with blocks, more complex building emerges as children build walls and floors, bridges, and enclosures. At first, playing with blocks is an end in itself but with more experience, blocks are used in a larger architectural plan. "I need to put these blocks on top of each other to build a second story to my garage," says 5-year-old Gian-Francesco. It is almost as if the first year of block building was a practice period to lay the foundation for more complex work.

So it is with how the young child's brain develops. Foundational concepts of brain development (National Scientific Council on the Developing Child, 2010) help us understand three basic blocks on which brain development is based. (See the video series, "Three Core Concepts in Early Development," available at www.developingchild.harvard.edu/resources/multimedia/videos/three_core_concepts/.)

Concept 1: Experiences build brain architecture. Through daily activities and experiences the brain cells (neurons) shape the neurological networks that create the foundation for emotions, logic, memory, motor skills, social-emotional behaviors, and vision. Each neuron creates an axon (which sends signals) and dendrites (which receive signals). Axons and dendrites join to form synapses. Simple circuits form the basis for more complex brain circuits. Electrical activity is triggered by sensory experiences and fine-tunes the brain's architecture. As you supervise block play, notice all the architecture there, and remember that the brain is being built as well.

Concept 2: "Serve and return" shapes the brain's architecture. If you have ever played tennis or ping-pong, you have participated in "serve and return." Your partner serves the ball to you and you hit it back, returning the serve. Now think of the image of new parents cooing, babbling, and smiling at their baby. That, too, is a "serve and return" activity and is key to forming strong brain architecture. The back and forth interactions between children and adults form the foundation of brain architecture on which all future development will be built. "Serve and return" interactions help create the neural connections between all the different areas of the brain, and they build the child's emotional and cognitive skills. The best advice for teachers and parents is to create "serve and return" interactions to enhance the child's growing brain.

Concept 3: Toxic **stress** hinders healthy brain development. Persistent adversity in young children, such as poverty, neglect, abuse, family violence, parental substance abuse, and severe maternal depression cause toxic stress. The body's stress management system is activated and sends the stress hormone cortisol into the body. The body's reaction to stress includes rapid increase of heart rate and a rise in blood pressure. These responses help the body deal with stress and then return to normal when the brain perceives that the stress is past. However, when stress is prolonged and the child is without supportive adult help, the stress level persists and affects the brain's architecture. The neural connections become reduced by stress overload at a time when they should be growing new ones. High levels of cortisol can disrupt the learning process by inhibiting reasoning abilities, which can lead to emotional and cognitive problems. These early experiences of deprivation and stress become hard-wired into the brain.

Questions

1. Aside from block play, what other experiences in an early childhood program helps to build the brain's architecture? List those that are appropriate for infants and toddlers, for preschoolers, and for school-age children.
2. How would you "serve and return" with a 3-year-old? A school-age child?
3. What is our role as early childhood educators in reducing persistent stress in children's lives?

3-1b Growth Is Interrelated

Although they are often discussed separately, the development domains (social-emotional, physical, language, cultural awareness, intellectual, and creativity) cannot be isolated from one another. Each makes a valuable contribution to the whole child.

The circularity of the child's growth and development is a key element to understanding the "whole" child. Figure 3-1 shows the connection of each developmental domain in relation to the others.

Children are alike in that they all have the same developmental goals yet differ in that they grow and develop at different rates. ◄

3-2 Developmental Ages and Stages: Major Milestones

Descriptions of children's common characteristics date back to a classic collection of research by Gesell and Ilg. (See Chapters 1 and 4 for related discussions.) Age alone does not determine a child's capabilities, but it does provide a guideline for establishing appropriate expectations. Despite the wide range of individual differences at all ages, common behaviors lend a perspective to help teachers prescribe programs, plan activities, and create curricula.

3-2a Word Pictures

Each developmental phase has characteristics traits. These are described in the following pages as Word Pictures. Word Pictures are designed to help classroom teachers plan learning experiences for a group of children. Word Pictures are a valuable teaching tool because they help teachers know what to expect and when to expect it. The developmental and learning theories in Chapter 4 and their classroom applications will help you understand the basis from which these Word Pictures are drawn. See Figure 3-2 for guidelines on using these tools. (Chapter 10 has more practical applications and examples for planning curriculum.)

In Behavior and Guidance

We base guidance and discipline strategies on the expected behaviors common to a given age range. Many so-called problem behaviors are normal behaviors of the age at which they occur. Two-year-olds are easily frustrated as they grow increasingly independent. The wise teacher accepts the child's developmental stage, drawing on the knowledge that 2-year-olds are easily distracted and enjoy a variety of play activities. After the 2-year-old is comforted, play is resumed.

Guidelines for Using Word Pictures

It is important to use these age-level charts with discretion. The following guidelines will help:

1. **Balance your impressions of the Word Pictures with classroom experience.** Observe children to add a measure of reality as you interpret the phrases.

2. **Make a profile of the whole child and resist the tendency to categorize or stereotype.**

3. **Get perspective on the range of developmental norms a child exhibits over time.**

4. **Remember that these norms of development refer to average or typical behavior. They should not be applied too literally.** These characteristics are approximations of norms and do not represent a picture of any one child.

5. **Keep in mind that children go through most of the stages described and in the same sequence, but they do so at their own rates of growth.**

6. **Focus on what a child can do rather than on what he or she cannot do. Use the characteristics to compare the child with himself or herself.**

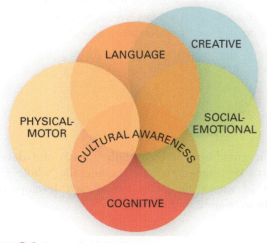

Figure 3-1 Areas of growth circles

Figure 3-2

In Curriculum Planning

Word Pictures can be used to tailor curricula on the basis of known developmental standards. When planning an activity, the teacher takes into account what she knows about each child's development and what she knows about the group as a whole.

Professionalism

Cultural Awareness and Identity

Children become aware of and form attitudes about racial and cultural differences at a very early age (Derman-Sparks & Edwards, 2010). Their experiences with their bodies, social environment, and cognitive-developmental stage combine to help them form their own identity and attitudes. As they develop cognitively, children become aware of differences and similarities in people. These cultural milestones are included in the Word Pictures to indicate how, as children come to a sense of themselves as individuals, their attitudes and behaviors toward others can be influenced.

truth or fiction?

T (F) Word Pictures are helpful when comparing one child with another.

Word Pictures are used to show an individual child's rate of growth and development and should not be used to compare one child with another. Each child is respected for his or her own growth pattern.

Word Pictures of an Infant

Ann Gordon

Social-Emotional

0–1 month	Cries to express emotions; bonding begins
4–10 weeks	Smiles socially and begins social games
3 months	Distinguishes familiar faces*
	Turns head toward human voices
	Kicks, smiles, waves in response
	Cries when left alone
	Recognizes parent
4 months	Laughs, smiles when spoken to, loves attention
5 months	Exhibits stranger anxiety* to 1 year
6 months	Distinguishes between voices
	Smiles, babbles at strangers
	Develops attachment
	Begins to play imitation games, plays peek-a-boo
	Sensitive to parental moods
8 months	Laughs out loud
9 months	Screams to get own way
	Play is activity only for present moment
	Fears unfamiliar: people, places, things*
	Beginning sense of separate self*

Language

0–1 month	Turns head in response to voices, cries to express needs
6–8 weeks	Coos
	Uses gestures to communicate: pushes objects away, squirms, reaches out to people,* pouts, smacks lips, shrieks, points
2 months	Makes voluntary vocal sounds
3 months	Babbles
6–12 months	Plays imitation sound games, responds to variety of sounds,* makes vowel sounds, acquires receptive language,* cries to communicate
12 months	Speaks first words

Physical-Motor

By 1 year	Grows 10 to 12 inches, triples birth weight, lengthens by 40%, doubles brain size, grows full head of hair, bounces in crib, uses whole-body motions

*Key characteristics of cultural awareness or identity.

4 months	Sees, grasps objects
5 months	Examines fingers, sits when propped
6 months	Rolls over, discovers feet, begins teething
7 months	Crawls
8 months	Sits up unaided, pulls to standing position, establishes pincer grasp
9 months	Creeps
10 months	Feeds self with spoon
11-12 months	Stands alone, cruises, takes first steps
Late infancy	Moves hands in rotation to turn knobs

Newborn motor activity is mostly reflexes.

Creative

Discovers and explores hands and feet
Expresses and discovers emotion, responds to facial expressions
Talks by babbling, cooing, and gurgling
Plays peek-a-boo

Cognitive

0–1 month	Responds to mother's voice
	Senses function, especially pain, touch*
10 weeks	Memory is evident*
4 months	Smiles on recognition
7–10 months	Solves simple problems (knocks over box to get toy)
8 months	Begins to believe in permanence of objects
	Follows simple instruction
8–12 months	Shows intentionality in acts
11 months	Begins trial-error experimentation
12 months	Plays drop and retrieve games, pat-a-cake
	Explores with hands and fingers
	Smiles, vocalizes at image in mirror*

Word Pictures of a Toddler

© 2016 Cengage Learning®

Social-Emotional

Almost totally egocentric
Has self-identity,* refers to self by name
Likes to be noticed, loves an audience
Lacks inhibitions
Insists on own way, assertive, strong sense of ownership
Likes doing things by self
Laughs loudly at peek-a-boo
Cries when left alone
Curious*
Active, eager
Relates to adults better than to children
Usually friendly
Mimics adult behavior*
Experiences and shows shame*

Language

Some two-word phrases, uses 5 to 50 words
Enjoys vocalizing to self, babbles in own jargon
Uses "eh-eh" or "uh-uh" with gestures
Names closest relatives*
Repeats adults' words*
Points to communicate needs, wants

*Key characteristics of cultural awareness or identity.

Shakes head "no" to respond*
Responds to directions to fetch, point
Asks "what's that?" or "whassat?"*
Understands simple phrases, obeys verbal requests

Physical-Motor

Awkward coordination; chubby body
Tottering stance, finds it difficult to turn corners
Creeps when in a hurry
Walks with increasing confidence with feet wide apart, arms out, head forward
Runs with stiff, flat gait
Goes up and down stairs holding on
Backs into chair to sit down, prefers standing to sitting
Can squat for long periods of time
Motor-minded: constant motion, always on the move
Loves to pull and push objects, holds objects in both hands
Uses whole-arm movements
Carry and dump is a favorite activity
Scribbles
Turns pages two or three at a time
Zips and unzips large zipper

Creative

Responds to mood of music, sings phrases of nursery rhymes
Freely examines every object
Loves to finger paint and explore texture
Stares, takes it all in
"Age of exploration"
Makes up nonsense syllables

Cognitive

Points to objects in a book
Matches similar objects, fits round block in round hole
Loves opposites: up/down, yes/no*
Imitates simple tasks
Interest shifts quickly, short attention span
Follows one direction
Gives up easily but easily engaged*
Conclusions are important: closes doors, shuts books
Thinks with feet; action-oriented
Builds tower of three or four small blocks

Word Pictures of a Two-Year-Old

Social-Emotional

Self-centered, refers to self by given name*
Has difficulty sharing, possessive
Clings to the familiar; resistant to change, ritualistic; insists on
    routines*
Dependent
Likes one adult at a time*
Likes people*
Quits readily; easily frustrated, impulsive; shifts activities suddenly
Goes to extreme, pushes, shoves
Easily distracted
Finicky, fussy eater; has some food jags
Dawdles; slow geared
Watches others, plays parallel to others, treats people as inani-
    mate objects*
Excited about own capabilities

Language

Uses telegraphic sentences of two or three words: "throw ball"
Has difficulty in pronunciation; "me," "mine" most prominent
    pronouns*
Spontaneous language; engages in rhythmic, repetitive, constant
    talking
Interested in sound

Sings phrases of song, not on pitch
Unable to articulate feelings, frustrated when not understood;
    may stutter
Asks "whassat?" about pictures*
Can match words with objects
Uses 50 to 300 words

Physical-Motor

Uses whole-body action, has difficulty relaxing
Pushes, pulls, pokes, climbs into things
Leans forward while running
Climbs stairs one by one
Depends on adults for dressing, can help undress
Has reached one-half potential height
Bladder and bowel control begins, cuts last teeth, feeds self
Thumb-forefinger opposition is complete, alternates hands;
    preference developing
Awkward with small objects, grasps cups with two hands
Lugs, tumbles, topples; unsteady
Can rotate to fit objects
Expresses emotions bodily*

Creative

Imitates other children
Combines parallel play and fantasy play
Plays with sounds; repeats syllables over and over
Enjoys simple finger plays, can follow simple melodies
Learns to scribble, uses art for sensory pleasure

Cognitive

Recognizes, explores physical characteristics, classifies people by
    gender*
Investigates with touch and taste; intrigued by water, washing
Likes to fill and empty things
Has limited attention span, does one thing at a time
Lives in present, understands familiar concepts*
Can tell difference between black and white*
Needs own name used
Likes simple make-believe
Remembers orders of routines, recalls where toys are left
Names familiar objects in books

Word Pictures of a Three-Year-Old

*Key characteristics of cultural awareness or identity.

Social-Emotional

Imitates adults, wants to please adults; conforms*
Responds to verbal suggestions; easily prompted, redirected
Can be bargained with, reasoned with; begins to share, take
    turns, wait
Avid "me-too"-er*
Exuberant, talkative, humorous
Has imaginary companion, nightmares, animal phobias, fears
Plays consciously, cooperatively with others* and plays spontane-
    ously in groups
Goes after desires; fights for them, asserts independence often
Often stymied, frustrated, jealous
Sympathizes*
Strong sex-role stereotypes*

Language

Talkative with or without a listener
Can listen to learn*
Likes new words* and puts words into action
Increases use of pronouns, prepositions
Uses "s" to indicate plural nouns and "ed" to indicate past tense
Uses sentences of 3 or more words and 300 to 1000 words
Says "Is that all right?" a lot
Talks about nonpresent situations
Moves and talks at the same time
Substitutes letters in speech: "w" for "r"
Intrigued by whispering

Physical-Motor

Has well balanced body lines, walks erect; nimble on feet
Gallops in wide, high steps; swings arms when walking
Alternates feet in stair climbing
Suddenly starts, stops, turns corners rapidly
Jumps up and down with ease, can balance on one foot
Uses toilet alone, achieves bladder control, washes hands unassisted
Loses baby fat
Rides a tricycle
Puts on, takes off wraps with help; unbuttons buttons
Grasps with thumb and index finger, has some finger control with small objects
Holds cup in one hand, pours easily from small pitcher, can carry liquids
Has activity with drive and purpose

Creative

Dramatizes play
Enjoys slapstick humor, laughs at the ridiculous
Experiments with silly language
Imaginary companion may appear
Tricycle becomes many objects in dramatic play
Acts out own version of favorite story
Enjoys simple poems
Learns color concepts

Cognitive

Matches people according to physical characteristics*
Estimates "how many"; has number concepts of one and two
Enjoys making simple choices, cannot combine two activities
Alert, excited, curious; asks "why?" constantly; sees vague cause- and-effect relationships*
Understands "It's time to . . . "Let's pretend . . ."
Enjoys guessing games, riddles
Has lively imagination*
Often overgeneralizes*
Has short attention span; carries out two to four directions in sequence
Often colors pages one color
Names and matches simple colors, understands size and shape comparisons
Can recognize simple melodies
Distinguishes between night and day

Word Pictures of a Four-Year-Old

© Cengage Learning®

Social-Emotional

Mood changes rapidly; easily overstimulated, excitable,
Tries out feelings of power, dominates; is bossy, boastful, belligerent
Assertive, argumentative; shows off; is cocky, noisy, explosive, destructive
Can fight own battles; hits, grabs, insists on desires
Impatient in large groups,* cooperates in groups of two or three*
Develops "special" friends* but shifts loyalties often, in-group develops, excludes others*
Resistant, tests limits
Exaggerates; tells tall tales, alibis frequently; tattles frequently
Teases, outwits; has terrific humor
May have scary dreams
Has food jags, food strikes

Language

Has more words than knowledge, joins sentences together
A great talker, questioner; asks "when?" "why?" "how?"*

Likes words, plays with them; exaggerates, practices words
Has high interest in poetry
Can talk to solve conflicts,* responds to verbal directions
Enjoys taking turns to sing along; interested in dramatizing songs, stories
Uses voice control, pitch, rhythm
Loves being read to

Physical-Motor

Has longer, leaner body build
Vigorous, dynamic, acrobatic, active until exhausted
"Works": builds, drives, pilots
Can jump own height and land upright
Hops, skips, throws large ball, kicks accurately
Hops and stands on one foot, jumps over objects
Walks in a straight line, races up and down stairs, turns somersaults
Walks backward toe-heel
Has accurate, rash body movements; alternates feet going down stairs
Copies a cross, square; can draw a stick figure
Holds paint brush in adult manner, pencil in fisted grasp
Can lace shoes, dresses self except back buttons, ties
Has sureness and control in finger activities

Creative

Adventurous, shows vivid imagination, exaggerates and goes to extremes
Displays great interest in violence in imaginary play, demonstrates more elaborate dramatic play, can put on elaborate plays with puppets
Loves anything new

*Key characteristics of cultural awareness or identity.

Makes up new words, sounds, and stories
Enjoys complexity in book illustrations, likes funny poetry
Tells spontaneous story with artwork, combines words and ideas
Finds ways to solve problems

Cognitive

Does some naming and representative art, gives art products personal value
Can work for a goal*
Questions constantly, interested in how things work, interested in life-death concepts

Has an extended attention span, can do two things at once
Dramatic play is closer to reality,* has imaginary playmates
Judges which of two objects is larger, has concept of three, can name more
Has accurate sense of time
Full of ideas, likes a variety of materials, has dynamic intellectual drive*
Begins to generalize; often faulty*
Calls people names*
Recognizes several printed words

Word Pictures of a Five-Year-Old

© Cengage Learning®

Enjoys dictating stories, tells a familiar story, makes up songs
Uses 1500 words
Answers telephone, takes a message
Thinks out loud*

Physical-Motor

Completely coordinated, has adult-like posture and tremendous physical drive
Likes to use fine motor skills; has accuracy, skill with simple tools
Learns how to tie bow knot, dresses self completely
Draws a recognizable person*
Handedness is evident
Cuts on a line with scissors, begins to color within the lines
Catches ball from 3 feet away
Skips using alternate feet; enjoys jumping, running, doing stunts
Rides a two-wheeler, balances on a balance beam
Jumps rope, skips, runs lightly on toes
Likes to dance, is graceful, rhythmic
Sometimes roughhouses, fights

Creative

Explores variety of art processes, has idea of what to draw—wants to make something recognizable, likes to copy, enjoys making patterns and designs
Becomes engrossed in details of painting, blocks
Fantasy is more active, less verbal
Thinks out loud, has ideas, loves to talk about them
Can learn simple dance routine
Puts on simple plays

Social-Emotional

Poised, self-confident, self-contained; has sense of self-identity*
Sensitive to ridicule*
Has to be right; persistent
May get silly, high, wild; enjoys pointless riddles, jokes
Enjoys group play, competitive games*; aware of rules; defines them for others*
Chooses own friends, sociable*
Gets involved with group decisions,* insists on fair play*
Likes adult companionship,* accepts and respects authority,* asks permission
Remains calm in emergencies

Language

Uses big words and complete sentences, can define and spell some words
Takes turn in conversation, has clear ideas and articulates them*
Uses words to give, receive information; asks questions to learn answers*
Insists "I already know that"

Cognitive

Curious about everything,* wants to know "how?" "why?"*
Likes to display new knowledge, skills; somewhat conscious of ignorance*
Attention span increases; makes a plan, follows it, centers on task
Knows tomorrow, yesterday; knows names, address, town
Can count 10 objects, rote-counts to 20
Sorts objects by single characteristic*
Understands concepts of smallest, less than, one-half
May tell time accurately, on the hour; knows what a calendar is used for
Seldom sees things from another's point of view*

*Key characteristics of cultural awareness or identity.

Word Picture of a Six- or Seven-Year-Old

Ann Gordon

Social-Emotional

Six-Year-Old
Likes to work, yet often does so in spurts, not persistent
Can be charming
Tends to be a know-it-all, free with opinions and advice
Brings home evidence of good schoolwork, tests and measures self against peers*
Observes family rules,* believes in rules except for self*
Gender-role stereotypes are rigid,* friends are of same sex*
Friends easily gained, easily lost*; makes social connections through play*
Active, outgoing, proud of accomplishments
Shows aggression through insults, name calling*

Seven-Year-Old
More serious, sensitive to others' reactions*; enjoys solitary activities
Eager for home responsibilities
Complaining, pensive, impatient; shame is common emotion*
Leaves rather than face criticism, ridicule, disapproval*; complains of unfair treatment, not being liked*
Shows politeness and consideration for adults*
Enjoys solitary activities
First peer pressure: needs to be "in"*; wants to be one of the gang*
Self-absorbed, self-conscious; relates physical competence to self-concept*

Language

Six- or Seven-Year-Old
Enjoys putting language skill to paper, learning to print and write
Talks *with* adults rather than *to* them,* chatters incessantly
Dominates conversations, speech irregularities still common
Acquisition of new words tapers off
Bilingual capacities nearly complete* if English is second language; ability to learn new language still present*

Physical-Motor

Six- or Seven-Year-Old
Basic skills developing, need refinement
Likes to test limits of own body, values physical competence*
Works at self-imposed tasks
Needs daily legitimate channels for high energy, susceptible to fatigue
Learns to ride two-wheel bike, skate, ski
Motor development is tool for socializing; boisterous, enjoys stunts and roughhousing
Visual acuity reaches normal
Hungry at short intervals, like sweets
Chews pencils, fingernails, hair

Creative

Six-Year-Old
Tries out artistic exploration seriously for the first time
Industrious, eager, curious, enthusiastic
Greater interest in process, not product; interested in skill and technique
Loves jokes and guessing games
Loves to color, paint
Understands cause and effect
Likes cooperative projects, activities, tasks

Seven-Year-Old
Likes to be alone listening to music, the age for starting music lessons
Wants work to look good
Driven by curiosity, desire to discover and invent
Intensely interested in how things work: takes apart, puts back together
Uses symbols in both writing and drawing
Interested in all sorts of codes
Likes to select and sort

Cognitive

Six- or Seven-Year-Old
Letter and word reversal common, learns to read, beginning math skills
Can consider others' point of view*
Use logic, systematic thinking; can plan ahead; can conceptualize situations*
Enjoys collecting: sorting, classifying; can sequence events and retell stories
Concepts of winning and losing are difficult*
Likes games with simple rules; may cheat or change rules*
Wants "real" things: watches and cameras that work
Sifts and sorts information*
Enjoys exploring culture of classmates*

Word Pictures of an Eight-Year-Old

Ann Gordon

Social-Emotional

Outgoing, enthusiastic, socially expansive
Enormously curious about people and things*
Judgmental and critical of self and others*
Ambivalent about growing up, struggles with feelings of inferiority
Often hostile but attracted to opposite sex, chooses same-sex playmates
Growing self-confidence, learns about self through others: peers, parents*
Is aware of and sensitive to differences in other children;* responds to studies of other cultures*

*Key characteristics of cultural awareness or identity.

Begins to evaluate self and others through clothing, physical attraction, social status*; joins clubs; likes to work cooperatively
Likes to meet new people, go new places*
Has emerging sensitivity to personality traits of others,* eager for peer approval and acceptance*
Growing sense of moral responsibility, has growing interest in fairness and justice*

Language

Talks with adults, attentive and responsive to adult communication*
Teases members of opposite sex
Talks about "self"*
Talkative, exaggerates, imitates language of peers
Likes to explain ideas
Enjoys storytelling and writing short stories

Physical-Motor

Begins to engage in team sports,* enjoys competitive sports*
Often a growth-spurt year
Speedy, works fast
Restless, energetic, needs physical release, plays hard, exhausts self
Eye-hand coordination matures, learns cursive handwriting
Hearty appetite, few food dislikes
Repeatedly practices new skills to perfect them

Creative

Has great imagination
Enjoys riddles, limericks, knock-knock jokes
Likes to explain ideas
Visual acuity and fine motor skills come together
Most productive in groups
Shows interest in process and product

Cognitive

Criticizes abilities in all academic areas
Seeks new experiences*
Likes to barter, bargain, trade
Enjoys creating collections of things
Interested in how children from other countries live*
Thinks beyond the here-and-now boundaries of time and space
Enjoys role-playing character parts*
Tests out parents to learn more about them
Needs direction, focus
Enjoys all types of humor
Full of ideas, plans
Concrete operations are solidifying*
Industrious, but overestimates abilities
Growing interest in logic and the way things work
Takes responsibility seriously*

*Key characteristics of cultural awareness or identity.

3-2b Cultural, Racial, and Ethnic Considerations

The answer to "Who is the young child?" takes on new meaning as we look at the ethnic mix of American life. There are more students in the classroom who are culturally and linguistically different from the teaching staff and from each other than ever before. Unless teachers are informed and educated about these differences, they may misinterpret a child's abilities, learning, and needs. Too often, language barriers between a teacher and a child lead to the conclusion that the child is a slow learner or has a disability.

Dual-language learners are those children who are growing up with two or more languages. Head Start research notes that over a quarter of the young children in their programs are growing up in families where English is not the primary language (Head Start, 2014). Early childhood professionals need to find ways to support children and their families so that home language and family and culture identity is preserved. Derman-Sparks & Edwards (2010) note that a lack of understanding about the culture, history, beliefs, and values of the children is harmful to a child's self-concept. Dual-language children can become successful learners when early childhood programs meet the challenge of responding to the unique background of each child.

3-3 Children with Diverse Abilities

Watching and working with young children exposes the individual diversities within the group. As you teach, you become aware of how each child grows and develops at a different rate and how his inner timetable monitors his readiness to learn.

3-3a Factors that Influence Growth

1. *Genetic makeup.* Each child is a unique combination of genes (nature) that determine eye and hair color, height, body shape, personality traits, and intelligence as well as the presence of certain diseases, such as Tay-Sachs, cystic fibrosis, and sickle cell anemia.
2. *Environment.* From conception, the brain is affected by environmental conditions. An individual child's rate and sequence of development reflects the interactions among the brain, the body, and the environment. The attitudes with which children are raised, their culture, their socioeconomic status, the kinds of caregiving

Diversity

they experience, and their community combine in countless ways to affect growth. Nutrition, safety, play space, adult relationships, neighborhood, and family stability affect individual development. Whether a child lives in poverty or affluence, environmental factors interact with genes to create a single, individual person.

3. *Gender and race differences.* Girls and boys differ in both the rate and the pattern of growth, especially in adolescence. Ethnic variations in growth are common. African American and Asian American children appear to mature faster than North American white children, who are more mature than European children (Berk, 2013). Growth "norms" should be used with caution and with respect to ethnic differences.

---

biracial. Having parents of two different races.

interracial. Relating to, involving, or representing different races.

children with special needs. Children whose development and/or behavior require help or intervention beyond the scope of the ordinary classroom or adult interactions.

3-3b Children with Special Needs

All early childhood programs serve children who exhibit a wide range of developmental abilities and extend the answer to, "Who is the child?" Two types of children come under the category of **children with special needs**: children who have various disabilities and children who are gifted.

The term *special needs* includes a great many conditions that may or may not be noticeable (Fig. 3-3). To be designated as having special needs, a child's normal growth and development is (1) delayed; (2) distorted, atypical, or abnormal; or (3) severely or negatively affected (Allen & Cowdery, 2012). This definition includes the physical, mental, emotional, and social areas of development.

Learning Disabilities

Children with learning disabilities that keep them from storing, processing, and producing information are found in almost every classroom and may include the following characteristics:

> Poor memory skills; difficulty in following directions; eye–hand coordination problems; and trouble discriminating between letters, numbers, and sounds

Educators must help all children develop a pride in their cultural heritage. **<**

Ann Gordon

Standards

Learning Styles

Differences in learning style are addressed when planning programs and curricula. Some children are quiet, others move around and talk, and others never seem to listen. While on a field trip to the farm, these children demonstrate three common **learning styles**:

Lorenzo watches and looks around. He calls to others, "See the goat!" and "Look at that!" Lorenzo is a *visual* learner.

Olivia chatters away to her friends as they enter the barnyard. "Listen to all the noise the sheep are making." "Hear the horses?" Olivia is an *auditory* learner.

As she runs ahead of the other children, Anna calls out, "Get over here so we can touch them." She begs, "Take me closer. I want to feel the sheep." Anna is a *kinesthetic* learner.

The children respond to the experience through their individual learning style. Lorenzo draws pictures and paints what he saw at the farm. Olivia repeats stories about the farm over and over as she integrates her experience. Anna plays out her farm experience by making clay animals and dancing a variety of animal dances. Think about these children as you plan to meet their learning needs. Lorenzo will need to see the teacher's facial expression and body language as well as pictures and diagrams. Olivia will need to hear the words, not just read the text. Anna will learn best through a hands-on approach. NAEYC Professional **Standards 1, 4, and 5** underscore the need for knowing each child's learning preferences and how to accommodate them when planning learning experiences.

> **Dyslexia**, the most common specific learning disability, which causes children to reverse letters (such as *d* and *b*) or words (such as *was* and *saw*), although many children who are not dyslexic do this
> A strength in one area, such as math, and yet a disability in another area, such as language

Use caution against early diagnosis of a young child as "learning disabled" because young children differ in their individual rates of growth, and many differences and delays are within the range of normal development. A learning disability does not mean that a child is intellectually impaired or delayed (Fig. 3-4).

> Fifteen to Twenty percent of children in the United States exhibit some form of atypical development and need special services (Bee & Boyd, 2011).

© iStockphoto.com/dalton00

Attention-Deficit Hyperactivity Disorder

Do you know a child who can never sit still— one who is constantly

---

A Variety of Special Needs Teachers May Encounter

1. *Speech and language:* hearing impairment, stuttering, articulation problems, cleft palate, chronic voice disorders, learning disabilities

2. *Physical-motor:* visual impairment, blindness, perceptual motor deficits, orthopedic disabilities such as cerebral palsy, spina bifida, loss of limbs, muscular dystrophy

3. *Intellectual:* cognitive delays, brain injury, brain dysfunction, dyslexia, learning disabilities

4. *Social-emotional:* self-destructive behavior, severe withdrawal, dangerous aggression toward self and others, noncommunicativeness, moodiness, tantrums, attention-deficit hyperactivity disorder, severe anxiety, depression, phobias, psychosis, autism

5. *Health impairments:* severe asthma, epilepsy, hemophilia, congenital heart defects, severe anemia, malnutrition, diabetes, tuberculosis, cystic fibrosis, Down syndrome, sickle cell anemia, Tay-Sachs disease, AIDS

6. *Specific learning disabilities:* difficulties with language use and acquisition, spoken and written language affected, perceptual handicaps, brain injury, minimal brain dysfunction, dyslexia, developmental aphasia

These disorders may range from mild to severe, and children will exhibit a wide variety of abilities and needs even if they are diagnosed with the same condition. For further information concerning a specific one, the student will want to consult a special education textbook.

© Cengage Learning®

Figure 3-3

---

truth or fiction?

Ⓣ Ⓕ There are two types of children who have special needs.

The two types of children considered to have special needs are those with some sort of exceptionality: those with disabilities and those who are gifted.

---

learning styles. A child's preferred method of integrating knowledge and experiences.

dyslexia. An impaired ability to read and understand written language.

Planning for Developmental Differences and Learning Styles

The learning environment can be arranged so that children of every skill level can work and play together:

> Make sure the materials and activities are in a variety of formats.

> Address the variations of development within a 1-year age span.

> Plan around the known similarities within the group and allow for the needs and interests of all the children.

> Small group work may help some children with the learning experience.

> Modify materials and activities to make them accessible to children with special needs.

Figure 3-4

on the move, talks excessively, and disrupts classroom activities? Those traits are typical of those with a condition known as **attention-deficit hyperactivity disorder (ADHD)**.

Medication with a drug (Ritalin®) is a common treatment for children with ADHD, but its effects are short term, and its side effects can be serious. The most effective treatment appears to be a combination of medication and individual behavior-management strategies. There is no easy solution for dealing with children who are hyperactive; further research into the cause and the development of safe and effective treatments is clearly needed (Fig. 3-5).

Asperger Syndrome

Asperger syndrome (AS) is a neurologic condition that is part of *autism spectrum disorder*. According to the National Association of Neurological Disorders and Stroke (2014), characteristics common to children with AS are the following:

> Impaired language and communication
> Repetitive patterns of thought and behavior
> Obsessive interest in a single object or topic in which they have great knowledge
> Repetitive routines and rituals
> Socially and emotionally inappropriate behavior
> Inability to interact successfully with peers
> Clumsy, uncoordinated motor movements

---

attention-deficit hyperactivity disorder (ADHD). A medical condition also known as attention-deficit hyperactivity disorder. It affects up to 3% to 5% of all school-age children. Children with ADHD can be difficult to manage, both at home and in the classroom. They are prone to restlessness, anxiety, short attention spans, and impulsiveness. Medication with a drug (Ritalin®) is a common treatment, but the most effective treatment appears to be a combination of medication and individual behavior management strategies.

Asperger syndrome (AS). A developmental disorder linked to autism and characterized by a lack of social skills, poor concentration, self-absorption, and limited interests.

Types of ADHD

The National Resource Center on ADHD (2014) notes three subtypes of ADHD that are common today:

1. ADHD predominately inattentive type (ADHD-1)

   > Makes careless mistakes
   > Does not pay close attention to details
   > Easily distracted; hard to maintain attention
   > Does not appear to listen; seems forgetful
   > Has trouble with follow-through
   > Loses things; has difficulty with organization
   > Might avoid tasks that take prolonged intellectual effort

2. ADHD predominately hyperactive-impulsive (ADHD-HI)

   > Fidgets, squirms
   > Has trouble staying seated, runs around
   > Talks excessively; has difficulty being quiet during activities
   > Blurts out answers; interrupts; intrudes on others
   > Has difficulty waiting to take turns

3. ADHD combined type (ADHD-C)

   > Meets criteria from both categories listed previously

Effective Guidance Strategies for Children with ADHD

Strategy	Example
Maintain regular and consistent routines and rules.	"Remember, Sitara, always wash your hands before eating lunch."
Have realistic expectations.	"I know it is hard for you to wait. Why don't you go over to the math lab and work until I am ready?"
Make eye contact when giving directions using clear and simple explanations.	"Look at me, Toby, so that I know that you are listening. Good. Now let's go over the assignment together."
Allow time for transitions by giving a plan for the next step.	"In 3 minutes it will be time to get read to go home. When the other children start to leave, I want you to get your coat and come back to the group."
Select jobs in which the child will be successful	"Connie, please pass out the napkins to this table today."
Recognize accomplishments	"Good job, Connie. You gave everyone a red napkin and then sat down with one for yourself."

Figure 3-5

He was lying on a rug in front of the blocks, his arm was curled around his head and he was rocking slowly and rhythmically. His name was Andy, he was three years old, and the only child with special needs in the classroom. Andy had been diagnosed with autism.

I was the teacher assigned to help Andy become more integrated into the life of the class. My first priority was to get to know Andy and for him to get to know me. I sat on the rug near him and began to talk with him about what I was seeing: some children were painting, others were reading, and others were in the dress up area. I asked Andy if he'd like to play with the blocks and took a few off the shelf. As I built and talked, Andy sat up and watched what I was doing. I handed him a block. He held

it for a few minutes and then put it on top of my blocks. We did this until he lay down again, curling his arm over his ears. That was our beginning.

One of Andy's favorite pastimes was to take a set of doll house figures and put them in various rooms in the large doll house. He sometimes mumbled a word or two and often called a doll by his sister's name or as "mommy" or "daddy." I would repeat his phrases and then ask him to tell me what they were doing or where they were going. As his language improved, he would elaborate on his stories. I would often call attention to what he was doing to invite other children into his scenarios, although this was not highly successful.

One thing that surprised me about Andy was his sense of humor. Although he could not verbalize well,

he listened to other children and to stories, and when he found something funny, Andy would laugh aloud.

I moved away when Andy was 5 years old and would hear about him from some teacher friends. I learned he went to elementary school and was enrolled in special education courses, and that he graduated from high school as well. The last I knew he was living in an adult community for people with special needs and had a job.

Andy had a strong impact on my life because he was the first person I knew who was handicapped in some way. I have taught many children with special needs throughout my career and find that they always have something to teach me.

Eileen Harris
Teacher

Many children with AS attend schools with normally developing children. Their behaviors may seem odd to their peers and disruptive to the class. Teachers can guide children with AS by using the following methods:

> Give simple and direct communication.
> Combine objects and actions: show the child the book and demonstrate where it goes in the shelf.
> Provide peer interactions with other children who are disabled and have similar levels of language and social development.
> Establish a predictable routine and environment; minimize distractions.
> Improve communication skills by having the child ask for something rather than point.
> Encourage frequent communication with the family.

3-3c Inclusion Strategies

Inclusion means that a child with special needs is a full-time member of an early childhood program with typically developing children. Teachers are a key factor in the successful integration of these children in the classroom. Their attitude is critical; they must be committed to teaching all children, regardless of the child's intelligence or skill levels, with equal caring and concern. Figure 3-6 lists appropriate and successful strategies for creating an inclusive classroom.

3-3d Who Is Gifted and Talented?

The U.S. Department of Education defines gifted and talented students as "children and youth with outstanding talent who perform or show the potential for performing at remarkably high levels of accomplishment when compared with others of their age, experience, or environment." The National Society for the Gifted & Talented (2014) identifies six areas in which giftedness is expressed. A child may be gifted in one or two of these areas, but not all six.

1. *Creative thinking.* Independent and original thinker in speech and writing, creates and invents, improvises, challenged by problem solving and creative tasks, has sense of humor, and does not mind being different from the crowd.
2. *General intellectual ability.* Observant and inquisitive, hypothesizes, formulates abstractions and processes information in complex ways, excited about new

---

inclusion. When a child with a disability is a full-time member of a regular classroom with children who are developing normally as well as with children with special needs.

gifted and talented. Children who have unusually high intelligence, as characterized by: learning to read spontaneously; being able to solve problems and communicate at a level far advanced from their chronological age; excellent memory; extensive vocabulary; and unusual approaches to ideas, tasks, people.

Ways for Teachers to Enhance Inclusion in the Classroom

> **Foster** healthy social relationships and interactions between children who are disabled and children who are not disabled.

> **Recognize** that every child with special needs has strengths and build on those.

> **Receive** training and guidance in working with children who have special needs and are developmentally disabled.

> **Work with** families to plan and implement the child's IEP.

> **Ensure that** children with disabilities are actively involved and accepted in the total program.

> **See that** children with special needs are helped to take advantage of, to the fullest extent of their capabilities, all the activities the school has to offer.

> **Address** children's individual disabilities in program planning and that procedures and curriculum are adapted to fit the children with special needs.

(Adapted from Allen & Cowdery, 2012)

Figure 3-6

ideas, learns rapidly, uses a large vocabulary, and is a self-starter.

3. *Specific academic ability.* High ability in memorization and comprehension, acquires basic skill knowledge quickly, widely read and high academic success in special interest area, pursues special interest with enthusiasm and vigor.

4. *Leadership.* Is fluent, concise in self-expression, self-confident, well-liked by peers and has high expectations for self and others, assumes responsibility and is well organized, has good judgment and foresees consequences and implications of decisions.

5. *Psychomotor.* Enjoys participation in various athletic opportunities and is well coordinated, has good manipulative and motor skills, high energy level, exhibits precision in movement, and is challenged by difficult athletic activities.

6. *Visual and performing arts.* Has unusual ability to express self, feelings, and mood through dance, drama,

Public Law 94-142. The Education for All Handicapped Children Act. This so-called Bill of Rights for the Handicapped guarantees free public education to disabled persons from 3 to 21 years of age "in the least restrictive" environment. In 1990 Congress reauthorized PL 94-142 and renamed it the Individuals with Disabilities Education Act (IDEA) (PL 101-576). Two new categories, autism and traumatic brain injury, were included, and children from birth to age 5 years were now eligible to receive services.

Public Law 99-457. The Education of the Handicapped Amendments Act of 1986. Sections of this law provide funding for children who were not included in the previous law: infants, toddlers, and 3- to 5-year-olds. This law also allows for the inclusion of "developmentally delayed" youngsters and leaves local agencies the opportunity to include the "at-risk" child in that definition.

Ethics

The Right to Be Included

During the past 50 years, there has been significant public recognition of and funding for education programs for people with special needs. Previously, public and private attitudes were ones of shame and segregation. Past generations hid adults and children with special needs in their homes or secluded them in institutions. Keeping special populations out of sight gave way to providing separate opportunities for them. Public consciousness is now sufficient to understand that not all people with special needs are necessarily mentally impaired. The current practice of integrating children with varying exceptionalities into ongoing programs in schools—and into the mainstream of American life—is a more humane practice. Significant legislation and practices that fostered the practice of inclusion include the following:

> 1972: Head Start required that a minimum of 10% of its enrollment be reserved for children with disabilities and led the way toward large-scale inclusion.

> 1975: **Public Law 94-142**, the Education for All Handicapped Children Act—the so-called Bill of Rights for the handicapped—was passed and guarantees free public education to disabled people from 3 to 21 years of age "in the least restrictive" environment. Parents of children with special needs are an integral part of the development of their child's Individualized Education Plan (IEP), in which the strengths and needs of the family are taken into consideration.

> 1986: **Public Law 99-457**, the Amendments to the Education for All Handicapped Children Act, provides funding for children who were not included in the previous law, including infants, toddlers, and 3- to 5-year-olds. This law also allows for the inclusion of "developmentally delayed" children and provides local agencies the opportunity to include at-risk children in that definition.

> 1990: Congress reauthorized Public Law 94-142 and renamed it the Individuals with Disabilities Education Act (IDEA) (**Public Law 101-476**). Two new categories were included: autism and traumatic brain injury.

> 1990: **Public Law 101-336**, the Americans with Disabilities Act (ADA), makes it unlawful to discriminate against people with disabilities and requires that they have equal access to public and private services as well as reasonable accommodations.

Each step taken during the past 50 years has given thousands of children the right to be included and promotes the dignity and worth of all individuals.

and music, has good motor coordination and high level of creative expression, has outstanding sense of spatial relationships, is observant, and likes producing own product rather than copying.

The inclusive environment fosters children's interactions with one another.◄

The teacher's role with children who are gifted is to provide challenge and stimulation. Children who are gifted need a learning environment that supports intellectual risk-taking, the use of logic and abstract concepts, and curiosity to enhance their specific talents. All the children in the classroom benefit from this enrichment; each responds according to his or her abilities, and a rich curriculum benefits the whole class. Children who are gifted may need scaffolding strategies to support their learning.

Families of children who are gifted need support and encouragement as well as guidance in dealing with their child's exceptionality. Together, teachers and parents can explore what will best suit each individual child so that this giftedness may be nurtured and challenged at home and at school.

Children with special needs cut across social, economic, and cultural lines.

3-3e Dealing with Bias and Stereotypes

One of the most important issues for a child with special needs is to be accepted. Young children are forthright in commenting on and asking questions about what confuses or frightens them. Children without special needs may be anxious about what another child's exceptionality may mean to them.

Although this is a common reaction and age appropriate, we need to guide children's interest and curiosity in ways that do not offend other children. Derman-Sparks & Edwards (2010) suggest the following strategies:

> The rejection must be handled immediately, with support and assurance given to the child who was rejected that this type of behavior will not be permitted.

> It is important to help children recognize how they are different and how they are alike.

> Children need to have their fears about other children's abilities and exceptionalities taken seriously and to have adults understand their concerns.

> Questions must be answered promptly, truthfully, and simply.

All children benefit when adults are willing to confront bias and deal with children's prejudice and misconceptions. When we provide opportunities for children to interact with people who look and act differently than they do, we actively foster acceptance and respect for the individual.

teachsource video case

Watch the TeachSource Video entitled, "5–11 Years: Developmental Disabilities in Middle Childhood." After you study the video clip, reflect on the following questions:

1. How did this teaching staff and environment adapt in order to include children with special needs?

2. What examples did you observe that foster children's interactions with children with special needs and how successful do you think they were?

3. Was there evidence of any gifted and talented students? How would you describe them?

summary

3.1 To articulate the concept of the whole child is to address all developmental dimensions: the physical, cognitive, social, emotional, and linguistic areas of development. Although they may be discussed separately, each area of growth is affected by and affects every other developmental area.

3.2 Word Pictures describe common behaviors and characteristics typical to an age group that help teachers look at specific areas of a child's development in order to plan appropriate experiences for the group as well as for the individual child.

3.3 Developmental differences include a variety of exceptionalities such as learning disabilities, dyslexia, ADHD, and AS. In an inclusive classroom, the environment and curriculum are adapted to fit the needs of each student who has a disability. Children who are identified as gifted and talented also require a learning environment that supports their unique talents.

web resources

Center for the Study of Biracial Children
   http://csbchome.org
Children and Adults with ADHD
   http://www.chadd.org/

Council for Exceptional Children
   http://www.cec.sped.org
National Association for Gifted Children
   http://www.nagc.org

references

Allen, K. E., & Cowdery, G. E. (2012). *The exceptional child: Inclusion in early childhood education* (5th ed.). Clifton Park, NY: Thomson Delmar Learning.

Bee, H., & Boyd, D. (2011). *The developing child.* Menlo Park, CA: Addison-Wesley.

Berk, L. E. (2013). *Child development.* Boston: Allyn & Bacon.

Derman-Sparks, L., & Olsen Edwards, J. (2010). *Anti-bias education for young children and ourselves.* Washington, DC: National Association for the Education of Young Children.

Head Start: Early Childhood Learning and Knowledge Center (ECLKC). *Report to Congress on Dual-Language Learners in Head Start and Early Head Start Programs.* Retrieved June 1, 2014 from **https://eclkc.ohs.acf.hhs.gov/hslc**

Kelly, R. (2009, February 2) Beyond just black and white. *Newsweek, 153,* 41.

National Institute of Neurological Disorders and Stroke. (2010). *What is Asperger syndrome?* Available at: **http://www.ninds.nih.gov/disorders/asperger.** Retrieved January 25, 2014.

National Resource Center of ADHD. (2014). **www.help4adhd.org**

National Society for the Gifted & Talented. *Giftedness defined: What is gifted and talented?* Available at: **http://www.nsgt.org/articles/index.asp#4.** Retrieved January 25, 2014.

4

developmental and learning theories

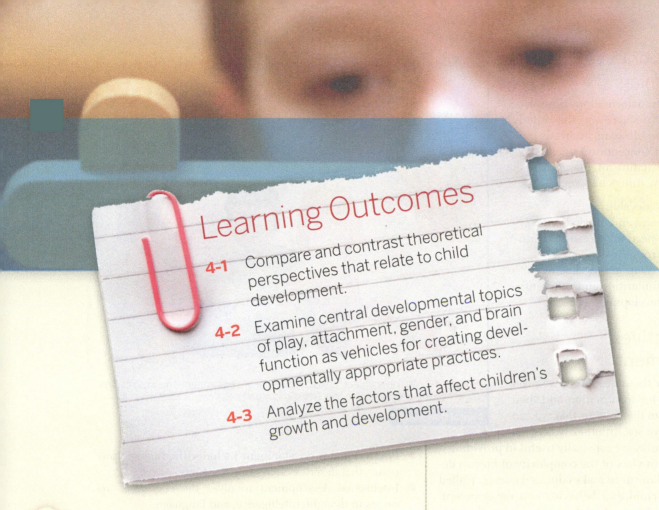

Learning Outcomes

4-1 Compare and contrast theoretical perspectives that relate to child development.

4-2 Examine central developmental topics of play, attachment, gender, and brain function as vehicles for creating developmentally appropriate practices.

4-3 Analyze the factors that affect children's growth and development.

Rainer Unkel/Vario images GmbH & Co.KG/Alamy

NAEYC Standards

The following NAEYC Standards for Early Childhood Professional Preparation are addressed in this chapter:

Standard 1: Promoting Child Development and Learning

Standard 5: Using Content Knowledge to Build Meaningful Curriculum

Standard 6: Becoming a Professional

truth or fiction

T F Smoking cigarettes and nail-biting are signs of conflict with parents in early childhood.

T F Instruction is more important than play in early education programs.

T F Emotions run the brain.

4-1 Theories of Development and Learning

Many remarkable transformations take place in the early years. Development, the orderly set of changes in the life span, occurs as individuals move from conception to death. We want to know the nature of these changes and the reasons why things happen:

> How do children develop?
> What do they learn, and in what order?
> What do people need to be ready to learn?
> What affects learning?
> Do all people develop in the same ways?
> What are the similarities and differences in growth and development?

4-1a Perspectives on Development

To begin to answer these questions, we need some way to look for information and then choose and organize the facts so that we can understand what we see. In other words, we need a theory. Theories are especially useful in providing a broad and consistent view of the complexity of human development. They allow us to make educated guesses (called hypotheses) about children's behavior and development. Because these theories are based on experience, their validity can be checked by teachers as they observe children every day.

The Nature of Development

A child is a blend of many parts that interrelate in different ways and change with growth over time. Such complexity and dynamic change is difficult to describe, much less predict. To simplify the study of development, we try to consider separately the aspects that make up the whole of development, as in Figure 4-1. We can then better understand the major processes of development that parallel these developmental areas.

---

development. The orderly set of changes in the life span that occurs as individuals move from conception to death.

theory. A group of general principles, ideas, or proposed explanations for explaining some kind of phenomenon; in this case, child development.

hypotheses. A tentative theory or assumption made to draw inferences or test conclusions; an interpretation of a practical situation that is then taken as the ground for action.

maturation. The process of growth whereby a body matures regardless of, and relatively independent of, intervention such as exercise, experience, or environment.

nature/nurture. The argument regarding human development that centers around two opposing viewpoints; nature refers to the belief that it is a person's genetic, inherent character that determines development; nurture applies to the notion that it is the sum total of experiences and the environment that determine development.

Figure 4-1 We use images, such as this rainbow of developmental areas, to capture the concept of the whole child as a sum of many parts. (© Cengage Learning 2013)

Digital Download

> Physical-motor development includes the biologic processes that describe changes in the body.
> Intellectual development involves the cognitive processes in thought, intelligence, and language.
> Affective development includes those socio-emotional processes that reflect changes in an individual's relationships with self and other people, emotions, personality, creativity, and spirituality.

Major Issues in Development

Is children's development due more to maturation or to experience? The changes we see in children over time may be due to internal or external influences. Some theories claim that children change because of innate, biologic, or genetic patterns built into the human being; others claim that they are shaped by the environment and life's experiences (due to parents, learning and play materials, TV, school, and so on). This argument is often referred to as the nature/nurture controversy, also known as the problem of heredity versus environment.

Is growth smooth and continuous or does is occur in stages? Some theories emphasize a gradual, cumulative kind of growth, more like "from an acorn, a giant oak will grow." This continuity of development is usually the viewpoint of those theories that emphasize experience (nurture). Others see children growing in stages that are clearly marked by distinct changes. As a caterpillar changes into a butterfly, it does not become more of a caterpillar, but rather turns into a different kind of organism. This viewpoint emphasizes the innate nature of development.

What can theory and research do for early childhood educators? Science has opened our eyes to the amazing complexity of the mind and the wondrous path of growth

Is it nature or nurture that influences development? Heredity and environment are involved in behavior, characteristics, and patterns, so the true answer is "both." **<**

in the body. In previous generations, little scientific information was available. Many beliefs were espoused by adults about children, such as "You'll spoil the baby if you respond to his demands too quickly," or "Children who suffer early neglect will never amount to much." These statements can be powerful, particularly as they are passed on by family and culture. However, some ideas are rooted in myth rather than reality. Researchers and theorists have accumulated a rich store of knowledge, based on scientific evidence. They can help sort fact from fiction. Figure 4-2 describes the 12 principles distilled from decades of research, theory, and practice.

No one set of principles encompasses all developmental and learning theories. We have chosen eight theories;

three [psychoanalytic, behaviorist-learning, and cognitive-developmental] are often considered the grand theories of child development; the others are essential additions that deepen our knowledge base. Because the field of child development is broad, encompassing a wide variety of opinion and fact, there is no one theory that describes everything. Moreover, these theories arose at different time periods, in various countries. Each theory will describe children and their processes in a different way. Teachers put together what has been historically and empirically learned about young children and develop programs that best respond to their needs and assist in their growth. As a teacher, you have a diversity of thought on which to establish a professional philosophy.

4-1b Psychoanalytic Theory

Psychoanalytic theory is about personality development and emotional problems. It looks at development in terms of internal drives that are often **unconscious**, or hidden from our awareness. These motives are the underlying forces that influence human thinking and behavior and provide the foundation for universal stages of development. In psychoanalytic terms, children's behavior can be interpreted by knowing their various stages and the tasks within those stages.

truth or *fiction?*

T **(F)** Smoking cigarettes and nail biting are signs of conflict with parents in early childhood.

While *true* according to psychoanalytic theory, there is no empirical evidence for it, so we call it *fiction*.

---

unconscious. Not conscious, without awareness, occurring below the level of conscious thought.

Basic Principles of Development

1. Domains of children's development—physical, social, emotional, and cognitive—are closely related. Development in one domain influences and is influenced by development in other domains.

2. Development occurs in a relatively orderly sequence, with later abilities, skills, and knowledge building on those already acquired.

3. Development proceeds at varying rates from child to child as well as unevenly within different areas of each child's functioning.

4. Early experiences have both cumulative and delayed effects on an individual child's development; optimal periods exist for certain types of development and learning.

5. Development proceeds in predictable directions toward greater complexity, organization, and internalization.

6. Development and learning occur in and are influenced by multiple social and cultural contexts.

7. Children are active learners, drawing on direct physical and social experience as well as culturally transmitted knowledge to construct their own understanding of the world around them.

8. Development and learning result from interaction of biologic maturation and the environment, which includes both the physical and the social worlds that children inhabit.

9. Play is an important vehicle for children's social, emotional, and cognitive development, as well as a reflection of their development.

10. Development advances when children have opportunities to practice newly acquired skills, as well as when they experience a challenge just beyond the level of their present mastery.

11. Children demonstrate different modes of knowing and learning and different ways of representing what they know.

12. Children learn best in the context of a community in which they are safe and valued, their physical needs are met, and they feel psychologically secure.

Figure 4-2 Developmentally appropriate practices are based on knowledge of how children develop, which is based on research, theory, and observation. (Source: Based on Bredekamp & Copple, 2009)

Freud's Theory of Psychosexual Development

Sigmund Freud began his career as a medical doctor and became interested in the irrational side of human behavior as he treated "hysterics." His technique, asking people to recline on a couch and talk about everything that was going on with them, was ridiculed by the medical establishment as the "talking cure." Then, as patients revealed their thoughts, fantasies, and problems, Freud began to see patterns.

According to Freud, people possess three basic drives: the sexual drive, survival instincts, and a drive for destructiveness. Of the first—childhood sexuality—Freud outlined development in terms of **psychosexual** stages, each characterized by a particular part of the body, with the sensual satisfaction associated with each body part linked to major challenges of that age. Toddler issues of biting or thumb-sucking and preschoolers' "doctor play" and gender stereotyping might be seen in a psychosexual context. Each stage also has its own

psychosexual. Freud's theory of development that outlines the process by which energy is expressed through different erogenous parts of the body during different stages of development.

conflicts between child and parent, and how the child experiences those conflicts will determine basic personality and behavior patterns (Freud, 1968) (Fig. 4-3).

Although Freud's interest was in abnormal adult behavior and its causes, his conclusions have had a major effect on our conception of childhood and its place in the life span. To Freud, the personality was the most important aspect of development, more central to human growth than language, perception, or cognition. His theory described the personality structures that were to develop and asserted that how children were treated determined whether they developed healthy or abnormal personalities. The mother–child relationship was considered particularly important. Thus, the interaction between the child's wishes and needs (by the mother or other adults) was a focal point for proper or arrested development.

All psychoanalytic explanations of human development emphasize the critical importance of relationships with people and the sequence, or stages, of personality development. The psychoanalyst Erik Erikson also expanded and refined Freud's theory of development.

Freud's Psychoanalytic Theory of Childhood

Stage	Age (years)	Description/Major Area
Oral	Birth to 2	Mouth source of pleasure Sucking, biting, eating and teething
Anal	2-3	Anus source of pleasure Bowel movements and toilet learning
Phallic	3-6	Genitals source of pleasure Sex role identification and conscience development
Latency	6-12	Sexual forces dormant Energy put into schoolwork and sports
Genital	12-18	Genitals source of pleasure Stimulation and satisfaction from relationships

© Cengage Learning®

Figure 4-3 Freud's psychoanalytic theory of childhood sexuality contends that each stage has its own area of pleasure and crisis between the child and parent/society.

Erikson's Theory of Psychosocial Development

Erik Homberg Erikson is perhaps the most influential psychoanalyst and key figure in the study of children and development. His interests in children and education included a teaching background in progressive and Montessori schools in Europe. After clinical training in psychoanalysis, he remained interested in the connections between psychotherapy and education. Erikson became the first child analyst in the Boston area and worked for years in several universities in the United States.

To Erikson, life is a series of **psychosocial** stages through which each person passes, each stage growing from the previous ones. Development is driven by the quest for personal meaning, a lifelong task of answering the question, "Who am I?" Personality is built through balancing a child's wishes with the demands of the environment. Positive growth allows the individual to integrate his or her physical and biologic development with the challenges that the social institutions and culture present; too many negative or traumatic events skew the child's resolution of the challenges of the stage. It isn't surprising to learn that Erikson coined the phrase *identity crisis* when you look at Figure 4-4 and read the emotional challenges of the eight stages.

Erikson differed from Freud in some fundamental ways:

1. The drive for identity and meaning occurs in a social context rather than always around sexual and aggressive drives.
2. Development occurs throughout the life span, in contrast to the notion that personality is shaped only in childhood. Rather than being "stuck" with arrested development, people bring the learning with them into the next stage.
3. Developmental struggles that occur during one's life can be overcome later. You *can* go back; problems of childhood can be dealt with in later stages so that the adult can achieve vitality by means other than hypnosis or talk therapy.

Everyone has certain biologic, social, and psychological needs that must be satisfied to ensure growth in a healthy manner. Medicine has learned much about physical needs—diet, rest, exercise. Basic intellectual, social, and emotional needs also must be met for an organism to be healthy.

psychosocial. Those psychological issues that deal with how people relate to others and the problems that arise on a social level; a modification by Erikson of the psychodynamic theories of Freud with attention to social and environmental problems of life.

Erikson's Theory of Psychosocial Development

Stage	Description	Challenge	Strength
Stage One	The newborn	Trust vs. Mistrust	Hope
Stage Two	Toddlers	Autonomy vs. Shame and Doubt	Willpower
Stage Three	Childhood	Initiative vs. Guilt	Purpose
Stage Four	School	Industry vs. Inferiority	Competence
Stage Five	Adolescence	Identity vs. Role Diffusion	Fidelity
Stage Six	Young adulthood	Intimacy vs. Isolation	Love
Stage Seven	Adults	Generativity vs. Stagnation	Care
Stage Eight	Old age	Integrity vs. Despair	Wisdom

Figure 4-4 Erikson's theory of psychosocial development centers on basic crises that people face from birth to old age. This stage theory of development proposes that these conflicts are part of the life process and that successful handling of these issues can give a person the "ego strength" to face life positively. (Adapted from Hubley & Hubley, 1975 & 2005)

Applications to Teaching

Play is a critical part of children's total development. Most schools for children younger than 6 years old have periods of time allotted for play called "choice time" or "free play." Freud contends that it is through fantasy play that children act out their impulses and thus discharge them. Erikson supports play explicitly by stating that autonomy and initiative are developed mainly through social and imaginative play. He suggests that child's play is "the infantile form of the human ability to deal with experiences by creating model situations and to master reality by experiment and planning. . . . To 'play it out' in play is the most natural self-healing measure childhood affords" (Erikson, 1963).

The adult is primarily an emotional base and a social mediator for the child. Teachers become interpreters of feelings, actions, reasons, and solutions. Teachers look at each child's emotional make-up and monitor their progress through developmental crises; each crisis is a turning point of increased vulnerability and also enhanced potential. The issues of early childhood, from psychoanalytic theory, are every person's life issues. Although the remnants of these stages stay with us all our lives, teachers who are aware of their own processes can fully appreciate the struggles of children.

4-1c Behaviorism

Behaviorism is the most pragmatic and functional of the modern psychological ideologies. Behaviorist theories describe both development and learning. Developed during the 1920s and continually modified, behaviorism is the most distinctively American contribution to psychology. It begins with Locke's notion that a child is essentially a clean slate on which events are written throughout life. The conditions of those events cause all important human behavior. Behaviorists often insist that only what can actually be observed will be accepted as fact. Only behavior can be treated, they say, not feelings or internal states. This contrasts with the psychoanalytic approach, which insists that behavior is just an indirect clue to the real self of inner feelings and thoughts.

---

classical conditioning. A form of learning in which one stimulus is repeatedly paired with another so that the second one brings forth a response.

stimulus–response. The kind of psychological learning, first characterized in the behaviorist theory of Pavlov, that takes place when pairing something that rousts or incites an activity with the activity itself in a way that the stimulus (such as a bell) will trigger a response (such as salivating in anticipation of food that usually arrives after the bell is sounded).

operant conditioning. A form of learning in which an organism's behavior is shaped by what is reinforced.

reinforcement. A procedure, such as reward or punishment, that changes a response to a stimulus; the act of encouraging a behavior to increase in frequency.

social cognition. Bandura's theory about learning that emphasizes the cognitive processes of observational learning.

socialization. The process of learning the rules and behaviors expected when in situations with others.

The Behaviorists

Ivan Pavlov, a Russian physiologist, was working in a laboratory, studying how animals digest food. He noticed that the dogs in his laboratory would anticipate their meals when they heard or saw their attendants making preparations. Instead of starting to salivate just when food was set in front of them, the dogs would salivate to a number of stimuli associated with food. He identified this simple form of learning as respondent conditioning. The association of involuntary reflexes with other environmental conditions became known as **classical conditioning**, a cornerstone of behaviorist theory.

John B. Watson was an American theorist who studied Pavlov's animal experiments. He then translated those ideas of conditioning into human terms. For instance, he showed a boy a white rat, then sounded a loud noise, and after only seven pairings, the boy cringed at the sight of the rat without the bell sounding at all. Watson made sweeping claims about the powers of this classical conditioning, declaring that he could shape a person's entire life by controlling exactly the events of an infant's first year. His work gave scientific validity to the idea that teachers should set conditions for learning and reward proper responses.

Edward L. Thorndike also studied the conditions of learning. Known as the "godfather of standardized testing," Thorndike helped develop scales to measure student achievement and standardized educational testing (see Chapter 6). He set forth the famous **stimulus–response** technique. A stimulus will recall a response in a person; this forms learned habits. **Operant conditioning** focuses attention on the response rather than the stimulus and concentrates on what **reinforcements** can be used to increase a behavior. Therefore, it is wise to pay close attention to the consequences of behavior and to the various kinds of reinforcement.

B. F. Skinner took the idea of the "clean slate" one step further to create the doctrine of the "empty organism." All behavior is under the control of one or more aspects of the environment, and a person is like a vessel to be filled by carefully planned experiences. Furthermore, Skinner maintained that there is no behavior that cannot be modified. Some people argue that Skinnerian concepts tend to depersonalize the learning process and treat people as puppets. Others say that behaviorist psychology has made us develop new ways to help people learn and cope effectively with the world.

Albert Bandura has developed another type of learning theory, called **social cognition**. As behaviorists began to accept that what people said about their feelings and internal states was valid, they looked at how children became socialized. **Socialization** is the process of learning to conform to social rules. Social cognitive researchers watch how children learn these rules and use them in groups. They study the patterns of reinforcement and reward in socially appropriate and unacceptable behavior. According to Bandura, children acquire most of their social concepts from models they observe in the course of daily life. Attachment affects the process because the most significant and influential people are those to whom the child is

Behaviorist Learning Processes

Learning Process	Kind of Behavior	Type of Learning	Role of Learner	Example
Classical conditioning	Reflective	Association	Passive	School bell rings, children slide papers into desk and put on their backpacks.
Operant conditioning	Voluntary	Reinforcement	Active or Passive	Teachers give attention, praise, smiles, hugs as social reinforcers [nonsocial ones include tokens, toys, food, stickers]
Modeling	Voluntary	Observation & Imitation	Active	Child is selected as leader in a group game of "Simon Says," and others follow her lead.

© Cengage Learning®

Figure 4-5 Classical conditioning, operant conditioning, and modeling are three ways to develop learned behavior. Each describes how certain kinds of behavior will be learned and what role the learner will take in the process.

emotionally tied. From this arose a new concept known as modeling, a special kind of observational learning.

Theory of Behaviorism and Learning

Learning occurs when an organism interacts with the environment. Through experience, behavior is modified or changed. In the behaviorist's eyes, classical and operant conditioning are based on the idea that learning is mostly the development of habit. People learn by a series of associations, thus forming a connection between a stimulus and response that did not exist before. Modeling is based on a more social approach. Figure 4-5 summarizes these three types of behaviorist learning processes.

Classical Conditioning Classical conditioning can be explained by reviewing Pavlov's original experiments. A dog normally salivates at the sight of food but not when he hears a bell. When the sound of a bell is paired with the sight of food, the dog "learns" to salivate when he hears the bell, whether or not food is nearby. Thus, the dog has been conditioned to salivate (give the response) for both the food (unconditioned stimulus) and the bell (conditioned stimulus). Children can be trained to start putting toys away when a cleanup song is played, signaling the end of playtime. Classical conditioning can also account for the development of phobias. Only a few painful visits to a childhood dentist can teach a lifetime fear of dental health professionals.

Operant Conditioning. Operant conditioning is slightly different from classical conditioning in that it focuses on the response rather than the stimulus. In operant conditioning, the process that makes it more likely that a behavior will recur is called *reinforcement*. A stimulus that increases the likelihood of repeated behavior is called a *reinforcer*. Most people are likely to increase what gives them pleasure (such as food or attention) and decrease what gives them displeasure (such as punishment, pain, or the withdrawal of food or attention). The behaviorist tries to influence the organism by

controlling these kinds of reinforcement. Operant conditioning is more complicated than classical conditioning. Reinforcers can be positive or negative, or can be considered punishment, and are effective only if they are meaningful to the learner. Reinforcement is a powerful tool, so it is important for adults to realize that it can be misused. An adult may not be gentle with a negative reinforcer when angry with a child's inappropriate behavior, and the child may end up feeling punished. Adults who neglect using positive words or actions are missing opportunities to shape and improve behavior.

Modeling. Modeling, also called *observational learning*, is the process of learning and teaching by example. For instance, children who see their parents smoking will likely smoke themselves. According to Bandura, children acquire most of their social concepts from models they observe in the course of daily life. The models, whether adult, peer, or nonhuman, most likely to be imitated are individuals who are nurturant—warm, rewarding, and affectionate. The most significant and influential people are those to whom the child is emotionally tied.

At the same time, any behavior can be learned by watching it, from language (listening to others talk) to fighting (watching violence on television). Bandura's studies showed that exposure to filmed aggression heightens aggressive reactions in children. "Subjects who viewed the aggressive human and cartoon models on film exhibited nearly twice as much aggression than did subjects in the control group who were not exposed to the aggressive film content" (Bandura, 1986). Pictorial mass media—television, video games, and computer activities—serve as important sources of social behavior. Bandura's theory has expanded into a social

---

modeling. The part of behaviorist theory, first coined by Bandura, that describes learning through observing and imitating an example. The model observed can be real, filmed, or animated; and the child mimics in order to acquire the behavior.

observational learning. The acquisition of skills and behaviors by observing others.

Modeling. Children learn from observing others; models can be adults, other children, nonhumans, and media images.◄

4-1d Cognitive Theory

Adult: What does it mean to be alive?

Child: It means you can move about, play—that you can do all kinds of things.

Adult: Is a mountain alive?

Child: Yes, because it has grown by itself.

Adult: Is a cloud alive?

Child: Yes, because it sends water.

Adult: Is wind alive?

Child: Yes, because it pushes things.

Cognitive theory describes what and how children think. The structure and development of human thought processes affect the way a person understands and perceives the world. Piaget's theory of cognition forms a cornerstone of early childhood educational concepts about children; others have developed this theory further into a **constructivist** theory of learning.

cognitive model of children thinking hard about what they see and feel. Thus, personal and cognitive factors influence behavior, as does the environment, and in turn children's behavior can affect the environment around them. Adding the factors of observation and thinking to behaviorist theory links it to Piaget's cognitive theory (next in this chapter).

Applications to Teaching

Behaviorist theories make a strong case for how the environment influences our behavior. Of all the theories, this one attends closely to the conditions for learning. Anyone who attempts to teach or guide a child by offering a toy, a piece of advice, or a different way to do something is, in part a behaviorist. The theorists describe development more in terms of nurture than nature, and tend to view development as continuous (Hauser-Cram, et al., 2014). A teacher arranges the environment so that positive learning is enhanced by paying close attention to how to arrange furniture, materials, and the daily schedule. If you believe that people learn or change their behavior because of the consequences of that behavior, then likely you will try to modify the environment to shape that behavior. Helping a school-age child overcome bedwetting, ignoring preschool whining so it doesn't get attention, smiling and babbling back at an infant to increase vocalization are all behaviorist learning tactics (Rathus, 2014). Further, how teachers interact with children is critical to shaping their behavior.

constructivist. A model of learning developed from the principles of children's thinking by Piaget and implemented in programs as those in Reggio Emilia, Italy, which states that individuals learn through adaptation. This model of learning posits that children are not passive receptacles into which knowledge is poured but rather are active at making meaning, testing out theories, and trying to make sense of the world and themselves. Knowledge is subjective as each person creates personal meaning out of experiences and integrates new ideas into existing knowledge structures.

Ethics

Staying Ethical while Using Behavior Modification

Adults are powerful reinforcers and models for children. A learning situation is composed of many cues; it is up to adults to know what those cues are and how to control them. Teachers who use behavior modification techniques know both what children are to do and how they will be reinforced in their behavior. The ethics of using this kind of control concern everyone.

What children learn is shaped by the circumstances surrounding the learning. Experiences that are enjoyable are reinforcing. From the peek-a-boo game with an infant to a 7-year-old's first ride on a skateboard, an experience is more likely to be repeated and learned if it is pleasant.

What children learn is also influenced by mood and tone. Social learning is particularly powerful in the lives of young children. Any behavior is learnable and can become part of children's behavioral repertoire. Harsh words and threats frighten children. An atmosphere of constant criticism or fighting can teach children antisocial and destructive behaviors. Chapter 7 deals with behavior management and has examples of appropriate behavior modification techniques.

Piaget's Theory of Cognitive Development

Jean Jacques Piaget was one of the most exciting research theorists in child development. A major force in child psychology, he studied both thought processes and how they change with age. Prolific his entire life, Piaget gave us a complex theory of intelligence and child development (1952). He recorded, in a systematic way, how children learn, when they learn, and what they learn.

Born at the turn of the 20th century, Piaget built on his childhood curiosity in science and philosophy by working with Dr. Theodore Simon at the Binet Laboratory in Paris (Simon and Alfred Binet devised the first intelligence test). While recording children's abilities to answer questions correctly, he became fascinated with their incorrect responses. He noticed that children tended to give similar kinds of wrong answers at certain ages.

Piaget then began studying his own children's thought processes. He noticed how actively children engage in their own development. He also developed a new method for studying thought processes. Rather than using a standardized test, he adapted a method of question and response, discussed in Chapter 6.

While others thought that the development of thinking was either intrinsic (nature) or extrinsic (nurture), Piaget thought that neither position offered a full explanation for these amazing and complex behaviors. His theory relies on both maturational and environmental factors.

> It is *maturational* because it sets out a sequence of cognitive (thinking) stages governed by heredity. Heredity affects our learning by (1) how the body and brain are structured biologically and (2) what automatic, or instinctive, behavior we present, such as an infant's sucking at birth.

> It is *environmental* because the experiences children have will directly influence how they develop. Thinking and learning compose a process of interaction between a person and the environment.

Piaget also believed that all species inherit a basic tendency to organize their lives and adapt to the world around them. Humans use three basic processes to think, known as the adaptive processes of assimilation (absorbing information into current understanding) and accommodation (adjusting understanding with new information) and the balancing process of equilibration (coming to equilibrium in one's understanding).

To think about and interact with ideas and objects, humans develop schemas, or mental concepts. Very young children learn perceptual schemas as they taste and feel; preschool children use language and pretend play to create their understanding; older children develop more abstract schemas, such as morality schemas that help them determine how to act. Children learn best when they are actually doing the work (or play) themselves, rather than being told or shown. Having studied Montessori methods, Piaget concluded that teachers could prepare a stimulating environment and also interact with the children to enhance their thinking.

Piaget identified four major stages of cognitive development: sensorimotor, preoperational, concrete operational, and formal operational. See Figure 4-6 for examples of the stages that encompass the early childhood years. Each person of normal intelligence will go through these stages in this order, although the rate will change depending on the individual and his or her experiences. Each stage of development has critical lessons for the child to learn to think and make sense of the world.

Applications to Teaching

Piaget never claimed to be an educator, so his writings do not apply directly to classroom methods or subject matter. However, Piaget's theories provide a framework for understanding children's thinking. Perhaps most important is the awareness on the part of all adults that all children have the capability to reason and be thinkers if they are given appropriate materials for their stage of development. Teachers must remember that young children:

1. Think differently from adults.
2. Need many materials to explore and describe.
3. Think in a concrete manner and often cannot think out things in their heads.
4. Come to conclusions and decisions based on what they see, rather than on what is sensible and adult logical.
5. Need challenging questions and the time to make their own decisions and find their own answers.

It is Piaget's genius for empathy with children, together with his true intellectual genius, that has made him the outstanding child psychologist in the world today and one destined to stand beside Freud with respect to his contributions to psychology, education, and related disciplines. Just as Freud's discoveries of unconscious motivation, infantile sexuality, and the stages of psychosexual growth have changed our ways of thinking about human personality, so have Piaget's discoveries of children's implicit philosophies, the construction of reality by the infant, and the stages of mental development altered our ways of thinking about human intelligence.

4-1e Sociocultural Theory

Since the end of the 20th century, many American early educators have turned their attention to another theorist. Because of the interest in the programs at Reggio Emilia, Italy, we now look closer at the works of Vygotsky. His sociocultural theory focuses on the child as a whole and incorporates ideas of culture and values into child development, particularly the areas of language and self-identity.

assimilation. A concept in Piaget's cognitive theory as one of two processes people use to learn and incorporate new information; the person takes new information and puts it together with what is already known in order to "assimilate" the new information intellectually, such as when a toddler shakes a toy magnet first, as with all other toys, in order to get to know this new object. Children usually first try to put new experiences into the "schema," or categories, they already know and use.

accommodation. A concept in Piaget's cognitive theory as one of two processes people use to learn and incorporate new information.

equilibration. To balance equally; in Piaget's theory, the thinking process by which a person "makes sense" and puts into balance new information with what is already known.

schemas. A plan, scheme, or framework that helps make an organizational pattern from which to operate; in Piaget's theory, cognitive schemas are used for thinking.

sociocultural. Aspects of theory or development that refer to the social and cultural issues; key descriptor of Vygotsky's theory of development.

Piaget's Theory of Childhood Cognitive Development

As a baby
Sensorimotor period
Key concept
Object permanence
Definition
—the understanding that objects continue to exist even when they are out of sight.
—essential to understanding the physical world.
Explanation
—birth to 4 months, infants respond to objects, but stop tracking them if they are covered.
—4 to 8 months, infants will reach for an object if it is partially covered.
—by 8 to 12 months, infants will search for hidden objects randomly, anywhere.
—by 12 to 18 months, toddlers will search for an object where they last saw it.
—by 18 to 24 months, toddlers will search for hidden objects in a systematic way.

As a preschooler
Preoperational
Key concept
Symbolic play and language
Definition
—the use of ideas, images, sounds, or symbols to stand for objects and events = symbolic play.
—the use of an abstract, rule-governed system of symbols that can be combined to communicate information = language.
—essential to developing the capacity to think.
Explanation
—from 18 to 24 months, first sentences appear.
—from 2 to 4 years, imaginary play emerges, using objects as symbols for play (doll stands in for a baby, blocks as pretend food in house play)
—from 3 to 5 years, social play develops to include pretend play and games.

As a primary child
Concrete operational
Key concept
Reasoning
Definition
—actions can be carried out mentally.
—logical reasoning replaces intuitive thinking in concrete situations.
—classification skills develop.
—essential to ability to think logically.
Explanation
—can coordinate several characteristics rather than a single property.
—reversibility emerges; can see the same problem from several perspectives.
—can divide things into sets and reason about their relationships.
—conservation skills emerge; an amount of liquid remains the same, no matter the container.

Figure 4-6 In cognitive theory, children's thinking develops in stages, with critical learning occurring at each stage.

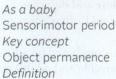

Vygotsky's Theory of Sociocultural Development

Born in 1896 in Byelorussia, Lev Vygotsky was educated in Moscow and worked there at the Institute of Psychology, where he focused on the problems of educational practice, particularly those pertaining to handicapped children. He studied the works of Freud, Piaget, and Montessori. Unfortunately, his career was cut short by tuberculosis; he died in 1934 at age 38.

Vygotsky's work focuses on how values, beliefs, skills, and traditions are transmitted to the next generation. Like Erikson, Vygotsky believed in the interpersonal connection between the child and other important people. Like Piaget, he asserted that much of children's learning takes place during play. Like Maslow (see Humanistic Theory),

he considered the child as a whole, taking a humanistic, more qualitative approach to studying children. His theory is rooted in experimental psychology and in the work of his own contemporaries Pavlov and Watson (see Behaviorism), but he differed from them in that he emphasized family, social interaction, and play as primary influences in children's lives, rather than the stimulus–response and schedules of reinforcement that were becoming so popular in his day.

Vygotsky promoted what later became the DAP principle that development and learning occur in and are influenced by multiple social and cultural contexts. The child is embedded in the family and culture of his community, and much of a child's development is culturally specific. Rather than moving through certain stages or sequences (think Piaget or Erikson),

Watch the three TeachSource Videos on "Piaget's Sensorimotor, Preoperational, and Concrete Operational Stages." After you study the video clips, reflect on the following questions:

1. How does children's thinking change over the early years, and how does this affect what is planned in early childhood education classrooms for the three age groups?

2. Why should teachers know developmental or learning theories before they create programs for young children?

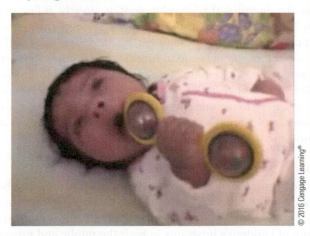

© 2016 Cengage Learning®

Belinda Images/SuperStock

Vygotsky's scaffolding. How and when children master a skill is influenced by the sensitive structuring they receive from adults and other children. Giuliana can ride a tricycle by herself and has hopped onto her brother's two-wheeler. Surely she will fall. But if her uncle scaffolds the learning by running alongside and helping her balance, she can do more. Of course, it will take many attempts, but with assistance, Giuliana can eventually ride on her own. ◄

children's mastery and interaction differ from culture to culture. Adults teach children the skills valued by the society from a very early age; children's learning is considerably influenced by their family's priorities and values.

Sociocultural theory is often compared to Piaget's cognitive theory.

Piaget	Vygotsky
Children need to interact with objects	Children need to interact with people
Stages of thinking are bound by nature	Children's thinking can be advanced by special interactions with others
Child speech is egocentric by nature	Child speech is simply tied to what they are thinking at that age

Vygotsky saw, during the years of 3 to 7, that speech and language are tied to what children are thinking. Children talk aloud to themselves; after a while, this "self-talk" becomes internalized so that the child can act without saying anything out loud. Vygotsky contended that children speak to themselves for self-guidance and self-direction and that this private speech helps children think about their behavior and plan for action. With age, private (inner) speech (once called "egocentric speech"), which goes from out loud to whispers to lip movement, is critical to a child's self-regulation.

Because language and development build on each other, the best way to develop competency is through interaction with others in a special way. Children learn through guided participation with others. This kind of apprenticeship helps with scaffolding, whereby a tutor supports the novice not only by instruction but also by building supports so that the novice can try doing the task with help. Other people create this helpful structure to support the child's learning. Just as a physical scaffold surrounds a building so that it might be worked on, so the child gets hints, advice, and structure to master a skill or activity. Social interactions between a teacher and a learner not only impart skills but also give the learner the context and the cultural values of that skill, teaching relationship building and language at the same time. When mentors sense that the learner is ready for a new challenge—or simply want the learner to

egocentric. Self-centered; regarding the self as the center of all things; in Piaget's theory, young children think using themselves as the center of the universe or as the entire universe.

scaffolding. Vygotsky's term for guidance, assistance, or cognitive structures that help a child learn.

come along—they draw the novice into a zone of proximal development (ZPD), the range of learning that is beyond what novices could learn alone but within the novice's grasp with help.

Applications to Teaching

Sociocultural theory has four implications for the classroom teacher:

1. Teachers understand and incorporate a child's family and culture into their teaching. Teachers provide a variety of ways for young dual-language learners and their families to participate throughout the program; thus the educational program incorporates each child's home language(s) and English-language development. This is also a growing specialty in psychology. Teachers and researchers have observed that children of color in this society are socialized to operate in "two worlds" and thus must achieve a kind of bicognitive development. Indeed, anyone relating to the dominant culture from another cultural or ethnic perspective must become *bicultural* in a sense to live in both worlds.

2. Teachers develop comfortable and cooperative relationships with their children. The teacher and learner adjust to one another; teachers use what they know about children to guide their teaching and plan their curriculum. Sociocultural theory supports both the "emergent curriculum" and the idea of spontaneous, teachable moments such as are advocated by proponents of an anti-bias curriculum.

3. Teachers realize that play is valuable. It is in play that the child can practice operating the symbols and tools of the culture. Vygotsky (1978) puts it this way:

   Action in the imaginative sphere, in an imaginary situation, the creation of voluntary intentions, the formation of real-life plans and volitional motives—all appear in play and make it the highest level of preschool development. The child moves forward essentially through play activity. Only in this sense can play be considered a leading activity that determines the child's development. For instance, children might build a structure with blocks; the teacher encourages them to draw the building and then map the entire block corner as a village or

neighborhood. The adult serves an important role as an intellectual mediator, enlarging the child's ZPD, continually shifting to another set of symbols to give children a different way of looking at the same thing.

4. Teachers in a Vygotskian classroom will encourage activity and an awareness of individual differences. Teacher Valeria plans her kindergarten class with time for older, third-grade "buddies" to read and invites siblings younger and older to join the class at pick-up time by asking for songs they know.

4-1f Ecological Theory

As with sociocultural theory, ecological theory is based on the premise that development is greatly influenced by forces outside the child. A general systems theory was applied to human development in the 1970s, just as the ecology movement began in America and Europe. Development became "a joint function of person and environment" (Bronfenbrenner, 2000), and human ecosystems were conceptualized to include both physical factors (climate, space, home, and school) and the social environment (family, culture, and the larger society).

Bronfenbrenner's Ecological Perspective

Urie Bronfenbrenner, a professor at Cornell University, began pursuing the study of psychology and developmental science in the late 1930s. He played an active role in the design of children's programs in both the public and private sectors, including being one of the founders of Head Start.

Bronfenbrenner's ecological model describes four systems that influence human development, nested within each other like a circle of rings. With the child at the center, these four are (1) the settings in which a child spends a significant period of time, (2) the relationships of those settings, (3) the societal structures, and (4) the larger contexts in which these systems operate. Figure 4-7 illustrates these systems. Just as in nature, activity in one part will affect all the other parts. A sudden income drop will affect the family in many ways: the parents may be preoccupied and unavailable to the child, who may then need more attention from the caregivers at school, who in turn may ask for more resources from the community for the family.

4-1g Applications to Teaching

The values of the community can influence social conditions and in turn be influenced by the individual family or program. For example, a neighborhood becomes full of families with young children. The community values shift to incorporate more issues for these families as parents get involved with creating a neighborhood playground. The community starts a parent participation nursery school in a local church, and a retired teacher opens a family child care home in the neighborhood for infants and toddlers. The city council lobbies the state legislature to adopt more "family-friendly" political policies and offers some pre-tax dependent care benefits to its employees.

---

zone of proximal development. The term in Vygotsky's sociocultural theory that defines which children can learn. Interpersonal and dynamic, the zone refers to the area a child can master (skill, information, etc.) with the assistance of another skilled person; below that, children can learn on their own; above the limit are areas beyond the child's capacity to learn, even with help.

bicognitive. A term coined by Ramirez and Casteneda (see Chapter 4) to describe a set of experiences and environments that promote children's ability to use more than one mode of thinking or linguistic system. Each of us grows up with a preferred cognitive style, such as global or analytic, field dependent or field independent, seeing the parts vs. seeing the whole, as well as a linguistic style. For true cultural democracy to take place, we need to develop a flexibility to switch learning styles or cognitive modes (i.e., develop bicognitive abilities) and have an awareness of and respect for differing cognitive styles.

ecological. Having to do with the relationships between people and their environment; Bronfenbrenner's theory is explained in terms of the balance and interplay of the child and the people and settings that influence development.

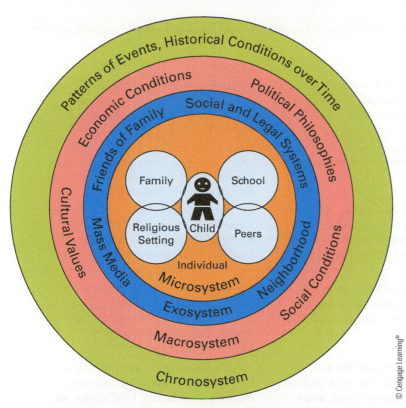

Figure 4-7 Bronfenbrenner's Ecological Theory. Ecological theory shows how the many influences in a child's life can affect development.

Teachers can use this theory to build an understanding of the systems that affect the families of the children they serve. The many systems in the child's physical and social world have a profound effect, both directly and indirectly, on the development of the child. This theory underscores the need to have a working partnership between early childhood programs and the families they serve.

4-1h Multiple Intelligences Theory

Intelligence, as Piaget saw it, reflected in more than academic abilities. Standardized and intelligence tests seemed inadequate to measure a broader view of intelligence. Howard Gardner, a professor of human development at the Harvard Graduate School of Education, has been very influential in the ongoing debate about the nature of intelligence. His work is influenced by that of Piaget and Jerome Bruner as well as brain-based research (see discussion in this chapter) and the study of genius.

Gardner's Theory of Multiple Intelligences

The theory of **multiple intelligences** (MI) asserts that there are at least nine basic different intelligences: "Human cognitive competence is better described in terms of sets of abilities, talents, or mental skills, which we call 'intelligences.' All normal individuals possess each of these skills to some extent; individuals differ in the degree of skill and the nature of their combination" (Fig. 4-8).

Everyone who has a functional brain will be able to demonstrate some skill in these areas. But the child who

has special "musical intelligence," for instance, will hear a concert and insist on a violin (as did Yehudi Menuhin). Or a culture that depends on running for its daily living (as do some people of Kenya) is more likely to have children well developed in body-kinesthetic intelligence. Gardner writes of Anne Sullivan, teacher of blind and deaf Helen Keller, as an example of someone with interpersonal intelligence because she could understand what Helen needed in a way no one else could.

Applications to Teaching

The MI theory has had a big impact on schools, transforming curricula and teaching methods from preschool to high school. Even the producers of *Sesame Street* have taken to applying the theory to developing programs. Teachers in early childhood use the theory daily as they individualize their environments, curricula, and approaches.

> The preschool class notices a child whose facility with puzzles excels that of his classmates (spatial intelligence); he is given a chance to try more complex ones, and works outdoors to create a maze for the group (naturalistic).

> The prekindergarten class gets a counting center in their room. There were materials to draw items for counting (spatial); the teachers worked with children to jump as they counted by twos (body-kinesthetic); music played to encourage counting in rhythm (musical). Chapter 10 includes examples of curriculum development using this theory.

4-1i Maturation Theory

As noted in Chapter 1, Arnold Gesell was a physician intrigued with the notion that children's internal clocks seemed to govern their growth and behavior. In the 1940s and 1950s, Gesell (1940) established norms for several areas of growth and the behaviors that accompany such development. The Gesell Institute continues to provide guidelines for how children mature from birth to puberty. The Word Pictures in Chapter 3 are an excellent example of the information that maturational theory and research have provided.

Gesell's Theory of Maturation

Maturation is the process of physical and mental growth that is determined by heredity. The maturation sequence occurs in relatively stable and orderly ways. Maturation theory holds that much growth is genetically determined from conception. This theory differs from behaviorism, which asserts that growth is determined by environmental conditions and experiences, and cognitive theory, which states that growth and behavior are a reflection of both maturation and learning.

multiple intelligences. A theory of intelligence, proposed by Howard Gardner, that outlines several different kinds of intelligence, rather than the notion of intelligence as measured by standardized testing, such as the IQ.

Area	Definition	Example
Musical Intelligence	The capacity to think in music, to be able to hear patterns, recognize them, and then remember them.	Gardner cites the importance of music in cultures worldwide, as well as its role in Stone Age societies, as evidence of this.
Bodily-Kinesthetic Intelligence 	The capacity to use parts or all of your body to solve a problem or make something.	We can see this in a person's ability in sport (to play a game), in dance (to express a feeling, music or rhythm), in acting, or in making a product.
Logical-Mathematical Intelligence **1 - 2 - 3 - 4 - 5**	The capacity to think in a logical, often linear, pattern and to understand principles of a system; most common intelligence tested with standard "IQ" tests.	Problem solving is often remarkably rapid (as in gifted children), and this thinking is often nonverbal (the familiar "Aha!" phenomenon).
Linguistic Intelligence **a - b - c - d**	The capacity to use language to express thoughts, ideas, and feelings and the ability to understand other people and their words.	The gift of language is universal; spoken language is constant across cultures, and the development of graphic language is one of the hallmarks of human activity.
Spatial Intelligence	The capacity to represent the world internally in spatial terms, as in problem navigation, in the use of maps, and in relying on drawings to build something.	Playing games such as chess and all the visual arts—painting, sculpting, drawing—use spatial intelligence, as do the sciences such as anatomy, architecture, and engineering.
Interpersonal Intelligence 	The capacity to understand other people and focus on contrasts in moods, temperaments, motivations, and intentions.	Master players in school notice how others are playing before entering; some children seem to be born leaders; teachers, therapists, religious or political leaders, and many parents seem to have the capacity to notice distinctions among others.
Intrapersonal Intelligence	The capacity to understand yourself, knowing who you are, how you react, and the internal aspects of one's self.	Often having access to their own feeling life, they draw on a range of emotions as a means of understanding and guiding their own behavior. Children with an innate sense of what they can and cannot do and often know when they need help.
Naturalist Intelligence	The capacity to discriminate among living things (plants, animals), as well as a sensitivity to other features of the natural world (clouds, rock configurations).	This intelligence is valuable for hunters, gatherers, and farmers and is important to those who are botanists or chefs.
Existential Intelligence	The ability to contemplate questions beyond sensory input, such as considering the infinite or unexplained phenomena.	Individuals who are drawn to issues of life and death and questions of morality, and ponder the meaning of existence and other matters of the spirit, such as clergy, shaman, and spiritual leaders.

Figure 4-8 Gardner's multiple intelligences theory describes a new way of looking at intelligence.

Maturation and growth are interrelated and occur together. Maturation describes the quality of growth; that is, while a child grows in inches and pounds, the nature (or quality) of that growth changes. Maturation is qualitative, describing the way a baby moves into walking, rather than simply the age at which the baby took the first step. Growth is what happens; maturation is how it happens.

Figure 4-9 Pyramid of Needs. Abraham Maslow studied healthy personalities and theorized that what people need for growth is a hierarchy of basic and growth needs. (Source: Adapted from Maslow, 1962)

Studies have established that the maturation sequence is the same for all children, regardless of culture, country of origin, or learning environment. But there are two vital points to remember:

> Although maturation determines the sequence of development, the precise age is approximate. The sequence of developmental stages may be universal, but the rate at which a child moves through the stages varies tremendously.

> Growth is uneven. Children grow in spurts. Motor development may be slow in some stages, fast in others. For instance, a baby may gain an ounce a day for 2 months, then only half a pound in an entire month. Usually there is a growth spurt at puberty, with some children at 13 nearly their adult height, others not yet 5 feet tall. Unpredictability brings individual variation.

Applications to Teaching

Maturation theory is most useful in describing children's growth and typical behavior. The charts known as Word Pictures in Chapter 3 help adults understand behavior better and will keep them from expecting too much or too little. Remember that there is great individual variation and uneven growth. Be cautious in overgeneralizing from these normative charts. Gesell's initial data were focused on a narrow portion of the population and were derived from American children only. Further work in the past two decades has adjusted the ranges with succeeding generations of children and an ever-larger and more diverse population. Maturation theory has inspired excellent developmental norms that help parents, teachers, and physicians alike determine whether a child's growth is within the normal range.

4-1j Humanistic Theory

As the field of psychology began to develop, various schools of thought arose. By the middle of this century, two "camps" dominated American psychological circles. The first was psychoanalytic theory, best known through Freud and

Erikson. The second was behaviorism. In the mid-1950s, Abraham Maslow articulated a third force in psychology. Humanism focused on what motivated people to be well, successful, and mentally healthy. This was a change from the study of mental illness, as in psychotherapy, or the study of animal behavior, in the case of much behaviorist research.

Maslow's Pyramid of Needs

Maslow's theory of self-actualization is a set of ideas about what people need to become and stay healthy. He asserts that every human being is motivated by a number of basic needs, regardless of age, gender, race, culture, or geographic location. According to Maslow (1962), a basic need has the following characteristics:

> Its absence breeds illness.
> Its presence prevents illness.
> Its restoration cures illness.

The basic needs are sometimes called *deficiency needs* because they are critical for a person's survival, and a deficiency can cause a person to die. Until those are met, no significant growth can take place. *Growth needs* can emerge when the basic needs have been met. *Higher needs* are dependent on those two primary ones. Higher needs are what we strive for to become more satisfied and healthy people.

This theory is described as a hierarchy, or pyramid, because there is a certain way these needs are interrelated, and because the most critical needs form the foundation from which the other needs can be met (Fig. 4-9).

Applications to Teaching

How well a teacher knows that a hungry child will ignore a lesson, or simply be unable to concentrate. A tired child often pushes aside learning materials and experiences until

humanism. Maslow's theory that describes the conditions for health and well-being in a pyramid of human needs.

self-actualization. The set of principles set forth by Abraham Maslow for a person's wellness or ability to be the most that a person can be; the state of being that results from having met all the basic and growth needs.

I often hear teachers talking about theories: "Aren't theories just opinions from a few people?" "Don't the theories come from someone who did research on a select group of children?" "I learned those way back in college; what does it have to do with my classroom now?"

Decision making in teaching can be difficult. Theoretical perspectives, along with personal experience and professional philosophies, affect how we work with children and families every day. In my program, I often find parents and teachers giving me their advice as to what is best or how to do something better. Everyone has an idea, just as the theorists do.

But theories have been put to the test of time; and time and again, so they inform my practice. For instance,

> It is 9:30 am. Fifteen-month-olds Kenya and Peter are crying and fussy this morning. Neither has eaten since breakfast at 7:00. They have been indoors all morning.

Maturation theory. Children's physical developmental needs affect their emotional states.

I schedule regular times for active movement. And I am sure to offer food and watch for signs of hunger.

> It is 11:30 am. Preschoolers Mario and Therese are beginners in how to make ice-cube paint; they stand next to me at the table and hesitate.

Sociocultural theory. Children's learning often needs a guide to show them the way to get started, and children need to feel part of the class culture in order to learn well.

Psychosocial theory. The children can identify with the teacher and feel encouraged to become successful.

They are beginners; I am an expert. I can scaffold their learning and enjoyment of the experience. With continued practice, they can learn to make their own ice-cube paint, and even create a new version that everyone else will want to try.

> It is 4:00 pm. Kindergartners Jared and Panya have been arguing about who has brought the "best" toy to my program. Others have heard the ruckus and have stopped to watch the two start a fight.

Cognitive theory. Their egocentric thinking prevents them from seeing any view other than their own. Also, they are unable to hold two ideas at the same time, so they cannot see that both toys are "good."

Behaviorist theory. The children can learn from watching others and applying another's example to their own behavior.

I must intervene as the conflict deteriorates into a shouting match. I engage the two of them in a conflict resolution method that gets all children to express their own ideas, both about the problem and for some solutions, so that they can practice hearing another's ideas while still holding their own. I praise each child's positive characteristics in the other's presence, showing other ways to behave appropriately and how the children and their toys can play together.

Keep in mind that there are strengths and limitations to every theory. This is why I never rely on just one perspective about children's learning and development. There is no ONE right way, but there is always a BETTER way. Effective early childhood education is developed by accurately tested and diverse theoretical views, which support rich outcomes for all children.

—Teresa

---

rested. Relevance to early childhood education can be seen in each level of the pyramid:

> The child who is deprived of basic physiologic needs may be able to think of those needs only; in fact, "such a man can fairly be said to live by bread alone" (Maslow, 1962). The humanists would strongly advocate a school breakfast or lunch program and would support regular rest and nap times in programs with long hours.

> The need for safety and security emerges once basic needs are met. Given an unpredictable home or school, a child cannot find any sense of consistency, and so is preoccupied with worrying and anxiety. Maslow would advise teachers to give freedom within limits, rather than either total neglect or permissiveness.

> Growth needs for love and belonging and for esteem are often expressed directly and clearly by young children.

Self-esteem includes such needs as a desire for confidence, competence, mastery, adequacy, achievement, independence, and freedom. Respect from others includes such concepts as prestige, recognition, acceptance, attention, status, reputation, and appreciation.

> Self-actualization is what gives a person satisfaction in life. From the desire to know and understand the world and people around us comes a renewal of self-knowledge. This is expressed in the enthusiasm, curiosity, and natural drive to learn and try. Humanistic psychology can be seen as being at odds with those cultures and religions that put "God" rather than "self" at the top of the hierarchy. An African world view might see the good of the community as the essential goal of being fully human. Cultures with more of a "collective" orientation, rather than an emphasis on the individual or self, would see the family or group as the ultimate goal of humanity.

4-2 Key Developmental Topics for Early Childhood Education

To expand our knowledge of child development, we include several important topics. Teachers well versed in these developmental topics will be able to make better decisions concerning classrooms and curricula and connect with families.

4-2a Identity

As children grow, **identity** formation becomes an important part of their development. Both psychoanalytic and humanist theories assert that self-concept is key to positive growth; cognitive and sociocultural theories note that children construct an understanding of self by way of race, ethnicity, gender, and ability. They develop a sense of self as families hand down beliefs, attitudes, and expected behaviors.

Ethnicity and Cultural Diversity

Ethnicity and cultural diversity affect education profoundly as described here (Lightfoot, 1978):

1. There are problems when the language that is spoken by the child is not understood by caregivers from another culture.
2. There are problems when caregivers have low expectations for children based largely on the children's membership in a low-status cultural group, rather than on the actual abilities of the children.
3. There are problems when caregivers are unprepared to deal with children whose general behavioral style is different from that of the caregivers.

4. There are problems when standard testing and assessment techniques are applied to certain cultural groups with insufficient recognition of, or respect for, the cultural patterns of the group.

Creating a culturally responsive education is the only way we can implement truly developmentally appropriate practices. Becoming familiar with the languages spoken by children and families invites families and colleagues to learn about the diverse linguistic and cultural experiences of all the children, especially those who are dual-language learners.

Gender

Gender is the sociocultural dimension of being female or male. There are two aspects of gender development that are particularly important in the early years: gender identity (the sense of being female or male, which most children acquire by 3 years old) and gender role (the set of expectations that define how a male or female should behave, think, and feel).

Gender has been important to several theories. Freud's stages of psychosexual development reflect the belief that gender and sexual behavior are instinctual. Erikson also claimed that anatomy was destiny: males were more intrusive because of genital structure, and females were more inclusive.

Cognitive theory emphasizes that children learn through observation and imitation, and behaviorists claim that through reinforcement children learn gender-appropriate behavior. Proponents of this view point to how parents and the media encourage girls and boys to engage in certain activities

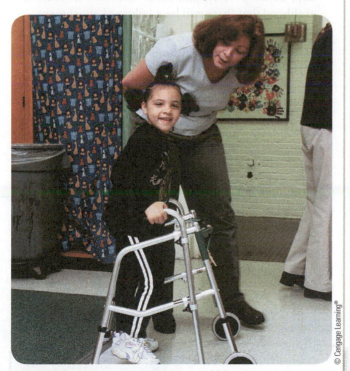

Identity formation. Developing a consistent definition of one's self as an individual is a lifelong process that involves roles, beliefs, and aspirations. ◀

© Cengage Learning®

Diversity

What Are the Differences, and Do They Make Any Difference?

Physically, males grow to be 10% taller than females, and girls are less likely to develop physical or mental disorders than boys. Boys are also more active than girls. There are sex differences in the amount of physical aggression; however, there are fewer differences in verbal aggression, although males do show less self-regulation than females. Research indicates that there are no significant differences between girls and boys in intelligence or reasoning behavior. Some cognitive functioning and personality differences do exist, but the differences are small, with no overall pattern.

So . . . does any of this make any difference? Gender-schema theory proposes that children use sex as one way of organizing their perceptions about the world (Campbell et al., 2004). If children learn that strength is linked to the male gender-role stereotype and weakness to the female stereotype, all children will try to live up to their respective roles. This can make a huge difference if the role is positive and adaptive, but is problematic if the role is repressive or limiting.

---

identity. The sense of self that develops and grows more complex over a lifetime.
gender. The sociocultural dimension of being female or male that includes identity and appropriate roles.

and types of play. The work of Eleanor Maccoby (1998) has provided both hard data and an open forum for discussions about how people grow and the complex interaction between heredity and environment that makes child development so fascinating.

Gender identity appears to follow a developmental sequence:

> Children generally acquire the ability to label themselves and others correctly by age 2 or 3 years; sex-typed behavior begins to appear; gender stability (the understanding of staying the same sex throughout life) is usually acquired by age 4 years, when children tend to choose same-sex playmates and sex-typed toy preferences.

> Gender constancy (a person keeps the same gender regardless of appearance) is acquired by about 5 or 6 years; playgrounds may look like "gender schools" with activity sorted by sex.

Because there is controversy about how similar or different the two sexes may be, teachers need to attend to both girls and boys fairly. To the extent that gender roles could become constricting, adults should pay careful attention to the messages they give children. Socialization accounts for much of the gender-typed behavior we see in children.

4-2b Attachment

Attachment is a term used particularly in the works of John Bowlby and Mary Ainsworth and a concept used in Burton White's descriptive work, Magda Gerber's Resources for Infant Educarers (RIE) programs for infants and toddlers, and WestEd/Far West Laboratory's Program for Infant and Toddler Caregivers (PITC). Attachment is emotional connection, an "affectional bond" (Bowlby, 1973) between two people. The child or adult who is attached to another uses that person as a "safe base" from which to venture out into the world, a source of comfort when distressed or stressed, and a support for encouragement. Attachment behaviors are any that allow a person to get and stay attached, such as smiling, eye contact, talking, touching, and even clinging and crying.

truth or fiction?

T (F) Instruction is more important than play in early education programs.

Play is child's work, a reflection of the child's growth, and a window into the child's world that enables teachers to create appropriate educational experiences and programs.

Infants are preprogrammed to form attachments to adults, thus ensuring their survival. "It is an essential part of the ground plan of the human species—as well as that of

attachment. The relational bond that connects a child to another important person; feelings and behaviors of devotion or positive connection.

many other species—for an infant to become attached to a mother figure. This figure need not be the natural mother but can be anyone who plays the role of the principal caregiver" (Ainsworth, 1979). Freud believed that infants become attached to those who fed them. Erikson asserted that the first year of life is critical for attachment, in the stage of trust versus mistrust.

The nature of children's attachment has been researched extensively. Studies show that human and animal babies send signals to their mothers very early on. The human infant's early signals include crying and gazing, both of which are powerful to adults, and a kind of rhythmic sucking that appears to keep the mother engaged. Although virtually all infants develop attachments, including to multiple caregivers, they differ in how secure they are in those attachments. Attachment can be measured by observing children's response to a stranger both in and out of the parent's presence. Researchers have found that most American infants tested in the stranger situation demonstrated secure attachment. Still, when attachment fails, children are placed at tremendous risk. The "dance" requires partners; both infant and parent (or caregiver) must have the skill to connect.

> Premature infants often lack these skills at first, and some traumatic conditions or highly difficult temperaments can cause parents to report children as quite unresponsive.

> Parents who themselves did not have secure attachments as children may not know the needed behaviors. Abuse and other neglectful conditions—such as depression, abject poverty, and other stresses—increase the likelihood that there will be a failure of attachment.

Not all developmental psychologists believe that attachment is so important to later competence and identity. Kagan (1978) believes that infants are resilient and that children can grow positively within wide variations of parenting. There are great cultural variations in attachment. German babies are more likely than American babies to be categorized as avoidant, but this might be because the culture encourages early independence. Japanese babies are more likely to be seen as avoidant, but this could also be a factor of the method used to record it, which calls for children to be left in a room without the mother, a situation that rarely occurs for most Japanese infants. European-Americans place high value on attachment, yet seem to hold their babies less than other ethnic groups.

Questions should be asked about child care, particularly for infants, wondering whether such

Most infants demonstrate secure attachment to their parents or a primary caretaker, although about one third appear insecure, avoidant, resistant, or disorganized as toddlers, and shifts in attachment status from one age to another are common.

© iStockphoto.com/dalton00

care undermines children's attachment to their parents. The debate has spurred research into both parent–child attachment and child care programs. Whether concerns about infant child care prove valid or not, as of this date we can conclude that children are not at any higher risk in high-quality child care.

4-2c Play

Play! What a wonderful word! "Will you play with me?" is one of the most expressive, expectant questions known. It carries with it hope and anticipation about a world of fun and make-believe, a world of adventure and exploration, a world of the young child.

City streets, parks and fields, tenements, huts, empty rooms, and backyards are all settings for play. Play is a way of life for children; it is their natural response. Play is universal to childhood experiences because it is intrinsically motivated and naturally satisfying to children. Play can be defined in the following ways:

> Play is relatively free of rules except for what children will impose themselves.
> Play is controlled and dominated by the children.
> Play is carried out as if the activity were real life.
> Play focuses on the activity—the doing—rather than on the end result or product.
> Play requires the interaction and involvement of the children.

It is what children do, and it is serious business to them. Any activity children choose to engage in is play; it is never-ending.

Educators and psychologists have called play a reflection of the child's growth, the essence of the child's life, a window into the child's world. It is a self-satisfying activity through which children gain control and come to understand life. Play teaches children about themselves; they learn how tall—or short—they are, what words to use to get a turn on the swing, and where to put their hands when climbing a ladder. Through play, children learn about the world: what the color purple is, how to make matzoh balls, and how to be a friend. Play helps children define who they are.

Play takes many forms. Play can be purely physical (running, climbing, ball throwing) or highly intellectual (solving an intricate puzzle, remembering the words to a song). Play is creative when crayons, clay, and finger paint are used. Its emotional form is expressed when children pretend to be mommies, daddies, or babies. Skipping rope with a friend, playing jacks, and sharing a book are examples of the social side of play.

Types of Play

There is a general sequence to the development of social play (Fig. 4-10). Babies and toddlers have a clearly defined social self. Infant play begins with patterns established at birth:

> Babies gaze, smile, and make sociable sounds in response to the quality and frequency of attention from a parent or caregiver. Socialization of infants occurs through interaction. By the end of their first year, infants smile at and touch one another and vocalize in a sociable effort.
> Toddlers play well on their own (solitary play) or with adults. They begin solitary pretend play at about 1 year of age. They still watch others (onlooker). As children become more aware of one another, they begin to play side by side, without interacting (parallel play).
> Preschoolers are aware of and pleased about, but not directly involved with, the other person. During this stage some form of coordinated play begins, doing something with another child (associative play).
> Older preschoolers begin to join forces with one another in an active way (cooperative play); they verbalize, plan, and carry out play. This becomes the most common type of peer interaction during kindergarten and school-aged years.
> Most play is unstructured and happens naturally when the curriculum is designed for play. Spontaneous play is the unplanned, self-selected activity in which children freely participate. When they are allowed to make choices in a free play situation, children will choose activities that express their individual interests, needs, and readiness levels.
> Dramatic play—or imaginative or pretend play—is a common form of spontaneous play. Three- and 4-year-olds are at the peak of their interest in this type of activity. In dramatic play, children assume the roles of different characters, both animate and inanimate. Children identify themselves with another person or thing, playing out situations that interest or frighten them. Dramatic play reveals children's attitudes and concepts toward people and things in their environment. This is the way children cope with their smallness or lack of strength. Superhero play is appealing because it so readily addresses a child's sense of helplessness and inferiority. Dramatic play provides the means for children to work out their difficulties by themselves. By doing so, they become free to pursue other tasks and more formal learning.

Sociodramatic play happens when at least two children cooperate in dramatic play. Both types of play involve two basic elements: imitation and make-believe. It is the most highly developed form of symbolic play. Vygotsky noted that in pretend play, the ZPD allows children to raise themselves to higher levels of behavior. In terms of Piaget's cognitive theory, such play assists the child in creating imaginary situations that are governed by rules. Erikson would remind us that much of play is wishful thinking, pretending great strength and deeds, building hope.

---

play. Human activities and behaviors that are characterized by being relatively free of rules except for what participants will impose themselves, that focuses on the activity—the doing—rather than on the end result or product, that is controlled by the participants, and that requires interaction and involvement.
sociodramatic. A type of symbolic play with at least two children cooperating in dramatic play that involves imitation and make-believe.

Unoccupied Play
> May stand in one spot
> Looks around the area
> Performs random movements that have no apparent goal

Solitary Play
> Plays alone
> Plays independently of others

Onlooker Play
> May watch while others play
> May talk but does not enter play
> Shows active interest in the play

Parallel Play
> Plays alongside others
> Plays separately from others but with toys or actions that are similar to the others

Associative Play
> Play involves social interaction but little or no organization
> Interested in each other without an agreed-on plan

Cooperative Play
> Socially interacts in a group with a sense of group identity
> Joins an organized activity, a prototype for games

Figure 4-10 Play categories developed by Parten in the 1930s are still accurate for children today.

Digital Download

A developmentally appropriate program filled with play opportunities should culminate in these three types of learning:

1. Children learn about themselves and develop a positive self-image and a sense of competence. They should know and feel good about themselves as learners. They should develop a sense of independence, a measure of self-discipline, and knowledge based on full use of their sensory skills.

2. Children learn about others and the world around them, developing an awareness of other people. Teachers want children to perfect their communication and social skills so that they will be more sensitive participants in the world in which they live. This means that children learn and appreciate the values of their parents, the community, and society at large. When children become aware of the demands of living in today's society, that awareness can help them become more responsible citizens. The emphasis on social interaction and group relationships in the early childhood setting underscores this goal.

3. To learn to solve problems, children need to be accomplished in observation and investigation. When exploring a puzzle, for example, children need to know how to manipulate it, take it apart, and put it back together, to see how other people solve puzzles, and to get help when the pieces do not fit together. They should know how to predict and experiment—such as the kindergartners who speculate on what will happen when a glass is placed over a glowing candle. Preschoolers need to learn how to negotiate, discuss, compromise, and stand their ground, particularly when they encounter and solve problems socially. The 3-year-old who wants the cart the 5-year-olds are using will need a teacher nearby to observe faces, voices, and bodies. Helpful phrases can be offered, aggression stopped, conflicts worked out, and plans made with the teacher's scaffolding. The use of DAP involves teachers helping children to become effective problem solvers through experience.

4-2d Brain Function

Some of the most exciting research discoveries in the 21st century have been in the area of brain research. **Neuroscience** research has developed sophisticated

neuroscience. The field of cognitive study that involves the brain, neural anatomy of the body, and the functions of the brain that affect development.

Neuroscience research is intertwined with basic principles of learning and appropriate practices of early childhood education. Rushton (2011) provides these four principles; we connect the dots to classroom practice, then ask you to do the same.

Principle #1: "Every brain is uniquely organized." . . . *Provide materials that match child skills at several levels.* For instance, alphabet awareness would call for writing materials in the art area, sandpaper letters in the library, sand trays with an alphabet chart in the sensory corner, and alphabet blocks in the block corner.

Principle #2: "The brain is continually growing, changing, and adapting to the environment." . . . *Provide a people-friendly environment.* Children are welcomed with a smiling greeting, have familiar places for their belongings, are invited to help create classroom space, and have teachers who are responsive to their changing mood and energy.

Principle #3: "A brain-compatible classroom enables connection of learning to positive emotions." . . . *Give children reasonable choices.* Allowing children to make some decisions ("Do you want to brush you teeth first or set up your nap space?") and some choices ("What game shall we play at outside circle today?") leads to feelings of positive power and competence.

Principle #4: "Children's brains need to be immersed in real life, hands-on, and meaningful learning experiences that are intertwined with a commonality and require some form of problem-solving." . . . *Set up time for small groups to get immersed in a topic without interruption.* If a child walks in with an interesting item, facilitate exploration and sharing instead of sending it to the cubby. Encourage children to elaborate—to you, to visitors, or anyone else who will listen—their explanations and critical thinking.

Questions

1. What play experiences encourage brain growth?
2. What hazards in a school day might be inappropriate to brain development?

---

technologies, such as ultrasound; magnetic resonance imaging (MRI); positron emission tomography (PET); and effective, noninvasive ways to study brain chemistry (such as the steroid hormone cortisol). Brain scans and other technologies have made it possible to investigate the intricate circuitry of the brain. Within the past decade, there has been much excitement and numerous publications concerning connections between the fields of neuroscience and education. "Neuro-education is a nascent discipline that seeks to blend the collective field of neuroscience, psychology, cognitive science, and education to create a better understanding of how we learn and how the information can be used to create more effective teaching methods, curricula, and educational policy" (Carew & Magsamen, 2010).

What do we know by now? The brain seems to operate on a "use it or lose it" principle. At birth, one has about 100 billion brain cells and 50 trillion connections among them. With use, these cells grow branches that reach out to make connections with other cells. With impoverishments, you may lose branches. Over the first decade of life, the number of connections begins to decline, and by the teenage years, about half have been discarded (this number will remain relatively stable throughout life). Galinsky (2010) notes that those connections that have been reinforced by repeated experience tend to remain, whereas those that are not reinforced are discarded, or pruned. Thus, a child's

early experiences—both positive and negative—help shape the brain.

Every environment has opportunities for interaction with a variety of objects, people, and circumstances that can stimulate brain growth. Conversely, any environment can be impoverished. This is less about toys than it is about interactions and the emotional atmosphere. Most recently, Dr. Stephen Porges has developed a comprehensive theory that shows how our conscious and adaptive brain works (Porges, 2011). He proposes that the various parts of the brain work with the body, combining the neuro-regulatory system to make both physiological and emotional connections. When the brain perceives a threat or stress, the body reacts. What was described 20 years ago as downshifting (Caine & Caine, 1994) compromise the brain's capabilities, triggering the body's systems that regulate the heart, facial expression, even loss of neural tone. Chronic threat of

---

neuro-education. The discipline that blends neuroscience, psychology, cognitive science, and education to apply knowledge of brain function with new ways of learning and teaching.

downshifting. A process by which the brain reacts to perceived threat. The brain/mind learns optimally when appropriately challenged; however, should the person sense a threat or danger (either physical or emotional), the brain will become less flexible and revert to primitive attitudes and procedures (downshift).

1. *Each brain is unique.* It develops on different timetables; normal brains can be as much as 3 years apart in developmental stages. We should not hold each age- or grade-level learner to the same standards.

2. *Stress and threat affect the brain in many ways.* They reduce capacity for understanding, meaning, and memory. They reduce higher-order thinking skills. Learners are threatened by loss of approval, helplessness, lack of resources, and unattainable deadlines.

3. *Emotions run the brain.* Bad ones flavor all attempts at learning. Good ones create an excitement and love of learning. More important, we only believe something and give it meaning when we feel strongly about it.

4. *The neocortex is strongly run by patterns, not facts.* We learn best with themes, patterns, and whole experiences. The patterns of information provide the understanding learners seek.

5. *We learn in a multipath, simultaneous style* that is visual, auditory, kinesthetic, conscious, and nonconscious. We do most poorly when we "piecemeal" learning into linear, sequential math facts and other out-of-context information lists.

6. *Our memory is very poor in rote, semantic situations.* It is best in contextual, episodic, event-oriented situations.

7. *All learning is mind–body.* Physiology states, posture, and breathing affect learning. Teachers should learn how to better manage students' states as well as teach students how to manage their own states.

8. *Feed the brain.* Our brains are stimulated by challenge, novelty, and feedback in our learning environments. Creating more of these conditions is critical to brain growth.

9. *Ritual is a way for the reptilian brain to have a productive expression.* More positive and productive rituals can lower perceived stress and threat.

10. *The brain is poorly designed for formal instruction.* It is designed to learn what it needs to learn to survive. It can usually learn what it wants to learn. By focusing on learning, not instruction or teaching, we can allow the brain to learn more.

11. *Cycles and rhythms.* Our brain is designed for ups and downs, not constant attention. The terms "on task" and "off task" are irrelevant to the brain.

12. *Assessment.* Most of what is critical to the brain and learning cannot be assessed. The best learning is often the creation of biases, themes, models, and patterns of deep understanding.

Figure 4-11 All early childhood education teachers can benefit from the knowledge of the brain and how it works.

Professionalism

Applying Research to Professional Practice

Research in neuroscience and brain function has important implications for the professional teacher. The following framework for action offers three guidelines:

> First, do no harm. Support strong, secure attachments. Provide education for families about what helps their children's brains to grow. Advocate to ensure high quality of child care and early education.

> Second, prevention is best, but when a child needs help, intervene quickly and intensively. The brain is a work in progress, and children can recover from serious stress. Many conditions are preventable; it is everyone's job to work toward eliminating the unnecessary traumas.

> Third, promote the healthy development and learning of every child. Risk does not mean poor outcomes. "The medical, psychological, and educational literatures contain a sufficient number of examples of people who develop or recover significant capacities after critical periods have passed to sustain hope for every individual" (Shore, 1997).

emotional embarrassment, social disrespect, or simply hurried, restrictive time settings can all trigger this response. (See Stress, Chapter 1.)

Figure 4-11 summarizes key brain function principles for teachers in early childhood classrooms. The Brain Box connects the dots between neuroscience and education.

4-3 How Factors Affect Growth and Development

As a teacher, you are responsible for applying theory to practice. No one theory tells us everything. Thoughtful teachers develop their own viewpoints. To integrate theory into your teaching practices, compare the major developmental and learning theories. Figure 4-12 reviews the highlights of each theory.

Most early childhood educators are eclectic in their theoretical biases. That is, they have developed their own philosophies of education based on a little of each theory. Each teacher has an obligation to develop a clear set of ideas about how children grow and learn.

Theory	Major Theorists	Important Facts
Psychosexual	Freud	Stage theory of personality; mind structures of id, ego, and superego Teacher: support of mother–child relationship
Psychosocial	Erikson	Stage theory of social and emotional development; key crisis/challenge at each stage Teacher: emotional base, social mediator
Behaviorist	Pavlov	Classical conditioning Teacher: pay attention to associations
	Watson	Environmental emphasis of conditioning Teacher: set conditions for learning and reward responses
	Thorndike	Standardized testing; stimulus–response technique Teacher: help children form learned habits
	Skinner	Empty organism; operant conditioning Teacher: carefully modify behaviors
	Bandura	Modeling; social cognition; self-efficacy Teacher: arranger of environment and reinforcer of behavior
Cognitive	Piaget	Stage theory of thinking; has both maturational and environmental emphasis Thought processes of assimilation, accommodation, and equilibration Teacher: provider of materials and time and supporter of children's unique ways of thinking
Sociocultural	Vygotsky	Development embedded in family and culture Children learn best through collaborative and assisted learning to increase their zone of proximal development; use private speech Teacher: scaffold children's learning
Ecological	Bronfenbrenner	Four systems that influence development, nested within each other Teacher: understand the systems that influence families and children; advocate
Multiple intelligences	Gardner	Nine kinds of intelligence, defined as problem-solving and product-creating Teacher: provides many ways to learn and express knowledge
Maturation	Gesell	Emphasis on heredity, norms of typical development and behavior Teacher: guider of behavior based on what is typical and normal
Humanist	Maslow	Hierarchy of needs that includes basic and growth needs, with pinnacle of self-actualization based on what is healthy Teacher: provider of basic and growth needs
Attachment	Bowlby, Ainsworth, Gerber	Attachment and categories research Teacher: support parent–child bonds
Identity	Lightfoot	Culture and language issues in education Teacher: work for cultural competence
	Maccoby	Sex differences and gender research Teacher: be aware of gender-schema and stereotyping
Play	Parten	Types of play and value of play in childhood Teacher: support play spaces and time in schedule; use to facilitate skill development
Brain function	Neuroscientists	New insights into early development with magnetic resonance imaging and other techniques; "use it or lose it" principle Teacher: warm and responsive care matters

© Cengage Learning®

Figure 4-12 The major theories of and research on development and learning describe children and their growth in different ways.

4-3a Applying Theory to Practice

Most educators agree on some basic tenets based on applying the various theories of development and learning:

1. Children's basic physiologic needs and their needs for physical and psychological safety must be met satisfactorily before they can experience and respond to "growth motives" (humanist, psychoanalytic, attachment, and brain function).
2. Children develop unevenly and not in a linear fashion as they grow toward psychosocial maturity and psychological well-being. A wide variety of factors in children's lives, as well as the manner in which they interpret their own experiences, will have a bearing on the pattern and rate of progress toward greater social and emotional maturity (psychoanalytic, sociocultural, behaviorist, maturational, and ecological theories).
3. Developmental crises that occur in the normal process of growing up may offer maximal opportunities for psychological growth, but these crises are also full of possibilities for regression or even negative adaptation (psychoanalytic, attachment, and brain function).
4. Children strive for mastery of their own private inner worlds as well as of the world outside them (psychodynamic, cognitive, and play research).
5. Interactions with significant persons play a major part in development (psychodynamic, behaviorist, sociocultural, humanist, and identity research).

4-3b Reaching Developmental Research Conclusions

Research, and the information it yields, must serve the needs of the practitioner to be useful. Teachers can combine research with personal observations and experiences. Figure 4-13 consolidates what developmental research has found and how it can be applied to teaching. Look back at Figure 4-2 on Basic Principles of Development. At the same time, be a critical consumer of research claims. Be skeptical of what is reported in popular media, and do not assume that research results automatically apply to an individual. Part of the scientific method involves having the experiment repeated, so do not generalize about one study or sample. Correlation is not cause; that is, just because things

truth or *fiction?*

T F Emotions run the brain.

Stress and threat affect brain function. Bad feelings flood the brain and can impair learning, whereas good emotions create excitement and curiosity.

go together does not mean that one caused the other. Finally, always consider the source of the information and evaluate its credibility.

4-3c Identifying Conditions for Learning

Developmental theory helps define conditions that enhance learning and from which positive learning environments are created. Research on all theories extends the knowledge of children and learning. Both theory and research have helped all to recognize the following:

1. Learning must be real. We teach about the children's bodies, their families, their neighborhoods, and their school. We start with who children are and expand this to include the world, in their terms. We give them the words—both in their home language and the dominant language of school—the ideas, the ways to question and figure things out for themselves.
2. Learning must be rewarding. Practice makes better, but only if it is all right to practice, to stumble, and try

Standards

Standard 1: Promoting Child Development and Becoming a Professional.
A professional teacher must know and understand multiple influences on development and learning and integrate these perspectives into the work. But there are so many theories; how can one make child development useful without overgeneralizing?
Former NAEYC President and Professor Emeritus Bettye Caldwell (1983) offers three ideas:

> First, all children have the same needs and rights, go through the same developmental stages, and have the same developmental goals. Cross-cultural research on Piagetian theory has demonstrated that a sequence of development holds true worldwide, although the ages vary among cultures and individuals.

> Second, children are like each other in some ways. Although all 2-year-olds are in the process of developing language, the actual rate of vocabulary increase will differ according to how important language expression is to the cultural and familial groups. Teachers without appropriate knowledge of their students' cultures run a risk of misapplying developmental theories and norms.

> Third, each child is like no other in many respects. What is unique comes from genetic make-up, temperament, energy level, sensory sensitivity, interests, and motivation, to name several. Theories have limits: they can foster a global outlook about children in general, but these theories must be viewed in light of both cultural diversity and a respect for individuality.

Developmental Research Tells Us:	Teachers Can:
1. Growth occurs in a sequence.	Think about the steps children will take when planning projects. Know the sequence of growth in their children's age group.
2. Children in any age group will behave similarly in certain ways.	Plan for activities in relation to age range of children. Know the characteristics of their children's age group.
3. Children grow through certain stages.	Know the stages of growth in their class. Note behaviors inconsistent with general stages of development.
4. Growth occurs in four interrelated areas.	Understand that a person's work in one area can help in another. Plan for language growth, while children use their bodies.
5. Intellectual growth: Children learn through their senses. Children learn by doing and need concrete experiences. Cognitive growth occurs in four areas: Perception, Language, Memory, Reasoning	Have activities in looking, smelling, tasting, hearing, and touching. Realize that talking is abstract; have children touch. Provide materials and activities in matching, finding same/different, putting a picture with a sound, taste, or symbol. Provide opportunities to find and label things, talk with grown-ups, friends, tell what it "looks like," "smells like," etc. Know that by age 3 years a child can often remember two or three directions. Know that memory is helped by seeing, holding objects and people. Recognize that it is just beginning, so children judge on what they see rather than what they reason they should see. Be sure adult explanations aid in understanding reasons. Practice finding "answers" to open-ended questions such as "How can you tell when you are tired?"
6. Social growth: The world is seen only from the child's viewpoint. Seeing is believing. Group play is developing. Independence increases as competence grows. People are born not knowing when it is safe to go on. Adult attention is very important. Young children are not born with an internal mechanism that says "slow down."	Expect that children will know their ideas only. Be aware that the rights of others are minimal to them. Remember that if they cannot see the situation, they may not be able to talk about it. Provide free-play sessions, with places to play socially. Understand that group play in structured situations is difficult because of "self" orientation. Know that children test to see how far they can go. Realize that children will vary from independent to dependent (both among the group and within one child). Understand that children will need to learn by trial and error. Know the children individually. Be with the child, not just with the group. Move into a situation before children lose control.
7. Emotional growth: Self-image is developing. Mind-brain-body interactions connect feelings and body responses.	Watch for what each person's self-image is becoming. Give praise to enhance good feelings about oneself. Know that giving children responsibilities helps self-image. Talk to children at eye level. Children learn by example. Model appropriate behavior by doing yourself what you want the children to do.
8. Physical growth: Muscle development is not complete. Muscles cannot stay still for long. Large muscles are better developed than small ones. Hand preference is being established.	Do not expect perfection, in either small- or large-muscle activity. Plan short times for children to sit. Give lots of chances to move about; be gentle with expectations for hand work. Watch to see how children decide their handedness. Let children trade hands in their play. Have materials available to be used often.
A skill must be done several times before it is internalized. Bowel and bladder control is not completely internalized.	Plan projects to use the same skill over and over. Be understanding of "accidents." If possible, have toilet facilities available always, and keep them attractive.

© Cengage Learning®

Figure 4-13 Developmental research tests theories of growth and learning to find out about children and childhood.

again. We include the time to do all this, by providing an atmosphere of acceptance and of immediate feedback as to what was accomplished (even what boundary was just overstepped). Also, practice can make a good experience even better because it reminds children in their terms of what they can do.

3. Learning must build on children's lives. We help connect the family to the child and the teacher. We realize that children learn about culture and language from family and knowledgeable members of the community, such as teachers, librarians, or grocers. We know important family events and help the family support happenings at school. For children, learning goes on wherever they may be, awake and asleep. Parents can learn to value learning and help it happen for their child.

4. Learning needs a good stage. Healthy bodies make for alert minds, so good education means caring for children's health. This includes physical health, and emotional and mental health, too. A teacher who is aware and available helps provide psychological safety and well-being. Mental health is both emotional and intellectual. Teachers have a variety of activities and a flexible schedule, when someone is pursuing an idea, building a project, or finishing a disagreement.

As long as we care for children, we will have our hands full. With the theoretical underpinnings presented here, we have the tools with which to make our own way into the world of children and of early childhood education.

summary

4.1 The "most excellent eight" are the major developmental and learning theories that provide useful theoretical perspectives that relate to child development. Psychoanalytic (Freud, Erikson); behaviorist (Pavlov, Watson, Thorndike, Skinner, and Bandura); cognitive (Piaget); sociocultural (Vygotsky) are considered grand theories of child development. Ecological (Bronfenbrenner), multiple intelligences (Gardner), maturational (Gesell), and humanist (Maslow) represent essential additions; together they comprise the eight theories that best inform early childhood education.

4.2 The four central developmental topics that affect early childhood are identity, attachment, play, and brain function. Both ethnic/cultural diversity and gender issues affect identity formation. Supporting attachment bonds between children and parents and also key care providers is crucial to early development. Types of play and what children gain from it help teachers capitalize on the natural and rich processes for learning. Key conclusions of current neuro-education research provide criteria in developing high-quality programs. These topics provide teachers with knowledge to use for creating developmentally appropriate practices.

4.3 Both maturational and environmental factors affect children's growth and development. Knowing how to apply theory to practice helps teachers notice these factors. Reaching reasonable conclusions about developmental research will aid in providing positive educational experiences for children. Teachers use theory and research for identifying the factors that affect growth and development and create adaptive conditions for learning.

web resources

Classics in the History of Psychology
http://psychclassics.yorku.ca

National Association for the Education of Young Children **www.naeyc.org.** (See the journals *Young Children* and *Teaching Young Children* for practical applications of research and theory.)

National Institute for Early Education Research
www.nieer.org

American Psychological Association **www.apa.org** (the APA has annual conferences and publications on research and applications)

references

Ainsworth, M. (1979, October). Infant-mother attachment. *American Psychologist*, pp. 131–142.

Bandura, A. (1986). *Social foundations of thought and action: A social cognitive theory.* New York: Prentice Hall.

Bowlby, J. (1973). *Attachment and loss* (Vol. 2). New York: Basic Books.

Brazelton, T. Berry, & Sparrow, Joshua D. (2006). *Touchpoints: Birth to three: Your child's emotional and behavioral development* 2e-. New York: Da Capo Press.

Bredekamp, S., & Copple, C. Eds. (2009). *DAP in early childhood programs serving children from birth through age eight, 3e,* Washington, DC: NAEYC.

Bronfenbrenner, U. (2000). Ecological system theory. In A. Kazdin (Ed.), *Encyclopedia of psychology.* Washington, DC: American Psychological Association/Oxford Press.

Caine, G., & Caine, R. (1994). *Making connections: Teaching and the human brain.* New York: Addison-Wesley.

Caldwell, B. (1983). *Child development and cultural diversity.* Geneva, Switzerland: OMEP World Assembly.

Campbell, S. B., et al. (2004). The course of maternal depressive symptoms and maternal sensitivity as predictors of attachment security at 36 months. *Development and Psychopathology, 16* (2), 231–232.

Carew, T. J., and Magsamen, S. M. (2010). Neuroscience and education: An ideal partnership for producing evidence-based solutions to guide 21st century learning. *Neuron, 67* (5), 685–688.

Erikson, E. H. (1963). *Childhood and society* (2nd ed.). New York: Norton.

Freud, S. (1968). *A general introduction to psychoanalysis.* New York: Washington Square Press.

continued

Galinsky, E. (2010). *Minds in the making: The seven essential life skills every child needs* (2010). New York: Harper Paperback.

Gardner, H. (1993). *Multiple intelligences.* New York: Basic Books.

Gesell, A. (1940). *The first five years of life.* New York: Harper & Row.

Gardner, H (2000). Intelligences reframed: Multiple intelligences for the 21st century. New York: Basic Books.

Hauser-Cram, P., Nugent, J. K., Thies, K. M., & Travers, J. F. (2014). *Development of children and adolescents.* New Jersey: Wiley & Sons.

Hubley, John, & Hubley, Faith (VHS, 1975; DVD, 2005) Pyramid Media.

Hyun, E. (1998). *Making sense of developmentally and culturally appropriate practice (DCAP) in early childhood education.* New York: Peter Lang Publishing.

Kagan, J. (1978). Perspectives on infancy. In J. D. Godowsky (Ed.), *Handbook on infant development* 2e. New York: Saxon (2001).

Lightfoot, S. L. (1978). *Worlds apart.* New York: Basic Books.

Maccoby, E. E. (1998). *The two sexes.* Cambridge, MA: Harvard University Press.

Maslow, A. H. (1962). *Towards a psychology of being.* New York: Van Nostrand.

Mooney (2000). *Theories of Childhood.* Beltsville, MD: Redleaf Press.

Nakahata, A. (2001, Fall). Identity is tied to culture. Interview by Marion Hironaka. *Connections: California AEYC Newsletter.*

Parten, M. B. (1932). Social participation among preschool children. *Journal of Abnormal & Social Psychology, 27,* 243–269.

Piaget, J. (1952). *The origins of intelligence in children* [M. Cook, transl.]. Oxford, England: International Universities Press.

Porges, S.W. (2011). *The polyvagal theory: Neurophysiological foundations.* New Jersey: Wiley & Sons.

Ramirez, M., & Casteneda, A. (1974). *Cultural democracy, biocognitive development and education.* New York: Academic Press.

Rathus, S.A. (2014). *Childhood & adolescence: voyages in development (5e).* Belmont, CA: Wadsworth Cengage.

Shore, R. (1997). *Rethinking the brain: New insights into early development.* New York: Families and Work Institute.

Vygotsky, L. S. (1978). *Mind in society: The development of higher psychological processes.* Cambridge, MA: Harvard University Press.

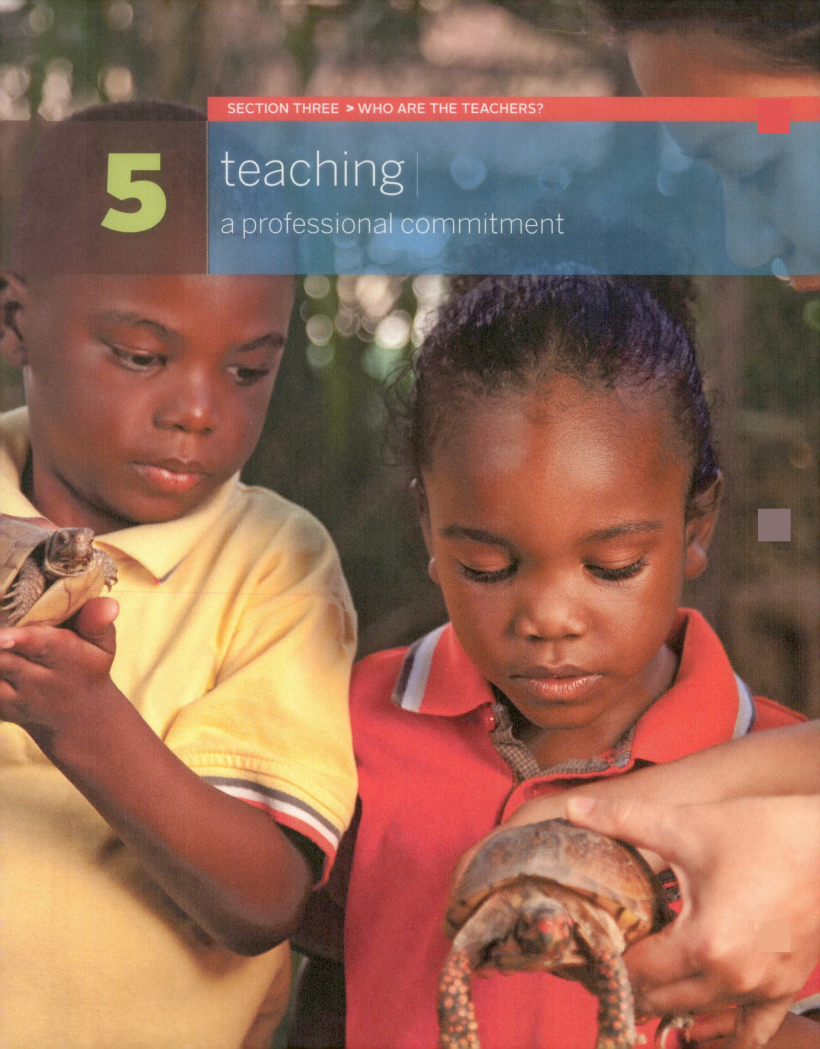

5 teaching | a professional commitment

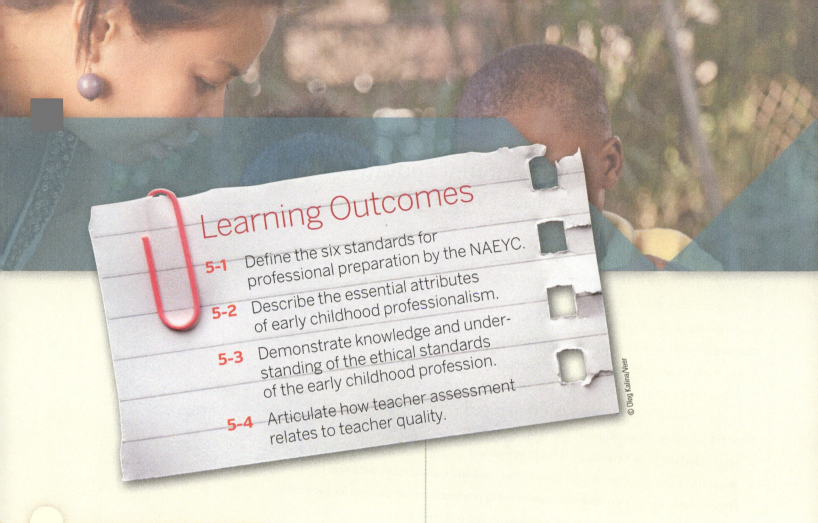

Learning Outcomes

5-1 Define the six standards for professional preparation by the NAEYC.

5-2 Describe the essential attributes of early childhood professionalism.

5-3 Demonstrate knowledge and understanding of the ethical standards of the early childhood profession.

5-4 Articulate how teacher assessment relates to teacher quality.

© Oleg Kalina/Veer

NAEYC Standards

The following NAEYC Standards for Early Childhood Professional Preparation are addressed in this chapter:

Standard 1: Promoting Child Development and Learning

Standard 2: Building Family and Community Relationships

Standard 3: Observing, Documenting, and Assessing to Support Young Children and Families

Standard 4: Using Developmentally Effective Approaches to Connect with Children and Families

Standard 5: Using Content Knowledge to Build Meaningful Curriculum

Standard 6: Becoming a Professional

Standard 7: Field Experiences

© iStockphoto.com/DanielBendjy

truth^{or}*fiction*

T F Each professional standard emphasizes the need for both knowledge and skills.

T F One of the essential attributes of an early childhood professional is parenting experience.

T F The core values are different from one's own personal values.

T F Teacher quality is improved through the use of a good assessment tool.

5-1 Six Standards for Early Childhood Professional Preparation

The National Association for the Education of Young Children (NAEYC) has developed a core set of standards to ensure that teachers receive the best possible professional preparation available and have a vision for how to pursue the education they need. The standards identify common expectations for professional knowledge and skills and are incorporated throughout this text to help teachers shape their professional goals. Each standard promotes inclusion and diversity and stresses knowledge as well as experience.

NAEYC's Standards for Initial and Advanced Early Childhood Professional Preparation

What Today's Teachers Should Know and Do

Standard 1: Promote Child Development and Learning

> Know and understand young children's characteristics and needs

> Know and understand the multiple influences on development and learning

> Use developmental knowledge to create healthy, respectful, supportive, and challenging learning environments

Standard 2: Build Family and Community Relationships

> Know and understand diverse family and community characteristics

> Support and engage families and community through respectful, reciprocal relationships

> Involve families and communities in their children's development and learning

Standard 3: Observe, Document, and Assess to Support Young Children and Families

> Understand the goals, benefits, and uses of assessment

> Know about and use observation, documentation, and other appropriate assessment tools and approaches

> Understand and practice responsible assessment to promote positive outcomes for each child

> Know about assessment partnerships with families and professional colleagues

Standard 4: Use Developmentally Effective Approaches to Connect with Children and Families

> Understand positive relationships and supportive interactions as the foundations of working with children

> Know and understand effective strategies and tools for early education

> Use a broad repertoire of developmentally appropriate teaching/learning

> Reflect on your own practice to promote positive outcomes for each child

Standard 5: Use Content Knowledge to Build Meaningful Curriculum

> Understand content knowledge and resources in academic disciplines

> Know and use the central concepts, inquiry tools, and structures of content areas or academic disciplines

> Use your own knowledge, appropriate early learning standards, and other resources to design, implement, and evaluate meaningful, challenging curricula for each child

Standard 6: Becoming a Professional

> Identify and involve oneself with the early childhood field

> Know about and uphold ethical standards and other professional standards

> Engage in continuous, collaborative learning to inform practice

> Integrate knowledgeable, reflective, and critical perspectives of early education

> Engage in informed advocacy for children and the profession

---

standards. The degree or level of requirement, excellence, or attainment, mandated by local or national government or private agencies that articulate the objectives necessary for teacher preparation.

NAEYC's Standards for Initial and Advanced Early Childhood Professional Preparation

5-2 Essential Attributes of Professionalism

The standards for early education teacher preparation are a road map toward teaching excellence and professionalism. Becoming a professional takes time, training, and experience, as noted in the following essential attributes.

5-2a Knowledge and Skills

There is a body of knowledge, an educational foundation that is assumed of anyone entering the early childhood education profession:

> Basic teaching skills are essential, including methods and techniques appropriate for teaching the very young child.

> The teacher's background includes studying child development and human behavior, family relations, parent education and development, and curriculum planning.

> Some practical teaching experience under the guidance of a master teacher is assumed, as is a familiarity with observation and recording techniques.

> Professional expectations mandated by the states provide some degree of professionalization of early childhood teachers through special certifications.

truth or **fiction?**

(T) F Each standard emphasizes the need for both knowledge and skills.

Each standard includes a key element requiring application of knowledge and skills that all early childhood educators should master in order to help young children reach their full potential.

Figure 5-1 is an example of a California statewide certification program. This career matrix has a number of

Childhood Development Permit Matrix

Level	Education Requirement	Experience Requirement
Assistant	6 units of ECE or CD	None
Associate teacher	12 units ECE or CD, including core courses	50 days of 3+ hr/day within 4 yr
Teacher	24 units ECE/CD, including core courses + 16 GE units	175 days of 3+ hr/day within 4 yr
Master teacher	24 units ECE or CD, including 16 GE units + 6 specialization units + 2 adult supervision units	350 days of 3+ hr/day within 4 yr
Site supervisor	AA (or 60 units) with 24 ECE or CD units, including core + 6 units administration + 2 units adult supervision	350 days of 4+ hr/day including at least 100 days of supervising adults
Program director	BA with 24 ECE or CD units, including core + 6 units administration + 2 units adult supervision	Site supervisor status and 1 program year of site supervisor experience

© Cengage Learning®

Figure 5-1 A combination of education and experience works to form a career ladder for early childhood education (ECE) professionals in California who want a child development (CD) permit. AA, associate in arts; BA, bachelor or arts; GE, general education.

levels, each with alternative qualifications for meeting the requirements. Within each level, there are varieties of roles available.

5-2b Understanding the Teacher's Role

Teachers wear many hats during the day, and among them are storyteller, carpenter, traffic director, musician, problem solver, poet, and janitor. The roles and responsibilities vary from one teaching situation to another but usually include the following:

In the Classroom

> Interacting with children to establish warm relation-ships, build trust, observe and listen, and model behavior.
> Managing the classroom to coordinate and supervise staff, care for the safety of the environment, and maintain the activity and program
> Setting the tone for the emotional framework of the class, the atmosphere that supports children's growth and learning
> Planning and evaluating curricula to ensure that learning goals are met and that the curricula remain meaningful and appropriate

Teachers model learning, listening, and loving. <

---

emotional framework. The basic "feeling" of a classroom that determines the tone and underlying sensibilities that affect how people feel and behave while in the classroom.

team teaching. Group-based model of teaching, whereby a group composed of people with varying skills, experience, and training teach jointly.

cultural competency. A teacher's cultural awareness and sensitivity in many contexts, such as in guidance, curriculum, family relationships, and interactions with children, families, and coworkers.

Outside the Classroom

> Keeping records on children's progress, health, and family information and, as a way to develop curriculum, documenting for accreditation and teacher training processes
> Attending meetings such as weekly staff meetings, family–teacher conferences, family education meetings, home visits, and conferences
> Organizing and collecting materials to use in classroom and in the curriculum
> Keeping in contact with families and other early childhood specialists through e-mail and telephone calls
> Working with families to plan fund raisers, field trips, and parenting classes

Team Teaching: A Collaborative Effort

Team teaching involves two or more adults working together in one classroom with a group of children and is common in many early childhood programs. State regulations often mandate the ratio of adults to children, with the number determined by the ages of the children. NAEYC (2005) suggests the following guidelines:

> In infant/toddler programs (birth to 30 months), optimal group size is 12 or fewer children with teacher-to-child ratios between 1:3 and 1:6.
> For preschoolers (30 months to 5 years), optimal group size is 20 or fewer children with ratios from 1:6 to 1:10 with the older children.
> For school-aged children (5 to 8 years), optimal group size is 30 or fewer children with ratios of 1:10 to 1:12.

Teaching teams are composed of people with varying skills, experience, and training. Each team may have a head or lead teacher, assistants, aides, student teachers, interns, and volunteers. If you have played on a sports team, you know that teamwork does not just happen. It takes intentionality, organization, and planning. Figure 5-2 highlights essential ingredients for successful team teaching.

5-2c Cultural Competency

Throughout this text, you will be exposed to cultural awareness and sensitivity in many contexts. The culturally competent early childhood professional will interact with cultural influences in guidance approaches, family relationships, immigrant family concerns, bilingualism, and almost every area of education today.

The ability to adapt to a diversified group of families, or cultural competency, is the challenge for the teachers of the 21st century. This is especially true for children who are dual-language learners. Teachers can learn what home languages are spoken and use that language around the classroom by labeling items, securing books and story CDs, and adding travel posters, menus from ethnic restaurants, and some display items that represent the language and traditions of the families. Focus on the specific families rather than their entire culture (Nemeth, 2012).

When I first started teaching, I found that I really liked the team-teaching approach in the early childhood programs where I worked. My friendships with my teammates inspired me to do my best and not let them down. I felt supported by the team whenever I got into a situation that was uncomfortable and I liked the way we all shared the teaching responsibilities. I learned a lot in those early years that helped make me a good teacher.

My biggest frustration has been the amount of gossip and backbiting that can go on among team members. I'm glad I was first influenced by a group of teachers who didn't do that, but later teaching experiences showed me how often infighting can occur. The issue becomes how to solve it in an ethical and sensitive way.

One director I worked for would tell anyone who had a complaint about another teacher to not bother her but go tell the other person. This is good advice to begin with, but what about teachers like me who do not like confrontation? In many cases, the problem just doesn't get dealt with.

The director I work for now has taken the suggestion of confrontation to another level. She is willing to hear about serious and well-founded criticism by the teaching staff. Depending upon the problem, she may choose to talk to the offending teacher alone. Mostly, though, she has the teacher who is making the complaint AND the teacher who is being criticized meet together with her to discuss the issue. In doing this, the director is giving both teachers an opportunity to voice their feelings and come to a fair conclusion. Doesn't this sound familiar? It is the same techniques we use to help children with their conflict resolution!

—Gina

Making these changes requires a pluralistic mindset and an ability to communicate across cultural and individual circumstances, as well as an ability to examine our values and beliefs and learn about the values and beliefs held by the children and families we serve.

5-2d Practice Intentional Teaching

Intentional teaching means that everything you do as a teacher has specific goals and purpose. Intentional teaching goes further than reflective teaching and alters your teaching strategies. It means that you have given your choices and actions a great deal of thought and that if anyone asks you why you have done something, you have a sound explanation (Epstein, 2007). Intentionality plays an important part when a teacher chooses the best kind of learning experiences for children.

We know that children can learn by choosing to work and play in areas that are of interest to them. We also know that there are concepts and content that is best learned through teacher-directed learning experiences. Both self-direction and teacher-direction are important to the growing child. Through intentional teaching, you set the goals, plan the lessons, select the teaching strategies, and focus on the most effective way to help children learn.

Professionalism

Role Definitions for the Early Childhood Teacher

Title	Description	Minimum Qualifications
Apprentice or teacher aide	Is responsible to teacher for implementing program	Entry level, no previous formal training but enrolled in early childhood education classes
Assistant or associate teacher	Is part of the teaching team under the direction of teacher; may implement curriculum, supervise children, and communicate with parents	Child Development Associate teacher (CDA) credential
Teacher	Is co-leader who plans and implements curriculum, works with parents, and evaluates children's progress	Associate degree in early childhood education or related field
Lead teacher	Creates a model classroom, applies good early childhood education practices, supervises other team members, develops new curriculum, provides leadership to team	Bachelor's degree in early childhood education or related field; supervised teaching experience; additional coursework in family life, assessment, supervision, etc.

---

intentional teaching. The ability to plan with purpose and intent and articulate the rationale for your decisions.

5-2e Engage in Reflective Teaching

Reflective teaching is thinking about the broader meaning of teaching by giving careful thought to your role, attitude, and behavior. Reflection is the inner thoughts that might follow any experience you have, or that occur before you plan a teaching experience, or while teaching. Reflection goes to the core of teaching: the relationship between self-understanding and its impact on your educational practices.

At each step of the way, reflection informs the teaching process and results from insightful examination, self-awareness, and self-assessment. Reflective dialogue with colleagues, fellow students, supervisors, and mentors provides the opportunity to challenge yourself, strengthen your professional knowledge, and gain greater depth of understanding about teaching.

truth^{or} *fiction?*

T (F) One of the essential attributes of an early childhood professional is parenting experience.

Basic teaching skills, a child development background, some teaching experience, and certification are the essential attributes for an early childhood professional.

5-2f Personal Qualities

If you were to answer the question, "What personal qualities should teachers have?" you would probably answer with some of these attributes: dedication, compassion, insight, flexibility, patience, energy, a sense of humor, responsibility, and reliability—all hallmarks of a good teacher. Good teachers continue to learn about themselves throughout their career through two other attributes:

1. *Self-awareness.* Answering the question, "Who am I as a teacher and how does that make a difference in the lives of the children I teach?" may be the first step toward self-awareness. Self-knowledge and self-awareness—examining values and personal qualities—take courage and patience. Reflective thinking promotes a healthy

attitude toward accepting oneself, and this a good way to begin to accept children.

2. *Attitudes and bias.* Attitudes and values weave their way into every relationship. Personal histories are filled with bias about race, culture, gender, abilities, and economic status and may negatively affect how we teach. The **anti-bias** approach to teaching (Derman-Sparks & Edwards, 2010) promotes the concept that all children are worthy of our respect and challenges teachers to examine beliefs, attitudes, and actions that might deny a child unconditional acceptance. Figure 5-4 poses questions that help address an awareness of our own biases.

5-2g Avenues for Professional Growth

Good teachers are lifelong learners. Creative and stimulating classrooms are the product of teachers who continue to learn more about how to teach. As NAEYC Standard 5 suggests, qualified teachers engage in continuous, collaborative learning to inform the practice of teaching. There are several ways to achieve professional growth.

Professional Development and Continuing Education

As you gain more experience teaching, you become ready to explore new ideas and resources. This is the time to take workshops and courses and attend regional or national conferences. Many early childhood settings provide periodic in-service training with local resource people, or members of the staff develop a presentation for the rest of the group. **Professional development**, which involves expanding your knowledge in group dynamics, cultural sensitivity, or child assessment portfolios will enhance your career choices and enlarge your contributions to your coworkers.

Professional Affiliations

There are a number of organizations concerned with young children, teachers, and issues related to the early childhood education profession. Abundant resources (print and Internet) are available from these groups. The NAEYC, one of the largest, has local and state affiliate groups through which one can become a member. NAEYC offers a range of services to its members, including conferences and publications such as the journal *Young Children.* The Association for Childhood Education International (ACEI) has a similar function, whereas the Society for Research in Child Development (SRCD) focuses on child psychology, research, and development.

Knowledge of Career Options

If you are considering a career in early childhood education, the options are many and varied. Figure 5-5 lists some of the possibilities that exist in this profession.

---

reflective teaching. Thinking about the broader meaning of teaching through reflection about your role, your attitude, and your behavior.

anti-bias. A phrase describing the development of curriculum that emphasizes an inclusive look at people and problems, extending the tenets of multicultural education and pluralism.

professional development. The process of gaining the body of knowledge and educational foundation that will help in career progression and acquiring further skills on the job.

Essentials of Team Teaching

Weaving a group of teachers into a coordinated and well-functioning team takes a commitment to and understanding of these six essentials.

Collaboration and collegiality. Each member of the team must have the skills to collaborate and work in tandem with the rest of the team. Together, it is the team that shapes and directs the program for children. Collegiality is the mutual respect, support, and trust within a group of teachers to work together on behalf of the children and families in their class.

Role definition and satisfaction. Each teacher is a unique resource with individual talents and experiences that should be appreciated and utilized. Written job descriptions help teachers to understand the scope of their own position as well as that of other team members.

Flexibility. Flexibility is the willingness to offer and accept negotiation and compromise among staff members. Just as effective teachers learn to adapt and change to children's interests and needs, so too do they accept the needs of their coworkers. The daily give-and-take among the staff is key to team effort.

Open and frequent communication. The ability to communicate thoughts, concerns, and feelings to others openly and honestly is perhaps the most important factor in creating a teaching team. The team needs to share information about children and their families, to contribute new ideas to the team, and to collaborate to solve problems. Communication is an ongoing process, and accepting differences of opinions, approaches, and personality traits is part of the challenge of working on a team. See Figure 5-3.

Self-awareness. The ability to be reflective is particularly significant as a member of a teaching team. The more you are aware of your strengths and weaknesses, the greater is your ability to use these attributes to enhance other members of the team and the team as a whole.

Mutual respect and acceptance. Appreciating and accepting the individuality of other team members is important to a team effort. The climate of trust gained through mutual respect allows each staff member to contribute his or her best.

Figure 5-2

Figure 5-3 Professional attitudes and behaviors enhance team teaching.

5-2h Advocacy

Every teacher can become a child advocate and demonstrate the vital importance of care and education for young children and their families. In accepting the challenge to become an effective advocate, you can take the following steps:

1. Make a personal commitment to advocacy and let others know what is at stake.
2. Keep informed about legislative issues that affect children and families.

Reflecting on Personal Beliefs and Bias

Ask Yourself These Questions:

Am I aware of my own identity and its influence on my beliefs and behavior?

Do I have a set of ethical beliefs I follow in relation to working with children and families who are different from me?

Do I foster respect for the values of those who are different from me?

Do I examine my biases and look at ways I can change my own attitudes? When? How?

Do I show a preference for children who mostly fit my own ethnic, cultural, and religious background? When? How?

Do I somehow pass along my biases to the children I teach? When? How? With whom?

Do I truly enjoy differences in human beings? When? With whom?

As you reflect on and confront your responses, your insights will help you become a better and more professional teacher.

Figure 5-4

---

advocate. Someone who furthers the principles and issues of the early childhood field by speaking to others about such issues.

"A teacher's moment-by-moment actions and interactions with children are the most powerful determinant of learning outcomes and development. Curriculum is very important, but what the teacher does is paramount" (Copple & Bredekamp, 2009). Developmentally appropriate practices are now supported by neuroscience. If you stick out your tongue at a baby, he does the same. The same portions of the human brain activate when a person performs an action as when that person is watching someone perform the action. Monkey see, monkey do. And children do, too.

It appears that certain brain regions contain "mirror neurons." These are neurological networks set up "so that a child's neurological synapses 'mirror' not only the teacher's actions and reactions . . . [but also] these same mirror neurons affect the mood of the individual observing the instructor (Rushton et al., 2009).

This implies that it is not just what the teacher presents that is important, but how and who does the presenting. "The irreducible core of the environment during early development is people" (Thompson, 2001). The greatest dangers to the developing brain in the early years are chronic stressors, including unavailable, depressed, or otherwise coercive or inconsistent adults.

The implications of the discovery of mirror neurons is staggering: Might the mirror neurons affect the mood of the child watching the teacher? "At a subliminal level, children observe the teacher's expressions and dispositions and internalize how the teacher is feeling. Neuroscientists believe that our ability to empathize with another human being is due, in part, to the activation of the mirror neuron networks being activated by what we observe" (Rushton et al., 2010).

Children's behavior and their mirror

neurons reflect their external world. Research suggests that "a positive, enthusiastic teacher sends signals to the child's mirror neurons, which, in turn, can impact how they receive the learning objectives being delivered. How we present not only ourselves, but also the phenomenal journey of learning, is critical to the child's emotional development" (Rushton, 2011).

Questions

1. What imitative behaviors might you see in young children that indicate mirror neurons are firing?
2. If the research recommends that curriculum be personally meaningful, what kinds of activities would likely be positively meaningful to toddlers? Prekindergartners?
3. Knowing that you influence children's developing mirror neuron networks, how should you behave with them?

---

3. Know the process and how to access it and express your view in appropriate places. Watch the implementation and its impact.
4. Be visible in your support and show appreciation for what is being done by others.
5. Build rapport and trust with those on all sides of the issue.
6. Educate your legislators about the needs of children, families, and teachers.

5-3 An Ethical Code of Conduct

Throughout your teaching career, you will be in the position of making difficult decisions about children, families, and coworkers. Many of these choices are related to ethical conflicts and moral principles.

5-3a What Are Ethics?

Ethics is the system or code of morals of a particular philosophy, religion, group, or profession and the moral guidelines by which we govern our own behavior and that of society.

---

ethics. A series or system of oral principles and standards; what is "right" and "wrong"; one's values; the principles of conduct governing both an individual teacher and the teaching profession.

When faced with ethical dilemmas, we are guided by our own ethical and moral values that we were taught by our families, friends, religion, and culture that helped us learn right from wrong. We reflect these ideals and principles in our everyday lives and when working with children, families, and coworkers.

Becoming a Whole Teacher

The knowledge and skills you acquire, your understanding of the teacher's roles and responsibilities, your cultural competence and personal qualities, and the results of professional growth opportunities eventually merge. The integration of knowledge, training, and experience reflects who you have become as a teacher: you have developed your own professional philosophy with strengths and convictions about what teachers do and what teachers are.

As you blend training and experience with your personal style and nature, you find your voice. This is the sum of one's response to teaching, and it is unique to you. The person blends with the professional, and the sum becomes greater than the two, allowing the whole teacher the freedom to grow in insight and understanding.

Diversity

Strategies for Dealing with Diversity

Ten Ways to Put Diversity into Action.

1. Look within: remember the first step in confronting bias begins with an understanding of your own roots, habits, and values.
2. There is not only one "best" or "right" way: accept and explore the suggestions of others rather than holding fast to your own "right" way.
3. Move from an "either/or" to a "both/and" perspective: help others feel included and valued through collaboration on ideas, processes, and programs.
4. Foster a climate of acceptance: everyone's beliefs have value and need to be heard.
5. Recognize bias in yourself, others, and institutions: when you see it and hear it, you can begin to deal with it.
6. Become competent in issues of diversity: learn all you can about the families you teach so that you can understand and recognize their value systems.
7. Create inclusive classrooms and programs: see that all aspects of diversity are included in the staff, curriculum, and environment.
8. Expand your teaching strategies: learn from your children and families and incorporate experiences into your teaching repertoire.
9. Promote equity in teaching teams: assistants, aides, and volunteers deserve the same respect as lead teachers and administrators.
10. Invite families into the process: help them find their voice within the educational system.

5-3b Ethical Situations

Doing what is right becomes difficult at times; knowing what is right may be elusive. Even identifying what is right—an ethical situation—may not be obvious.

Some cases are clearly ethical dilemmas: suspected child abuse, loose talk about children and their families outside school, or the firing of a staff member without due cause. Others may not seem as obvious. Some everyday examples include the following:

When parents:

1. Ask to advance their child into the next class against your advice
2. Want you to use discipline practices common to their family and culture but at odds with your own values
3. Attempt to gossip with you about another child, family, or staff member

When a teacher:

1. Suggests a private meeting outside school with a select group of teachers
2. Refuses to take a turn cleaning out the animal cages
3. Regularly misses staff meetings
4. Disagrees with the school's educational philosophy and continues to teach in ways that differ from the approved methods in that setting

Options for the Early Childhood Professional

Direct Services to Children and Families

Teacher in early childhood program
Director of child care facility, nursery school, Montessori program
Family day care provider
Nanny or au pair
Foster parent
Social worker/adoption agent
Pediatric nurse/school nurse
Family therapist/parent educator
Pediatrician
Parent educator
Early intervention specialist
Recreation leader
Play group leader
Home visitor

Indirect Services to Children and Families

Curriculum specialist
Instructional specialist—computers
Child development researcher
Early childhood education specialist
Program consultant
Consumer advocate
Teacher trainer, 2- and 4-year colleges
Consultant
Resource and referral programs
State and national departments of education and/or human services

Community Involvement

State/local licensing worker
Legislative advocate
Child care law specialist
ECE environmental consultant
Interior designer for children's spaces
Government planning agent on children's issues consultant
Consultant in bilingual education, multiculturalism
Nutrition specialist for children
Child care referral counselor

Other Options

Communications consultant
Script writer/editor
Freelance writer
Children's book author
Children's photographer
Microcomputer specialist/program

(Adapted from Eyer, D. *Career Options in Early Childhood Education* [2011].)

Figure 5-5

> Provides teachers with a known, defined core of professional values—those basic truths that any early childhood educator should consider inviolate

> Protects teachers and administrators from having to make hard ethical decisions on the spur of the moment, possibly on the basis of personal bias

> Supports the teacher's choice by saying,"It isn't that I won't act this way: No early childhood educator should act this way" (Kipnis, 1987)

5. Goes to the school administrator with a complaint about a staff member

When the administrator:

1. Insists on adding one more child to an already over-enrolled class
2. Makes personnel decisions based on friendship, not performance
3. Backs a parent who complains about a teacher without hearing the teacher's side of the story

5-3c NAEYC'S Code of Ethical Conduct

NAEYC adopted a revised Code of Ethical Conduct and Statement of Commitment in 2005. The four sections of the code cover ethical responsibilities to (1) children, (2) families, (3) colleagues, and (4) the community and society. The Code of Ethical Conduct may be found in Appendix A at the back of this text.

5-3d Reasons for a Code of Ethics

A professional code of ethics:

> Provides collective wisdom and advice from a broad professional base
> States the principles by which each individual can measure and govern professional behavior
> Says that a group or association has recognized the moral dimensions of its work

---

code of ethics. A code of ethics is a set of statements that helps an educator deal with the temptations inherent in that occupation. It helps her or him act in terms of what is right rather than what is expedient.

assessment. An evaluation such as of a teacher's effectiveness.

5-4 Teacher Assessment: A Key to Quality

In many early childhood settings, an annual performance **assessment** is a professional requirement and becomes a road map for professional growth. Assessments are one of the best ways to ensure the highest quality of teaching.

teachsource video case

Watch the TeachSource Video Case entitled "Teaching as a Profession: An Early Childhood Teacher's Responsibilities and Development." After you study the video clip, view the artifacts, and read the teacher interviews and text, reflect on the following questions:

1. One of the primary values in the NAEYC Code of Ethical Conduct is that children are best understood in the context of their family, culture, and society. Where and how does teacher Samantha Brade weave this into the interview?

2. In the case, Samantha defines many roles and responsibilities that challenge her as a professional. Comment on her ability to be self-reflective as she talks about teaching.

Ethics

Ten Reasons for Teacher Assessment and Evaluations

Knowing the reasons for an assessment creates a climate of trust and mutual accountability. Ten reasons follow:

1. To uphold professional standards in the field of early childhood education
2. To maintain accountability and professional responsibility
3. To identify strengths and limitations
4. To benefit everyone: teachers, children, families, and programs
5. To promote reflective teaching
6. To achieve reasonable goals
7. To increase skill level
8. To assess whether or not goals are achieved
9. To promote healthy change
10. To increase self-confidence

Adapted from Browne & Gordon (2009).

An annual assessment gives you an opportunity to address specific goals and how they will improve your teaching. A professional assessment that is a continuous process with follow-through creates the opportunity for long-lasting improvement to take place. Figure 5-6 shows how teaching goals and performance are part of a continuous loop.

truth or fiction?

T F The core values are different from one's own personal values.

Core values represent agreement within the profession about standards of ethical behavior and are not the same as one's personal values.

5-4a Types of Assessments

Assessments begin with goal setting and reflection: a time to look at where you are, what you think, and how you would like to improve your teaching. The next step is to set a few achievable goals, such as to improve group time skills, learn more about the culture of the children and their families, or improve and expand guidance strategies. During the assessment process, you will discuss your goals with your supervising teacher or director and together develop specific strategies to achieve

Figure 5-6 A feedback loop is a continuous cycle in which teacher behavior is observed for a performance evaluation. The evaluation is offered through growth goals, which are set to affect teacher behavior. Thus, the cycle is continuous, with each part helping the next.

your goals within a given timeframe. The **feedback loop** outlines this process (see Fig. 5-6). There are several formats for assessing teacher performance, and these are often used in tandem.

---

core values. Basic purposes or issues a professional group acknowledges as common concerns to all its members.

feedback loop. In terms of evaluations, a feedback loop is used to describe the process whereby an evaluator gives information to a teacher, who in turn uses this information to improve teaching skills.

Teacher Goal	Example
To help each child develop a positive self-concept	I greet each child with a smile and a personal comment.
To help each child develop socially, emotionally, cognitively, and physically	I have goals for each child in each developmental area, Fall and Spring.
To help provide many opportunities for each child to be successful	My parent conference sheets have examples; for instance, Charlie didn't want to come to group time, so I had him pick the story and help me read it—he comes every day now!
To encourage creativity, questioning, and problem solving	This is my weak point. I tend to talk too much and tell them what to do.
To foster enjoyment for learning in each child	I do great group times and give everyone turns.
To facilitate children's development of a healthy identity and inclusive social skills	I participated in our center's self-study and am taking an antibias curriculum class.

© Cengage Learning®

Figure 5-7 Performance-based assessment ties the goals of the program to a teacher's work. This example asks the teacher to do a self-assessment; a director, parent, or peer could observe and make a second assessment.

Self-Assessment

A **self-assessment** is critical to your own professional worth because it provides you with an opportunity to improve your effectiveness as a teacher. Your own assessment of your strengths and weaknesses prepares you to hear how others assess your teaching skills. Figure 5-7 is an example of a teacher's self-assessment that links the teacher's goals to the program philosophy.

Supervisory Evaluation

Job performance is an administrator's responsibility; therefore, teachers can expect their supervisors to be involved in their evaluation. There are a number of formats, including observations, conferences, videotapes, reports, portfolios, and storytelling.

truth or fiction?

T F Teacher quality is improved through the use of a good assessment tool.

A teacher's professional growth—and therefore the quality of teaching—is enhanced by an annual evaluation that provides information and feedback that promotes best teaching practices.

Sometimes a single form that combines a teacher's self-assessment and the supervisor's evaluation is used, such as the one in Figure 5-8.

Cultural Awareness and Sensitivity

Cultural awareness needs to be taken into consideration when assessing a teacher's performance. Insight about a teacher's social and cultural background is critical if the evaluator is a member of the majority population and the teacher is not.

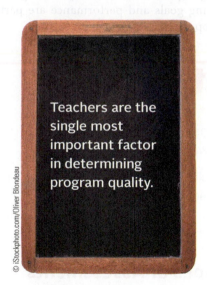

Teachers are the single most important factor in determining program quality.

© iStockphoto.com/Oliver Blondeau

Cultural factors that can affect communication include a sense of time, personal space, eye contact, body language, facial expressions, the use of silence, and concepts of authority. The evaluator has a rare opportunity to create bridges of understanding between and among many cultures. Within the assessment process, they can create a two-way interchange about culturally relevant issues that affect teacher performance.

---

self-assessment. A teacher's own evaluation of his or her performance, strengths, and challenges for personal and professional growth.

Staff Evaluation

Employee _____

Evaluation Period _____

	C (90–100%)	F (60–89%)	O (30–59%)	N (0–29%)
General Work Habits				
1. Arrives on time				
2. Reliable in attendance; gives ample notice for absences				
3. Responsible in job duties				
4. Alert in health and safety matters				
5. Follows the center's philosophy				
6. Open to new ideas				
7. Flexible with assignments and schedule				
8. Comes to work with a positive attitude				
9. Looks for ways to improve the program				
10. Remains calm in a tense situation				
11. Completes required written communication on time				
Professional Development, Attitude, and Efforts				
1. Takes job seriously and seeks to improve skills				
2. Participates in workshops, classes, groups				
3. Reads and discusses distributed handouts				
4. Is self-reflective with goals for ongoing development				
Attitude and Skills with Children				
1. Friendly, warm, and affectionate				
2. Bends low for child level interactions				
3. Uses a modulated, appropriate voice				
4. Knows and shows respect for individuals				
5. Is aware of development levels/changes				
6. Encourages independence/self-help				
7. Promotes self-esteem in communication				
8. Limits interventions in problem solving				
9. Avoids stereotyping and labeling				
10. Reinforces positive behavior				
11. Minimal use of time out				
12. Regularly records observations of children				
Attitude and Skills with Parents				
1. Available to parents and approachable				
2. Listens and responds well to parents				
3. Is tactful with negative information				
4. Maintains confidentiality				
5. Seeks a partnership with parents				
6. Regularly communicates with parents				
7. Conducts parent conferences on schedule				
Attitude and Skills with Class				
1. Creates an inviting learning environment				
2. Provides developmentally appropriate activities				
3. Develops plans from observation and portfolio entries				
4. Provides materials for all curriculum components				
5. Provides an appropriate role model				
6. Anticipates problems and redirects				
7. Is flexible and responsive to child's interests				
8. Is prepared for day's activities				
9. Handles transitions well				
Attitude and Skills with Co-Workers				
1. Is friendly and respectful with others				
2. Strives to assume a fair share of work				
3. Offers and shares ideas and materials				
4. Communicates directly and avoids gossip				
5. Approaches criticism with learning attitude				
6. Looks for ways to be helpful				

Comments:

Figure 5-8 The quality and effectiveness of teaching is affected by the quality and effectiveness of the evaluation process. This form is useful for a self-evaluation and supervisory evaluation.

DAP

> ### Portfolio-Based Assessments
>
> **Portfolio-based assessments** are becoming popular tools for helping teachers make sense of their teaching experiences. A portfolio is an intentional compilation of materials and resources, collected over a period of time. A portfolio is not an assessment tool in and of itself; it is the display or collection system used to demonstrate evidence of professional growth.
>
> Documentation is an important part of creating a portfolio because it provides concrete evidence of how a teacher understands and implements developmentally appropriate teaching practices and translates theory into action.
>
> The portfolio is ever-changing and reflects the individuality of the teacher by virtue of what it contains. By what is included and what is omitted, a portfolio shows evaluators tangible evidence of a teacher's abilities, provides a framework for setting new goals, and gives a more personal sense of the teacher's commitment and professionalism.
>
> A portfolio may include but may not be limited to the following:
>
> > Materials developed by the teacher for use in the classroom
>
> > A videotape of the teacher's performance
>
> > Lesson plans with an evaluation of a specific activity
>
> > Samples of materials developed for the classroom
>
> > Articles written for newsletters, parents, and colleagues
>
> > A journal of teaching experiences
>
> > Photos of field trips or projects
>
> > Self-reflective notes on teaching
>
> > Professional articles
>
> Creating a portfolio is a developmentally appropriate practice that reflects a teacher's professional growth and knowledge of the nature of teaching.

© Cengage Learning®

Evaluations are a professional responsibility that help to clarify job performance, professional growth, and challenges. <

© Cengage Learning®

portfolio-based assessment. An evaluation of a teacher's work using materials, journals, and other resources compiled over a period of time.

summary

5.1 Becoming a professional teacher means that there are professional guidelines and standards to follow. The six NAEYC Standards for Professional Preparation (promoting child development and learning; building family and community relations; observing, documenting, and assessing; using developmentally effective approaches to connect with children and families; using content knowledge to build meaningful curriculum; and becoming a professional) serve as a challenge for what today and tomorrow's teachers should know and be able to do.

5.2 The essential attributes of an early childhood teacher are knowledge and skills, understanding the teacher's role in and out of the classroom and on a teaching team, and cultural competency. Personal qualities are self-awareness,

attitudes and bias, awareness of professional growth opportunities, professional affiliations, and advocacy. Combined, these attributes contribute to the making of the whole teacher.

5.3 A professional code of ethics sets out standards of behavior based on core values and commitments that all early childhood professionals share.

5.4 An annual assessment that is linked to professional growth is a key to maintaining quality programs for young children. The process includes a self-evaluation and an assessment by a supervisor in order to set professional goals. Understanding the cultural context of the teaching staff is an important aspect of the assessment process.

web resources

Center for Child Care Workforce **http://www.ccw.org**
Council for Professional Recognition (CDA)
   http://www.cdacouncil.org

National Association for the Education of Young Children **http://www.naeyc.org**

references

Browne, K. W., & Gordon, A. M. (2013). *Early childhood field experience: Learning to teach well: An early childhood practicum guide.* Upper Saddle River, NJ: Pearson Learning.

Derman-Sparks, L., & Olsen Edwards, J. (2010). *Anti-bias education for young children and ourselves.* Washington, DC: National Association for the Education of Young Children.

Gordon, A., & Browne, K. (2014). *Beginning and beyond: Foundations in early childhood.* Belmont, CA: Wadsworth Cengage Learning.

Kipnis, K. (1987, May). How to discuss professional ethics. *Young Children,* pp. 26–30.

NAEYC. (2005). *Code of ethical conduct.* Washington, DC: Author.

NAEYC (2005). *Early childhood program standards and accreditation criteria.* Washington, DC: Author.

Nemeth, K. N. (2012). *Basics of Supporting Dual Language Learners: An introduction for educators of children from birth through age 8.* Washington, DC: National Association for the Education of Young Children.

6 observation and assessment
learning to read the child

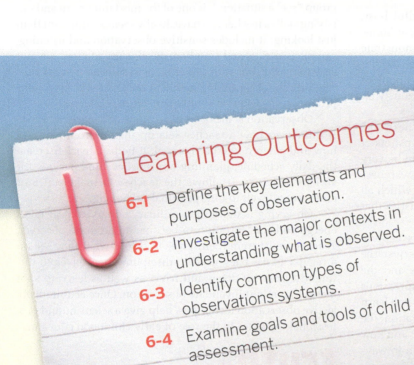

Learning Outcomes

6-1 Define the key elements and purposes of observation.

6-2 Investigate the major contexts in understanding what is observed.

6-3 Identify common types of observations systems.

6-4 Examine goals and tools of child assessment.

NAEYC Standards

The following NAEYC Standards for Early Childhood Professional Preparation are addressed in this chapter:

Standard 3: Observing, Documenting, and Assessing to Support Young Children and Families

Standard 6: Becoming a Professional

truth or *fiction*

T F Observation is as easy as looking and remembering what you see.

T F Understanding what is observed includes learning about children as individuals and in groups.

T F Narratives are the most common type of observation.

T F Testing young children is an effective assessment method.

6-1 Defining Observation

Children are fascinating. They are charming, needful, busy, creative, unpredictable, and emotional. At school, at home, in the grocery store, and in the park, children demonstrate a variety of behaviors. There is the happy child who toddles toward the swing. The angry, defiant child grabs a book or toy and runs away. The studious child works seriously on a puzzle.

These pictures of children flash through the mind, caught for an instant as if by a camera. Such snapshots of children working, playing, and living together can be very useful to teachers. A skilled observer, with an awareness of our diverse world, is reminded of the ways in which all children are the same as well as of the characteristics that make each child unique.

Good observational skills can help teachers capture those moments in a child's life. Memory leaves just the impression. Documentation with visual samples and the written word provides opportunities to check impressions and opinions against the facts. In this chapter, you will learn the key purposes, elements, and contexts of observation; the many types of observation and recording systems; and how to document and assess child behavior and growth in ways that reflect and evaluate children well, without falling prey to the problems of inappropriate assessment.

6-1a What Is Observation?

Teachers learn to make mental notes of the important details in each interaction:

> That's the first time I've seen Karen playing with Bryce. They are laughing together as they build with blocks.

> For 5 minutes now, Ninoy has been standing on the fringes of the sand area where the toddler group is playing. He has ignored the children's smiles and refused the teacher's invitation to join in the play.

> Antonio stops climbing each time he reaches the top of the climbing frame. He looks quickly around, and if he catches a teacher's eye, he scrambles down and runs away.

Through their behavior, these three children reveal much about their personalities. The teacher's responsibility is to notice all the clues and put them together in meaningful ways. The first child, Karen, has been looking for a special friend. Now that she has learned some ways to approach other children that do not frighten and overwhelm them, children want to play with her. Ninoy's parents separated 2 weeks ago. It appears he is just beginning to feel some of that pain and has become withdrawn at school. At home, Antonio is expected to do things right the first time. Because climbing over the top of the frame might be tricky, he does not attempt it at all. At school, he generally attempts only what he knows he can do without making a mistake.

objectivity. The quality or state of being able to see what is real and realistic, as distinguished from subjective and personal opinion or bias.

bias. A personal and sometimes unreasoned judgment inherent in all our perceptions.

The ability to observe—to "read" the child, understand a group, "see" a situation—is one of the most important and satisfying skills a teacher can have. Really *seeing* is different than just looking; it includes sensitive observation and listening, careful assessing, and simultaneous documentation. It is not easy to master, but with practice, the results are remarkable. The process of becoming a skilled observer will keep your primary focus where it should be—on the children.

Observation is the basis of so much of a teacher's work. It influences how a teacher sets up the environment and how and when it will be changed. It helps a teacher create the daily schedule, planning appropriate time periods for various activities. It allows the teacher to make sense of and respond well to interpersonal exchanges.

Observing is more than ordinary supervising. It takes energy and concentration to become an accurate observer. Teachers must train themselves to record what they see on a regular basis. They need to discipline themselves to distinguish between detail and trivia as well as learn to spot biases that might invalidate observation. Once acquired, objective observation techniques help give a scientific and professional character to the role of early childhood educator.

truth or fiction?

T F Observation is as easy as looking and remembering what you see.

Accurate observation involves skill and practice. Learning to watch carefully, avoid conclusions or judgment during the observation, and collect what is important instead of tangential details is a scientific method that is complex and challenging.

6-1b Why Observe?

To Improve Your Teaching

The most effective teachers are those who are thorough in their preparation and systematic in evaluating their own work. It takes a certain level of awareness—of self, of the children, and of the environment—to monitor our own progress. Observing children helps teachers become more objective about the children in their care. When making observational notes, teachers look first at what the child is doing. This is different from looking at how a child ought to be doing something. The teacher becomes like a camera, recording what is seen without immediately judging it. This **objectivity** can balance the intense, personal side of teaching (see Figure 6-1).

Bias is inherent in all our perceptions. We must acknowledge this truth without falling prey to the notion that because our efforts will be flawed, they are worthless. Observing can never be totally objective because everything passes through the filter of the observer's beliefs, biases, assumptions, history, understanding, and knowledge.

Poor Observation

A. Julio walked over to the coat rack and dropped his sweater on the floor. He is shy (1) of teachers, so he didn't ask anyone to help him pick it up. He walked over to Cynthia because she's his best friend (2). He wasn't nice (3) to the other children when he started being pushy and bossy (4). He wanted their attention (5), so he nagged (6) them into leaving the table and going to the blocks like 4-year-old boys do (7).

Analysis and Comments

(1) Inference of a general characteristic
(2) Inference of child's emotion
(3) Observer's opinion
(4) Inference with no physical evidence stated
(5) Opinion of child's motivation
(6) Observer's inference
(7) Overgeneralization; stereotyping

Good Observation

B. Emilio pulled out a puzzle from the rack with his right hand, and then carried it with both hands to the table nearby. Using both hands, he methodically took each piece out of the frame and set it to his left. Sara, who had been seated across from Emilio with some table toys in front of her, reached out and pushed all the puzzle pieces onto the floor. Emilio's face reddened as he stared directly at Sara with his mouth in a taut line. His hands turned to fists, his brown furrowed, and he yelled at Sara in a forceful tone, "Stop it! I hate you!"

Analysis and Comments

Emilio was clearly *angry*, as demonstrated in his facial expressions, hand gestures, and body movements. The way a child speaks is as revealing as what a child says when one wants to determine what a child is feeling. Muscular tension is another clue to the child's emotions. But the physical attitude of the child is not enough; one must also consider the context. Just seeing a child sitting in a chair with a red face, one doesn't know if he is embarrassed, angry, feverish, or overstimulated. We need to know the events that led to this appearance. Then we can correctly assess the entire situation. By being open to what is happening without judging it first, we begin to see children more clearly.

© Cengage Learning®

Figure 6-1 Example A contains numerous biases, which are underlined in the left column and explained in the right column. Example B has clear descriptions and is relatively free of biases.

Teachers are influenced in their work by their own early childhood experiences. They have notions about how children learn, play, grow, or behave because of the way they were raised and trained (see Diversity box). Moreover, when teachers are in the thick of activity, they see only a narrow picture. To pull back, take some notes, and make an observation gives the teacher a chance to see the larger scene.

Teams of teachers help each other gain perspective on the class, an individual, or a time of the day. All teachers develop ideas and impressions about children when they spend time with them. Some children seem shy, some helpful, some affectionate, aggressive, cooperative, stubborn, and so on. These opinions influence the way teachers behave and interact with children. Observations can be a means of validating—or adjusting—one teacher's point of view. By checking out an opinion or idea through systematic observation, teachers use the reflective process to establish a professional level of teamwork.

If we teach ourselves to be available and focused on children, we engage in a kind of "slowing down" that serves both children and teacher well. Regular observation prompts teachers to ask important questions (Jones & Reynolds, 2013), such as:

> What is happening for this child in this play?
> What is his agenda?

> Does the child have the needed skills and materials to accomplish her intent?

To answer these questions, teachers and families need to practice taking the child's perspective. Careful observation of children at play enables one to do just that.

To Construct and Apply Theory

Observations are a link between theory and practice. Early childhood education is the one level of teaching that systematically bases its teaching on child development. If we are to develop programs that work for young children—what they can do, how they think and communicate, and what they feel—we need to be able to apply sound child development knowledge to the classroom. Further, we can use what researchers have learned to understand the individual children in our care.

Recall Antonio who runs away when teacher Gabriel starts to watch him climb. Gabriel is reminded that Erikson's stage of psychosocial development at preschool, which involves balancing "Initiative vs. Guilt," is the challenge here. Antonio worries that he might do something wrong while he is climbing, so teacher Gabriel will have to find a way to endorse Antonio's "good ideas" in trying something new and help him feel less "guilty" about slipping or going slowly.

Diversity

Check Your Lenses!

Observers watching the same scene, seeing the same behavior, think of it in very different terms. Seeing through a different pair of cultural eyes, each of us is thus affected in our reactions and assessments. (Gonzalez Mena in Gordon & Browne, 2014)

What we see is in the eye of the beholder. What do you behold?

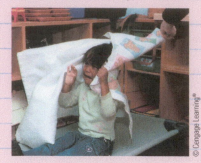

A 2-year-old screams "Mine!" and fends off a boy trying to grab the blanket she's holding.

You see: "She's obviously protecting her security blanket; she is standing up for herself."

> Believing in private property.

Or: "Look at that selfish child; she disturbs the group and is unkind."

> Believing in group harmony.

A 4-year-old shouts at another, "No; don't knock it down; we just built it ourselves!"

You see: "He's protecting his space; he takes pride in what he creates."

> Believing in self-expression and low frustration tolerance.

Or: "He is rude; he hurts others' feelings and is unfriendly."

> Believing in group affiliation and building community.

Close observation can also reveal the growing brain at work, and see when it is at risk of overload. See Brain Box for an explanation and example.

To Build Curriculum

Observation helps a teaching team record what they do in the curriculum. In contrast to traditional planning, which tends to be teacher dominated and planned ahead of time, this kind of curriculum involves observing the children to see their interests, then building activities that evolve from the interaction of the children and adults.

Consider the observations teachers made in this example. A nearby construction site brought keen interest in building activities to the classroom. The discovery center turned into a workshop, a woodworking table became a regular station outdoors, and weekly field trips by small groups resulted in stories and drawings that were then put on a documentation panel for parents to see children's learning in action. Imagine the class's excitement when members of the construction crew arrived one day for snack and donated hardhats to the dramatic play corner!

Professionalism

The Scientist Who Waits

For the professional teacher, two guidelines come to mind as one begins to observe:

> **Practice intensive waiting.** Cultivate an ability to wait and see what is really happening instead of rushing to conclusions about what it means, where such behavior comes from, or what should be done.

> **Become part scientist.** A good observer makes a clear distinction between fact and inference, between real behavior and an impression or conclusion drawn from it. See something and wonder why. After developing hunches or intuitions about the problem, generate alternatives and then test the hypothesis. This kind of "action research" is easily adaptable to teaching.

To Help Families

Families benefit from observations. A collection of notes about an individual child can be used in parent conferences. The teacher shares fresh, meaningful examples that demonstrate the child's growth and abilities and gains perspective when the notes are discussed and compared with family observations at home. Problems become clearer, and plans can be made to work together between home and school. Results can be further

> Become part scientist. A good observer makes a clear distinction between fact and inference, between real behavior and an impression or conclusion drawn from it. Slow down and see more!

Brain Research *says*

Early childhood education is built on the belief that the whole child, in all developmental domains, provides a greater understanding than only a narrow or single-domain view. Information about the brain has provided new insights into the biological basis of behavior and development. Stress and its impact on children's behavior is of special interest, along with the role that caregivers can take to respond to stress.

The human stress system has two branches, the hypothalamic-pituitary-adrenocortical system (HPA) axis and the autonomic nervous system. The HPA axis stimulates the production of the stress hormone cortisol, which can be influenced by "the Big Three:" [which are] controllability, predictability/familiarity, and social support (Gilkerson & Klein, 2007). Knowledgeable teachers can use this information to work with families to provide for these three factors in early experiences.

A second application involves the autonomic nervous system, which gives physical cues to the observant teacher about a child's stress level. Specifically changes can be seen with heightened stress. "Fluctuations in skin color, breathing patterns, sweating, yawning, or the need to go to the bathroom can be cues to the burden a current demand places on a particular child. Similarly, observation of the quality of motor behavior and attention offers insight into how the child experiences the complexity of the task and what support he needs" (Gilkerson, 2001).

So, when a child is wiggly, unco-operative, or inattentive, consider the child's behavior to be important clues to that child's experience. Observing closely can reveal brain activity and help understand and respond well to a child's individual sensory profile.

Questions

1. What might it feel like to be that child in those moments?
2. How can observation assist the teacher in ascertaining a child's capacity to engage?
3. Do you remember being overloaded in school? And what did that feel/look like?

---

tested through continuing observation. Authentic assessments such as child portfolios (discussed later in this chapter) are ideal tools for communication.

To Assess Children

Assessment is a critical part of a teacher's job, and evaluating children includes observing and assessing their behavior and their development. Authentic assessment, done when children are in their natural setting and performing real tasks, fits best with the overall goal of developmentally

Learning to assess children's skills and behavior and to document them is becoming increasingly important to the early childhood educator. Testing is commonplace in educational systems for older children, and appropriate assessment is a challenge in the early years. ◄

appropriate practice. Teachers are called on to set specific goals for the children in their classes and for the overall class performance. They document children's progress. In this way, teachers are accountable to their clients: the children, the parents, and the public. Assessment techniques, such as portfolios and screening, are described later in this chapter.

6-2 Understanding What Is Observed

The goal of observing children is to understand them better. Observational data help adults know children in several significant ways. There are several major contexts that a teacher comes to understand in observing and recording child behavior.

6-2a Children as Individuals

How do children spend their time at school? What activities are difficult? Who is the child's best friend? By watching individual children, teachers can choose activities and materials to match interests and skills. This is called **differentiated instruction**: tailoring what is taught to what a child is ready and willing to learn. This kind of teaching gives children educational experiences that offer connected knowledge that is real and relevant (see Chapter 10) and is part of developmentally appropriate practices.

Observing helps a teacher spot a child's strengths and areas of difficulty. Once these are known, teachers plan intervention measures, helping to make the school experience successful for the child.

---

differentiated instruction. Using different methods to teach the same concept, used to accommodate the different learning styles of individual children.

Observing to offer differentiated instruction is part of programs for children with special needs; in these cases an individualized education plan (IEP) is developed jointly by teachers, education specialists, and parents to better serve the child.◄

6-2b Children in Groups

When recording behavior, teachers see growth patterns emerge. Both Piaget and Erikson used observation to learn how children think and develop socially and emotionally. Gesell studied large numbers of children to get developmental **norms** of physical growth (see Word Pictures in Chapter 3).

Observation gives a feeling for group behavior as well as a developmental yardstick to compare individuals within the group. Observing children can provide the answer to these questions:

truth or *fiction?*

Ⓣ F Understanding what is observed includes learning about children as individuals and in groups.

By observing individual children, teachers both learn the child's skills and challenges and also collect data about what to expect from children of that age group.

> What might you expect when 2-year-olds pour juice?
> How will the second-grade class behave on a field trip?
> What is the difference in the attention span at story time of 3-year-olds vs. pre-kinders?
> How will children likely react when left at kindergarten the first day?

---

norms. An average or general standard of development or achievement, usually derived from the average or median of a large group; a pattern or trait taken to be typical of the behavior, skills, or interests of a group.

DAP

Observing on Three Levels
Observation of a child can be made on three levels:

> Report exactly what the child does: note exactly what actions the child takes.

> Express how the child seems to feel about what happened: note facial expressions, body language, and the quality of the behavior.

> Include your own interpretations: add as a last and separate step some of your own personal responses and impressions.

Note the three levels in the teacher's journal:
Matthew has some issues—he has been here only 3 weeks and I have to shadow him most of the day.

> Today he was knocking down children's block buildings during indoor free play, turning over the chairs at the snack table, and pushing William on a tricycle backward as fast as he could. *(Level 1)*

> You should have seen the look of terror on W's face. And then I looked at M, and he appeared puzzled—even surprised—when I asked him to look at William. He even relaxed into me as I put my arms around them both to "talk it out." *(Level 2)*

> Something is going on here that I don't get. I talked with his mom after class, just telling her the incidents. She gives him a chair to push around at home, so now I see where some of the pushing comes from. Not only that, she is having him tested next week for sensory processing problems with an occupational therapist. Phew! *(Level 3)*

> It is safe to say that whenever a teacher encounters a problem—whether it is a child's behavior, a period of the day, a set of materials, or a puzzling series of events—the first step toward a solution is systematic observation.

Teachers then determine age-appropriate expectations for their group. For example, experienced teachers of toddlers will not put out watercolor sets, whereas the second-grade teacher will do so routinely. Teachers learn that it is typical of 4- and 5-year-olds to exclude others from their play because teachers see it happen countless times. Three-and-a-half-year-old Kailani is sure she is "too little" to use the toilet; this will not concern the knowledgeable teacher, who knows that this is developmentally appropriate behavior! Decisions about *single* children come from watching and knowing *many* children.

6-2c Developmental Relationships

Observing brings about an understanding of the various developmental areas and how they are related. Children's behavior is both a mix of several distinct developmental domains (see Chapter 4) and an integrated whole whose parts influence each other. By "the whole child" we mean a consideration of how development works in unison.

Observing helps teachers see how the pieces fit together. Experienced teachers will tell you that children's developmental profiles usually encompass skills of 2 to 3 years. Antonio has the physical coordination of a 3-year-old, the language skills of a 5-year-old, and the self-regulation skills of a 2-year-old, all bound up in the body that is 4!

6-2d Influences on Behavior

Careful observation gives us insight into the influences and dynamics of behavior.

Standards

Observing, Documenting, and Assessing to Support Young Children

Bryce's midyear report shows that he lacks dexterity in running and climbing and that he is exceptionally strong in verbal and listening skills. This influences his development in the following areas:

Emotionally. He appears to lack self-confidence, and his self-esteem deteriorates the longer he feels inept at physical skills. He may even be afraid to master the art of climbing and running for fear he will fail.

Socially. Children tease Bryce because he often cannot keep up with them while playing outside. He often ends up playing alone or watching the other children in more active pursuits.

Intellectually. There is a lack of risk-taking in Bryce's whole approach to play. Because of his slow physical development, he seems unlikely to challenge himself in other ways.

Bryce's progress report thus sets a primary goal in physical/motor skills, with the knowledge that such growth can positively affect learning in other areas.

The classroom arrangement and daily schedule affect children's behavior because children are highly influenced by their environment.

6-2e Understanding of Self

Observing children can be a key to understanding ourselves. People who become skilled at seeing small but important facets of human personality increase their self-awareness. "It is difficult to be objective about yourself, but as you watch your own behavior and interactions you can learn more about how you feel and respond in various situations and realize the impact of your behavior

Observation	Influences and Outcomes
Boaz has separation anxiety when he enters his child care each morning, yet he is competent and says he likes school. Close observation reveals that his favorite areas are climbing outdoor games and the sandbox. Boaz feels least successful in the construction and creative arts areas, the primary choices indoors.	Boaz feels unsure of himself in the activities offered, and he shows his discomfort by crying and clinging to his dad. Since Farsi is his home language, the teacher asks his father to provide a list of key words and phrases the staff can use with Boaz right away. By adding something he enjoys, such as a sand table indoors, the teacher changes the physical environment to be more appealing and positive. Boaz's difficulties in saying goodbye disappear as he hears his own language spoken at school, finds success, and can be comfortable.
Mari starts the day happily but cries frequently throughout the day. Is there a pattern to her outbursts? Watch what happens to Mari when free play is over and group time begins. She falls apart readily when it is time to move outdoors to play, time to have snacks, time to nap, and so on.	The cause of Mari's problem is difficult to detect. The physical environment seems to interest and appeal to her. On closer observation, her crying and disruptive behavior appear to happen just at the point of change, regardless of the activities before or afterward. It is the time aspect of the environment that causes difficulty for her. The teacher makes a special effort to signal upcoming transitions and to involve her in bringing them about. Telling Mari, "Five more minutes until nap time" or "After you wash your hands, go to the snack table" gives her the clues she needs to anticipate the process of change. Asking her to announce cleanup time to the class lets her be in control of that transition.

on others," (Feeney et al., 2012). For example, a teacher whose own experience of school authority was problematic may react to a program's "rules" by making frequent exceptions for children. She may not intend to undermine class guidelines, but her inconsistency results in uncooperative behavior. Becoming aware of her own action—and being introspective about its motivation—improves her teaching.

6-3 Documenting What We See

The second part of the observation process is recording children's behavior fully and vividly, capturing the unique qualities, culture, and personality of each child and the group. In recording what you observe, you need to learn how to look and to learn the language of documentation.

documentation. The furnishing and use of documentary evidence; the written comments, graphical illustrations, photos, dictation, and other work samples.

Common Elements of Observation Systems

Element	Definition	Example
Focus	What do you want to know? Whom/what do you want to observe? What aspects of behavior do you want to know about? What is your purpose?	What's going on at nap time? Child(ren), teachers Social interaction, impulse control, problem-solving skills Study environment, check effectiveness of daily schedule, deal with negative behavior
System	What will you do? How will you record the information you need?	Define the terms, decide how long to record Level of detail, units of measure
Tools	What will you need for your observations?	Video/audio tape recorder(s), camera, chart, pencil
Environment	Where will you watch? What restraints are inherent in the setting?	Classroom, home Other people, interruptions

© Cengage Learning®

Figure 6-2 All types of observations have the four key elements of focus, system, tools, and environment.

> **Learning to look.** Although it is true that teachers rarely have the luxury of observing uninterrupted for long periods of time, they can often plan shorter segments. Practice by paying attention to the content of children's play during free periods—theirs and yours. Carry a small notebook in your pocket, and jot down who is playing together whenever you can. At the end of the day, spread out your notes and see what you learned about your group's play partners.

> **Recording to document.** Try your hand at jotting down some notes about the play. It is easy to get discouraged, especially if you are unaccustomed to writing, but it gets easier as you practice finding synonyms for common words. For instance, children are active creatures; how many ways do they run? They may gallop, dart, whirl, saunter, skip, or hop. Or think of the various ways children talk to you: they shriek, whisper, whine, shout, demand, whimper, lisp, and roar.

Be sure to record what you see in the language that comes easiest to you. Once you have mastered a descriptive vocabulary, recording important behavior will become easier.

---

narratives. A major observation technique that involves attempting to record nearly everything that happens, in as much detail as possible, as it happens. Narratives include several subtypes such as baby biographies, specimen descriptions, diary descriptions, and logs or journals.

running record. The narrative form of recording behavior that involves writing all behavior as it occurs.

baby biographies. One of the first methods of child study, these narratives were written accounts by parents of what their babies did and said, usually in the form of a diary or log.

diary descriptions. A form of observation technique that involves making a comprehensive narrative record of behavior, in diary form.

specimen description. A form of narrative technique that involves taking on-the-spot notes about a child or behavior (the "specimen").

6-3a Common Elements

All types of observations used in recording children's behavior have the key ingredients of defining and describing the behaviors and repeating the observation in terms of several factors, such as time, number of children, and activities. All observational systems have certain elements in common (Figure 6-2).

6-3b Types of Observations

There are four major methods of observing and documenting child growth and development. Each captures behavior in unique ways, and teachers select the method that best collects data for them to use.

Narratives

At once the most valuable and the most difficult to compile of records, narratives are attempts to record nearly everything that happens. In the case of a young child, this means all that the child does, says, gestures, seems to feel, and appears to think about. Narratives maintain a running record of the excitement and tension of the interaction while remaining an accurate, objective account of the events and behavior. Observers put into words what they see, hear, and know about an event or a person.

Narratives are the oldest and often most informative kind of report. Gesell used mothers' baby biographies as diary descriptions and doctors' narratives to set basic developmental norms. These specimen descriptions are a standard technique in anthropology and the biologic sciences, and Pestalozzi, Darwin, and Piaget used logs and journals to record in minute detail children's growth.

Running records are the most common classroom form of narrative. This means describing every action observed within a given time period. It might be a 5-minute period during free play to record what a preschooler does

Narrative Form of Observation

The Child Alone

Unoccupied Behavior. SH slowly walks from the classroom to the outside play area, looking up each time one of the children swishes by. SH stops when reaching the table and benches and begins pulling the string on the sweatshirt. Still standing, SH looks around the yard for a minute, then wanders slowly over to the seesaw. Learning against it, SH touches the seesaw gingerly, then trails both hands over it while looking out into the yard. (*Interpretive comments.* This unoccupied behavior is probably due to two reasons: SH is overweight and has limited language skills compared with the other children. Pulling at the sweatshirt string is something to do to pass the time because the overweight body is awkward and not especially skillful.)

Onlooker Behavior. J is standing next to the slide watching her classmates using this piece of equipment. She looks up and says, "Hi." Her eyes open wider as she watches the children go down the slide. P calls to J to join them, but J shakes her head "no." (*Interpretive comments.* J is interested in the slide but is reluctant to use it. She has a concerned look on her face when the others slide down; it seems too much of a challenge for J.)

Solitary Play. L comes running onto the yard holding two paintbrushes and a bucket filled with water. He stops about 3 feet away from a group of children playing with cars in the sandbox and sits down. He drops the brushes into the bucket and laughs when the water splashes his face. He begins swishing the water around with the brushes and then starts wiggling his fingers in it. (*Interpretive comments.* L is very energetic and seems to thoroughly enjoy his outside playtime with water. He adds creative touches to this pleasurable experience.)

© Cengage Learning®

Figure 6-3 The narrative gives a rich sample of children's behavior; even though it risks teacher bias, it still records valuable information.

or during a reading period to document exactly how a first-grader decodes words. Another way to use this type of narrative is to watch an activity area to record how children use the materials (Figure 6-3).

The procedure is to take on-the-spot notes each day. This task lends itself easily to most early childhood settings. The teachers carry with them a small notebook and pencil, tucked in a pocket. They jot down whatever seems important or noteworthy during the day. These anecdotal notes are the most familiar form of recording observations. They often focus on one item at a time:

> A part of the environment: how is the science area being used?
> A particular time of day: what happens right after naps?
> A specific child: how often is Karen hitting other children?

These notes then become a rich source of information for report writing and family conferences. They are also part of curriculum documentation as children's behavior and conversations become part of documentation panels alongside photos and artwork.

Because this is time consuming and needs to be done without interruption, narratives are challenging to manage. Diary descriptions in the form of a log/journal are often used with infants and toddlers. A page is set aside for each child in the class. It helps to write immediately after the program is over or to organize the teaching teams to enable one member of the staff to observe and record during class time.

Another challenging part of the narrative is to be able to write enough detail so that the reader will be able to picture whole situations later. Whatever notes the teachers use, however brief, need to be both clear and accurate. This includes being aware of the personal biases that can influence observation. It is a given that we all have biases. It is not realistic to think that one can be bias free. The goal is to be conscious of the bias we bring to our work and to be open to multiple interpretations of observed behavior. In this way we do not let our individual bias dictate our observations and interactions with children from diverse backgrounds.

Even though the narrative remains one of the most widely used and effective methods of observing young children today, many teachers prefer more structured procedures, such as those that follow.

Time Sampling

The time sampling method is an observation of what happens within a given period of time. Developed as an observational strategy in laboratory schools in the 1920s, time sampling was used to collect data on large numbers of children and to get a sense of normative behaviors for particular age groups or sexes. It has been used to record autonomy, dependency, task persistence, aggression, play patterns, and nervous habits (nail biting or hair twisting). In a time sample, behavior is recorded at regular time intervals. To use this method, one needs to sample what occurs fairly frequently. It makes sense to choose those behaviors that might occur at least once every 10 minutes. The definitive study using time sampling defined children's play patterns (Parten, 1932). The codes developed in this study have become classic play patterns used throughout this text and in the professional field to describe the interactions of children (Figure 6-4).

---

log/journal. A form of observation technique that involves making a page of notes about children's behavior in a cumulative journal.

time sampling. An observation technique that involves observing certain behavior and settings within a prescribed time frame.

Play with Others
P = Parallel
A = Associative
C = Cooperative
Time Unit

Child	9:00			9:10			9:20			9:30			Total		
	P	A	C	P	A	C	P	A	C	P	A	C	P	A	C
Jamal															
Marty															
Dahlia															
Keith															

© Cengage Learning®

Figure 6-4 Time sampling involves defining the behavior and making a coding sheet to tally observations.

Time sampling helps teachers define exactly what it is they want to observe and is ideal for collecting information about the group as a whole. Developing a category and coding system reduces the problem of observer bias. Yet diminishing this bias also eliminates some of the richness and quality of information. It is difficult to get the whole picture when one divides it into artificial time units and with only a few categories.

Event Sampling

With the event sampling method, the observer defines an event, devises a system for describing and coding it, then waits for it to happen. As soon as it does, the recorder moves into action. Thus, the behavior is recorded as it occurs naturally.

Teachers can use event sampling to examine behaviors such as bossiness, avoidance of teacher requests, or withdrawal. The classic analysis of preschool children's quarrels used event sampling (Dawes, 1934). Whenever a quarrel began, the observer recorded it. Like time sampling, event sampling looks at particular behaviors or occurrences (Figure 6-5). But the unit is the event rather than a prescribed time interval. Event sampling is a favorite

event sampling. An observation technique that involves defining the event to be observed and coding the event to record what is important to remember about it.

checklist. A modified child study technique that uses a list of items for comparison, such as a "yes/no" checklist for the demonstration of a task.

frequency count. A modified child study technique that records how often a behavior occurs within a certain time frame.

evaluation. A study to determine or set significance or quality.

rating scales. A modified child study technique similar to a checklist that classifies behavior according to grade or rank, such as using the descriptors "always, sometimes, never" to describe the frequency of a certain behavior.

shadow study. A modified child study technique that profiles an individual at a given moment in time; similar to diary description, the shadow study is a narrative recorded as the behavior happens.

of classroom teachers. They can go about the business of teaching children until the event occurs. Then they can record the event quickly and efficiently.

Modified Child Study Techniques

Because observation is the key method of studying young children in their natural settings, it makes good sense to use more than one kind of documentation. Questions arise that need fast answers, and modified child study techniques can define the scope of a problem fairly quickly. Some of the techniques are checklist systems, rating scales, and shadow studies. Experimental procedures and the clinical technique can study both a group and the individuals in it.

Checklists contain a great deal of information that can be recorded rapidly. A carefully planned checklist can tell a lot about one child or the entire class. The data are collected in a short period of time. The Checklist (Figure 6-6) can be collected on a number of children over a week, or modified into mini-checklists that are done during the time the behaviors may occur ("eating" for snack/lunch, "gross motor" for outdoors). A frequency count is a type of checklist that gives a broad picture of how children spend their time and what activities interest them. Tracking where children play gives a team a sense of how the environment is used and what curricular areas to enhance.

Checklists can vary in length and complexity depending on their function. To develop one, teachers first determine the purpose of the observation. Next they define what the children will do to demonstrate the behavior being observed. Finally comes the task of designing an actual checklist that is easy to use and simple to set aside when other duties take precedence.

Although they make it easy to record, checklists lack the richness of the more descriptive narrative. They can tally broad areas of information but miss context. Checklists are often used in evaluation.

Rating scales are like checklists, planned in advance to record something specific. They extend checklists by adding some quality to what is observed. They differ from checklists in that they require teachers to make refined decisions. A rating scale may use word phrases or a numerical key. For example, a rating scale measuring attention at group times could be set up. On a scale of 1 to 3, teachers rate children's attention:

Never: *wiggles, distracts others, wanders away*

Sometimes: *imitates some hand gestures, watches leader about half the time*

Always: *enthusiastically enters group, eagerly imitates leader.*

The advantage is that more information is gathered. A potential problem is added because the observer's opinions are now required and could hamper objectivity.

The shadow study is a third type of modified technique. It is similar to the diary description and focuses on one child

Time	Children	Antecedent Event	Behavior	After Effects
8:30 45 sec	Shelly, Mike	Play dough table; S. picks up roller M. had been using & set aside; no one else @ table.	M. yells, "Gimme that back!" and grabs it out of S. hand. S. stares, then picks up cookie cutter.	S. looks at teacher, tells her "He took it away" and starts to cry; M. ignores & continues rolling.
9:40 2 min	Tasauna, Yuki, Lorena	T. & Y. are building farm house; L. runs through & kicks over blocks & animals.	T. shouts "Don't kick it, we don't like you anymore." Y. sits back, watches T., then picks up animals & starts to play. L. turns back and sticks out her tongue. T. says "Get out of here, you can't come to my birthday." Teacher approaches for problem solving.	Teacher engages all three in conflict resolution process; both T. & L. frown, then state their feelings, Y. listens & whispers when asked, "I want to play." L & T agree to "fix it," and all three play for 5 minutes afterwards.

© Cengage Learning®

Figure 6-5 Sampling of events can be helpful in determining how frequently a specific event takes place.

Skills Checklist

Motor Skills Observation (ages 2–4)

Child Age: _____

Date: _____

Observer: _____

	Yes	No
Eating:		
1. Holds glass with one hand		
2. Pours from pitcher		
3. Spills little from spoon		
4. Selects food with pincer grasp		
Dressing:		
1. Unbuttons		
2. Puts shoes on		
3. Uses both hands together (such as holding jacket with one hand while zipping with the other)		
Fine Motor:		
1. Uses pincer grasp with pencil, brushes		
2. Draws straight line		
3. Copies circles		
4. Cuts at least 2 inches in line		
5. Makes designs and crude letters		
6. Builds tower of 6 to 9 blocks		
7. Turns pages singly		
Gross Motor:		
1. Descends/ascends steps with alternate feet		
2. Stands on one foot, unsupported		
3. Hops on two feet		
4. Catches ball, arms straight, elbows in front of body		
5. Operates tricycle		

© Cengage Learning®

Figure 6-6 A checklist gives specific information about an individual child's skills.

at a time. An in-depth approach, the shadow study gives a detailed picture. Each teacher attempts to observe and record the behavior of one particular child. Then, after a week or so, the notes are compared. Although the notes may be random, it is preferable that they have some form and organization. The data in a shadow study are descriptive, so it shares the advantages of narratives. One interesting side effect often noted is how the behavior of the child being studied improves while the child is being observed. Disruptive behavior seems to diminish or appear less intense. It would appear that in the act of focusing on the child, teacher attention has somehow helped to alter the behavior. Somehow the child feels the impact of all this positive, caring attention and responds to it. (See Digital Download for a shadow study example.)

Two additional strategies are used to obtain

information about a child. Because they involve some adult intervention, they do not consist strictly of observing and recording naturally occurring behavior. Still, they are very helpful techniques for teachers to understand and use.

Experimental procedures are those in which adult researchers closely control a situation and its variables. Researchers create a situation in which they can do the following:

1. Observe a particular behavior
2. Make a hypothesis, or guess, about that behavior
3. Test the hypothesis by conducting the experiment

For instance, an experimenter might wish to observe fine motor behavior in 7-year-olds to test the hypothesis that these children can significantly improve their fine motor skills if given specific instruction in sewing. Two groups of children are tested. One group is given an embroidery hoop, thread, and needle and asked to "try 10 stitches." The other receives a demonstration of how to stitch, coached while attempting , then given the identical task. The embroidery hoops created by both groups are then compared for quality of stitching, level of persistence, and response to task.

Few teachers working directly with children will use the stringent criteria needed to undertake a true scientific experiment. However, it is useful to understand this process because much basic research conducted to investigate how children think, perceive, and behave uses these techniques. In addition, the teacher-as-researcher approach is common in classrooms with a professional focus on continual improvement.

The clinical method is the final information- gathering technique that involves the adult directly with the child. This method is used in psychotherapy and in counseling settings as the therapist asks probing questions. Piaget mastered the clinical method (la méthode clinique) as he observed and questioned or tried out new ideas with children. For instance, a group of preschoolers is gathered around a water table. Teacher Miho notices two cups, one deep and narrow, the other broad and shallow, and asks, "I wonder which one holds more, or if they are the same?" The children say what they think and why. Then, one of the children takes the two cups and pours the liquid from one into the other.

Teachers do more than simply observe and record what happens. Rather, they intervene in the children's natural play to explore a question systematically with them, then listen for and observe the answers. The clinical method is not strictly an observational method, but it is an informative technique that when used carefully, can reveal much about children's abilities and knowledge.

experimental procedure. Observation technique that gathers information by establishing a hypothesis, controlling the variables that might influence behavior, and testing the hypothesis.

clinical method (la méthode clinique). An information-gathering technique, derived from therapy and used by Piaget, in which the adult observes and then interacts with the child[ren] by asking questions and posing ideas to see the reaction and thinking.

Observation and its various methods are used extensively in early childhood education programs and, increasingly, in elementary education to assess children. Figure 6-7 summarizes these systems. By practicing observing—what it takes to look, to see, to become more sensitive—teachers can learn to record children's behavior fully and vividly, capturing the unique qualities, culture, and personality of each child and the group.

6-3c How to Observe Effectively

To make observing workable in a program, keep in mind that there are many ways to observe and record.

> **Certain times of the day may be easier than others.** Many prefer to document during free play; others choose to record what they see after the program is over. The professional team that is committed to observation will find ways to support its implementation.
> **Finding an opportunity for regular observations is challenging.** Centers are rarely staffed so well that one teacher can be free from classroom responsibilities for long periods of time. A parent may supervise an activity so a teacher can record, or teachers can team up so that one can run an activity while the other documents children's skills.
> **Children may respond self-consciously at first but will resume normal activity once observation is done regularly.** When children know they are being observed, they may ask pointed questions of the observer, even change their behavior as if they were on stage momentarily. Once part of the routine, observation fades into the background and helps keep most of the attention child centered rather than teacher directed and increases children's and adult's communication.
> **Teachers can improve their assessment skills outside the classroom.** Taking an "Observation & Assessment" course or workshop is helpful; so is visiting other programs in pairs and comparing notes afterward. Staff meetings take on added dimension when teachers role-play what they think they have seen and others ask for details.

The teacher who makes notes during class time has other considerations. Be ready to set aside your recording when necessary. Wear clothing with at least one good pocket. Take care not to leave notes out on tables for others to see. They should be kept confidential until added to the children's records. Whether with notepads or video cameras, teachers must organize themselves for success in the following ways:

> **Gather and prepare the materials ahead of time.** This may mean getting everyone aprons with large pockets or a set of cards or labeled spiral notebook.
> **Consider where you will observe.** Set up observation places (chairs, stations); in a well-equipped yard and room, you can plan strategically.

Observational Techniques

Method	Observational Interval	Recording Techniques	Advantages	Disadvantages
1. Narratives				
Diary description	Day to day	Using notebook and pencil; can itemize activity or other ongoing behavior; can see growth patterns	Rich in detail; maintains sequence of events; describes behavior as it occurs	Open to observer bias; time-consuming
Specimen descriptions/ running record	Continuous sequences	Same	Less structured	Sometimes need follow-up
Journal	Regular, preferred daily/weekly	Log, usually with space for each child; often a summary	Same as narratives	Difficult to find time to do
"On-the-hoof" anecdotes	Sporadic	Ongoing during class time; using notepad in hand	Quick and easy to take; short-capture pertinent events/ details	Lack detail; need to be tilled later; can detract from teaching responsibilities
2. Time sampling	Short and uniform time intervals	On-the-spot as time passes; prearranged recording sheets	Easy to record; easy to analyze; relatively bias free	Limited behaviors; loss of detail, loss of sequence and ecology of event
3. Event sampling	For the duration of the event	Same as for time sampling	Easy to record; easy to analyze; can maintain flow of class activity easily	Limited behaviors; loss of detail; must wait for behavior to occur
4. Modifications				
Checklists	Regular or intermittent	Using prepared recording sheets; can be during or after class	Easy to develop and use	Lack of detail; tell little of the cause of behaviors
Rating scales	Continuous behavior	Same as for checklists	Easy to develop and use; range of behaviors	Ambiguity of terms; high observer bias
Shadow study	Continuous behavior	Narrative-type recording; uses prepared recording sheets	Rich in detail; focuses in depth on individual	Bias problem; can take away too much of a teacher's time and attention
Experimental procedures	Short and uniform	May be checklists, prearranged recording sheets, audio or video tape	Simple, clear, pure study; relatively bias free	Difficult, hard to isolate in the classroom
Clinical method	Any time	Usually notebook or tape recorded	Relevant data; can be spontaneous, easy to use	Adult has changed naturally occurring behavior

Figure 6-7 A summary chart of the major observational techniques that the early childhood professional can use to record children's behavior. (Adapted from Irwin, D. M., and Bushnell, M. M. [1980]. *Observational strategies for child study.* New York: Holt, Rinehart, and Winston.)

> **Plan when you will observe.** In a well-planned day, teachers can have the freedom to practice observing regularly during play time.

> **Prepare every adult to be an observer.** Give every teacher some regular opportunities to observe and reflect on children's play.

truth or fiction?

(T) **F** Narratives are the most common type of observation.

Of the four major types of observation methods, narratives are the most commonly used method of documentation, capturing the richness and context of children's behavior as well as being easily used in most settings with the simple tools of paper and pencil.

Respect the privacy of the children and their families at all times. Any information gathered as part of an observation is treated with strict confidentiality. Wherever an observation is planned, it is critical to maintain professional **confidentiality**. Teachers and students are careful not to use children's names in casual conversation. They do not talk about children in front of other children or among themselves. It is the role of the adults to see that children's privacy is maintained. Telling tales out of school is tempting but unprofessional.

In some programs, observers are a normal part of the school routine. In colleges where there are laboratory facilities on campus, visitors and student observers are familiar figures. At parent cooperatives, children are used to many adults in their room. It becomes easy to follow established guidelines for making an observation (Figure 6-8).

The success of the observation depends on how inconspicuous the observer can be. Children are more natural if the observer blends into the scenery. By sitting back, one can observe the whole scene and record what is seen and heard, undisturbed and uninfluenced. This distancing sets up a climate for recording that aids the observer in concentrating on the children.

There are two main reasons for an observer to be **unobtrusive**. First, it allows for a more accurate recording of the children's activities. Second, it does not interfere with the smooth functioning of the classroom, the children, or the teachers. In the case of teachers observing their own programs, you must

---

confidentiality. Spoken, written, or acted on in strict privacy, such as keeping the names of children or schools in confidence when discussing observations.

unobtrusive. Not noticeable or conspicuous, in the background.

assessment. An evaluation or determination of the importance, disposition, or state of something or someone, such as in evaluating a child's skills, a classroom environment, or a teacher's effectiveness.

plan ahead with colleagues and have materials at hand that can be set aside quickly if necessary.

6-4 Assessment: Goals and Tools

Children are evaluated because teachers and parents want to know what the children are learning. Evaluations set the tone for a child's overall educational experience. Highlighting children's strengths builds a foundation from which to address their limitations or needs. Evaluation processes can help teachers discover who children are, what they can (and cannot) do, and how we can help children grow and learn.

In assessing children, teachers first decide what it is they want to know about each child, and why. Goals for children stem from program objectives. For instance, if the school philosophy is, "Our program is designed to help children grow toward increasing physical, social, and intellectual competencies," an evaluation will measure children's progress in all three developmental domains. A primary school program focused on teaching language skills assesses how speaking, listening, reading, and writing are being accomplished.

Evaluations provide teachers with an opportunity to distance themselves from the daily contact with children and look at them in a more detached, professional way. Teachers can use the results to share their opinions and concerns about children with each other and with parents. Charting individual growth sets the child apart as a unique human being.

Assessment must:

> Occur in a variety of settings over time, drawing on many sources of information
> Focus on essential skills and dispositions valued by the program, families, and communities
> Have teacher-designed tools and methods that demonstrate the child in action and in a familiar setting

Observing young children in action is the key to early childhood assessment; most of the child evaluation instruments described in this chapter are based on what children do spontaneously or in their familiar, natural settings. For an evaluation to be reliable and valid, multiple sources of information should be used.

In general, assessments are made to:

> Establish a baseline of information about each child
> Monitor the growth of individual children
> Have a systematic plan for intervention and guidance
> Plan the curriculum
> Provide families with updated information on their child
> Provide information for making administrative decisions

6-4a To Establish a Baseline

One purpose of evaluating children is to establish a starting point of their skills and behavior. It shows where the

1. Please sign in with the front office and obtain a visitor's badge. Your badge must be worn and visible at all times while at the center.

2. Inform the front office when you have completed your visit.

3. Be unobtrusive. Please find a spot that does not infringe on the children's space.

4. If you are with a small group or another person, do not observe together; consciously separate and space yourselves. Do not talk to other visitors during observation, please.

5. Respond to the children, but please do not initiate conversations with them.

6. If a child seems upset that you are near him/her, please remove yourself from the area. If you receive direct requests from a child to leave, please respond that you realize that he said you are in *his* space and will move.

7. Please do not interfere with the teaching/learning process during your observation. Save your questions for the end of your observation. Either ask when you check out in the front office or leave a note in the teacher's mailbox requesting a time to meet. Please understand that we welcome questions but cannot interrupt the program to answer them immediately.

8. Walk around the periphery of the outdoor area or classrooms rather than through them.

9. When possible, do not stand. Please do not hover over children. Sit, squat, or bend down at the knees so you are at the children's level.

10. Taking photographs is not permitted. In special cases, permission for photographs may be given by the Dean of Child Development and Education.

Thank you for your help and consideration in making your visit to the center a pleasant one for everyone involved.

Figure 6-8 Establishing guidelines for observers and visitors helps remind us of the importance of teaching as watching, not just telling. (Courtesy of K. Burson of De Anza College Child Development Center)

child is in relation to the program objectives. Baseline data give a realistic picture of a child at that moment in time, but there is a presumption that the picture will change.

A Baseline Tool

The beginning of the school term is an obvious time to start collecting information. Records of a child are established in the context of the child's history and family background. Families frequently submit this information with an application to the school. It is critical to be sensitive about how to ask for personal information and to understand family reluctance to share details with adults they have only just met. Teachers can gather the data by visiting the child at home or holding a conference and speaking directly and frequently with the family about the child's development. Additionally, more will be revealed as trust and communication build the relationship over time.

An entry-level assessment made during the first few weeks of the program can be informative, particularly when added to the child's family history. Some agencies or states require a specific time period in which this assessment must be completed. The evaluation itself should be done informally, with teachers collecting information as children engage naturally with materials and each other (Figure 6-9, and Digital Download).

Application

Teachers use this information to understand a child and identify any concerns right away. One must remember, however, that the entry assessment is only a first impression. Avoid creating a self-fulfilling prophecy by labeling children so that they become shaped into those beginning patterns. Still, so much happens in the beginning that rich information is gained from documenting this short period of time.

Goals and Plans

Teachers use baseline data to set realistic goals for individual children. They tailor the curriculum to the needs and interests they have observed. For instance, after setting a baseline of Mariko's language ability in English, teachers plan activities to increase her understanding and use of language. Then, they make periodic checks on her increased vocabulary as the school year progresses.

6-4b To Monitor Children's Progress

Teachers use evaluations to document children's growth. Data collected provide evidence of children's growth or lack of progress.

> Karen has mastered the brushes at the easel. Now we can encourage her to try the smaller brushes in table painting.

1. Child's name _____ Teacher _____

   Age _____ Sex _____
   language _____ Fluency in English? _____
   Any previous school experiences? _____
   Siblings/others in household _____
   Family situation (one/two parents, other adults, etc.) _____

2. Separation from parent:

   Smooth _____ Some anxiety _____ Mild difficulty _____ Unable to separate _____
   Did parent have trouble separating?
   Comments:

3. How does child come to and leave from school?

   Parent _____ Car pool _____ Baby-sitter _____ Bus _____

4. Physical appearance:

   General health _____ Expression _____
   Nonrestrictive clothing _____ Body posture _____

5. Self-care:

   Dressing: Alone _____ Needs assistance _____
   Toileting: By self _____ Needs help _____
   Eating: Independent_____ Asks to be Fed_____
   Toothbrushing _____ Sleeping/resting:
   Allergies/other health-related problems:

6. Child's interests:

   Indoors:

   Clay _____ Books _____ Puzzles _____ Water play _____ Easels _____ Language _____ Table/
   rug toys _____
   Sensory _____ choices _____ Art _____ Cooking _____ Science _____ Blocks _____
   Outdoors:
   Swings _____ Climbers _____ Sandbox _____ Water play _____
   Wheel toys _____ Animals _____ Group games _____ Woodworking _____
   Group times (level of participation):

7. Social-emotional development:

   a. Initiates activities _____ Plays alone _____ Seems happy _____ Has to be invited _____ Brings
      security object _____ Seems tense _____
   b. Plays mostly with children of: Same age _____ Younger _____ Older _____
   c. Moves into environment: Easily Hesitantly Not at all Wanders
   d. Special friends:
   e. Does the child follow teachers? _____ Anyone in particular? _____

8. Language/Cognitive development:

   Language: Follows directions _____ Clear pronunciation _____ Holds conversations _____ Words/
   phrases _____ Dual-Language _____
   Cognitive: Curiosity _____ Symbolic/Pretend _____ Problem-solving_____ Pattern/Classification ___ _____
   Number _____ Shapes ___ Memory _____

9. Physical development:

   Climbs safely _____ Runs smoothly _____ Foot preference _____ Handles body well _____
   Uses scissors _____ Hand preference _____ Uses pens, brushes _____

10. Goals/points to remember: _____

Figure 6-9 Baseline information is collected. Once teachers and children have had some time together, these first impressions can be documented.

Digital Download

> Bryce has been asking how to spell simple words. Let's see that he gets some time away from the blocks to work at the writing center.

A Progress Tool

Midyear evaluations are common and are intended to build a profile of the whole child. Teachers note the intervention and guidance steps they plan, where appropriate. Many states have created assessment tools, such as California's Desired Results Developmental Profile (DRDP), that refer to specific age groups, including what the child will do to show a suitable level of behavior in each developmental stage.

Application

Information about a child will be used to assess growth and change. How often this happens can vary. Although many changes occur in rapid succession in these early years, it takes time for a child to integrate life experiences and for teachers to see them expressed as a permanent part of behavior. Evaluating too frequently does not reveal sufficient change to make it worthwhile and places an added burden on the teaching staff as well. For centers operating on a year-round basis, an assessment should be done every 6 months. In programs with a shorter calendar, this would mean establishing a baseline in the fall and checking progress in the winter or spring, or both.

Goals and Plans

Goals are established for children as a result of an assessment. These goals are changed as growth takes place. A good assessment tool monitors progress in each developmental domain so that plans can be made to challenge and support growth. (See the Education CourseMate website for an example of progress monitoring tool.)

6-4c To Plan for Guidance and Intervention

A third purpose for evaluation is to help teachers determine guidance procedures. When teachers see a problem behavior or are concerned about a child, they plan for further assessment. If a developmental screening is needed to assess whether a child has a learning problem or needs special services (in order to develop an **Individualized Education Plan [IEP]** and provide intervention and accommodations), teachers will refer the family to a proper specialist or agency such as the local school district. Developmental screening tests will be discussed further in this chapter.

A Guidance Tool

Once a need has been pinpointed, the teaching staff decides how to proceed. Individual problems are highlighted when teachers make a point of concentrating on the child's behavior. Used at a team meeting, such a tool can outline the steps to be taken and clarify how to talk to families.

teachsource video case

Watch the TeachSource Video Case entitled "Communicating with Families: Best Practices in an Early Childhood Setting." After you study the video clip, view the artifacts, read the teacher interviews and text, and reflect on the following questions:

1. How does preschool teacher Mona Sanon find out important information about her children and their families?
2. Why is child assessment important in early care and education and how is it best implemented?

© 2016 Cengage Learning®

Application

The following case study demonstrates how information from evaluations can be used for guidance and intervention:

> Karen's recent evaluation revealed an increase in the number of toilet accidents she has had. The staff noted a higher incidence during midmorning snacks but came to no conclusion as to the cause. They agreed to continue to treat her behavior in a relaxed manner and have one teacher remind Karen to use the toilet before she washes her hands for snack. At the same time, they made plans to contact the parents for further information and insights. They will confer again afterward and agree on an approach.

Goals and Plans

An evaluation tool helps teachers set goals for children and for adults. Narrowing the focus to include only those behaviors that concern the staff enables the staff to review quickly the needs of many children. In Karen's case, the conference report shows the following results:

Individualized Education Plan (IEP). A written plan designed to meet the individual, unique needs of a child, usually 3 years and older, with identified special needs; this is done in accordance with federal IDEA act and is developed and revised by an IEP team that identifies the child's learning needs, goals, accommodations, and services that will be provided.

Karen B.	Teacher Observations	Family Observations
Toilet accidents	Three times before snack	Always take her to bathroom before meals at home
Plan: teacher will take her before snack	Tried for 2 weeks	Remind her to go with teacher
Results: no accidents week 2!	Resistant week 1, cooperative week 2	Glad that this is working at school

6-4d To Plan Curriculum

Teachers plan the curriculum on the basis of children's evaluations. Translating the assessment to actual classroom practice is an important part of the teacher's role. A thorough evaluation helps teachers plan appropriate activities to meet children's needs.

Planning Tools

All the previous evaluation tools can be used to plan the curriculum. Entry-level assessments and midyear reports are often summarized in a group chart, as in Figure 6-10.

Application

Evaluation results assist teachers in seeing more clearly the strengths and abilities of each child in the class. Curriculum activities are then planned that will continue to enhance the growth of that child. Also, areas of difficulty will be identified.

Teachers plan curriculum to build on children's interests in an emergent way and to assist with skill building.

Goals and Plans

By analyzing both group and individual skills through periodic assessment, teachers maintain a secure and challenging environment. One such chart, made at the end of the first semester of a prekindergarten class, revealed this pattern:

> At least one third of the class was having trouble listening at circle time, as evidenced by the group chart that identified "Group Time" and "Language Listening Skills" as areas for growth for nearly half the children. The staff centered their attention on the group time content. It was concluded that a story made the group times too long; the children were restless throughout most of the reading. It was agreed to move story time to just before nap and shorten the group time temporarily.

6-4e To Communicate with Families

Once a child's needs and capabilities are identified, families are entitled to hear the conclusions. The teaching staff has an obligation to provide a realistic overview of the child's progress and alert families to any possible concerns.

A Tool with Families

Teachers and families need to talk together, especially when problems are revealed by the evaluation. As knowledge and insights are shared, a fuller picture of the child emerges for both. Each can then assume a role in the resolution of the problem. Evaluation tools can help identify areas in which a child may need special help.

Group Chart

Summary of Development/Fall Progress Reports (see forms for details)
Developmental Area: 1 5 fine; 2 5 needs work; ? 5 don't know

Child	Physical	Language	Cognitive	Social	Emotional	Creative
Greg	2	1	1	1	2	?
Anwar	?	2	1	2	2	1
San-Joo	1	?	?	2	1	?
Reva	1	1	1	1	1	1
Katy	2	1	?	?	?	2

Group Goals for Winter:

Emphasize social and emotional areas of curriculum.
Plan physical games (indoor games because of weather).

Individual Goals for Winter:

Greg: Encourage some creative arts, games. Observe creativity in intellectual activities.
Anwar: Needs to be helped to feel confident and express himself; don't push too hard on physical risks yet.
San-Joo: Need assessment of language and cognitive skills; observe use of table toys, receptive language at group time.
Reva: What is the next step? Is she ready for helping the others? Involve her with 100-piece puzzles and the computer.
Katy: Need to focus on her overall development; too many unknowns—is she getting enough individual attention?

Figure 6-10 Teachers can use individual assessment tools to plan for the entire group and for each child in the class.

© Cengage Learning®

Verna and Chris are the Kinder Team for a public elementary school. Verna has been teaching kindergarten for 5 years. Chris is the associate teacher, having spent 2 years in his own child's preschool while getting his teaching certificate and then 3 years in a transitional kindergarten class across town. They want you to meet Jody, age 5.

Verna's Observations: "I can see Jody struggling; two things I notice are:
> He uses scissors in a hedge clippers fashion.
> He has an awkward grip when using a pencil.
Chris' Observations: "I see him on more of a par with the preschoolers I used to work with; what I see is:
> He finds it difficult to fit puzzle pieces together.
> He does not choose the woodworking table, manipulative table, or cooking project during free choice."
Both are concerned: they notice he is "acting up" during writing time, and is avoiding some of the high-interest activities that most of the boys enjoy.

Assessment. Verna usually talks with Jody's father Sam when he drops off Jody in the morning, and Chris just did the regular Fall home visit where he was able to chat a few extra minutes with Aurora. These revealed two important facts: Jody has trouble handling table utensils and "goes into a meltdown" and refuses to button his sweater. There is no special provision at home for him to pursue fine motor activities, and now his parents worry that he has a motor disability.

Goals and plans. Verna and Chris suggest to Jody's parents that a first step of intervention would be to find ways to build in interesting experiences that "just happen" to include fine motor work.

*Chris uses Jody's interest in airplanes to draw him into areas of the curriculum he does not ordinarily pursue. Small airplanes are added to the block corner, and airplane stencils are placed near the art table. A large mural of an airport is hung on the fence, and children invited to paint on it. Another day children cut airplane pictures out of magazines and use them in a collage. Simple airplane puzzles are placed on the puzzle table. Felt shapes and small plastic airplanes in the water table draw Jody toward activities requiring fine motor skills.

* Jody's parents supplied him with a special art box at home, full of crayons, scissors, pens, watercolors, and stencils. His dad takes him to the small plane airport, where they get a chance to get into a cockpit and try the many levers and buttons. His mom gets an origami kit and they start to try paper-folding. They decide to make paper airplanes and bring the kit to school for sharing time.

Results. As his fine motor skills increased and were refined, Jody became a more confident and happier child. By the end of 3 weeks, everyone sees a change.

*Chris: "Now he is more involved with the other boys, and is totally ready to come join us at the woodworking table."

*Verna: "He is a regular participant in all areas of the school, and really enjoys his newfound interest in art materials."

*Sam & Aurora: "We were afraid that Jody was going to have to go to a special school, and he was starting to resist getting ready in the morning. Now he is the first up and dressed, and runs from the car into the classroom. What a change! "

Application
Aside from identifying normal behavior problems, evaluations may raise questions concerning a child's physical development, hearing and visual acuity, or language facility. Potentially serious emotional or social problems may emerge from the evaluation, and parents can be encouraged to seek further professional guidance.

Goals and Plans
Because evaluation is an ongoing process, reevaluation and goal setting are done regularly. Whether or not a child has an identified special need, communicating both progress and new goals is critical for the feedback loop of an evaluation to be effective. (See Teacher Talks, as well as chapters Chapters 7 & 8).

6-4f To Make Administrative Decisions
Evaluation results can help a school make administrative decisions. They can lead to changes in the overall program or in the school's philosophy. For example, a child care component

might be added to the half-day program after learning that most children are enrolled in another child care situation after nursery school. Or an evaluation might reveal that there is too little emphasis on developing gross motor skills and coordination, so the administration might decide to remodel the play yard and purchase new equipment.

In the early childhood education setting, both informal and formal methods are used for evaluating children. Informal and homemade methods include observation, note taking, self-assessments, parent interviews and surveys, samples of children's work, and teacher-designed forms.

An Administrative Tool

Some teachers conclude the year with a summary report. This evaluation serves as an overview of what a child has accomplished, what areas of strength are present, and what future growth might occur.

Application

Making administrative decisions based on evaluation results is a sound idea. Assessments give administrators specific and verifiable information on which to base decisions. A summary of their child's learning experiences is useful for families. Teachers may use such summaries as references should they ever be consulted by another program about the child. Again, it is critical to administer these assessments in a sensitive and accepting manner, to keep the time period as brief as possible, and to communicate the results in the same tone. If this is not done, the child's self-esteem may be

Ethics

Considering a "No Testing Zone" in Preschool

When most of us think of testing, we are reminded of the standardized tests in elementary school. Such whole-group or one-size-fits-all kind of assessment is a controversial method that is widely used in the K-to-12 system as a means of screening or retention. Young children typically do not show what they know in strange situations, such as test time, or with adults whose interactions are about standardized instructions only. Children whose home language differs from what is used in the test or whose culture is not included in test material are at a disadvantage.

The National Association for the Education of Young Children (NAEYC) Code of Ethical Conduct states: "We shall not participate in practices that discriminate against children by denying benefits, giving special advantages, or excluding them on the basis of their race, ethnicity, religion, sex, national origin, language, ability."

One of the most important roles the early childhood educator has is helping families—and the general public—understand how to see children's learning in their daily educational experiences and ensuring that early education programs assess children's learning effectively while still providing a positive and engaging environment in which to grow.

damaged, and the parents' trust may be lost. The disadvantages of these tools parallel those of standardized tests.

The issue of readiness or placement of children is difficult and complex. The next section describes the potential problems and misapplications of tests in this regard. Whether or not a child is ready to succeed in a program affects families and children personally. Having a good evaluation tool helps in making such decisions equitably, and in communicating results in a clear and kind manner.

Goals and Plans

The evaluation tool that gives a specific profile of a child's skills will allow an administrator to share information with a family clearly and honestly. By carefully choosing a tool, administrators give the parents information they can use to plan for the child's development.

6-4g Concerns about Child Assessments

Assessment is challenging! Of all the functions performed by teachers, probably none calls for more energy, time, and skill than evaluation. Anyone involved in evaluation should avoid the following:

> **Unfair comparisons.** Evaluations should be used to identify and understand the child involved, not to compare one with another in a competitive manner.
> **Bias.** Evaluations can label unfairly or prematurely the children they are intended to help. Typecasting will not produce a useful assessment. Insufficient data and overemphasis on evaluation-tool results are two areas that need close monitoring. Evaluation tools should be free of language or other cultural bias. For instance, an evaluation of children should not include experiences unfamiliar to the cultural group being assessed.
> **Overemphasis on norms.** Most evaluation tools imply some level of normal behavior or performance, acceptable levels of interaction, or quantities of materials and space. People involved in an evaluation must remember to individualize the process rather than try to fit a child into the mold created by the assessment tool.
> **Interpretation.** Evaluations evoke a tendency to over-interpret or misinterpret results. It must be clear what is being evaluated and how the information will be used. It is particularly important to be sensitive to the feelings of those being evaluated when communicating the results of the assessment.
> **Too narrow a perspective.** An evaluation tool may focus too much on one area and not enough on others. No single occasion or instrument will tell teachers all they need to know about a child's abilities. It is essential that information be gathered in many ways and on several occasions. An imbalanced assessment gives an incomplete picture.
> **Too wide a range.** An evaluation should be designed for a single level or age group and not cover too wide a range. It is appropriate to measure a child's ability to

Evaluations should avoid unfair comparisons of children and try to individualize the process rather than attempt to fit children into a mold created by an assessment tool.◄

print at age 6 but not at age 2. What is expected of the person or task should be taken into account.

> **Too little or too much time.** The amount of time necessary to complete an evaluation must be weighed. The evaluation that is too lengthy loses its effectiveness in the time it takes. Time for interpretation and reflection must be included in the overall process.

> **"Teaching to the test."** Too much attention on an evaluation can change what happens in the program. Teachers may shape their instruction to match a test's specific focus. This is known as "measurement-driven instruction" and narrows the curriculum.

6-4h Testing and Screening

The practice of testing and screening for readiness and retention has increased dramatically in the past two decades. The theoretical basis of "testing" is steeped in Western methods of thought. Hale-Benson & Hilliard (1986) have long cautioned all teachers to pay close attention to tests in light of cultural diversity.

With the passage of Public Law 94-142 (the Education for All Handicapped Children Act) and the early childhood education amendment to the law (Public Law 99-457), states now have the responsibility to establish specific procedures and policies to identify, evaluate, and provide services to all children with learning problems.

Testing for admittance to kindergarten or promotion to first grade has become more common. The results are that more children are being denied entrance to a school system, being put into extra-year or pull-out programs or placed in kindergarten twice.

Ironically, standardized tests fail to reflect adequately what children learn. Children know so much more than they are taught, and what is tested may not be the important

learning that the children have done. Contemporary theorists and psychologists confirm this concern for young children. "Over the past several decades the assumptions underlying the current testing edifice have been challenged by developmental, cognitive, and educational studies. There's a considerable body of scientific findings telling us that if we want to understand people's competence or knowledge about something, we should not examine them in an artificial way in an artificial setting" (Gardner, 1988). Moreover, most formal testing engages only two (linguistic and logical mathematical) of the eight intelligences Gardner has identified.

Testing raises both practical and serious philosophical issues, such as the following:

> Young children do not function well in common test situations, nor do the test results necessarily reflect children's true knowledge or skills.

> These practices (often based on inappropriate uses of readiness or screening tests) disregard the potential, documented long-term negative effects of retention on children's self-esteem and the fact that such practices disproportionately affect low-income and minority children (NAEYC, 2010).

> Although the most needed and appropriate tests (teacher-made tests) are the hardest to create, the standardized ones are frequently misused and misunderstood by teachers and parents (Meisels & Atkins, 2005).

> Teachers are pressured into running programs that overemphasize the testing situation and test items (NAEYC, 2013).

> Most tests focus on cognitive and language skills; such a narrow focus ignores other areas of development.

The practice of standardized testing has caused early childhood education curricula to become increasingly academic. Early childhood educators and parents are alarmed that many kindergartens are now structured and are "watered-down" first grades, emphasizing workbooks and other paper-and-pencil activities that are inappropriate for 5-year-olds. The trend further trickles down to preschool and child care programs that feel that their mission is to get children "ready" for kindergarten. Too many school systems, expecting children to conform to an inappropriate curriculum and finding large numbers of "unready" children, react to the problem by raising the entrance age for kindergarten or labeling the children as failures.

Teachers and schools are now responding to the overuse and inappropriate use of tests. The National Association of Elementary School Principals urges limited use of formal tests and retention. The Texas Board of Education has barred retention before first grade, and in the state of New York, a coalition of groups is urging a ban on mass standardized testing of children before grade three.

Standards

Does testing have appropriate uses in the early years? Some claim that there are valid screening tests to identify children who, because of the risk for possible learning problems or a handicapping condition, may need more intervention or accommodation (see the Standards feature for suggestions).

Perhaps most important is the reminder to all teachers that tests have no special magic. Testing is not a very effective way of evaluating *any* child, but assessment is.

Assessment is not testing; it is so much more than that. A standardized test, a homemade tool, or a screening instrument should be only one of several measures used to determine a child's skills, abilities, or readiness. Any result should be part of a multitude of information, such as direct observation, parental report, and children's actual work.

6-4i Authentic Assessment: The Portfolio

In light of the concerns about the mis-assessment of young children and the "test mania" that standardized tests in the primary grades have fomented, early childhood professionals have looked for alternative assessment measures.

The 2011 *Oxford American Dictionary* defines *authentic* as "of undisputed origin, genuine . . . made or done

in a way that faithfully resembles an original." For a child assessment to be authentic, it must try to capture who the child is and what that child knows (or does not know) and can (or cannot) do. Many early childhood educators have embraced the idea that a **portfolio** of children's work samples is an excellent way to document children's learning and faithfully capture their development.

There are three types of portfolios:

1. Display portfolios—scrapbooks that collect items without teacher comments
2. Showcase portfolios—the best pieces of the child's work
3. Working portfolios—selections of typical work along with teacher documentation to show the child's progress

truth or *fiction?*

T (F) Testing young children is an effective assessment method.

Young children do not respond well to a strange "testing" situation and often will not answer correctly the questions posed to them even if they know the information or have mastered the skill being tested.

Most early childhood programs use working portfolios because they document growth over time.

Collection Plan

Because simple collection of work is not enough, do not try to collect everything. Look for work samples that demonstrate your educational objectives and a child's progress over time on a goal. Make collection a natural extension of your day and what you do with children. Some teachers keep clipboards at activity areas; others use self-sticking notes and cameras at the ready. Be organized when storing work samples; ideas include pocket folders or even pizza boxes (Figure 6-11).

---

readiness. The condition of being ready, such as being in the state or stage of development so that the child has the capacity to understand, be taught, or engage, and thus be successful.

portfolio. An assessment method that tracks children's growth and development.

Items to include:

> Art samples
> Cutting samples
> Dictated stories
> Invented writing
> Sketches/photos of constructions
> Written samples of children's language and conversations
> Social interactions with peers and adults

Use self-sticking notes as a convenient, quick way to capture revealing moments. These notes are easily transferred to individual portfolios. Photographs can also supplement written documentation.

Courtesy of Wiggins-Dowler, 2004

All samples and records need names of those involved, time, and date. As you become more proficient, your observation skills become more specific, and the samples you choose will not be just the best work of children but the work that is indicative of their developmental process.

Use a folding document with separate sections for each developmental domain. Each labeled section has a cascading file of several pages, and on each are examples of developmental landmarks or unique attributes of the child. The most historical work is on the bottom page, with each overlap showing the child's progressive development. Then, on the top of each file is a developmental checklist or a summary of growth.

Figure 6-11 The portfolio can be an excellent visual "unfolding" of the child, presenting amazing images of each child as a competent learner who actively constructs knowledge within a social and cultural context. (Courtesy of Wiggins-Dowler, 2004)

Teacher's Evaluation

Teachers add their written comments to the work samples. Teacher commentary becomes a critical source of information to tell how the child did the samples, what they mean, and how they show growth or lack of it. The commentary enhances the work sample by explaining the process of learning that is going on. A picture may be worth a thousand words, but for assessment purposes, the words are essential, not just the artwork!

Portfolios can provide a history of learning, a structured record of a child's accomplishments, of who the child is, as well as a method for assessing progress. Although they take considerable planning—in their organization, storage, and selection of what to collect to show educational goals—they help you collect children's work intentionally. You can evaluate children on their work and play, as they are spontaneously, rather than with standardized tests or unnecessary screening.

summary

6.1 The major purposes of observation are to improve teaching, construct theory, build curriculum, help families, and assess children.

6.2 Five key contexts that observations help to understand are children as individuals, children in groups, developmental relationships, influences on behavior, and understanding of self.

6.3 The four major types of observation are narratives, time and event sampling, checklists, and modified child study techniques such as shadow study, experimental procedures, and the clinical method.

6.4 Assessment can fulfill the goals of establishing baselines, monitoring progress, focusing on guidance and intervention, assisting in planning curriculum, helping communication with families, and making administrative decisions. Concerns about child assessment are substantial, and testing and screening are problematic. Authentic assessments such as a child portfolio both describe and assess children in the early years.

web resources

California Department of Education **http://www.cde.ca.gov** (search for the Desired Results Developmental Profile)

Council for Exceptional Children **http://www.cec.sped .org**

National Association for the Education of Young Children **http://www.naeyc.org** (search for Position Statements on Screening & Assessment, Early Learning Standards, School Readiness, and Trends in Kindergarten Entry & Placement)

National Institute for Early Education Research **http://www.nieer.org**

references

Dawes, H. C. (1934). An analysis of two hundred quarrels of preschool children. *Child Development, 5,* 139–157.

Feeney, S., Moravicik, E., & Nolte, S. (2012). *Who am I in the lives of children?* (9e). Englewood Cliffs, NJ: Prentice-Hall.

Gardner, H. (1988, September/October). Alternatives to standardized testing. *Harvard Education Letter.*

Gilkerson, L. & Klein, R. (2007). *Early development and the brain: teaching resources for educators.* Washington, DC: Zero to Three.

Gonzalez-Mena, J. (2014). Figure 6-1. Understanding what we observe: A multicultural perspective. In A. M. Gordon & K. Williams Browne (Eds.), *Beginnings and beyond,* 9e. Clifton Park, NY: Thomson Delmar Learning.

Hale-Benson, J. A. & Hilliard, A. (1986). *Black children: Their roots, culture, and learning styles.* Baltimore, MD: The Johns Hopkins University Press.

Irwin, D. M., & Bushnell, M. M. (1980). *Observational strategies for child study.* New York: Holt, Rinehart & Winston.

Jones, E., & Reynolds, G. (2013). *The play's the thing: Teachers' roles in children's play, 2e.* New York: Teachers College Press.

Meisels, S. J., & Atkins-Barrett, S. (2005). *Developmental screening in early childhood education,* 5e. Washington, DC: NAEYC.

NAEYC [National Association for the Education of Young Children]. (2010). Position statement on standardized testing of young children 3 through 8 years of age. *Young Children,* 43.

NAEYC (2013). Using documentation and assessment to support children's learning. *Young Children,* 46.

Parten, M. B. (1932). Social participation among preschool children. *Journal of Abnormal and Social Psychology, 27,* 243–269.

Wiggins-Dowler, K. (2004). Focus box. The portfolio: An "unfolding" of the child. In A. M. Gordon & K. Williams Browne (Eds.), *Beginnings and beyond* (6th ed.). Clifton Park, NY: Thomson Delmar Learning.

Wortham, S.C. (2011). *Assessment in Early Childhood Education,* 6e. Pearson.

7 | guidance essentials

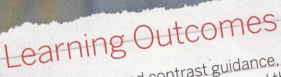

Learning Outcomes

7-1 Compare and contrast guidance, discipline, and punishment and their appropriate uses.

7-2 Demonstrate an awareness of what influences children's behavior.

7-3 Identify developmentally and culturally appropriate guidance techniques.

7-4 Examine effective guidance strategies that promote positive interactions, social learning, and problem-solving skills.

NAEYC Standards

The following NAEYC Standards for Early Childhood Professional Preparation are addressed in this chapter:

Standard 1: Promoting Child Development and Learning

Standard 2: Building Family and Community Relationships

Standard 4: Using Developmentally Effective Approaches to Connect with Children and Families

Standard 5: Using Current Knowledge to Build Meaningful Curriculum

truth or fiction

T F Discipline and guidance are similar concepts.

T F Children's temperament can be determined in infancy.

T F Developmentally appropriate guidance is based on age appropriateness and family culture.

T F Giving children choices confuses them.

7-1 Guidance, Discipline, and Punishment: Is There a Difference?

The children we meet in early childhood education programs are just learning how strong their emotions can be and what impact they have on their own behavior and on others. Understanding the distinctions among guidance, discipline, and punishment will help you assist children in managing their behavior and building positive relationships with others.

7-1a What Is Guidance?

Guidance is an ongoing system of strategies to help children learn to manage impulses, express feelings, channel frustrations, solve problems, and learn the difference between acceptable and unacceptable behavior (Browne & Gordon, 2013). The guidance process is an intentional course of action based on the adult's knowledge of the age group, the individual child, and the family context.

A guide points out directions, answers questions, and helps you get where you are going. This is what teachers do when helping children learn appropriate behavior. Three key elements to consider are the child, the adult, and the situation. Figure 7-1 shows how these three basic ingredients are reflected throughout the chapter in guidance theories and practice.

7-1b What Is Discipline?

The word **discipline** stems from *disciple:* a pupil, a follower, and a learner. This suggests an important concept,

that of following an example versus following rules. Adults help children learn appropriate behavior by setting good examples.

Discipline and guidance are similar, and the words are often used interchangeably. Positive discipline has the same foundation as positive guidance. Each stresses thoughtful, nonpunitive techniques that promote children's empathy and moral reasoning (Browne & Gordon, 2013). When discipline is confused with punishment, it loses its effectiveness and becomes a negative rather than a positive interaction. Linking discipline and guidance provides opportunities for the experience to become a learning situation that fosters thinking skills and problem solving. The adult's attitude is about, "What can I do to help a child learn from this experience?" rather than, "How can I punish this child?"

guidance. Ongoing system by which adults help children learn to manage their impulses, express feelings, channel frustrations, solve problems, and learn the difference between acceptable and unacceptable behavior.

discipline. Ability to follow an example or to follow rules; the development of self-control or control in general, such as by imposing order on a group. In early childhood terms, discipline means everything adults do and say to influence children's behavior.

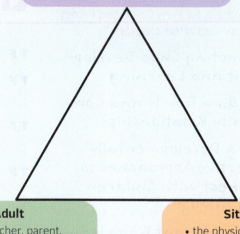

The Guidance Triangle

In establishing effective guidance practices, adults take into consideration three important elements: the child, the adult, and the situation. For instance, a 2-year-old needing assistance is more likely to respond to the intervention of a familiar teacher than one who is substituting for the day.

Child
as an individual
- level of development
- unique style/temperament
- "whole child": physical, emotional, social, intellectual

as a member of
- a family
- a race/ethnic/cultural group
- the group of children in this class

Adult
- the role (teacher, parent, coach, advocate, friend)
- relationship to the child
- values, biases
- skills and guidance techniques

Situation
- the physical environment
- time of day
- who, what is involved
- what else is happening
- what is unique about it

Figure 7-1 The Guidance Triangle. Source: From Ann Gordon & Kathryn Williams Browne, *Guiding Young Children in a Diverse Society.* Published by Allyn and Bacon, Boston, MA. 1996 by Pearson Education.

Digital Download

Standards

truth or fiction?

T F Discipline and guidance are similar concepts.

Both discipline and guidance require a positive approach to helping young children learn appropriate social behavior, and the terms are used synonymously.

7-1c What Is Punishment?

Punishment is a consequence for inappropriate behavior. To be effective, punishment should be related to the behavior and help children learn from the situation. Inappropriate punishment:

> Shames, frightens, and humiliates a child
> Is often physically and emotionally abusive
> Threatens children with the loss of affection
> Has consequences that are too long, too punitive, or postponed
> Has consequences that are often not related to the incident

To some, the words discipline and punishment are synonymous. They are not, as Figure 7-2 demonstrates.

7-1d The Goal Is Self-Discipline

One of the goals of a positive guidance process is to help children achieve **self-discipline** by allowing them to work out solutions to their problems. This happens when adults support children's developing ability to control themselves. When children have the opportunity to govern

their own actions, they become more confident of their inner controls.

7-2 Influence on Children's Behavior

Children act out their frustration and anger until they learn more appropriate ways to express their needs. For any guidance technique to be successful, a teacher must first understand the reasons why children behave the way they do.

7-2a Developmental Influences

The key to planning guidance strategies is to find strategies that fit with each child's developmental level. In that way, teachers have the confidence to support children's

Difference between Guidance and Punishment

Discipline	Punishment
Emphasizes what the child should *do*	Emphasizes what the child should *not* do
Is an ongoing process	Is a one-time occurrence
Sets an example to follow	Insists on obedience
Leads to self-control	Undermines independence
Helps children change	Is an adult release
Is positive	Is negative
Accepts child's need to assert self	*Makes* child behave
Fosters child's ability to think	Thinks *for* the child
Bolsters self-esteem	Defeats self-esteem
Shapes behavior	Condemns misbehavior

Figure 7-2 A guidance approach to discipline encourages children's interaction and involvement; punishment is usually something that is done to a child. (© Cengage Learning®)

positive guidance. Method based on caring, respectful, and supportive relationships.

punishment. The act of inflicting a penalty for an offense or behavior.

self-discipline. Gaining control over one's own behavior.

For guidance to be successful, a teacher must first understand children's behavior. ◄

DAP

Children's Temperament

Classic research by Thomas and Chess (1977) identifies three types of temperament in babies: the easy child, the difficult child, and the slow-to-warm-up child. The children were classified according to activity level, regulatory and rhythm of bodily routines, adaptability, physical sensitivity, intensity of reaction, ease of distraction, mood, and attention span. These differences were observed in very young infants and seem to remain consistent as the child grows.

An easy child is effortless to respond to; a slow-to-warm-up child may be harder to interact with; difficult children may be blamed for things they did not do. If parents and teachers come to know the nature of a child's temperament they can accept that as part of the child's developmental make-up. Guidance measures can be tailored to meet the unique needs of a slow-to-warm-up child, for instance, or for a difficult child. Those strategies will be different from techniques used to discipline the easy child.

Developmentally appropriate practices ensure that we take into account a child's individuality, including temperament, and build guidance techniques by matching developmental theories to our work with young children.

---

emerging self-control as they grow and develop. Group times that are too long set the stage for unwanted behavior. Lack of outside play activity prevents children from working off their pent-up energy and tensions, causing misbehavior back in the classroom.

7-2b Environmental Influences

Through the intentional use of the environment, the teacher indirectly influences the behavior in the classroom.

> The *physical setting* tells children clearly how to act in that space, such as where to sit, read, write, or play with blocks.
> *Materials and equipment* should be adequate and interesting to the age group. When children are occupied with stimulating, age-appropriate materials, there are fewer opportunities for misbehavior.
> The *daily schedule and timing* of events indirectly influence classroom behavior. When there are blocks of time in which to choose activities, children can proceed at their own pace without feeling hurried.
> The *interpersonal relationships* between and among children and adults should be accepting and supportive. Class size and teacher-to-child ratios that allow for interactions help to create an atmosphere of trust.

truth or fiction?

Ⓣ F Children's temperament can be determined in infancy.

Three types of temperaments have been identified in babies, and they remain consistent as the child grows.

Chapter 9 contains a more detailed discussion of the factors that need to be considered when designing spaces for children. Many of these aspects directly influence how children will behave. Use the classroom checklist in Figure 7-3 to evaluate how the environment is related to your guidance philosophy and to children's behavior.

7-2c Individual Influences

Many factors can trigger a behavior issue in a young child's life. A new baby, a grandparent's visit, divorce, moving to a new house, starting a new school, and illness are just some of the factors that can lead to upsets; others include when children are hungry, tired, bored, or restless. Individual differences in temperaments are innate and will affect the choice of guidance strategies.

Time

_____ Does the daily schedule provide enough time for unhurried play?

_____ Are those periods that create tension—transitions from one activity to another—given enough time?

_____ Is clean up a leisurely process built in at the end of each activity, with children participating?

Program Planning and Curriculum

_____ Is there enough to do so that children have choices and alternatives for play?

_____ Is the curriculum challenging enough to prevent boredom and restlessness?

_____ Is the curriculum age appropriate for the children in the class?

_____ Are there activities to help children release tension? Do the activities allow for body movement, exploration, and manipulation of materials?

_____ Are children included in developing the rules and setting guidelines? How is their inclusion demonstrated?

Organization and Order

_____ If children are expected to put things away after use, are the cabinets low, open, and marked in some way?

_____ Are the materials within easy reach of the children, promoting self-selection and independence?

_____ Are there enough materials so that sharing does not become a problem?

_____ Are the areas in which activities take place clearly defined so that children know what happens there?

_____ Does the room arrangement avoid runways and areas with no exits?

_____ Do children have their own private space?

_____ Are children able to use all visible and accessible materials? Are there materials about which children are told, "Don't touch"?

Personnel

_____ Are there enough teachers to give adequate attention to the number of children in the class?

_____ Are the group size and make-up balanced so that children have a variety of playmates?

_____ Are the teachers experienced, and do they seem comfortable in setting limits and guiding children's behavior?

_____ Do teachers use their attention to encourage behavior they want, and do they ignore what they want to discourage?

_____ Do all adults consistently enforce the same rules?

Figure 7-3 By anticipating children's needs and growth patterns, teachers set up classrooms that foster constructive and purposeful behavior. (© Cengage Learning®)

Digital Download

7-2d Social and Emotional Influences

Some behavior problems stem from the child's attempt to express social and emotional needs, such as to feel loved and cared for, to be included, to be considered important and valued, to have friends, and to feel safe from harm. Young children are still working out ways to express these needs and feelings. Typically, because they are only just learning language and communication skills, it is often through nonverbal or indirect actions that children let us know what is bothering them. Guidance strategies that help children learn to recognize their emotions, feelings, and words let them know we understand that they can be angry, jealous, or hurt.

Culturally influenced child-rearing practices range from the timing of toilet training to the use of physical punishment.

Professionalism

Young children have a range of emotional skills such as happiness, interest, surprise, fear, anger, sadness, and disgust. More complex emotions of shame, guilt, envy, and pride, emerge later as children's social experiences widen and they observe these emotions in others. These expressions of emotions appear in a wide range of cultural and ethic groups.

Children learn to respond to situations, and to react, both very emotional experiences. Effective teachers stimulate an emotional response to themselves and the curriculum that is a balance between interest and overwhelming anxiety. Creating the "right" emotional conditions is a primary way to gain access to a child's capacity to learn.

Young children are not yet limited by standards of conduct that prevent them from truthful and sincere self-expression. Teachers observe children and learn from them how they face their own feelings and the feelings of others and assess the child's range of skills that fosters emotional growth.

Family Patterns

Family Culture	Child's Experience and Behavior	Guidance Strategy
Democratic: family members share in decision making	Child is encouraged to negotiate and compromise.	Offer real choices; use problem-solving techniques
Authoritarian: one family member makes all of the decisions	Child is expected to obey, follow commands, and respect adult authority. Child may be unable to choose activities, look adults in the eye, or call them by name.	Don't insist on eye contact. Child may need help in selecting an activity. Work with the family members who make the decisions.
Strong, close-knit family	Child learns that the family comes first; the individual sacrifices for the family.	Recognize that family matters may take precedence over school.
Honor, dignity, and pride	Child's behavior reflects family honor; child is disciplined for rudeness and poor manners.	Share achievements with parents; help child learn manners; be sensitive when discussing child's behavior problems.
Expressing feelings is accepted	Child is allowed to cry, scream, throw temper tantrums.	Accept child's crying as you give comfort; stay with child until he is calm.

Figure 7-4 Sample of culturally diverse family patterns that affect guidance and discipline. Knowledge of culturally diverse family patterns and guidance strategies to parallel these child-rearing styles can allow you to begin a dialogue with the children you teach. (From S. York, *Roots and wings*, revised ed. St. Paul, MN: Redleaf Press, 2003. Copyright © 2003 by Stacey York. Adapted with permission from Redleaf Press, St. Paul, Minnesota, www.readleafpress.org.)

7-2e Cultural Influences

Discipline and guidance are deeply embedded within the values and beliefs of the family. Children reflect the context in which they are being raised in their family, culture, ethnicity, religion, socioeconomic status, and neighborhood. When we are aware of these influences, we are better able to match the child with the most effective guidance approach.

In some families, a sense of community is valued over individualism, a concept that can create difficulty in the early childhood classroom unless it is understood and appreciated. This is at odds with families in which cooperation and sharing are valued concepts. Teachers will need to become culturally sensitive to each family's values. Figure 7-4 shows how different family cultural patterns relate to a child's behavior and to an appropriate guidance strategy.

Strategies for Guiding Dual-Language Learners

Retaining their home language and learning a new one can be stressful for young children. Behavioral issues may compound or create those anxieties. As programs prepare to serve DLL students and their families, the following suggestions will help to ensure that children's social-emotional needs are being met with appropriate language and meaning:

> Pre- and in-service training for all staff that includes developmentally and age- appropriate techniques to support effective policies within the school for maintaining home languages and scaffolding learning English;

> Ensure that every classroom has a teacher who speaks the language of each DLL child and/or provide volunteer bi-lingual aides;

> Encourage teachers to learn the language of one of the DLL children through the use of storybooks and CDs in that child's language;

> Enlist the families of DLL children to help the staff learn basic words and phrases in the child's language;

Children's home languages are part of their identity and self-esteem (Nemeth, 2012). Respecting and supporting the needs of DLL children has a positive influence on their behavior and social development.

7-3 Developmentally and Culturally Appropriate Guidance

The key ingredient to developmentally appropriate practices is to start where children are and help them reach their potential. We achieve this by making guidance decisions based on what is developmentally and culturally appropriate.

7-3a Developmentally Appropriate Guidance

The three areas that must be considered for a developmentally appropriate approach to guidance are as follows:

1. Age appropriateness. These are behaviors common to a specific age group and provide a context in which to understand the child. Behavior then can be seen as normal and predictable and can be responded to accordingly. For instance, first and second graders have an ability to consider others' points of view, so the teacher would help them problem-solve by reflecting on how their behavior affects others.

2. Individual appropriateness. The teacher considers what is known about each child: his or her strengths, challenges, and interests. The guidance strategy then matches the capabilities of each child, and the adult expectations are reasonable for that child. For instance, Francie is an only

child of older parents and has difficulty playing with her age-mates. The teacher's guidance approach should include teaching and modeling social skills for Francie and suggesting compatible children for play dates.

3. Responding to family culture, as noted earlier under "Cultural Influences," is an integral part of planning guidance strategies for each child.

7-3b The Language of Guidance and Discipline

The language and communication techniques in guidance are both spoken and unspoken. Adults discover how potent the voice can be, what words will work best and when, and the effectiveness of body language, physical presence, and attitude.

truth or fiction?

T F Developmentally appropriate guidance is based on age appropriateness and family culture.

The three criteria on which developmentally appropriate guidance is based include individual appropriateness as well as age-appropriateness and family culture.

The language of guidance and discipline is most effective when:

> You use your voice with intentionality to talk to children in the same way you talk to other people, and use good speech patterns for children to imitate. Get close enough to speak in a normal tone and get down to the child's level. Often, lowering volume and pitch is effective enough to stop the behavior.
> Think before you speak. If you say, "Danny, run and get me the sponge," do you really want him to run? To have the greatest impact, use your words wisely with simple, clear statements, spoken once.
> Ask, don't tell. Encourage problem solving by asking, "What's happening here?" or "What's not working?" Then enlist the children's cooperation to solve the situation by asking, "How do you think we could handle this? What could you do to make this better?"
> Children are aware of your physical presence. Place yourself so you can see all or most of the room and the other teachers. A touch on the shoulder will tell a child you are near to help or to stop an inappropriate action.
> Keep an open attitude. Attitudes affect expectations. Check to see whether you have any assumptions about how children behave depending on their size, age, race, gender, or culture.
> Acknowledge and express children's feelings. "You sound angry/hurt/sad. How can I help?" "I know it is hard for

you to wait for a turn." Recognize and acknowledge positive behavior: "Looks like you found a good book to read while you are waiting for a turn at the computer."
> Use humor. "Oh no! The Legos don't remember how to put themselves back on the shelf."
> Accentuate the positive by making supportive comments that tell children what they are doing well. Avoid global praise ("Good job!") and be specific about what a child is learning. ("I've noticed that you are walking very carefully around Gina's block building. That's being a good friend.")

7-4 Essential Guidance Strategies

Some guidance methods are subtle; others are obvious. Every situation requires a strategy that best matches the needs of the child, the adult, and the situation. Remember the Guidance Triangle on page 142? No one method applies to all situations. The techniques that follow are based on **inductive guidance** principles that include the following:

> Asking open-ended questions
> Providing appropriate choices

inductive guidance. A guidance process in which children are held accountable for their actions and are called on to think about the impact of their behavior on others. Reasoning and problem-solving skills are stressed.

Getting down to the child's level provides for greater impact and involvement. ◄

> Communicating trust and confidence
> Modeling guidance as an interactive process
> Holding children increasingly responsible for their actions
> Teaching thinking and reasoning skills

7-4a Indirect Guidance

Children's behavior is influenced by the people and places where they work, live, and play. A classroom sends out indirect messages of where to play, sit, work, eat, and learn. Desks lined up in a row or a circle say, "Sit here and work." A room with a long corridor cries out for children to run through the space. Rigid time schedules cause anxiety and tension to rush through play, clean up, or eat. The presence of too few teachers leaves many children unsupervised or ignored. All of these are a sure recipe for misbehavior.

A productive environment does not just happen. Part of a teacher's professional role is to anticipate children's behavior and create an environment that fosters positive behavior. **Indirect guidance** is the teacher's way of setting up and controlling the environment to maximize learning and minimize disruptions. In Chapter 9, you will see the impact of space arrangements, schedules, and materials on children's behavior, and in Chapter 10, you will learn how an appropriate and challenging curriculum enhances optimal behavior.

---

indirect guidance. Creating conditions that promote optimal behavior through the intentional use of the environment and overall classroom climate.

power assertive methods. Harsh, punitive discipline methods that rely on children's fear of punishment rather than on the use of reason and understanding. Hitting and spanking are examples of power assertion.

direct guidance. Methods used while interacting with children.

guidance continuum. A range of guidance techniques starting with the least intrusive and moving to the most intervening strategies.

Watch the TeachSource Video Case entitled, "Elementary Classroom Management: Basic Strategies." After you study the video clip, view the artifacts, and read the teacher interviews and text, reflect on the following questions:

1. Kindergarten teacher Amy spoke of building teamwork. What examples did you observe in this video case that supported teamwork as a way to promote positive behavior?

2. How do you think Amy's attitude toward behavior problems affects her relationship with the children in her class?

At the other end of the guidance spectrum are **power assertive methods**, which rely on children's fear of punishment rather than the use of reason and understanding. Spanking, hitting, calling children names, and otherwise using demeaning punishments exclude the opportunity for teaching and learning to take place or to promote problem solving.

The techniques that follow use both direct and indirect guidance. They range from the least intrusive methods to those that require greater adult involvement, and they should be used in that order. They are valuable tools for enlarging the child's capacity to become increasingly self-directed and self-reliant.

7-4b Direct Guidance and the Guidance Continuum

Direct guidance techniques are those teachers use when interacting directly with children. Figure 7-5 outlines a **guidance continuum** that ranges from the least intrusive guidance methods to those requiring greater intervention.

After a teacher analyzes a problem situation, the guidance continuum serves as a reference for selecting the most appropriate strategy for addressing the child's behavior. Each of the techniques should be used in the context of the goals and guidance philosophy of the program.

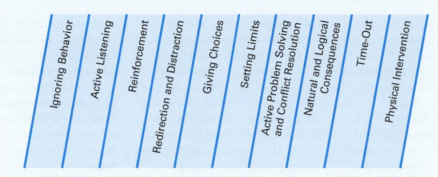

Figure 7-5 Follow the Guidance Continuum from left to right for the least intrusive to the most intervening strategies. Source: From Ann Gordon & Kathryn Williams Browne, Guiding Young Children in a Diverse Society. Published by Allyn and Bacon, Boston, MA. 1996 by Pearson Education.

Choose the least intrusive strategy to allow children time to work out the problem themselves. At each step of the continuum, there is greater expectation for the child's involvement in problem solving.

Ignoring the Behavior

When misbehavior is mildly annoying but not harmful, it may be best to ignore it. A child's whining or calling, "Teacher, teacher, teacher" without pause are two examples. The adult chooses not to respond to the child in any way and may even become occupied elsewhere while the behavior persists. This method is based on the learning theory that negative reinforcement (the adult ignoring the child) will eventually cause the child to stop the undesirable behavior. As soon as the whining or calling stops, pay attention to the child and, depending on the child's age, you might even say, "I like to talk with you when you aren't whining or calling at me. When you stop, I'll know that you are ready to talk and play again."

Active Listening and "I" Messages

With this method, you are looking to respond to a child's feelings as well as words. Listen carefully, then reflect back to the child what you think he or she is really saying. The child has an opportunity to correct any misinterpretations. For example:

Rita: I hate school!

Teacher: Sounds as if you are really disappointed you didn't get a turn cooking. today. I know how long you waited for a turn.

Rita: I really wanted to help make pancakes.

Teacher: Let's put your name over on the cooking list so that you'll be sure to get a turn tomorrow.

"I" messages are also an adult's way of reflecting back to children how their actions have affected others. "I" messages are honest, nonjudgmental statements that place no blame on the child but state an observation of the behavior and its results.

Ethics

Feelings: What if the Messages Are Different?

Young children observe the many different ways people express their feelings, preferences, likes and dislikes, and opinions. Early childhood educators can inadvertently use practices that counter parents' efforts. Families often have strong ideas about their children's display of emotions. Encouragement to act out every emotion is not appropriate in some cultures which may challenge your usual way of guiding children to express feelings.

Strong expression of feelings may be seen as a sign of disrespect to adults, particularly those in authority, such as teachers. Praising a child for self-expression and avoiding making negative remarks may seem appropriate to some teachers, but Chinese parents may see it as their duty to tell children their errors in such direct language (Chua, 2011).

In these early years, if the difference between home and school expectations are too great, children can be confused, which leads to difficulties and misunderstandings. It helps if you think of yourself as a learner rather than an expert and inquire about family practices regarding expressing emotions. Work with the family toward a solution acceptable to both of you. The most important element in bridging children's worlds is for the adults who care for them to be comfortable and accepting of differences.

Adult: I feel sad when you tell me you don't like me.

Adult: I get upset when I see you hitting other children. Let's sit down and remember what we agreed about hitting.

Adult: I'm disappointment no one cleaned up the reading area. What can we do to see that this doesn't happen again?

negative reinforcement. Response to a behavior that decreases the likelihood that the behavior will recur; for instance, a teacher's glare might stop a child from whispering at group time, and from then on, the anticipation of such an angry look could reinforce not whispering in the future.

Brain Research says

When you achieve a goal you feel good when someone says, "Well done!" or "Here's a smiley-face sticker." As teachers, we constantly encourage children's behavior through such positive—or negative—reinforcement. But does it work?

The brain makes its own rewards through the "pleasure pathway" and emits good feelings every day (Jensen, 2005). The brain may have different types of reward systems (Fiorillo, Tobler, & Schultz, 2003), one of which predicts pleasurable outcomes, activates the pleasure network (Tremblay & Schultz, 2000) and produces dopamine, the neurotransmitter that produces pleasure. The brain stores

these experiences of prediction and pleasure and learning improves after the first experience. However, student performance drops as they are rewarded time and again because the dopamine is activated as much by the anticipation of pleasure as by the pleasure itself (Berridge & Robinson, 2002). The brain is in a constant state of change and what worked as a reward one or two times, may not work long-term (Koob & LeMoal, 1997). In other words, a piece of candy escalates into a cheeseburger with french fries.

Most brain-related research on rewards has been for simple tasks, and the findings suggest that rewards

can be used successfully for short-terms tasks. The best use of rewards (Jensen, 2005) is for short lengths of time and for a specific reason; the use of tokens or boxes of raisins that are concrete and inexpensive. Consider using more abstract rewards, such as certificates, notes, verbal compliments, and privileges, to reinforce behaviors.

Questions

1. Describe how you feel when someone rewards you.
2. How does this research alter your thinking about giving out rewards and the concept of reinforcement?

Reinforcement

Positive reinforcement is a method of rewarding positive behavior based on the belief that children tend to repeat the same action in the future because it has been noticed. "Janie, I saw that you put your jacket in your locker right after you took it off. That's a good way to make sure you know where it is when it is time to go outside." Social **reinforcers**, such as smiling, taking interest, and giving attention, are useful tools to emphasize desired behaviors. Note that the reinforcement is on the action taken by Janie, not Janie herself. The teacher was specific about what she noticed so that Janie knows what behavior she needs to maintain.

Redirection and Distraction

There are times when the adult will want to change the activity in which the child is engaged to one that is more acceptable. If Pia and Elena are throwing books off the reading loft, the teacher will want to redirect them and may suggest throwing soft foam balls into a makeshift basket. **Redirecting** is

an alternative that permits the desired activity while changing the expression or form it takes: "It looks as if you two are enjoying dropping things from up there. Let's figure out a way you can do that so that books don't get damaged and no one gets hurt." The substitute activity must be a valid one, acceptable to the adults and fulfilling to the children.

Distraction is related to redirection but with some basic differences. Distraction is used to help focus a child's attention to another activity that may or may not relate to the previous behavior. Very young children, especially infants and toddlers, can easily be distracted from undesirable actions. While playing with blocks, 2-year-old Tyrese grabs a truck from Damon. As Damon yells "No!" the teacher approaches the boys: "Tyrese, there's a place for you at the clay table. Let's

---

positive reinforcement. A response to a behavior that increases the likelihood that the behavior will be repeated or increased; for instance, if a child gets attention and praise for crawling, it is likely that the crawling will increase—thus, the attention and praise were positive reinforcers for crawling.

reinforcers. Rewards in response to a specific behavior, thus increasing the likelihood that behavior will recur; reinforcers may be either social (praise) or nonsocial (food) in nature and may or may not be deliberately controlled.

redirecting. Calls for the adult to make an accurate assessment of what the children really want to do, then consider alternatives that permit the desired activity while changing the expression or form it takes.

distraction. A guidance method that helps a child focus on another activity.

© iStockphoto.com/GreenPimp

Teachers are called on to deal with a variety of emotional needs. **<**

walk over there together and you can pound with the clay." This method calls for well-timed intervention.

Giving Choices

Choices are one of the easiest and most successful methods for helping children who are being resistant. Choices help children maintain some control over the situation as well as practice self-direction and self-control.

Suggest two choices when there is the possibility of resistance. This lets children know that you expect them to comply with the request but allows some decision making on their part. "It is nearly time to go home. Do you want to put your jacket on now or wait until after the story?" The choice must be a valid one that acknowledges children's growing ability to deal with responsibility and help them practice making reasonable choices. Choices have consequences, and children should know what they are before they make a decision. "If you choose to use the computer now, you won't have time to finish your rain forest project." Helping children make reasonable choices gives them a foundation for decision making throughout their lives.

T F Giving children choices confuses them.

Giving children choices actually empowers children to have some control over what they can do and enables them to participate in the guidance process.

Setting Limits

Limits are the boundaries set up to help children know what behavior will or will not be acceptable. Limits are like fences; they are protective structures that help children feel secure. There are generally two reasons for setting limits:

1. To prevent children from injuring themselves or others
2. To prevent the destruction of property, materials, or equipment

Active Problem Solving and Conflict Resolution

Active problem solving helps children confront their differences and work together to solve their problems. By posing open-ended questions, such as "What might happen . . ." or "How might she feel if . . .," the adult helps children keep focused so that they can suggest alternative solutions and solve their own problem.

Figure 7-6 shows how teachers help children to clarify what happened and to think through a number of alternatives that will lead to an agreeable resolution. Several other guidance techniques are embedded in this approach, such

as **active listening**, reinforcement, making choices, and setting limits. This method of **conflict resolution** helps children see how their behavior influences and affects others. This is an early lesson in a lifelong quest to become responsible for one's own behavior.

Natural and Logical Consequences

Natural and logical consequences allow children to see the real-life outcomes of their own actions because they let children

limits. The boundaries of acceptable behavior beyond which actions are considered misbehavior and unacceptable conduct; the absolute controls an adult puts on children's behavior.

active problem solving. A principle in which adults actively engage children in confronting their differences and working together to solve their problems. The adult guides children toward solutions but does not solve problems for them. Posing open-ended questions, the adult helps children keep focused so that they can suggest alternative solutions.

active listening. A child guidance technique of reflecting back to the speaker what the listener thinks has been said.

conflict resolution. Helping children solve disagreements nonviolently and explore alternative ways to reach their goals. By following such a process, children learn to respect others' opinions, to express their own feelings in appropriate ways, and to learn tolerance for doing things in a different way.

natural consequences. The real-life outcomes of a child's own actions.

logical consequences. Consequences that adults impose upon a child's actions.

The Six Steps to Problem Solving

Step 1: Approach (Initiate Mediation)
___ Approach the conflict, signaling your awareness and availability.
___ Get close enough to intervene if necessary; stop aggressive behavior or neutralize the object of conflict by holding it yourself.

Step 2: Make a Statement
___ Describe the scene: "It looks like you both want the ball."
___ Reflect what the children have said: "You both say you had it first."
___ Offer no judgments, values, solutions.

Step 3: Ask Questions (Gather Data, Define the Problem)
___ Do not try to pinpoint blame, such as "Who started this?"
___ Draw out details; define problems: "What is happening here?" "What seems to be the problem?"
___ Help children communicate: "How did this happen?" "What do you want to tell her?" "How did that make you feel?"

Step 4: Generate Alternative Solutions
___ Help children think of ways to figure this out: "Who has an idea of how we could solve this?"
___ Let children offer suggestions: "We could take turns." "We could use it together." "We could tell her she can't play here."
___ Ask questions: "How do you think it would work if you took turns?" "What would happen if you didn't let her play?"
___ Avoid the common mistake of rushing this stage; give it the time it deserves.

Step 5: Agree on Solution
___ When both children accept a solution, rephrase it. "So, you agree that you will work together?"
___ If any solution seems unsafe or unacceptable, you tell the children: "It is not safe for you both to stand up and ride the wagon downhill together. What is another way you can agree?"

Step 6: Follow Through
___ Monitor the activity to make sure agreement is going according to plan. If the decision involves turn-taking, you may need to be a clock watcher. "OK, Maggie. Your 3 minutes are up. It's Leo's turn now."
___ Make a positive statement to the children who were in conflict and to others who might have witnessed it: "Looks as if you solved your problem!"
___ Use the power of language to reinforce the idea that solutions can be found and that children are capable of solving their problems.

Figure 7-6 Using these guidelines to help children solve problems, teachers can listen more than talk, allow children the time to make mistakes and figure out solutions, and point out that diversity of viewpoints is natural, normal, and workable. (© Cengage Learning®)

"I know you both want that book. Who has an idea about how we can solve this problem?" ◄

experience the natural consequence of their behavior. For instance:

> "If you don't eat your lunch, you may be hungry later."

> "You won't be able to go to the ball game if you do not finish your homework."

> "When you don't learn your spelling words, you don't pass the test."

This method allows adults to define the situation for children without making judgments and lets children know what to expect. The consequences rest with the child and the choices he or she makes.

Logical consequences, on the other hand, are a function of what adults impose. A logical consequence of disrupting group time is removal from the

teacher talks

Active Problem Solving: It Works!

As I looked around during outside free-choice play, I noticed that Peter and Lucas were engaged in a physical altercation. I approached in time to see Peter lift his arm to take a swing at Lucas. I was able to separate the boys before any physical damage occurred.

When I asked them what was happening, Peter told me that Lucas had pulled him down the ramp leading to the tree ship. Because these boys tend to use physical behavior to solve problems, I wanted to spend some quality time talking with the children about the situation.

I decided to first talk with Lucas alone. We sat side-by-side with a relaxed body posture. "I noticed that Peter was pretty angry with you, Lucas," I began. "Was Peter right when he told me that you pulled him down the ramp?" Lucas said yes, but explained this was only after Peter had blocked the entrance to the tree ship at the top of the ramp. "I see why you would be unhappy with that situation. You really wanted to go into the tree ship, didn't you?" Lucas nodded. "What did you say to Peter when he was blocking the way?"

Lucas replied, "I asked Peter to move, but he wouldn't so I pulled him down."

"I notice that a couple of our rules were forgotten. Lucas, what is the rule

about children wanting to play in the ship?"

"Anyone who wants to play there is allowed to."

"That's right, and what is the rule about our hands at school?"

"Our hands need to stay on our own bodies."

"That's right. So when Peter was blocking the entrance, you tried to solve the problem by asking. When he didn't move it sounds like you solved the problem by pulling him down the ramp. Is that right?" Lucas agreed. "What would be a way you could have solved the problem without pulling?" At first Lucas did not respond, so I offered a prompt: "When a problem can't be solved between the children by using words, who can you go to for help?"

"A teacher," Lucas responded. "You remembered what to do, Lucas! Let's go get Peter so we can practice the rules and solve the problem in a better way."

In Peter's mind, he had been perfectly reasonable: "There is a terrible storm and no one is allowed in because it is too dangerous." Of course Lucas was not privy to this information! I repeated the conversation with Peter, going over the rules, validating their feelings, and asking Peter to tell me a better way to solve the problem.

We then went back to the ramp to practice—what we call a "do-over." I positioned Peter at the top of the ramp and Lucas just below him. "Let's pretend Peter is blocking the ramp. Lucas, what could you say to Peter?"

Lucas: "Can I please go in the tree ship?"

Teacher: "That is a nice way to ask, Lucas. Now Peter, what would you say?"

Peter: "There is a storm and no one can come in."

Teacher: "Ok. I see that Peter is playing a game about a storm. Peter, I think that Lucas doesn't know the game you are playing and really wants to go into the ship.

Lucas, what would you say next?"

Lucas: "I just want to go down the slide, let me in the ship."

Teacher: "Peter?"

Peter: "Ok, fine. Come in the ship."

Peter moved out of the way and Lucas entered the ship and went down the slide. I asked the boys to tell me once more what they could do in a similar situation. I ended by saying, "Wow! You both know the rules about solving problems. Let's remember to keep practicing using our words and keeping our hands on our own bodies. Thanks for helping me figure out what was going on."

—Kathy

group. For the adult, this means a commitment to follow through; consequences, once stated, must be enforced. It is important to give children an opportunity to choose a course of action for themselves once they have some understanding of what is likely to happen, making the link between cause and effect. Consequences are not punishments when they are related to the action, are respectful, and are reasonable (Nelsen, 2006).

Time Out

When a child is removed from the group and placed in a chair or an isolated part of the room, it is referred to as **time out**. There are times, in order to protect themselves or

others, when young children need to be removed from the situation.

Taking children away from the scene of intensity and emotion to allow them time to cool off and settle down is used with a positive attitude and approach, not as punishment for misbehavior. Too often, time out is punitive: children are pulled from an activity, seated in a chair, and told to "watch how the other children are playing nicely," or "sit there until you can behave."

---

time out. Removing a child from the play area when, owing to anger, hurt, or frustration, the child is out of control. It is a brief respite and a chance to stop all activity and regroup.

Any time-out period should be like those used in athletic events: a brief respite and a chance to stop all activity and think about what has happened. During this time, the teacher and the child talk about the incident, giving the child an opportunity to gain self-control. Children can monitor themselves and choose when they are ready to return to classroom activity. Noah, who persists in calling children offensive names, might be told, "You may come back to the play when you think you are ready to play without hurting children's feelings." Noah can then assume some responsibility for how he will behave and when he is ready to return to play.

Physical Intervention

There are times when a teacher must physically intervene to prevent children from injuring themselves, others, or property. Jude often gets out of control, and his playing becomes too rough. Today, Ramon pushed him away after telling him to stop. Jude retaliated by punching Ramon. The teacher intervened immediately, pulling Jude off Ramon and saying, "Stop hitting Ramon!" Jude raises his arms toward Ramon again, and the teacher puts her arms around him to hold his arms at his side. "I can't let you hurt other children. Let's go over here and talk about this." The teacher gives Jude time to calm down before she talks with him.

Almost simultaneously, the teacher has assessed Ramon to see if he is hurt. If so, she calls another teacher over to provide comfort and assistance to him. There may be times when it is appropriate to talk with both boys together or deal with each of them separately. Once the sequence of events has been sorted out, the teacher can begin the conflict resolution process. Ideally, both boys would be able to participate in this discussion as they learn to solve problems without hitting and fighting.

For children who have a history of aggression, a more long-term approach is required that would include regular observations and assessments of the child. Outside professional advice may be necessary if the aggression persists.

7-4c Selecting Strategies

Helping children learn new behaviors is a challenging prospect for teachers. Think of these 10 strategies as a "tool kit" for guiding young children. Figure 7-7 summarizes options for using these strategies.

7-4d Behavior that is Challenging

Children with a high degree of energy, stress, and short attention spans and who are easily distractible and demanding are the children who challenge our skills in guiding

The Teacher's Role in Children's Anger Management

1. Create a safe emotional climate . . .
   by having clear, firm, and flexible boundaries.
2. Model responsible anger management . . .
   by acknowledging when you are upset.
3. Help children develop self-regulatory skills . . .
   by giving children age- and skill-appropriate responsibilities and encouraging problem solving with support.
4. Encourage children to label feelings of anger . . .
   start with "mad" and expand to include "upset, annoyed, irritated, furious, steamed," etc.
5. Encourage children to talk about anger-arousing interactions . . . by talking about situations when they aren't happening. "I felt mad when . . . " can start a lively conversation; cards with realistic scenarios can do the same, as can puppets.
6. Use appropriate books and stories about anger to help children understand and manage anger.
7. Communicate with parents. . . . Introduce the books or puppets, let them borrow them overnight. Tell them what you do in your program, and ask what they do.

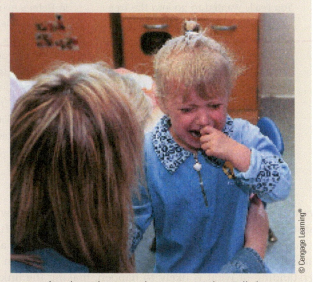

© Cengage Learning®

Figure 7-7 When children come to grips with their strong feelings, their emotional growth is encouraged. (categories from Marion, 2011)

Variety of Guidance Techniques

If This Is the Behavior	Try This	For Example
Whining	Ignoring	Do and say nothing while whining persists. Pay attention to child when whining stops.
Playing cooperatively	Positive reinforcement	"You two are sure working hard on this garden! What a good team you make."
Refusing to cooperate	Provide a choice	"Reva, do you want to pick up the Legos off the floor or help Charlie empty the water table?"
Restlessness, inattentiveness	Change the activity	"This story seems long today; we'll finish it later. Let's play some music and dance now."
Daydreaming	Indirect suggestion	"As soon as you get your coat, Winona, we'll all be ready to go inside."
Arguing over the use of a toy	Active listening	"You really wanted to be the first one to play with the blue truck today, didn't you, Lief?"
Dawdling, late for snacks	Natural consequences	"Sorry, Nate, the snacks have been put away. Maybe tomorrow you'll remember to come inside when the other children leave the yard."
Pushing, crowding, running inside	Change room arrangement	Create larger, more open spaces so children have greater freedom of movement and do not feel crowded together.
Unable to take turns, to wait	Review daily schedule, equipment	Buy duplicates of popular equipment. Allow enough time for free play so children won't feel anxious about getting a turn.
Boisterous play	Positive redirection	"You and Sergio seem to want to wrestle. Let's go set the mats out in the other room. If you wrestle here you disturb the children who are playing quietly."

Figure 7-8 The astute teacher selects from the options available and individualizes the responses. (© Cengage Learning®)

them toward appropriate behavior. These children often do not respond to the usual guidance strategies and need teachers with extra effort, patience, and perseverance.

We begin to address these problems by seeing the uniqueness in each child as we look at the five factors that influence children's behavior.

> We build caring relationships with children and their families and strengthen the collaboration between home and school.
> We make observations of each child's behavior, noting not only when the inappropriate behavior begins, but also the situation immediately before.
> We modify the classroom and schedule as necessary to help children adapt to new behaviors.

> We pay attention to disruptive, nonattentive, aggressive children when they are behaving appropriately.
> We follow through and support children in finding activities that require energy (woodworking) or is more calming (water play, reading, painting), depending on what the child needs at the time.

With patience, positive interactions, and appropriate guidance practices, teachers find creative and individual ways to help each child grow in social competence and self-assurance. There are times, however, when a child's behavior is beyond the scope of the early childhood classroom and teachers need to help parents find further professional help for their child's behavior.

summary

7.1 The terms guidance and discipline have similar meaning and are used interchangeably. Guidance is the ongoing system or process by which adults help children learn what is acceptable and unacceptable behavior. Positive guidance is based on helpful, caring, and supportive relationships between adults and children. Discipline is the action or strategy used to guide children's behavior. Punishment is a consequence for behavior an adult thinks is inappropriate and often includes negative and harmful methods.

7.2 There are at least five different influences that affect children's behavior: their developmental and maturity levels, the environment, their individual temperament and style, their social and emotional needs, and the family and culture in which they are raised.

7.3 Developmentally and culturally appropriate guidance are based on three criteria that teachers use to make decision about behavior and guidance. These three are: the age appropriateness (what we know about how children learn and grow), the individual appropriateness (what we know about the strengths and challenges of each child), and the cultural and family responsiveness (what we know about the child's family and culture, including dual-language learners).

7.4 Effective guidance strategies are on a continuum that begins with the least intrusive methods that require the minimal amount of teacher intervention to those that have the greatest teacher involvement. Some of these strategies are ignoring the behavior, active listening, positive and negative reinforcement, redirection and distraction, giving choices, setting limits, active problem solving and conflict resolution, natural and logical consequences, time out, and physical intervention.

web resources

American Academy of Pediatrics
   http://www.aap.org
National Network for Childcare
   http://nieer.org/link/national-network-child-care

Responsive Discipline
   http://www.k-state.edu/wwparent/courses/rd/

references

American Academy of Pediatrics (AAP). 2004. *Policy statement: Guidance for effective discipline.* Available at: http://aappolicy.aappublications.org/cgi/content/full/pediatrics;101/4/723. Retrieved December 10, 2010.

Browne, K. W., & Gordon, A. M. (2013). *Early childhood field experience:* To teach well. Upper Saddle River, NJ: Pearson.

Chua, A. (2011). *Battle hymn of the tiger mother.* New York: Penguin Books.

Gonzalez-Mena, J. (2008). *Multicultural issues in child care.* Menlo Park, CA: Mayfield.

Gordon, A. M., & Williams Browne, K. (2014). *Beginnings and beyond: Foundations in early childhood education.* Belmont, CA: Wadsworth Cengage Learning.

Gordon, A. M., & Williams Browne, K. (1996). *Guiding young children in a diverse society.* Boston: Allyn & Bacon.

Nelsen, J. (2006). *Positive discipline.* New York: Ballantine Books.

Nemeth, K. N. (2012). *Basics of supporting dual language learners: An introduction for educators of children from birth through age 8.* Washington, DC: National Association for the Education of Young Children.

Thomas, A., & Chess, S. (1977). *Temperament and development.* New York: Brunner/Mazel.

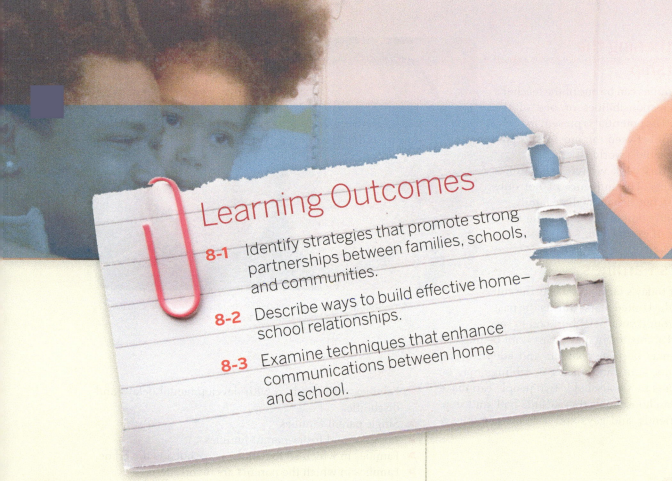

Learning Outcomes

8-1 Identify strategies that promote strong partnerships between families, schools, and communities.

8-2 Describe ways to build effective home–school relationships.

8-3 Examine techniques that enhance communications between home and school.

NAEYC Standards

The following NAEYC Standards for Early Childhood Professional Preparation are addressed in this chapter:

Standard 1: Promoting Child Development and Learning

Standard 2: Building Family and Community Relationships

Standard 5: Using Content Knowledge to Build Meaningful Curriculum

Standard 6: Becoming a Professional

truth *or* fiction

T F A family consists of a mother, father, and children.

T F A family-centered approach to family–school relationships supports the family as well as the child.

T F The primary purpose of a family–teacher conference is to discuss the child's inappropriate behavior.

8-1 Strengthening the Partnership

Working with families can be one of the teacher's most satisfying responsibilities or one of the most frustrating. The potential is present for a dynamic partnership between the most important adults in a young child's world.

Throughout this book we refer to families rather than parents. The influence of not only the child's parents, but also immediate family, extended family, and community, forms the identity and behavior of every child.

8-1a Today's Families

The definition of today's families reflects the cultural changes in the United States during the past 50 years. Look around your neighborhood to see what is a **family**. Parents today may or may not be married to one another, may be foster parents and adoptive parents. Grandparents, aunts and uncles, or siblings may be the parental figures in a household. Two people can make up a family. So can households that include half- and step-siblings, close friends, and gays and lesbians (Browne & Gordon, 2014).

truth ^{or} *fiction?*

T Ⓕ A family consists of a mother, father, and children.

Families are made up of the many people who live together and care for one another and who may or may not be related.

The term **parent** usually means a mother, father, or someone who is a legal guardian. That definition now includes those individuals who are raising their own biological children, foster children, adopted children, and children of other family members or friends.

8-1b Diversity of the American Family

There are many types of families who face additional challenges in child-rearing and who may need added support from teachers and the school:

---

family. A family unit [15]may consist of parents who may or may not be married to each other, or who may be adoptive or foster parents, as well as grandparents, aunts, uncles, and step- or half-siblings. Two people can be considered a family, as can a collective or commune.

parents. Those individuals who are raising their own biological children as well as those who are raising foster children, adopted children, or children of other family members or friends.

Many grandparents are responsible for raising their grandchildren and may need additional teacher support. ◄

© iStockphoto.com/Manuela Krause

> Families with children with developmental delays and disabilities
> Single-parent families
> Adoptive and foster parent families
> Families in which all the adults work outside the home
> Families in which the parents are divorced
> Families with LGBTQI children and/or parents
> Families who are homeless
> Teenage-parent families
> Families in which grandparents are raising grandchildren
> Families raising their children in a culture not their own and in which English is not the primary language
> Multiracial families
> First-time older-parent families

Many of these families do not have access to an extended support system to help them meet the challenge of raising children. Teachers should be aware of the unique needs of each family and work with them to find additional support, such as:

> Help them locate community resources to address their needs.
> Connect them with other families that have similar circumstances.
> Assist them in exploring appropriate school settings for the future.
> See that they are included in all school functions.

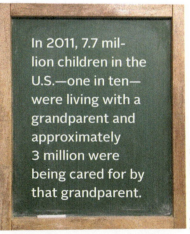

In 2011, 7.7 million children in the U.S.—one in ten—were living with a grandparent and approximately 3 million were being cared for by that grandparent.

© iStockphoto.com/dalton00

Professionalism

Meeting the Needs of Single Parents

Faced with the economic necessity to work, single parents must cope not only with raising children alone but also with child care arrangements and costs. Particularly hard hit are those who head single-parent households. They are more likely to live below the poverty level and to be members of a minority population.

The number of single father households with minor children in the U.S. has reached 2.6 million, nine times what it was in 1960. In that same time period, the number of single mother households rose more than four times to 8.6 million. (Livingston, 2013b)

Early childhood educators must be sensitive to the unique aspects of raising children alone. This means re-examining school policies and attitudes that may overlook the needs of single parents, such as:

1. What kind of involvement in a child's classroom is possible for a working single parent?

2. How can I help parents feel connected even if they are unable to be at the center?

3. What is appropriate support for single parents?

4. Am I judgmental about single parents? About single mothers? Single fathers?

5. How do I help families and children deal with issues concerning the absent parent?

6. What are some of the best strategies for helping children cope with the transitions when they visit one parent or the other?

These and other similar questions must become part of the agenda at staff meetings, in-service days for teachers, and parent–family group meetings.

> Learn about their special needs.
> Seek their help and advice.
> Help them establish contact with other families that may be willing to assist in translating, transporting, babysitting, and sharing friendship.

8-1c Valuing the Culture of the Family

Children's growth and development can be understood only within the context of their family's culture, so it is important that their values and attitudes be recognized and respected. This is an essential element in building strong family–school relationships.

Children learn best in settings that reflect and support their families. Families sense whether an early childhood environment is truly inclusive and supports and celebrates all varieties of families.

Successful partnerships with families of various cultures are built on teacher's self-knowledge of their own heritage,

Cultural Characteristics of Families

Cultural Dimension	Questions for Reflection
Values and Beliefs	How is *family* defined? What roles do adults and children play? How does the family make sense of the child's behavioral difficulties? How does culture inform the family's view of appropriate and inappropriate ways of dealing with problem behavior and guidance? What is most important to the family?
Historical and Social Influences	What strengths and stressors does the family identify? What barriers do they experience?
Communication	What is the family's primary language? What support is required to enable communication? How are needs and wants expressed? How is unhappiness, dissatisfaction, or distress experienced or expressed?
Attitudes Toward Seeking Help	How does the family seek help and from whom? How do members view professionals, and how do professionals view them?

Figure 8-1 J. Bradley, & P. Kibera, (2007). Closing the gap: Culture and the promotion of inclusion in child care. In D. Koralik (Ed.), *Spotlight on young children and families*. Washington, DC: National Association for the Education of Young Children. (© Cengage Learning®)

experience, and attitudes. Any prejudice and bias that teachers may have toward cultural groups different from their own must be examined and addressed so that they can fully connect with the families of the children in their class. Different perspectives about schedules, eating, toileting, sleeping, and ways of showing respect, for instance, could become barriers in working together. When viewed within a cultural context, these issues can become understood and respected as teachers and families work toward mutually acceptable resolutions.

Eisenbud (2002) suggest some ways to create an environment that supports family diversity:

> Ask families what names the child has for his or her caregivers and use these names with the child;
> Create enrollment forms that allow for answers other than "mother" or "father" to indicate the person who is legally responsible for the child;
> Find out what the child has been taught about his or her family situation and discuss with the family how you can support their position;

- If one or the other parent is absent, find out if and how that parent is involved with the child's life;
- Be aware of any drug use/addiction related to the child's health and welfare;
- Review the curriculum, books, and physical environment on a regular basis to ensure that all types of families are represented in the classroom;
- Adapt your conversations with children to reflect the diversity of families; for instance, "two mommies, stepbrother, foster dad," and so forth.

Think about the many ways you can strengthen all family units, no matter their makeup.

8-1d Families of Dual-Language Learners

Many young children are learning English as they continue to learn and speak their native home languages. This presents a challenge to early childhood teachers, who must collaborate with families to help children learn both languages in developmentally appropriate ways.

Maintaining a home language while learning English supports a child's self-esteem and cognitive development, along with strengthening family ties and promoting social interactions (Nemeth, 2012). To this end, teachers' professional development and in-service should include learning more effective strategies for working with DLL students and their families.

8-1e Understanding Parenthood

The role of a parent is ever changing. Every family has its own unique systems and patterns for raising their children. Two of them are worth exploring as you focus on working with parents and families.

Patterns of Child-Rearing

Baumrind's classic work (1972) defined three types of parental styles: authoritative, authoritarian, and permissive.

- The most successful approach is *authoritative* parents who foster the highest levels of self-esteem, self-reliance, independence, and curiosity in children. They provide a warm, loving atmosphere with clear limits and high

---

authoritative. Parents whose child-rearing patterns are associated with the highest levels of self-esteem, self-reliance, independence, and curiosity in children. They provide a warm, loving atmosphere with clear limits and high expectations.

authoritarian. Parents whose child-rearing patterns reflect high control and strict maturity demands combined with relatively low communication and nurturance. Authoritarian parents are dictatorial; they expect and demand obedience, yet lack warmth and affection.

permissive. A child-rearing pattern that is essentially the reverse of authoritarian parents. There is a high level of warmth and affection but little control. Clear standards and rules are not set, nor are they reinforced consistently.

Diversity

Immigrant Families

In 2012, nearly 13 million children in the U.S. were from immigrant families (KidsCount, 2014) and they come from a wide variety of nations and cultures.

Nearly 50% of immigrants are from Latin America, 41% are from Asia, and 8.5% are from Europe. The largest individual populations of immigrants come from Mexico, China, India, and the Philippines (U.S. Bureau of Census, 2012). Nearly 17% of all immigrants are children under age 16 (U.S. Department of Homeland Security, 2012).

The percentage of children who are Hispanic has increased faster than that of any other racial or ethnic group and will continue to reach 25% of the school-age population by 2020. Asians are also are a fast-growing ethnic group (U.S. Census Bureau, 2012).

These data, added to existing ethnic populations already present in the United States, challenge the early childhood teacher to a multicultural sensitivity not yet realized. A willingness to learn various cultural norms and a knowledge of languages will be helpful for teachers to communicate with children and parents whose primary language is not English.

Miscommunication may be a problem when teaching a classroom of children with such diverse backgrounds. When cultural perspectives of the family and the school differ markedly, teachers can easily misread a child's attitude and abilities because of different styles of languages and behaviors. For example, in some preschool settings, children are encouraged to call their teachers by their first name. This informal style of addressing authority figures may make some parents uncomfortable. Learning the meaning of behavior from another perspective will help expand our own view of the world.

The early childhood professional must aggressively recruit and train early childhood professionals within the immigrant cultures. Communicating across cultures is a challenge early childhood teachers will need to meet.

---

expectations. Authoritative parents are consistent in reinforcing rules and allow their children to make reasonable decisions appropriate to their age and experience.

- In contrast, *authoritarian* child-rearing patterns reflect high control and demands combined with relatively low communication and nurturance. Authoritarian parents are strict; they expect and demand obedience and may lack warmth and affection. They exert control through belittling, threats, and criticisms and may resort to force.
- With *permissive* parents, there is a high level of overindulgence or inattentiveness, warmth, and affection but little control. Clear standards and rules are not set, nor are they reinforced consistently. Permissive parents allow children to make decisions that are not appropriate for their age.

Fathers often bring children to child care as they take on more responsibility in working families. ◀

The positive effects of the authoritative parent model demonstrate that using reason over power, maintaining appropriate limits yet supporting appropriate autonomy, and encouraging give-and-take create more successful children.

Stages of Parent Development

Just as children have various stages of development, parents, too, grow and change throughout the course of raising their children. The parent of one child has different knowledge and feelings than does a parent with three children. Older first-time parents' experiences differ from those of teenage parents. Galinsky (1987) defined six distinct phases that parents go through as they and their children grow.

The earliest stages begin during pregnancy as parents fantasize about what kind of parent they would like to be and prepare for the inclusion of a child in their lives. During the first 2 years, attachment is a key issue, as is matching their child-rearing fantasies with the actual experience. From toddlerhood to adolescence, parents establish their authority style and family rules and clarify the values, knowledge, and skills they want for their children. In the teenage years, parents and children create new relationships with one another and renegotiate family rules. Another redefinition of roles occurs when children leave home and parents reflect on their sense of accomplishment and relationships with their children. The role of the parent changes and adapts as they and their children grow.

Depending on the size of the family, parents may be going through several stages at once. Boundaries are being readjusted, relationships are in flux, and issues of autonomy are being questioned; these may be happening all within the same time period. Each family will have different needs, concerns, and experiences depending on the age of their children and their own stage of parent development. The early childhood professional's role is to support and understand the various forces within the family that affect their journey of parenthood.

Standards

Reggio Emilia: An Exemplary Partnership

One of the best examples of a successful school–family partnership is the schools of Reggio Emilia, Italy. Strong and active family involvement is found at every level of school functioning. This is not surprising because the schools were originally founded as parent cooperatives, part of the philosophy that continues to uphold a model of equal and extended partnership. Malaguzzi, the founder and guiding force behind the schools, refers to this balanced responsibility of teachers, parents, and children as a "triad at the center of education" (Edwards, Gandini, & Forman, 1993).

School-based management fosters meaningful participation of all families because all decisions are made by the teachers and parents within each school setting. No area seems the exclusive property of either parents or teachers. Curriculum planning, for instance, depends on the family's involvement, interest, and contribution.

Parents are the core of the individual school boards and on the city-wide school board as an integral part of the decision making process. Frequent meetings inform families of the school's program and bring them up to date on what their children are doing. Smaller groups of parents meet throughout the year with the teachers to talk about their children and the program; individual parent–teacher conferences, which either can request, are held to deal with specific concerns.

There are opportunities to be actively involved in the daily life of the school. Family members, teachers, and town residents build furnishings and maintain materials for the classrooms and the schoolyard and rearrange the space to accommodate program needs. In sessions with teachers and **pedagogistas**, parents learn various educational techniques necessary to the program, such as photography and puppet making, and they use these new skills in the classroom with their children. Using the whole town as a backdrop, families participate in many of the field trips to city landmarks or as small groups visiting a child's home. Recording and transcribing children's activities and projects are often a parent's responsibility (see Chapter 10). Photographs of children and families abound. These elements are the vehicles used to ensure a rich flow of communication.

The schools of Reggio Emilia exemplify the basic tenets of developmentally appropriate practices in the unique relationship with the families they serve. Families have influence and help affect change; in turn, the schools influence and change families. Each becomes a stronger voice for what is in the best interest of the child.

My first teaching position was as an assistant teacher in the 3-year-old group. I remember one child distinctly.

Rebecca spent much of her school day on a teacher's lap or shadowing a teacher as she moved around the classroom and yard. At many staff meetings, Rebecca was the main topic of conversation. The head teacher met with Rebecca's mother on many occasions and talked about the child's need for attention. She suggested strategies to implement at home and she shared the techniques that were being used in the classroom.

What I remember about this story is not so much what the teachers did to help Rebecca become less dependent on adults and more involved with her peers, but how I felt about the mother! I could not understand why Rebecca's mother didn't make the changes we suggested that would give Rebecca the attention she wanted from an adult. After all, we were trying to help and we knew what would work.

I moved on from this classroom to other preschools until I got married and started my own family. A few years later, when my first child was in nursery school, Rebecca's story came back to haunt me. Like Rebecca's mother, I had a younger child. My days were often overloaded: carpooling to nursery school, grocery shopping, home for the baby's morning nap. Then back to nursery school to pick up the carpool, delivering two other children to their homes, and then home to fix lunch. Laundry, scheduling dentist appointments, fielding phone calls, playing with the children after their naps, and dinner preparation made up the rest of the day. At other times, playdates had to be scheduled or a sick child had to get to the doctor. By the time the kids were bathed and put to bed at night, I was exhausted.

That's when I remembered Rebecca's mother. How arrogant of me to judge her for not going right home and doing what a teacher suggested. Her life was already full of schedules and things to do for her family. She didn't have the time or space to take on anything else. I pledged then and there, that when I was teaching again, I would remember that story and be very, very careful of judging parents. I didn't know what they had to deal with until I became one of them.

—Ann

8-2 Building Effective Home–School Relations

A **family-centered approach** to parent–school relationships supports the growth of the family as well as the child. When parents have a meaningful partnership with their children's teachers, it raises their sense of importance and diminishes some of the isolation and anxiety of child-rearing.

truth or fiction?

T F A family-centered approach to family–school relationships supports the family as well as the child.

A family-centered approach recognizes the needs and interests of the family and supports their values and culture.

8-2a What Families Contribute

Families know the child's physical, medical, social, and intellectual history. They know the child as a member of a family and the role that child plays in the family group, the extended family, and the community. Families bring a sense of continuity about the child and provide the context with which the teacher can view the whole child.

Families are the child's teachers too. They teach by word, by example, by all they do and say. Through closer home–school relationships, families can be helped to see that their everyday experiences with their children provide teachable moments and opportunities for educating their children. Teachers support families by keeping them informed about each stage of their child's development, by showing them how to encourage language and thinking skills, and by educating them to children's social needs at any given age.

8-2b What Teachers Contribute

Teachers bring another point of view to the partnership. As child development professionals, they see the child in relation to normal milestones and behaviors. They notice how each child plays with other children in the group and how they relate to other adults. When families need help, teachers become resources and work with them to find psychologists, hearing and speech specialists, or other educational programs, if warranted.

8-2c What Children Gain

Decades of research show the positive effects on achievement when children's parents are involved in their education. Family visibility is especially important for low-income and minority children; their family's presence can

family-centered approach. An approach to parent–school relationships that supports the growth of the family as well as the child.

A true partnership happens when parents and teachers share their strengths with one another for the benefit of the children they love and care for. ◀

A Checklist for Making Your School "Parent Friendly"

> Hold an orientation for parents at a convenient time.
> Provide a place for parents to gather.
> Create a parent bulletin board.
> Give annual parent awards for involvement.
> Create a parent advisory committee.
> Allow parents to help develop school policies and procedures.
> Schedule events on evenings and weekends.
> Provide child care for meetings.
> Establish a book or toy lending library.
> Make informal calls to parents, especially to share a child's successes.
> Provide transportation for parents who need it.
> Provide translators for parents who need them.
> Send appropriate duplicate mailings to noncustodial parents.
> Survey parents for issues of interest and need.
> Develop links to health and social support services.
> Provide resource and referral lists.
> Publish a school newsletter on regular basis.
> Provide multilingual written communications as needed.
> Hire teachers with a strong commitment to supporting families and parents.
> Provide in-service training for teachers in working with parents.
> Hire teachers who are respectful of social, ethnic, and religious backgrounds of parents.
> Hire staff that is reflective of the cultural background of students and parents.
> Encourage regularly scheduled conferences between parents and teachers.
> Offer a variety of family support programs.
> Provide many opportunities for parents to volunteer.
> Provide frequent opportunities for parents to air their concerns.
> Encourage parents to ask questions, to visit, and to call.
> Encourage parents to know what goes on in the classroom.
> Encourage parents to report back on what works well.
> Encourage parents to attend social events.
> Encourage teachers to make home visits.

Figure 8-2

heighten a sense of belonging and motivation. Children's gains are increased when parents are able to monitor their children's progress and reinforce the mission of the school at home. Look at Figure 8-2 to see what schools can do to encourage a family's presence and involvement.

8-3 Enhancing Communication between Home and School

Reaching out to families to establish ongoing interaction is a complex and time-consuming task. Some interactions are planned; some are spontaneous. Good communications

teachsource video case

teachsource video

Watch the TeachSource Video Case entitled, "Communicating with Families: Best Practices in an Early Childhood Setting." After you study the video clip, view the artifacts, and read the teacher interviews and text, reflect on the following questions:

1. A family-centered program acknowledges the critical influence of the family unit on the child's growth and development. What examples does teacher Mona Sanon talk about and model that strengthen the family-centered relationship?

2. What lessons can be learned from the discussion Mona had with a father about his son's block-building skills?

A parent's participation in the child's school life can heighten that child's sense of belonging. ◀

© Cengage Learning®

are at the core of the family–school relationship and go a long way to promote a true partnership.

Active Involvement

There are many options for family involvement in a child's education. Some family members may want to work directly with children and volunteer in the classroom; others may want to help out in the office, the schoolyard, or the kitchen. Some families prefer working with their hands, so they offer to sew, type, build, and paint. For those wanting greater involvement, serving on school boards or parent committees is a good option.

DAP

Scaffolding Parent Involvement

Scaffolding is a developmentally appropriate technique to support learning by giving advice or help on mastering a skill. For families who may feel uneasy about getting involved in the program, scaffolding their experience may offer needed reassurance. From low to high levels of involvement, teachers (*in italics*) support families' involvement (in regular type) by scaffolding their participation (Adapted from Browne & Gordon, 2013):

Low———————————————————————————————Moderate———————————————————————————————High

Take leadership position
Support parent leaders
Participate weekly in classroom
Prepare, observe, support
Create class newsletter
Jointly publish newsletter
Work in the office or library
Visit when parent is there
Help with school events
Send appreciation notes, assist parent
Collect or make materials for class
Have "helping hands" meetings
Participate in parent–teacher conferences
Plan conference carefully, send follow-up note
Attend class or school event
Plan welcoming, send home appreciate notes
Visit the class or help with an activity
Invite parent to work along side you; offer feasible tasks
Stay to observe on arrival or before departure
Be available to talk with parent

Ethics

Bulletin boards. Posted where parents can see them, these boards contain notices about parent meetings, guest speakers, community resources, child care, babysitting, clothing and furniture exchanges, and library story hours. Information regarding health programs, automobile and toy safety, and immunization clinics is also publicized. Post information on cultural events appropriate to the ethnic make-up of the school community.

A parents place. Some schools provide space for a parent lounge, complete with a library of resource books on child rearing. If there is no available space, set up a coffee or juice bar in the office or hall.

Informal contacts. All it takes is a phone call, a note, an e-mail, or a brief talk on a daily basis.

Home visits. The visit might be set up to focus only on the relationship between the teacher and the child, or it might be a way for teachers to meet the whole family and for the family to get acquainted with the teachers. The teacher can use this as a bridge to build a pleasant, casual beginning with this family.

8-3b Family–Teacher Conferences

Family–teacher conferences provide a way of coming together to focus on the needs of the individual child and can be a mutually supportive link between the adults who most want to help the child reach his or her fullest potential possible.

Conferences between family members and teachers are held for many reasons. The initial conference may focus on the child's development, daily habits, and interests, as well as the parents' view of the child and their expectations. Further into the school year, both the family

8-3a Keeping in Touch

Five of the most common ways teachers can involve and inform parents are:

Classroom newsletters. Weekly or monthly, a newsletter gives a general idea of what the children are doing, any special events taking place in class, and personal information about new babies, vacations, or other important events in the lives of the children. Be sure the newsletter is written in the language of the parents of the children in the class.

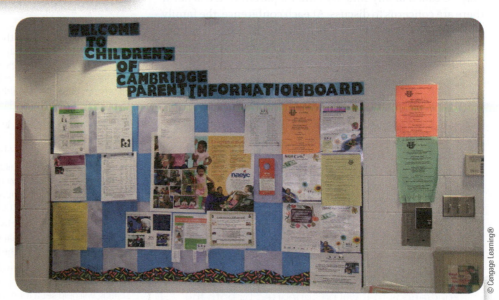

© Cengage Learning®

Bulletin boards provide valuable information and resources for children and their families. ◄

The Importance of a Classroom Newsletter

Why	Newsletter Example
To Keep Families Informed	Next Thursday is our first nature walk around the school and the neighborhood. Make sure your child wears boots or waterproof shoes to keep feet dry while we explore. Join us on our walk, if you can.
For Insights into Learning	The nature walk is part of our science curriculum. We want the children to explore the out-of-doors to stimulate their natural curiosity and delight in their discoveries. Firsthand experiences with the texture of tree bark or birds' nests help a child create a base of knowledge on which to build their understanding of the natural world around them.
To Bring Learning Home	You might want to try this at home with the whole family. Walk around your neighborhood and look at what is growing. Take a bag or basket to collect leaves and other natural materials. The children can make a collage out of them when you return home. Comment as the children make discoveries: "I wonder what makes the leaves so green." "What do you think happens to that flower when it snows?" Open-ended questions such as these help children clarify their own thinking and learning.
To Keep Communication Flowing	Several questions about our guidance philosophy came up at the last family meeting. We are putting together an insert for next month's newsletter and we would like your help on one of the topics. How do you deal with bedtime issues (delaying tactics, such as one more story, another glass of water, etc.) in your home? What works for you? Talk with Mrs. Olga or Miss Leona if you want to participate.

© Cengage Learning®

Figure 8-3 Classroom newsletters enlarge a family's understanding of what their child is experiencing and extends the learning between home and school.

Digital Download

and teachers will want an up-to-date assessment of the child's progress, noting especially the strengths of the child and areas in which improvement is needed. A conference may be called at any time by either a parent or a teacher if there are concerns to discuss. At each conference, the family and the teacher establish mutual goals and expectations. For a conference model that is satisfying and productive to both parties, see Figure 8-4.

truth or fiction?

T (F) The primary purpose of a family–teacher conference is to discuss the child's inappropriate behavior.

Family–teacher conferences cover many subjects, including behavior. The conference is primarily used to establish mutual goals and expectations that will be supported by both the family and the teacher.

Steps to Successful Parent/Family–Teacher Conferences

Be prepared, be organized, and have a clear purpose. Use a written format to maintain focus. Ask for staff input and up-to-date examples of child's work or behavior. Ask parents to help build the agenda.

Put the family at ease with a warm welcome and thanks for attending. Help them relax by stating some of their child's strengths, citing examples. Complement them on something you have noticed, either with their own child or when in the classroom with other children. Be sensitive to any cultural difference that may arise.

Ask, don't tell. Begin with an open-ended question ("How is that new schedule working out?" or "Can you tell me more?"). Learn how to listen carefully to what family members say.

Keep the focus on the child. Keep the conversation based on mutual concerns and how to help each other. Create mutual goals. Make a plan of action together and discuss ways to follow through and stay in touch.

Write a brief report after the conference. Make a special note of the important issues that were discussed, solutions that were agreed to, and dates for checking progress.

Successful conferences are a result of a good process and clear communications. A quiet space, sufficient time, and comfortable seating will help set a tone for open and honest dialogue.

Figure 8-4

© Cengage Learning®

Brain Research says

What is it that families really need to know about their children's brain development? Thanks to the media and popular press, brain research stories abound, and parents' interest is captured by headlines that call out "Make your baby smarter through Mozart!" and "These toys will increase your child's brain power!" We can help families understand what they most need to know by telling them a few simple facts.

First, families need to know the *significant role of the parent/family/ caregiver* in providing the kind of stimulation and care babies and young children need for their brains to grow and be healthy. Parents are the child's first caregivers and teachers and through their sensitive nurturing, they build secure attachments with their child. Babies are wired to feel, think, respond, and move, and the gestures, reactions, and touching by their families is critical to their brain development and learning. Parents need to respond quickly to their children's cues when they cry for attention or support because this builds children's trust in their caregivers, in themselves, and in the world about them. Touching is important. Children feel more secure and reassured when they are held, cuddled, and snuggled.

Too much stress elevates cortisol levels in the brain to a degree that can destroy or reduce brain cells. Encourage families to reduce and/or remove as much stress from their children's lives as possible. This often means that families need to address their own stressful situations as well.

Second, families need to know the *significance role of the environment.* Nature and nurture do not operate separately but in partnership in the brain's architecture. Genes and the environment work together to influence learning. The brain is in constant motion, growing new connections based on the activities and experiences of the child.

Families can be encouraged to provide an enriched learning environment that offers hands-on activities that include the five senses. Daily activities offer challenges for growth. When a parent asks, "How can we make more room for your new puzzles?" this helps children learn to think, solve problems, and listen to other people's suggestions. Children love repetition (How many times do you read "Goodnight Moon" or sing "Eensy Weensy Spider"?). The brain loves repetition too, because

it creates more neural pathways for learning. Language, and lots of it, also help the brain grow new connections, so parents should talk, sing, make up silly songs, recite poetry, talk, chat, and play language games with their young children. Music—all kinds of music—stimulates all aspects of the brain. Art activities prompt the part of the brain that deals with cognition, memory, and emotion. All physical activity stimulates brain growth and helps to fight obesity.

Families are fundamental teachers in every day situations. They need to know that much of what they are already doing is helping their children's brain activity in just the right way. They should feel confident that they are able to provide the stimulation for brain growth. Expensive toys and CDs are not the answer. Parents are.

Questions

1. What do you think of the claims being made about enhancing a child's brain power? Which ones make sense to you after reading through the articles in this text?
2. How would you encourage families to support their child's expanding brain?

8-3c Maintaining Privacy and Confidentiality

The more involved families are in the workings of the school, the more important it is to establish guidelines for protecting the privacy of all the families enrolled. Family members who volunteer in the office, the classroom, or on a field trip must understand that they cannot carry tales out of school about any of the children, the teachers, the administration, or other families. The school must be clear about its expectations for ensuring such privacy and communicate policies. Family members who work on advisory boards, planning committees, or other activities that allow them access to the school office should be sensitive to the confidentiality issue and respect the privacy of every family enrolled in the school.

summary

8.1 Family–school partnerships are strengthened as teachers come to know who makes up today's families. The definition of parent and family is broadly interpreted to include all who care for and nurture young children in their homes. The wide diversity of families calls on teachers to adapt their attitudes and programs to meet the needs of single, adoptive, homeless, divorced, working, gay and lesbian, teenage, grandparents, multiracial, and non-English-speaking families. Understanding and valuing family culture is an important way to strengthen the relationship, as is knowing stages of parenthood and child-rearing practices.

8.2 Home–school relations are most effective when families and teachers each understand and appreciate the unique contribution and role they play in the life of the child. Families provide the history and intimate knowledge of each child, whereas teachers bring a larger perspective based on years of teaching many children. The positive effects on children's achievement are well documented.

8.3 Communications between families and schools are enhanced when family members become actively involved in the life of the school. Keeping in touch through phoning, e-mail, newsletters, and bulletin boards helps teachers support open communication. Family–teacher conferences provide opportunities to set mutual goals for children, resolve conflicts, and problem-solve together.

web resources

National Coalition for Parent Involvement in Education
  http://www.ncpie.org
Zero to Three **http://www.zerotothree.org**

The Fred Rogers Company:
  http://www.fredrogers.org

references

Baumrind, D. (1972). Socialization and instrumental competence in young children. In W. W. Hartrup (Ed.), *The young child: Review of research* (Vol. 2). Washington, DC: National Association for the Education of Young Children.

Browne, K. W., & Gordon, A. M. (2013). *Early childhood field experience: Learning to teach well.* Upper Saddle River, NJ: Pearson Education.

Eisenbud, L. (2002, March). Working with nontraditional families. *Child Care Information Exchange,* pp. 16–20.

Galinsky, E. (1987). *Between generations.* Reading, MA: Addison-Wesley.

Hyun, E. (1998). *Making sense of developmentally and culturally appropriate practice (DCAP) in early childhood education.* New York: Peter Lang.

KIDSCOUNT data center (2014). *Children in immigrant families.* Annie B. Casey Foundation.

Livingston, G. (Sept. 4, 2013a). *At grandmother's house we stay.* Pew Research Center. Retrieved February 13, 2014 at **www.pewresearch.org**

Livingston, G. (July 2, 2013b). *The rise of single fathers.* Pew Research Center. Retrieved February 13, 2014. At **www.pewresearch.org**

Nemeth, K. (2012). *Basics of supporting dual language learners: An introduction for educators of children from birth through age 8.* Washington, DC: National Association for the Education of Young Children.

U.S. Bureau of the Census. (2012). *Populations estimates and projections (2012).* Washington, DC: U.S. Government Printing Office. Retrieved February 14, 2014.

U.S. Department of Homeland Security. *Yearbook of immigration statistics: 2011.* Washington, DC: U.S. Department of Homeland Security Statistics, 2012. Retrieved February 14, 2014.

9 creating environments

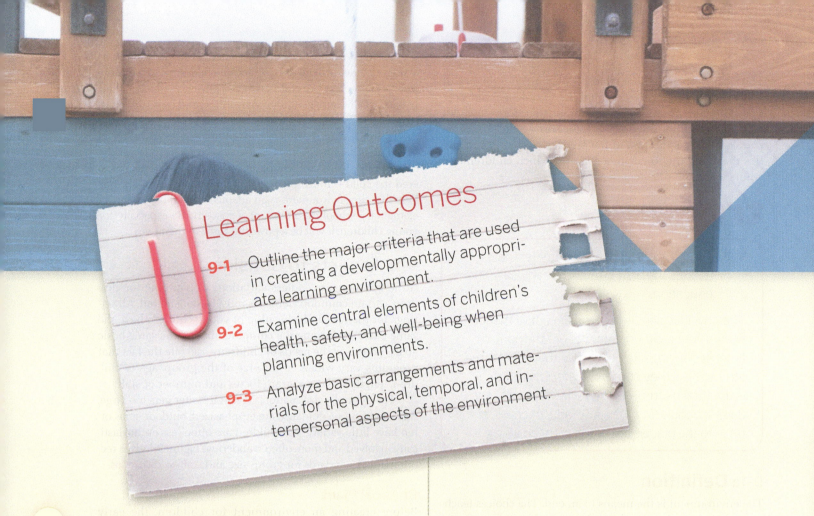

Learning Outcomes

9-1 Outline the major criteria that are used in creating a developmentally appropriate learning environment.

9-2 Examine central elements of children's health, safety, and well-being when planning environments.

9-3 Analyze basic arrangements and materials for the physical, temporal, and interpersonal aspects of the environment.

© iStockphoto.com/Realitybytes

truth or fiction

T F The physical plant of a center is what defines the environment in early care and education.

T F Health and safety are relatively simple to prepare for in an early childhood environment.

T F Daily schedules define the structure of programs.

9-1 Creating the Environment

The **environment** is where children play out the themes of childhood: their interests, triumphs, problems, and concerns. An environment for children, therefore, includes all of the conditions that affect their surroundings and the people in it. It is the sum of the physical and human qualities that combine to create a space in which children and adults work and play together.

truth*or* *fiction?*

T (**F**) The physical plant of a center is what defines the environment in early care and education.

The physical plant is just one aspect of the environment. Other elements are the content teachers arrange, the schedule they create; the atmosphere they communicate. Environment is the total picture—from the traffic flow to the daily schedule, from the numbers of chairs at a table to the placement of the guinea pig cage.

9-1a Definition

The environment is the means to an end. The choices teachers make concerning the physical setting (the equipment and materials, the room arrangement, the playground, and the facilities available), the **temporal** setting (timing for transitions, routines, activities), and the interpersonal setting (number and nature of teachers, ages and number of children, types and style of interactions among them) combine to support the program goals. Teachers plan a program in which the goals are reflected in the environment in the following ways:

1. The *room and yard* are arranged to give maximal exposure to the materials and equipment teachers want children to use.
2. The *daily schedule* is arranged in ways that provide the time blocks needed to teach content when and how they want to teach it.
3. The *relationships and interactions* among the teachers, between families and staff, and with children are warm and meaningful.

---

environment. All those conditions that affect children's surroundings and the people in them; the physical, interpersonal, and temporal aspects of an early childhood setting.

temporal. Having to do with time and time sequence; in the early childhood setting, refers to scheduling and how time is sequenced and spent, both at home and in school.

staff-to-child ratio. A numerical description of the number of staff to children, which will vary depending on the age of the children and the type of program activity and is established to provide for adult supervision of children at all times.

Each environment is unique. There is no such thing as a single model or ideal setting for all children. The environments adults create for children have a powerful effect on their behavior. Children's play is strongly influenced by settings and materials. Any set of behaviors can be fostered—or discouraged—by the ways the indoor and outdoor spaces are designed and used. The environment is sometimes referred to as "the curriculum's textbook" (Heroman, et al., 2010) and is considered the child's "third teacher" (after parents and caregivers). Whether the environment is an adapted church basement, an elementary school classroom, or a space made especially for young children, it will be a powerful force in their lives.

9-1b Aspects to Consider

Although there are endless variations in planning for children, certain common elements must be considered. All settings for the care and education of young children have the same basic environmental components and the same basic goals—meeting the needs of children—despite the fact that programs vary widely in the size of the group, age of children, length of day, program focus, and number of staff.

For example, size matters. When a center gets too large, rules and routine guidance are emphasized, outdoor areas often have little variety, and children are often less enthusiastically involved and more often wandering. Figure 9-1 gives recommended standards for group size and **staff-to-child ratios**.

Physical Plant

Before creating an environment for children, the early childhood education teacher must analyze the physical plant. A building that is inviting and beautiful beckons children to enter; a space with color and light encourages children to play with both. Many settings use space designed for other purposes, such as a family home, a church basement, or an empty elementary school classroom. The size and shape of the designated space determine how to plan for safe and appropriate use.

Resources

In planning the environment, the teacher must know what kinds of resources are available:

> *The first is financial assets.* Priority should be given to teacher salaries and benefits, equipment and materials, and other related services (maintenance, office help, bus service). By knowing the extent of the fiscal boundaries and budget limits, a teacher can plan a complete environment.

> *The second is community options.* Good environmental principles do not depend on numerous or expensive materials, buildings, or pieces of equipment. Some equipment can be made, borrowed, or purchased secondhand. In church-based schools, annual rummage sales provide dress-up clothes, books, toys, and some appliances. Families can provide computer or photo supplies, wood scraps, or materials for dramatic play kits. Community sources, such as the public library storyteller or a seniors group, may be available for extended experiences for the

Recommended Staff-to-Child Ratios within Group Size*

Ages of Children	Group Size										
	6	8	10	12	14	16	18	20	22	24	28
Infants (birth–12 mo)	1:3	1:4									
Toddlers (12–24 mo)	1:3	1:4	1:5	1:4							
Two-year-olds (24–30 mo)		1:4	1:5	1:6							
Two-and-a-half-year-olds (30–36 mo)			1:5	1:6	1:7						
Three-year-olds					1:7	1:8	1:9	1:10			
Four-year-olds						1:8	1:9	1:10			
Five-year-olds						1:8	1:9	1:10			
Six- to 8-year-olds								1:10	1:11	1:12	
Nine- to 12-year-olds										1:12	1:14

*Smaller group sizes and lower staff-to-child ratios have been found to be strong predictors of compliance with indicators of quality, such as positive interactions among staff and children and developmentally appropriate curriculum.

Figure 9-1 These two aspects of the environment affect the quality of children's education experience (NAEYC, 2005).

Two- to 5-year-old stature shows they can use and notice up to about 3 feet.

For crawling infants and toddlers, space consists primarily of the floor.

School-aged children can use and learn from the space up to about 5 feet, roughly their own height.

© Cengage Learning®

To rescale the space, teachers shift from an adult perspective to a child's scale. Getting on one's knees provides a glimpse of the environment from the child's point of view; child space is measured from the floor and playground up.

children. Effective fund-raising provides an added source of revenue in many schools and centers.

> *The third is the human resources.* Adults do their best with children when their abilities, experience, and availability are matched with what is expected of them. First-year teachers' resources are best expended in the classroom, whereas master teachers are ready to use their expertise in other ways, such as orienting parents or evaluating curriculum materials. The teachers themselves are the most responsive part of the environment; it is they who converse with, smile at, appreciate, give information to, and see the individuality of each child. They are the ones who create the space, the time, and the atmosphere that will engage children's curiosity and involvement. Just as we try to match children's developing skills to the tasks at hand, so too should we consider individual people as part of an environment's resources.

Program Goals

The program must be defined in relationship to the physical space because the goals and objectives of the program are expressed directly in the arrangement of the environment.

The specific goals of an early childhood education program will vary widely because early childhood settings contain such a wide range of ages and educational philosophies. Three general goals in designing environments (Harms et al., 2004) are:

> To plan soft and responsive settings that avoid behavior problems
> To set up predictable environments that encourage independence
> To create a stimulating space for active learning

When children walk into a classroom, the environment should communicate how they are to live and work in that setting (Figure 9-2). Children should receive clear messages about what they can and cannot do there, as well as cues that tell them:

> Where they are free to move to and where they cannot go
> How they will be treated
> Who will be there with them
> What material and equipment they can use
> How long they may play
> That they are safe there
> What is expected of them

For instance, when it is time to go outside, the doors are opened. If children need to stay off of a piece of equipment, it is marked by dividers or a flag, and a teacher stationed nearby explains the instruction. Children know that they matter when they are welcomed each day, and they know their time is valued when teachers tell them how long they have to complete a project or play sequence and when that time is nearly up. It is the teacher's understanding of all the environmental factors and how they are related to one another that indicates the quality in a program.

9-1c Developmentally Appropriate Learning Environments

We are all affected by our environment, and for young children, this is especially so. Although some children are particularly sensitive to stimulation (noise, light, clutter), all children's behavior is affected by what is in front of them. Therefore, we must pay attention to what is in their environment and what happens during their stay there. High quality programs will have important elements that work well for the children and teachers (Copple, 2010).

Key Elements

Developmentally appropriate environments will have most of the following key elements:

1. *Create a high-activity, low-stress, and brain-compatible environment.* Positive changes occur in the brain when a child is engaged in a learning experience, and the brain under threat will flood with cortisol and downshift to a defensive stance. Centers that allow small groups to form and focus will stimulate learning without pressure or stress to perform or too long of a wait (Figures 9-5 through 9-7).

2. *Build culturally and linguistically responsive environments.* First and foremost, it is important that the environment reflect the cultures of the children in the classroom. If the spaces do not look like home, or the teachers do not look like the children, it is critical that the interpersonal and temporal aspects of their environment complement their home culture and home languages as much as possible. (Figure 9-2).

3. *Be sure that children have access to enough toys and materials.* Make sure that supplies are stored in such a way that adults do not have to hand them to children each time they will be used. Equipment placed at a child's height on open, low shelving permits children to proceed at their own pace and to select materials without depending on adults to serve them. "A developmentally appropriate learning environment is designed for individual children to be messy, noisy and quiet, alone and social, and active and still," says Greenman (2004). "It is designed to accommodate much STUFF—loose parts—the raw materials of discovery for active hands and minds."(Figures 9-8 & 9-9).

4. *Give children an opportunity to make choices.* Choosing where to play helps children practice self-direction. Children should also be able to decide with whom they would like to play and with which teachers they would like to establish close relationships. (Figure 9-11).

5. *Consider the developmental level of the children.* Be developmentally aware; know what children in the class are capable of, where they are now in their development, and what the next step should be. Three-year-olds who just learned about zipping will still need a teacher at their level to hold the housing so that they can get the zipper going.

6. *Give children ways to identify their space.* Label cubbies with their names, a photo, or a familiar picture of

The Environment Mirrors the Goals of the Program

Children Need To . . .	So the Environment Should . . .
Be treated as individuals, with unique strengths and developmental goals	Ensure that the staff-to-child ratio supports one-to-one interactions so that they can be observed for goal-setting
	Provide private as well as public spaces so that children can experience group and solitary play
	Ensure that children have ready access to teachers and materials that will match the developmental level of the group
	Provide a balance of quiet and active times
See themselves and their family culture represented positively in the environment; be exposed to cultural diversity in meaningful ways	Include pictures, books, dolls, dramatic play materials, activities, and people that reflect many cultures and life experiences
	Staff teachers who understand and value the children's home cultures and family practices
	Provide opportunities for various cultural habits, activities, and celebrations to occur
Have an opportunity to make choices and participate in independent learning	Be arranged to encourage free exploration and a clear view of what is available
	Offer a variety of activity centers so that children can explore, manipulate, probe
	Allow large blocks of time for child-initiated free play so that children can make more than one choice
	Provide an adequate number of trained teachers to support self-discovery
Learn to be part of a group	Be set up for group play with chairs around the tables, easels adjacent to one another
	Facilitate regular scheduling of small and large group times, which children are encouraged to attend and participate in
	Include trained staff who select developmentally appropriate group activities for the group
Become responsible for the setting and take care of the equipment and materials	Schedule clean-up times as part of the daily routine
	Include teachers and children working together to restore order
	Allow time for children to be instructed in the proper use of materials and be made aware of their general care
Be aware of the behavioral limits of the school setting	Ensure that the teachers and the daily schedule reflect the important rules of behavior
	Include teachers who deal with behavior problems in a fair and consistent way
	Allow plenty of time during transitions so that children can move from one activity to another without stress
	Be arranged to avoid runways and dead ends created by furniture
Be with adults who will supervise and facilitate play and encourage learning throughout the day	Be set up before children arrive so that teachers are free to greet them
	Encourage teacher–child interactions through the use of small groups and a time schedule that allows for in-depth interactions

© Cengage Learning®

Figure 9-2

their family so that they can see where to put up their wraps, artwork, and other personal belongings.

7. *See that children are responsible for caring for the equipment and materials.* Establish a clean-up time in the daily schedule and allow children time to help restore the room and yard. Label shelves and cupboards with pictures of what is stored there so that children can readily find where things belong.

8. *Involve children in the process of planning and setting up the environment.* Let the children help decide what they want to learn by developing areas and units around what they bring into class. For instance, Fu-Ning's guinea pig had babies, so teacher Tanya arranged with his

mother to bring the pet family to school for a visit, and then sent a newsletter to families asking for other pets to visit. Small groups took field trips to a pet store, and the dramatic-play corner became a pet shop and animal hospital.

9. *Provide children with enough time.* One of the ways children learn is to repeat an activity over and over again. Large blocks of time in the daily schedule—especially for routines—let children proceed to learn at an unhurried pace.

10. *Allow children to solve their own problems without adult intervention whenever possible.* The Montessori method believes children have a drive for mastery, so

Simple/Complex

"Play equipment can differ in its holding power; i.e., the capacity to sustain attention. . . . A simple unit has one manipulable aspect; a complex unit has two different kinds of materials combined; and a super unit has three different kinds of materials that go together."

Simple: swings, climbers, sand pile with no toys

Complex: dramatic play with only a kitchen

Super: climbers with slides and ropes, playhouse with kitchen, dress-up clothes, dolls, and/or playdough; sand area with equipment and/or water

Adding features increase complexity. Make simple playdough more complex by offering cookie cutters; add toothpicks or a garlic press and it becomes a super unit.

Open/Closed

Open (many ways to use): sand and water, dress-up, collage materials, painting

Closed (one way to manipulate): puzzles, many board games, most Montessori equipment

In-between: Toys such as Legos®, TinkerToys®, blocks, balls

Softness/Hardness

Soft: rugs, pillows, playdough, finger paints, grass, sand, swings

Hard: tile floor, wooden furniture, asphalt, cement

Intrusion/Seclusion

Intrusion (places where children can enter or go through easily): housekeeping, table toys, even the entire environment are often highly intrusive areas

Seclusion (places where children can be alone or with only one other): cubbies, a fort, or under a table become secret places

High mobility/Low mobility

High (whole-body places and activities): outdoors, climbers, bike lanes, gym mats

Low (sitting-still places and activities): puzzles and games, story and group times, nap time

In-between: dramatic play, block corner, woodworking

© Cengage Learning®

Figure 9-3 Key dimensions when considering an early childhood environment. (Adapted from Prescott, 1994)

encourage children to find out for themselves what is or is not successful.

11. *Accept children's efforts.* To support children in their quest for independence, be ready to accept how children may put shoes on the "wrong feet."

12. *Communicate expectations.* Let children know what they are expected to do. Prompt children by giving them clues that indicate how to proceed: "If you pull up your underpants first, it will be easier to get your shorts up," the teacher tells Raymond, who is waiting for an adult to dress him. "Good. You've got the back up. Now reach around the front." By pointing out how he is succeeding, the teacher communicates confidence in a child's ability to accomplish the task.

13. *Be sure staff expectations are consistent.* The teaching team should set common goals for each child and reinforce them consistently. Children are confused if one teacher expects them to get their own cots ready for nap and another teacher does it for them.

14. *Make it safe to make a mistake.* We learn from experience. Let children know it is perfectly acceptable, indeed inevitable, that they will make mistakes. Help them deal with the consequences of their actions. Chelo spills her juice, so Dina points to the sponge and mop in the bucket. She watches and assists Chelo clean up the table, reinforcing her efforts by commenting on her scrubbing ability. Soon, the rest of the snack group is helping with napkins and sponges, too.

15. *Give credit where it is due.* Provide feedback so that children will know when they have been successful. Let children take some credit for their own accomplishments.

16. *Let children teach one another.* Encourage children to share the skills they have mastered with their peers. Those who can tie shoes enjoy helping their friends with stubborn laces or slippery knots. Encourage those who share home languages to help each other understand and communicate.

A well-planned environment opens up infinite possibilities for children to achieve a feeling of self-satisfaction while they explore the boundaries of their own beings.

Core Values

Putting a program's values to work is essential for an environment to be effective in achieving its goals. At the heart of all good early childhood education programs is the recognition that each child is unique, deserving of respect, and a part of a family. Such environments encourage children to learn tolerance and acceptance of the diversity in our world.

Each child has the right to achieve full potential and to develop positive self-esteem. Each family deserves support for the unique role it plays. Part of the commitment of the early childhood teacher is to help children learn to value one another's uniqueness, the differences as well as the similarities. Three core values in early childhood education are anti-bias, self-help, and inclusion. All blueprints in this chapter reflect these values.

The Anti-Bias Environment. The anti-bias environment encourages children and adults to:

> Explore the differences and similarities that make up our individual and group identities
> Develop skills for identifying and countering the hurtful impact of bias on themselves and their peers (Derman-Sparks & Olsen Edwards, 2010)

Because culture consists of the various ways people do similar activities, the physical environment is used to explore the many ways people do the basic human tasks of everyday life. The anti-bias approach to creating environments has its roots in the theories of Erikson, Piaget, Vygotsky, and Maslow (see Chapter 4). Because children begin to notice and construct classifications and evaluative categories as early as 2 to 3 years of age, educational environments must develop a child's basic sense of trust and mastery so that children can learn to understand themselves and become tolerant and compassionate toward others. The environment develops from three sources: the children and their activities, the teachers' awareness of the developmental needs and learning styles of the group, and societal events.

The anti-bias approach takes a broad view of a classroom, as a kind of "mini-society" in which children and adults work together to form a just world. The prevalence of stereotyping in society affects children's development, so teachers try to counteract such bias formation. A kindergarten teacher shows the children a magazine picture entitled "Brides of America." All of the women pictured are Caucasian. She asks, "What do you think of this picture?" Sarita responds, "That's a silly picture. My mom was a bride, and she's a Filipina."

The Self-Help Environment. The self-help environment promotes independent behavior in children and is a widespread practice in early childhood education programs. Self-concept is based on what we know about ourselves, which includes the ability to take care of our own needs. To care for oneself, to feel capable of learning, and to solve problems all are related to feelings of self-esteem. Self-esteem is the value we place on ourselves—how much we like or dislike who we are. Helping children achieve a positive self-concept and self-esteem is the most important part of teaching. The development of a strong sense of self-esteem is a lifelong process; its origins are in the early years.

Diversity

Why Diversity?

Why stress how we are different, when it is more comfortable to create an environment in which everyone does the same thing and gets along fine?

Culturally relevant and anti-bias environments helps teachers work with children and families by aligning what happens in a program with how children live in their home culture. It helps at a fundamental level to address issues of discrimination and prejudice with a proactive approach that can help children develop the following:

> **Positive self-concept.** Curiosity and creativity stem from being able to affect the environment and what is in it. When Jamal says his baby's hair is fuzzy like his, his smile tells how good he feels about it.

> **Awareness.** All people have interests and feelings, both about themselves and about others. Yoko notices that her classmate Julie runs and throws her arms around her dad, but she prefers a less demonstrative greeting.

> **Respect for diversity.** This stems from the ability to classify similarities and differences and then to appreciate both. Children making self-portraits for their class books choose different colors of paper for drawing faces, but all of them use the same markers to draw in their features.

> **Skills in communication and problem solving.** Learning how to express thoughts and feelings includes being able to hear others and finding peaceful ways to resolve conflicts. Jim and LaNell are quick to tell Eben that he can't play, but they find out that telling him he is "too little" is not a good enough reason to leave him out, and they must either try to include him or make a claim for privacy.

Quality environments for children will be *high-activity, low-stress, and brain-compatible* if kids can be messy and neat, noisy and quiet, alone and social, active and still. There need to be loose parts to play around with—both for the body and the mind.

©iStockphoto.com

anti-bias. A phrase describing the development of curriculum that emphasizes an inclusive look at people and problems, extending the tenets of multicultural education and pluralism.

A **self-help** environment has as one of its fundamental goals the development of children's own skills—fostering their mastery of basic abilities that will allow them to become responsible for their own personal care, their own learning, their own emotional controls, their own problem solving, and their own choices and decisions. A self-help environment has its roots in the Euro-American belief that **autonomy** and independence are important.

In planning a self-help environment, teachers look at self-care skills of dressing, eating, toileting, and resting as cornerstones for self-help. There will be materials for learning fastening and zipping; shelves will be low and well-marked so that toys are available and attractively displayed. Children will participate actively in snack time—their teachers sitting with them—and learn to manage some of their own nap items.

The Inclusive Environment. The inclusive environment addresses the practice of placing children with disabilities in the same classroom as children without disabilities. Known as **full inclusion**, it reflects the law in the United States that mandates that children with special needs be placed in the **least restrictive environment** and that all children need an environment that is safe, secure, and predictable with materials and activities that provide for their development (Allen & Cowdery, 2015).

When a child with disabilities has different developmental needs than other children of the same age, **accommodations** must be made. These changes may require either adding something to the environment that is not already there or using something in the environment in a different way. Children with motor disabilities need different adaptations than those with hearing or language disabilities or with visual impairments. Physical changes may be necessary, modifications in the schedule may be recommended, or individualizing activities may be best. Parents will be the best source of information about the child, and other readings or specialists can be further guides.

Three key concepts are helpful to remember: access, usability, and maximizing learning. Figure 9-4 is an abbreviated checklist for adaptations to create an inclusive environment.

---

self-help. The act of helping or providing for oneself without dependence on others; in early childhood terms, activities that a child can do alone, without adult assistance.

autonomy. The state of being able to exist and operate independently, of being self-sufficient rather than dependent on others.

full inclusion. Providing the "least restrictive environment" for children with physical limitations.

least restrictive environment. The least restrictive environment (LRE) is a special education term meaning that the child should be educated in the environment that is the least different from the regular classroom as long as the child can learn in that environment.

accommodations. Alterations in the way tasks are presented or activities experienced that allow children with learning disabilities to compete the same as other children.

9-2 Central Elements in Planning

Many people live and work in the early childhood education environment.

Directors and office personnel, maintenance people, cooks or food delivery services, bus drivers, and families have tasks that make special demands on the environment. But teachers and children use the environment the most. In the environment, the health, safety, and well-being of those participating is critical to its success as a place to learn.

> Who are the *children* who will use this space and what are their needs? Basic needs and educational goals are met through focused attention on the environment.

> What needs of the *teachers* are addressed? The quality of the working environment is an important predictor of a program's effectiveness.

> How are *families* made welcome in the environment? In settings where adults are free to stay, a comfortable place to talk or read is desirable, whereas those who participate need a place to put their belongings.

> Is the school environment *accessible*? All adults who come to the site need adequate and safe parking facilities. They need to know how to reach teachers and children in emergencies, including how to reach school authorities after hours, and they need to have a place for community notices and for written communication to parents and among families.

truthor*fiction?*

T (**F**) Health and safety are relatively simple to prepare for in an early childhood environment.

Health and safety issues are varied and complex. Teachers much be properly trained and programs well stocked with readily accessible materials at all times.

Keeping Children Healthy

Regardless of how many children are in the setting or for how long, the first priority is to provide for their health and safety. Health, safety, and nutrition are closely related because the quality of one affects the quality of the others (Marotz, 2015). Therefore, programs for children must establish policies that provide for the protection, service, and education of child health and safety at all times. Government regulations and professional recommendations vary, but all establish some kind of standards to ensure good health and safety practices.

Checklist for an Inclusive Classroom

	Challenges	Accessing the Environment	Learning through the Environment
Physical	How to enhance or adapt for those with difficulties moving or who move too much Consult a physical and/or occupational therapist	Wide doorways Ramps, stairs with handrails Door ad drawer handles Chairs with armrests or cube chairs	Varied surfaces and heights Space for gross-motor activity Quiet and comfortable spaces
Visual	How to enhance visuals for those with low or no vision Consult orientation and mobility specialist	Contrasting colors on edges and when surfaces change Eliminate glare and clutter Use spot lighting	Visual displays at eye level Large-print materials available Daily schedule in words and pictures Seat children close to center of activity
Auditory	How to enhance auditory aspects for deaf, hearing impaired, or poor auditory discrimination skills Consult parents about sign language	Dampen background noise Use nonauditory (silent) signals	Pair auditory messages with visuals Seat children so they can see faces Consider sign language
Social	How to adapt social environment for impulsive behaviors, attention deficits Consult with school psychologist or behavior specialist Creative use of staffing may be needed	Provide predictable schedule Offer program that can accept a range of activity levels	Note experiences for positive self-esteem Check materials and toys to include representation of all kinds of people Offer times for pairings of children with complementary abilities

Figure 9-4 When designing an inclusive environment, keep in mind that the environment needs to be safe and to invite everyone to participate, learn, and communicate. (Adapted from Haugen, 1997)

Sanitation

When groups of people live in close quarters, proper sanitary conditions are imperative to prevent the spread of disease. For an early childhood center, the physical plant must have adequate washing and toileting facilities for both children and adults. The number and size of toilets and wash basins are usually prescribed by local health or other regulatory agencies.

Teachers must engage in the daily practices of preventive health care. These include hand washing (the number-one way to prevent unnecessary spread of germs) and an approach known as *universal*, or *standard, precautions*. Through gentle reminders and role modeling, teachers help children learn the habit of washing their hands at important times such as before snack and mealtimes. All programs should be equipped with sets of latex gloves and plastic bags to properly handle and dispose of anything with blood or fecal material. Intact skin is a natural barrier against disease, and it may not always be possible to use gloves. However, it is essential that hands be washed immediately after any toileting activity. All areas for eating, diapering, and toileting must be cleaned and sanitized, using a bleach solution after cleaning away visible soiling.

The classrooms require daily cleaning, and equipment that is used regularly should be sanitized on a periodic basis. Nontoxic paint must be used in all circumstances, including outdoor equipment, cribs, and for art activities with children. Classroom dress-up clothing, pillows, nap blankets, and cuddle toys all need regular laundering, either at school or at home.

Temperature, Ventilation, and Lighting

Heating and ventilation should be comfortable for the activity level of the children and should change when weather conditions do. Adequate, non-glare lighting is a necessity. Studies indicate that uniform, fluorescent lighting may not be the best environment for children; therefore, a mixture of lighting such as is in homes is preferable. Rooms should have some means of controlling light (shades, blinds). Cross-ventilation is necessary in all rooms where children eat, sleep, or play. Proper heating and insulation are important.

Communicable Disease

Some people question the advisability of early group care on the grounds that it exposes children to too much illness. Others claim that such exposure at an early age helps children build up resistance, and that they are actually stronger and healthier by the time they enter primary grades. The Centers for Disease Control and Prevention (2014) has concluded that although infants and toddlers face a higher risk for colds and viruses, day care does not increase children's illnesses at older ages and is not a risk overall.

Parents should be notified when normal childhood diseases (such as chickenpox) or common problems (such as head lice) occur in the classroom. Infections of special concern to adults include chickenpox, hepatitis A, and cytomegalovirus (CMV). A description of the symptoms and the dates of exposure and incubation period may be helpful to parents. They can then assist in controlling the spread of the disease.

Professionalism

What's a Teacher to Do?

Teachers need to be professionally trained in first aid and cardiopulmonary resuscitation (CPR). In addition, there are several common health conditions (Needlman & Needlman, 1995) that require informed and responsive action.

Condition	Professional Response
1. Allergies and asthma	Post a list of all children with chronic conditions; check ingredient lists on foods; watch what triggers reactions.
2. Scrapes and cuts	Reassure and sympathize with child; supervise child's washing with soaped pad and caring comments; use packs of ice or frozen peas in towel for swelling.
3. Bumps on the head	Notify parents of any loss of consciousness and watch for signs for 2 to 3 days.
4. Sand in eyes	Remind child "Do not rub!"; have child wash hands and cover eye with tissue; normal eye tearing will bring sand to inside corner of eye; remove with clean tissue.
5. Splinters	Clean area with alcohol and remove with tweezers or cover with adhesive strip and let parent remove.
6. Conjunctivitis	"Pinkeye" is highly contagious; watch for excess eye rubbing and red eyes; have child wash hands; isolate with washable toys until parent takes child home and gets treatment.
7. Head lice	Distressing but not dangerous; wash shared clothing, stuffed animals, bedding; vacuum rugs and furniture; remove hats, combs, and brushes from dramatic-play area; send notices home and inspect children's hair for 2 to 3 weeks.
8. Chickenpox	Isolate child until parents pick up; alert all parents about contagious period; watch for signs on all children for 3 weeks after exposure.
9. Strep throat	Send home notices; wash all equipment that might carry germs.
10. Lingering coughs	At onset, send child home until evaluated; frequent drinks will soothe; coughs may last up to 2 weeks; if longer, may suggest infection or allergy.

Health Assessment and Program Policies

Every early childhood center should establish clear health policies and make them known to families. Most schools require, under state or local laws, a doctor's examination and permission to participate in an early childhood education program before a child can enter the program. This includes a record of immunizations and the child's general health. Parents, too, should submit a history of the child, highlighting eating, sleeping, and elimination habits. It is critical to note any dietary restrictions or allergies and then post them in the classrooms for a reminder.

A daily inspection of each child will help adults spot nasal discharge, inflamed eyes, and throat and skin conditions of a questionable nature. This daily check will screen out more serious cases of children too ill to stay. Educating families about the warning signs of illness will encourage sick children to be cared for at home. Every program should have explicit and consistent procedures about what happens when children are refused admittance or become ill during the day. Sick children need a place where they can be isolated from others, kept under supervision, and made comfortable until they are picked up. Teachers must be sensitive to parents' feelings and situations when sending a sick child home. This situation often produces guilt feelings and work-related stress in parents. Working families may need support in locating alternatives for care of a sick child.

Nutrition

What children eat is also important for proper health. Places where food is prepared and stored must be kept especially clean. The child who has regular, nutritious meals and snacks will likely be healthier and less susceptible to disease. Many children do not have the benefits of healthy meals and snacks. Some do not receive adequate food at home; others are accustomed to sugar-laden treats and "fast foods." Education about nutrition becomes the responsibility of a school that is concerned with children's health and physical development. The need for educating parents regarding child nutrition exists in virtually all early childhood education programs, regardless of social or economic status. Some centers establish food regulations in an attempt to ensure that nutritionally sound meals are served to children.

Most schools attempt to provide a relaxed atmosphere at meal and snack time. Children are asked to sit and eat, sharing conversation as well as food. Because lifelong eating patterns are established early in life, teachers of young children have a responsibility to understand the critical role nutrition plays in the child's total development.

Clothing

The health and safety of children are affected by the clothing they wear. A simple way to be sure children stay healthy is to encourage them to dress properly for play and for varying weather conditions. Children need clothing in which they can be active—clothing that is not binding and is easy to remove and easy to clean. To promote a self-help environment, parents and teachers should provide clothes the children can manage themselves (elastic waistbands, Velcro ties, large zippers). Pants are a good choice for both boys and girls; long dresses can become a hazard when climbing, running, or going up and down stairs. The safest shoes for active play should have composition or rubber soles. Whenever possible, it helps to keep changes of clothes at school.

Staff Health

A responsible early childhood center is one that supports and maintains a healthy staff. Teachers should be in good physical and mental health to be at their best with children. It is wise to check the health regulations and benefits of the individual school when employed there. Many states require annual chest x-rays and regular tuberculosis (TB) clearance as a condition of employment. Sick leave policies should be clearly stated in print.

Early childhood education is an intense job involving close interpersonal contact. Most teachers work long hours, often with low wages and few health benefits, and with clients in various stages of health. Such working conditions produce fatigue and stress, which can lead to illness or other stress-related problems.

Guarding Children's Safety

Creating a hazard-free environment that still allows for risk and challenge for children takes careful observation and attention to detail. A quick walk around the room and yard can reveal potential problems of sharp edges, rules about spillages and children's use of tools, and adult use of outlets, extension cords, and equipment.

Safety rules should be explained to children and upheld by adults, and traffic flow should be monitored.

First Aid

Every school should establish procedures for dealing with children who are injured on the property. First aid instructions should be required of all teachers and made available as part of their in-service training. Teachers should know how to treat bumps and bruises, minor cuts and abrasions, bleeding, splinters, bites and stings, seizures, sprains, broken bones, and minor burns. All teachers should receive training in using universal health precautions with all children. Teachers should not make assumptions about who is at risk and who is not for HIV infection or hepatitis.

Each classroom should be equipped with two first-aid kits. One is for use in the classroom and yard; the other should be suitable for taking on field trips. Each kit should be readily available to adults, but out of children's reach, and supplies should be replenished regularly.

Emergency numbers to be posted near the telephone in each room include those of the ambulance squad, fire department, police, health department, nearest hospital, and

Ethics

What's a Teacher to Do?

Sara's grandmother brings her to preschool in lacy dresses and patent leather shoes. You see that her clothing prevents her from climbing, and she tends to avoid messy activities such as art, woodworking, the sandbox, and even sensory play. A core value of the National Association for the Education of Young Children (NAEYC) Code states that we must engage in practices that "support the right of each child to play and learn in inclusive early childhood programs to the fullest extent consistent with the best interests of all involved." (See Appendix.)

The ethical dilemma indicates two different ways of resolving the issue with benefits and costs to both solutions:

> If the teacher changes the child's clothes, the grandmother will be unhappy because her choice of clothing is not honored and her way of preparing her grandchild for school is interfered with.

> If the teacher keeps the child clothed as is, she will not have the full educational experience the school is expected to deliver.

The teacher thought carefully about the ethical responsibility to create safe and healthy settings and also to respect the dignity of each family and its culture, language, customs, and beliefs. He then spoke with his director and a colleague before asking with both grandmother and parents about how to help Sara get the most out of play and also be presentable at school.

a consulting physician (if any). All families enrolled at the school should be aware of school policy regarding injuries at school and should provide the school with emergency information for each child: the name of the child's physician, how to locate the parents, and who else might be responsible for the injured child if the parents cannot be reached. The school in turn must make sure they notify parents of any injuries the child has incurred during the school day.

Disasters and Threats

Many adults are familiar with the most common disaster preparation, the fire drill. Local fire regulations require that fire extinguishers be in working order and placed in all classrooms and the kitchen area. Fire exits, fire alarms, and fire escapes should be well marked and functioning properly. Children and teachers should participate in fire drills regularly. Other natural disasters vary by geographic location; helping children prepare for earthquakes, tornadoes, hurricanes, floods, and snowstorms will include participating in drills for those disasters. Proper preparedness will include eliminating potential hazards (e.g., bolting down bookcases), establishing a coordinated response plan (a "Code Blue" emergency plan should involve children, parents, all staff, and local emergency agencies), and drills (such lock-down procedures). These experiences can reinforce the need for similar procedures at home.

Automobile Safety

The use of approved car seats and restraints for children riding in automobiles has received national attention in recent years. Some states have passed legislation requiring the use of specific devices to ensure safer travel for young children. Whether or not they walk to school, children should also be aware of basic rules for crossing streets. There are potential risks when cars and children occupy the same space. Children should not be left unattended in parking lots.

Maintaining Children's Well-Being

A final factor in children's care and education is their well-being. Young children are growing up in a world threatened by violence abroad and at home, drug abuse, unresolved conflicts among adults, and constant bombardment of television and other media. Because young children do not distinguish between the home and school parts of their lives, they readily talk about family details. Teachers are often at a loss as to what to do, either with information that a child shares or with the child's behavior in the program. Yet a situation does not need to be a crisis to affect a child's well-being. As a rule of thumb, when you feel the child's physical or emotional development is in jeopardy, you have a responsibility to take further action. This is a key role of the teacher (Chapter 5) and an element of guidance (Chapter 7).

Children's well-being can be threatened by a difficult situation at school, such as being bitten, left out,

or ridiculed. They are also at risk for a variety of crises from home—problems with family members, separation or divorce, violence, or substance abuse. Although much of our response will be with adults—parents, community resources, professional supports—we are also responsible for trying to provide a psychologically safe and positive environment. By design and by responsiveness, teachers provide an interpersonal environment that soothes and cares for young children.

9-3 Basic Arrangements and Materials

Every educational setting is organized fundamentally around physical space. The building itself may be new and designed specifically for young children. More often, however, the space is a converted house or store, a parish hall, or an elementary classroom. A program may share space with another group so that furniture is moved daily or weekly. A family child care program is housed in a private home; therefore, adaptations are made in the space both for the children and for the family that lives there. There may be a large yard or none at all. Some playgrounds are on the roof of the building, or a park across the street may serve as the only available playground.

Weather conditions must be considered when planning programs for children. Outside play—and therefore large-muscle equipment—may be unavailable during the winter, so room for active, vigorous play is needed inside during that time. Hot summer months can make some types of play difficult if there is little or no shade outdoors.

Ideally, the setting should have enough space to house the various activities separately. In practice, however, rooms are multipurpose, and more than one event takes place in the same space. A playroom doubles as an eating area because both require the use of tables and chairs. When a room serves many functions (playing, eating, sleeping), convenient and adequate storage space is a necessity.

The Physical Environment

It is important to have environmental supports for these areas (Harms et al., 2004):

1. Space and furnishings (indoors and outside)
2. Personal care routines (throughout the day)
3. Language and reasoning (between teachers and children)
4. Activities (motor, cognitive, creative)
5. Interaction (social, emotional)
6. Program structure (schedules)
7. Parents and staff (personal and professional needs)

Organizing Space

There are many different ways to arrange and organize space in an early childhood setting. Most environments are arranged by interest areas, also known as learning centers.

> *The amount of space devoted to any one activity says a great deal about its value.* For instance, a dramatic-play area with plenty of space encourages active use, and play is promoted with four telephones and three doll buggies.

> *The environment must be flexible to respond to the developing needs and interests of the children.* A group with great interest in block building may need to have the indoor and outside block area expanded for several weeks. As interests change, so do the room and yard—someone brings in a hamster, and the discovery area blossoms, or interest in family camping brings out tents around the grassy outdoor areas.

> *The physical environment speaks volumes to children.* Room and yard arrangement and choice of materials play an important role in their educational experience. A developmentally appropriate toddler room needs the simplicity of a large-motor zone, a pretend play space, a messy zone for fluid materials, and some kind of quiet spot where children can unwind and just relax.

> *The placement of the interest centers is important.* Balance the number of activities, both indoors and out. Some activities are noisier than others, so place the noisier centers together and cluster the quieter ones together. Quieter activities, such as puzzles, language games, and storytelling, take place in areas away from blocks, water play, or dramatic play because the last three tend to kindle animated, active, and sometimes noisy behavior. Outdoors, be sure there is a space for reflection and watching, not just places for running and shouting.

A room or yard that is arranged well with enough interesting materials will give children choices and open their eyes to possibilities. Teachers who evaluate their materials so that they encourage non-stereotyped activity are committed to an anti-bias environment. A yard with a sand toy storage box and small brooms with dustpans nearby puts self-help as a priority at clean-up time. A program that has prop boxes with materials for children with visual or auditory disabilities is one that is making real strides to be an inclusive environment.

General Requirements

Ground-floor classrooms are preferable for young children, to ensure that they can enter and leave with relative ease and safety. For noise reduction, the walls and ceilings should be sound-proofed. Carpeting, draperies, and other fireproof fabrics in the room will help absorb sound. Floors must be durable, sanitary, and easily cleaned. They should be free from drafts. Rugs should be vacuumed each day. Room size should be sufficient to allow for freedom of movement and the opportunity to play without interference. Some licensing agencies may suggest minimum room and yard size standards.

Many local and state agencies have regulations regarding the use of space for children in group care settings. The fire and health departments must be consulted and their regulations observed. The NAEYC (2007) has developed guidelines for indoor and outdoor facilities that promote optimal growth. Besides floor and play space (minimum 35 square feet indoors and 75 square feet outdoors), the guidelines suggest how to arrange activity areas to accommodate children and what kinds of activities and materials are safe, clean, and attractive. The Creative Curriculum (Heroman, et al., 2010) has been used extensively to help programs organize their environments for free choice and active learning as well as to focus on the learning potential in each area of the room and outdoors. Environmental rating scales (Harms et al., Cryer, et al., 2004) have been developed for family child care, infant-toddler, preschool, and school-age centers that detail materials and furnishings throughout the area.

There are several key dimensions to any environment that are helpful to consider. If we are to offer children both balance and variety, these criteria need to be included in developing space both indoors and out (Figure 9-3).

Indoors

Deciding what interest centers you want and what kind of space you will need is good preparation for making a basic floor plan and sketching in the interest centers. Infant and young toddler centers devote plenty of space to diapering and sleeping, with carpeted areas for crawling and playing. Classrooms for 2- through 8-year-olds (in school-age centers) usually have several areas outlined for a variety of activities.

Interest Areas. Interest areas likely to be seen in most early education centers include the following:

> Art
> Blocks
> Dramatic-play and house corner
> Library and literacy center
> Manipulatives and table toys
> Science and discovery
> Music and movement, and group time
> Computers

Figure 9-5 shows a preschool child care room, and Figures 9-6 and 9-7 demonstrate school-age and toddler environments.

Bathrooms. Bathrooms should be adjacent to the play and sleeping areas and easily reached from outdoors. Child-sized toilets and wash basins are preferable, but if unavailable, a step or platform may be built. In most early childhood settings, the bathrooms are without doors, for ease of supervision. Toileting facilities for children should be light, airy, attractive, and large enough to serve

---

interest areas. Centers in a classroom or yard that are organized for learning or experiences that will interest children.

learning centers. Areas of a classroom or yard that are organized to draw attention to specific objects or an activity.

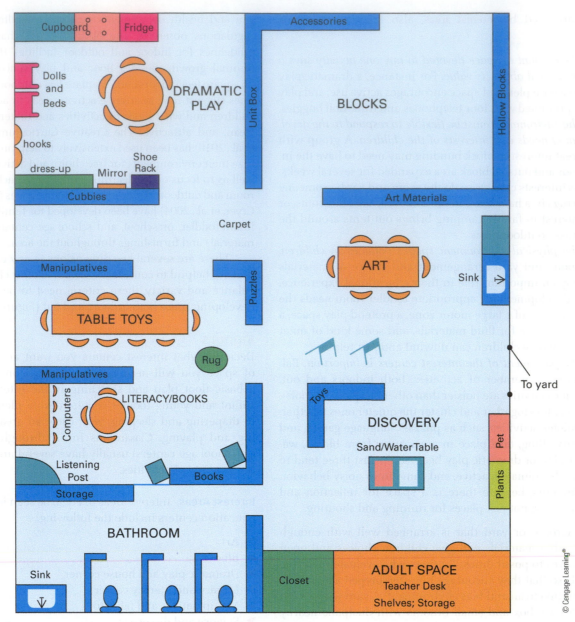

Figure 9-5 Preschool Environment. A preschool child care center needs clearly defined boundaries and obvious pathways to make it easy for children to use this space independently.

several children at a time. An exhaust fan is desirable. Paper towel holders should be at child height and waste baskets placed nearby.

If diapering is part of the program, areas for this purpose should be clearly defined and close to hand-washing facilities. Hand-washing regulations for the staff should be posted, and an area should be provided for recording children's toileting and elimination patterns. Closed cans and germicidal spray must be used, and diapering materials should be plentiful and handy.

Room to Rest. Room to rest is critical for all full-day programs; schools that provide nap time require adequate storage space for cots and bedding. Sleeping facilities are usually for children younger than 2 years who need to rest throughout the day; for preschools, movable screens,

low enough for teacher supervision, will divide the classroom space to allow for privacy and help reduce the noise level.

Cots or cribs should be labeled with children's names and washed regularly. They should be placed consistently and in such a way that children feel familiar, cozy, and private—not in the center of the room or in rows. Teachers can develop a "nap map" that places children so they can get the rest or sleep they need while still feeling part of the group.

Food Service. Food service is important for all programs. "Small children need nutrients for growth and energy. . . . [R]egardless of the guideline selected, the common factor necessary for good nutrition is the inclusion of a wide variety of foods" (Marotz, 2015). Routines and choices around

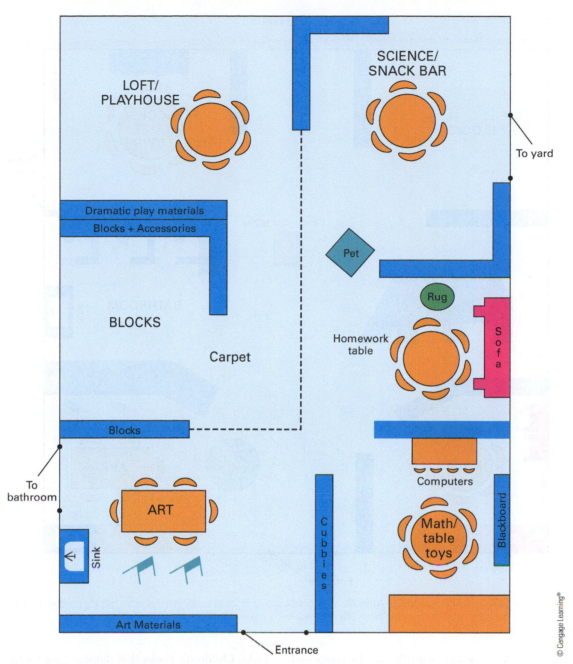

Figure 9-6 School-Age Environment. A school-age center has learning centers to allow children to make clear choices and engage in active learning through play.

food must take into consideration families' cultural practices and preferences.

Each age has its unique food service needs. Whether food service involves a light snack or full meal program, the center must adhere to the most rigid standards of health protection and safety provisions. Infants will need to be held or seated near an adult. Toddlers should not be fed popcorn, nuts, or raw carrots because of the hazard of choking. All children must be served food on disposable dishes or on dishes cleaned in a dishwasher with a sanitation cycle. Lunches brought from home by school-age and full-day children must be checked for spoilage. Information about eating patterns, proportions, and nutritional needs should be regularly shared with families.

Daily cleaning and proper disinfecting of equipment, counters, floors, and appliances is a necessity.

Adult Space. Adult space is often missing in early childhood education programs that dedicate nearly all the available space to child use and materials storage. Programs sometimes have an adult space or teacher resources space in the director's area. An adult bathroom is also common. However, professionals deserve environmental support for their work. A safe place for their belongings, space for first-aid emergency materials and information for families, and an area for teacher curriculum development goes a long way toward respecting the teachers' lives

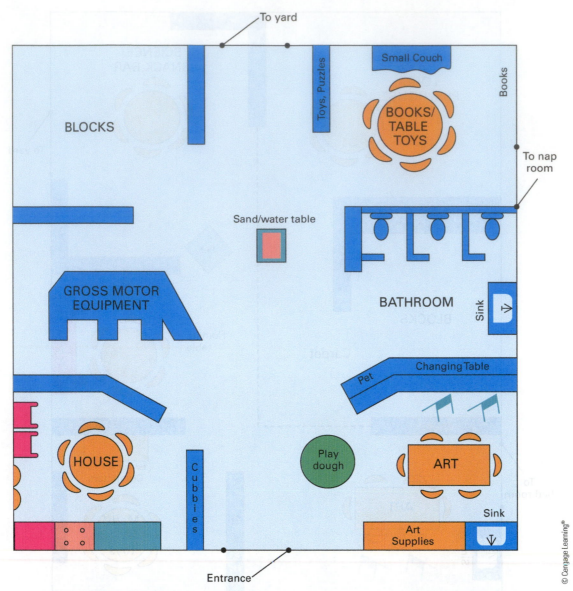

To yard

Small Couch

Toys, Puzzles

Books

BOOKS/
TABLE
TOYS

BLOCKS

To nap
room

Sand/water table

GROSS MOTOR
EQUIPMENT

BATHROOM

Sink

Changing Table

Pet

HOUSE

Cubbies

Play
dough

ART

Art
Supplies

Sink

Entrance

© Cengage Learning®

Figure 9-7 Toddler Environment. A toddler center has safety and accessibility in mind, while helping children to work in small groups so that they can be maximally involved, with a minimum of distraction from others.

in the classroom. We show our priorities by the space and time we give them.

Materials and Equipment

Selecting equipment and toys to support development is important because young children typically will try to play with everything in their environment (Figure 9-8). Out of necessity, most budgets have limited money available for such purchases. Try to avoid toys that have limited play value. Steer away from toys that:

> Make electronic technology the focus of play
> Lure girls into focusing on appearance
> Model violent and sexualized language or behavior
> Are linked to commercial products and advertisements

With self-help in mind, dressing frames and plenty of workable doll clothes will help children learn those self-care

tasks. Children's books that demonstrate social values and attitudes that expand gender roles and family lifestyles show a value for an anti-bias environment. Puzzles with magnets glued on the back of pieces can be used on a cookie sheet, and large knobs for toys with lids are modifications in the environment that promote inclusiveness.

Outdoors

"Children's access to outdoor play has evaporated like water in sunshine. It has happened so fast, along with everything else in this speed-ridden century, that we have not coped with it. . . . Some of our deepest childhood joys—those of field and stream, rocks and vacant lots; of privacy, secrecy, and tiny things that creep across or poke out of the earth's surface" can be experienced out of doors, and nowhere else (Rivkin & Schein, 2013). Time for fresh air and open space outdoors is often a child's favorite spot in

Preschool program

Art supplies: easels, paints, watercolors, play dough, clay pens, pencils, brushes, scissors, hole-punchers, glue, paste, collage materials, assorted paper

Infants/toddlers: Limit materials. Use open shelves with few choices.

School age: Have self-help table and teacher-guided projects.

Discovery and science: nature materials, textured materials, water/sensory table and materials, magnifying glasses, mirrors, scales, small pets

Infants/toddlers: Simplify, watch for safety. Aquarium.

School age: Display to read, computer.

Dramatic play: Safety mirrors; child-sized, versatile furniture; variety of nonstereotypic clothing; variety of dolls and accessories; *cooking utensils; food items; purses, suitcases, briefcases, backpacks*

Infants/toddlers: Limit the choice, add hats or dolls that can get wet.

School age: Add varied units such as prehistoric cave, moonscape.

Blocks: unit blocks, hollow blocks (may also be outdoors); props, such as people and animal figures, doll house, transportation toys; accessories like transportation signs, doll furniture, gas pumps, cloth scraps

Modifications

Infants/toddlers: Substitute soft blocks and cardboard blocks for unit blocks; limit props and accessories for safety; push-pull toys.

School-age: Include "village" or "castle" blocks; pattern blocks; increase number and types of unit blocks, add paper and pencils for child-made signs; make homemade blocks from milk cartons.

Manipulatives/table toys; puzzles; construction toys such as Legos and Tinkertoys; math toys like Unifix cubes, Cuisenaire blocks, attribute blocks, colored cubes, lacing, stringing toys, peg-boards; dressing frames; Montessori materials such as pink tower, graduated cylinders, golden cube; collectibles like buttons, keys, shells; cooperative games like lotto, dominoes, matching games

Infants/toddlers: Provide a few simple puzzles with knobs or soft pieces; eliminate math toys and replace with large plastic beads, nesting boxes, stacking toys, easy dressing frames for toddlers.

School-age: Emphasize construction, math toys, and cooperative games. Add cards, board games.

Language and books: books; flannel board; accessories; photos; lotto games; records; tapes; writing center including typewriter, pads, and pencils

Infants/toddlers: Cardboard books; use others with adults only.

School age: Readers, listening post

© Cengage Learning®

Figure 9-8 Although not comprehensive, this list starts to organize the environment for a variety of play. Note the adjustments that must be made to accommodate different ages. See the textbook's website for ideas about anti-bias materials.

a program. Indeed, many a preschooler has been able to say goodbye more easily when the great outdoors beckon.

The traditional playgrounds—typically on a flat, barren area with steel structures such as swings, climbers, a slide, perhaps a merry-go-round or seesaws, fixed in concrete and arranged in one row—are poor places for children's play from both safety and developmental perspectives. Children prefer spaces that have a variety of fixed and movable equipment. Raw materials, such as sand, water, tires, spools, sawhorses, bowls, or pans, in combination with larger superstructures or open-air "houses" with some flexible parts, stimulate a wide variety of both social and cognitive play (including constructive, dramatic, and games play). Figure 9-9 is a list of basic outdoor materials.

A wide porch or covered patio is ideal for rainy days or days when the sun is too severe. Many activities can be extended to the outside area with this type of protection. The physical plant should include adequate playground space adjacent to the building. A variety of playground surfaces makes for more interesting play and provides suitable covering for outdoor activities. Tanbark can be used in the swing area, cement for wheel toys, and grass for under climbing

DAP

Criteria for Selecting Materials

To prepare a developmentally appropriate environment, be sure the materials and equipment:

> Are age appropriate and can be used with a wide range of skills

> Are related to the school's philosophy and curriculum

> Reflect quality design and workmanship

> Are durable

> Offer flexibility and versatility in their uses

> Have safety features (e.g., nontoxic paints, rounded corners)

> Are aesthetically attractive and appealing to children (and adults)

> Are easy to maintain and repair

> Reflect the cultural make-up of the group and the diversity of the culture overall

> Are nonsexist, nonstereotypic, and anti-bias

"Play to Learn: Making Space for Games in School-Age"

Board and card games are an essential part of an after school program. Older children are ready for the strategy and competition that board games can offer. Games assist children in both social skills and academic practice. And as school-age children move into more formal intellectual thinking, they become more rule-oriented. The games that a school-age program provides are interactive and fun in healthy ways, and balance the technology-driven ones that are becoming a large part of elementary children's game-playing experience.

At the same time, when working with older children, it is likely that the group itself will be substantial, the adult-child ratio will be larger, and the schedule will allow for less intense supervision. The game area will be a popular place in your physical environment, but will require some special attention. Keeping pieces from going missing and boards from falling apart can be a challenge. Although nothing is indestructible, or loss-proof, here are some tips to extend the life of your games.

Boxes

> At your local office supply store, you can find durable plastic boxes of all sizes.

> There should be some just the right size for a deck of cards. Use those instead of the flimsy box they come in, or rubber bands.

> Invest in a nice wood checker/chess board and put all of the pieces in one of the boxes.

> For any game with small pieces, find a small box to fit them. Make sure it fits right in the game box so that the pieces stay with the game.

> If you have the budget for it, invest in larger boxes to put each of the whole games in board, pieces and all.

Game Management

> Make time to teach the students how to play the games. Problems arise when children don't know the rules. Instructions, corrections, and even variations can be done by the children themselves if they are taught properly in the first place.

> Make a separate folder for all of the rules and instructions. If you do lose them, you can almost always find them on the internet.

> Monitor how the games are going while in progress. Pieces most often disappear when kids don't know how to play the game and they use the pieces for other things.

> Check in about how the games are going over time. Make time throughout the school year to remind children of the game rules and introduce new games.

> If you don't have a check-out system, be selective over which games are out for all to reach. Games for older kids in the program can be kept in a separate place where they are accessible, but they have to ask for them. They will feel privileged and more inclined to return it with all the pieces.

The Game Spot

> Find a place in the room that can be both sheltered and handle noise. The game-playing will likely be both lively and studious, so the space needs to tolerate both.

> Mark shelves so the games can be put back by the players, and prep the kids to do that as a habit.

> When card decks have missing cards and are no longer full, put old cards in a separate bin for card-house building where children can bend and tape them for construction and art.

> Rotate some of the games over time, rather than having everything there year-round. The few that are always available should be a couple of favorites (in our program, that's Mancala and cards) and a few that need more playing time to learn strategy (for us it's Clue).

By following these guidelines, you will have a place and time for the school-age children to relax, to interact with each other, to operate independently and to learn while playing. Game On!

—Michele

---

equipment. Sand is used for play in a large area and also in a sensory table. No matter what the surface, the yard should be constructed with a good drainage system. Trees, bushes, and other plantings will allow for both sunshine and shade. Fences are *mandatory*. They must be durable and an appropriate height, with no opportunity for a child to gain a foothold.

Because there are no legal standards for the manufacture of play equipment, adults who work with children must assume responsibility for playground design.

Environments must be arranged so that there are enough play spaces for the number of children in the group.

By calculating the play space, a teacher can see whether there is a place for everyone to play. Clearly defined boundaries and obvious pathways make it easy for children to play. There should be enough space for larger groups to gather together as well as small groups. Figure 9-10 shows a playground suitable for 4- to 8-year-olds.

The Temporal Environment

The temporal environment describes the time aspects of a program. The daily schedule defines the structure of each program. These time aspects create the format for how

Basic Materials for Outdoor Playground or Play Yard

Grounds: Various surfaces (grass, asphalt, gravel/sand, tanbark), as much natural habitat as possible

Equipment: Climbing apparatus with ramps, slide, pole, ladder; swings (various types); house/quiet area; ramps and supports to build; tires, "loose parts"

Sand/water area and toys

Riding area and various wheel toys

Large building blocks

Dramatic-play props

Balls and game materials

Workbench and woodworking/clay materials

Easel and drying rack

Dancing/parachute/tumbling mat materials

Pet and garden areas

Infant-toddler: Have plenty of simple riding toys, eliminate woodworking, have apparatus correct size and simplicity and/or foam wedges

School-age: Increase game area, may eliminate number or kinds of wheel toys; substitute a stage, mural, boat, creek; increase "loose parts" for child-created forts

© Cengage Learning®

Figure 9-9 The possibilities of creating outdoor space are endless; remember that children need space to run and group together, to experience nature firsthand, and to be reflective and alone to watch.

children will experience the events of the day—in what order and for what length of time. No two schedules are alike because each reflects the program it represents. The amount of time devoted to specific activities communicates clearly what value the school places on them.

Daily Schedule: Time to Learn

In developing a schedule, teachers first decide what is important for children to learn, how that learning should take place, and how much time to allow in the daily program. A children's program must be for children and on their timetable as much as possible. The golden rule for child care is to treat children as we want them to treat us.

The physical plant may dictate a portion of the daily schedule. If toilet facilities are not located adjacent to the classroom, more time must be scheduled to travel to and from the bathrooms. If the yard is shared with other groups, some portion of the schedule may be modified.

Two aspects of the daily schedule are especially important: routines and transitions (Fig. 9-11).

truth or fiction?

T F Daily schedules define the structure of programs.

The time aspects of a program create the format for how children experience the events of the day—when certain things will occur, for how long, and in what order.

Routines

A routine is a constant. Each day, certain events are repeated, providing continuity and a sense of order to the schedule. Most routines are personal and individual rituals in children's daily lives. Children bring to school a history firmly established around routines, one that is deeply embedded in their family and culture. Routines are reassuring to children, who take pride in mastering them; they are also a highly emotional issue for some.

Routines are the pegs on which to hang the daily calendar. When children should eat, sleep, play, or be alone or together is determined by the placement of routines. The rest of the curriculum—art activities, field trips, woodworking—works around them. Routines in an early childhood education setting include the following:

> Self-care (eating, rest/sleeping, dressing, toileting)
> Transitions between activities
> Group times
> Beginning and ending the day or session
> Making choices
> Task completion
> Room clean up and yard restoration

Everyone can recall vivid memories associated with at least one routine. They seem to become battlegrounds on

routines. Regular procedures; habitual, repeated or regular parts of the school day; in early childhood programs, routines are those parts of the program schedule that remain constant, such as indoor time followed by cleanup and snack, regardless of what activities are being offered within those time slots.

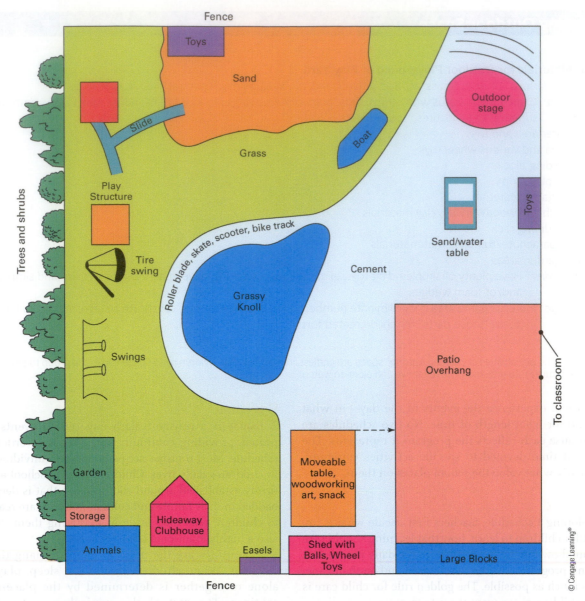

Figure 9-10 Playground Space. A playground or yard suitable for ages 4 and older will give children a sense of security and adventure, providing freedom of movement, contact with the natural world, and many opportunities for social play.

which children and adults often struggle. Many times this is where children choose to take their first stand on the road to independence. The teacher must be able to deal with the issue of self-care routines in sensitive and understanding ways. Children adjust to routines when they are regularly scheduled in the daily program and when there are clear expectations.

When the time sequence is clear, everyone can go about the business of learning and teaching. Children are more secure in a place that has a consistent schedule; they can begin to anticipate the regularity of what comes next and count on it. They can freely involve themselves without fear of being interrupted. Adults, too, enjoy the predictability of a daily schedule. By knowing the sequence of events, they are then free to flex the timing when unforeseen circumstances arise.

And it is the unforeseen that often does happen. For instance, Chad unexpectedly decides that he does not want Dad to go—just as the teacher was helping Shana onto the toilet for the first time. Flexibility to handle these situations comes from creating a humane schedule in the first place.

Transitions

As a species, humans are known for their adaptability. And yet we are resistant to change. For young children, too, change is difficult. Teachers and caregivers can make the necessary changes easier for children if they focus their attention on those times. Rather than trying to rush through quickly to get to the next event, allow for enough transition time. Helping children anticipate, figure out, work through, and successfully manage the changes in their day guides them to maturity.

Half-Day Toddler Program

9:00–9:30	Greet children
	Inside activities
	> Play dough and arts/easel
	> Home living
	> Blocks and manipulatives
	> Books
9:30	Door to outdoors opens
9:45–10:20	Outdoor play
	> Large motor
	> Social play
10:20	Music/movement outdoors
10:30	Snack/"Here We Are Together" song
	> Washing hands
	> Eating/pouring/cleanup
10:45–11:45	Outside
11:15	"Time to Put Our Toys Away" song
	> All encouraged to participate in clean up
11:20	Closure (indoors)
	> Parent–child together
	> Story or flannel board

Full-Day Program for Preschoolers

7:00	Arrival, breakfast
7:30	Inside free play
	> Arts/easels
	> Table toys/games/blocks
	> Dramatic-play center; house, grocery store, etc.
9:00	Clean up
9:15	Group time: songs/fingerplays and small-group choices
9:30	Choice time/small groups
	> Discovery/math lab/science activity
	> Cooking for morning or afternoon snack
	> Language art/prereading choice
10:00	Snack (at outside tables/cloths on warm days) or snack center during free play
10:15	Outside free play
	> Climbing, swinging, sand and water, wheel toys, group games

12:00	Hand washing and lunch
12:45	Get ready: toileting, hand washing, toothbrushing, prepare beds
1:15	Bedtime story
1:30	Rest time
2:30	Outdoors for those awake
3:30	Clean up outdoors and singing time
4:00	Snack time
4:15	Learning centers; some outdoor/indoor choices, field trips, story teller
5:30	Clean up and read books until going home

Half-Day Kindergarten Plan

8:15–8:30	Arrival
	Getting ready to start
	> Checking in library books, lunch money, etc.
8:30	News telling
	> "Anything you want to tell for news"
	> Newsletter written weekly
9:00	Work assignment
	> Write a story about your news, *or*
	> Make a page in your book (topic assigned), *or*
	> Work in math lab
9:30–10:15	Choice of indoors (paints, blocks, computer, table toys) *or* second-grade tutors read books to children
	When finished, play in loft *or* read books until recess
10:15	Snack
10:30	Recess
10:45	Language: chapter in novel read *or* other language activity
11:15	Dance *or* game or visitor
11:45	Ending: getting ready to leave
	> Check out library books
	> Gather art and other projects
12:00–1:30	For part of group each day
	Lunch, then:
	> Field trips
	> Writing lesson
	> Math or science lab

© Cengage Learning®

Figure 9-11 Daily schedules reflect the children's needs and ages while meeting the program's goals. The time and timing of the school day show what is valued in the program.

Good teachers prepare children for upcoming **transitions**, using a song or strumming of an instrument and the words, "Get ready to clean up soon." And they are also prepared for children's perceptions of time, immediacy, and closure to collide with the schedule. So if Chad does not want his Dad to go, perhaps getting Shana on the toilet will have to wait, or Dad can read him another story until Shana's "all done now."

---

transition. A change from one state or activity to another; in early childhood terms, transitions are those times of change in the daily schedule (whether planned or not), such as from being with a parent to being alone in school, from playing with one toy to choosing another, from being outside to being inside, etc.

Jim West/Alamy

> Sequencing of activities and allocating enough time are major scheduling factors in inclusive classrooms.

> *Example*: Changes in routines are especially difficult for children with developmental problems. Garrett, who has autistic-type behaviors, is obsessively attached to the daily schedule; therefore, the routines of greeting the teacher, hanging up his jacket, and washing his hands are rituals that must be held constant and in that order so that he feels secure and can start the day well.

> The content of group activities changes with age.

Example: In the toddler class, group times are simple: a short fingerplay, story with a flannel board or puppets, or a song to dismiss is adequate. The preschool group times include several songs, a dramatization of a favorite fingerplay, and a short story. In the kindergarten, circle lasts 15 to 20 minutes, with announcement and weather board, children's news telling, longer dramas, and even chapter stories.

Thus, the temporal environment mirrors the children's age and individual interests. A special note: many programs divide the day into small segments of time in the belief that young children have such short attention spans that they cannot remain at an activity for long. However, we know that children can stay focused for long periods of time on activities of *their* choice or interest. Although they may last only a short time in teacher-planned, structured activities, children need and thrive with more time to get their own creative juices flowing. Consult Figure 9-11 to see how the temporal environment allots time for successful free-play time.

Developmentally Appropriate Schedules

Just as the arrangement of space should reflect the group of children within, so does the daily schedule allow for appropriate growth at the developmental level of the group. There are common factors to consider for all children in the early years, as well as some developmental distinctions at the various ages.

> More choices are available to children as they grow.

Age-related differences can be seen in schedules, as described here:

Example: Two-year-olds could be overstimulated by the selection of materials that is appropriate for school-aged children.

> Transitions are handled differently in the various age groups.

Example: Older children can move through some transitions as a group, such as going out in a single file. This is difficult for younger children, who would push or wander away. For them, the door to the yard opens quietly, allowing children to go out slowly.
Example: A preschool child care class is dismissed from circle time to snack tables by the color of people's shirts, or the first letter of their names, rather than as one whole group.

> The structure of the day shifts with age.

Example: The balance of free-play and teacher-directed activities will change with the age range of the group, from relatively few directed activities for younger children to several in a preschool day. The kindergarten schedule provides more structure both in individual work projects and teacher-focused time, and school-age children are more ready for a lecture-type demonstration and whole-group instruction.

The Interpersonal Environment

A child responds to everything in school: the color of the room, the way the furniture is arranged, how much time there is to play, and how people treat one another. The feeling in a room is as real as the blocks or the books. Thus, the interpersonal aspects of an early childhood setting are powerful components of the environment.

Defining the Tone

Children are the most important people in the setting; they should feel safe and comfortable. A warm, interpersonal environment invites children to participate and to learn. When children feel secure with one another and with the setting, they will be able to engage more fully in the total program.

Teachers will be the key ingredient in determining the atmosphere of a group. The first component of the National

interpersonal. Relating to, or involving relationships with, other people; those parts of the environment that have to do with the people in a school setting.

Standards

Creating a Schedule with Standards

When creating the total environment for young children, teachers must know and understand the standards to use in developing an effective daily schedule. Knowing the multiple influences on development and learning shows an understanding of sound child development principles. There are many schedules that can work for children (see Figure 9-11), and professionals keep in mind that it is the sequence, not the exact number of minutes on the clock, that is meaningful for children. Effective strategies provide the framework on which the daily schedule is structured. Use these standards to create a schedule that promotes connections with children and families:

> Be consistent. Consistency brings security and closure, allowing for teacher authority and expertise to assert themselves.

> Provide for flexibility so that children's interests can be maintained and emergencies met. Flexibility invites sensitivity to individuals and respectful agreements to be reached.

> Include time for routines as well as time for transitions.

> Alternate quiet and active play and work to help children pace themselves.

> Provide opportunities for both inside and outside play.

> Allow children to participate in structured activities, as well as those of their own choosing. This often includes whole-group times (circle time to begin the day, song time for announcements, or story time as closure).

> Make it possible for children to work individually, in small groups, or in larger ones.

> Gear the time to the age and developmental levels of the group.

> Have a beginning and an end. Some provisions must be made for children to be met and greeted when they enter. Allow time for dismissal and transition, bringing the children closure with a review of the day's activities and anticipation of what will come tomorrow.

> Involve the adults in daily planning and review; include a regular meeting time for more substantial discussion of children, long-range planning, and evaluation.

> Include time for clean up and room restoration.

> Incorporate the teachers' roles and assignments so that they know their responsibilities.

> Be posted in an obvious place in the classroom for all to see.

Academy's criteria for high-quality early childhood programs (NAEYC, 2007) is the interactions among the staff and children and the role of the teacher is pivotal in establishing his human component of the environment. The connections among the people in a center or a home make all the difference to young children because they are the barometers of interpersonal tension or openness and freedom.

Family engagement is critical to the life of school, especially in the early years. The way people feel about each other and how they express their feelings have an effect on children. Teachers have to see children within their family and social context; to do so, they must invite families into the schooling process (see Chapter 8). Note the impact on all three aspects of the environment in these situations:

> Every day, Maryam brings her lunch, and it is so difficult to manage. These Iranian foods are not the same as the other children's, and there is often teasing that you have to keep redirecting. You wonder if you should simply tell her Auntie to send her with a sandwich . . . only you realize that everyone wants to eat familiar foods, and letting Maryam eat what her parents want her to should also be coupled with having the other children learn some tolerance, too. You *change the physical environment* by adding cooking activities that encourage everyone to become curious and interested in new foods.

> You can't believe it; no matter how many times you tell Kai's Chinese grandfather that school starts at 9 am, he continues to bring him between 9:30 and 10 . . . until you find out that in China, people respect the slower-paced habits of the elderly. You *flex your schedule* to allow for this late arrival and support this family custom.

> Elena's father speaks with such an accent that you can hardly understand him, and rarely talks with you. You'd like to just avoid talking, too, but then you'd connect only when there's a problem . . . and you discover that, in Guatemalan culture, "good parents" are expected to talk with teachers. You need to overcome your discomfort to establish positive *interpersonal feelings* and ask him respectfully to repeat what he is saying a bit more slowly.

Researchers have found a pattern of positive relationships between children's sensitive, involved interactions with teachers and children's enhanced development. The effect of these types of interactions is likely to be seen in children's cognitive, social-emotional, and language development (CA Department of Education, 2008). Further, the nature of the classroom atmosphere contributes greatly to children's success in learning English as a second language (Chang, et al., 2007). Such research confirms the findings of recent brain-based research and theories of Erikson, Bandura, and Vygotsky (see Chapter 4).

Young children develop best through close, affectionate relationships with people. This is particularly important for children younger than 3 years and for children whose primary language is not the dominant one spoken in the program. "The interpersonal aspect of environment is the central element affecting the quality of toddler play, more important than elaborateness of physical setting," declares Zeavin (1997). "It is through their play that they externalize troubling feelings, work out emotional conflicts, and gain control of their world. . . . Every issue is a relationship issue."

Positive Interpersonal Environments

Questions teachers can ask themselves as they evaluate the quality of the interpersonal environment include the following:

> Is there a feeling of mutual respect between children and adults?
> Do teachers pick up on nonverbal and verbal expressions of both girls and boys? Of children with varying abilities? Of children of color?
> How do children treat one another?
> Do teachers model cooperative behavior with other adults and children? Do they show by example how to work through a disagreement or problem?
> Does the physical set-up allow the teacher to focus on the children?
> Do housekeeping details keep teachers disconnected from children?
> Do teachers encourage children to use one another as resources?
> Do teachers take time to show children how to accomplish a task by themselves?
> Are girls complimented only on appearance and boys just for achievement? Are all children helped to appreciate similarities and differences?
> Do teachers use reasoning and follow-through?
> How and when do teachers interact with children?
> What are the teacher's posture and facial expression when involved in a problem situation?
> If I were a child, would I like to come to school here?

The answers to these questions help teachers gauge how well they are maintaining an atmosphere of positive social interaction. The most important thing to remember is that the way people feel about each other and how they express their feelings have an impact on children. Teachers must focus as much attention on the interpersonal part of the environment as they do on buying equipment or arranging the room.

teachsource video case

Watch the TeachSource Video entitled, "Space: Planning, Equipment & Facilities Management" and then answer the following questions:

1. How should teachers fill the "blank canvas"? In other words, how should the physical environment be arranged so that children's learning is enhanced?

2. What kind of daily schedule would be best for development in all 4 domains of learning?

3. What kinds of interpersonal strategies should adults use to help children learn?

4. In purchasing equipment, what specific notes and questions would you list under the categories of Safety, Maintenance, and Size/Age of Children?

© 2016 Cengage Learning®

summary

9.1 The major criteria that are used in creating developmentally appropriate environments are the physical plant, available resources, and program goals. Key elements put core values to work that help the environment.

9.2 Central elements in planning environments for children are keeping children healthy, guarding children's safety, and maintaining children's well-being.

9.3 Basic materials and arrangements for environments include analyzing the physical, temporal, and interpersonal aspects of the environment. Planning the physical environment involves organizing space and stocking both indoors and outdoors with appropriate materials. Addressing the temporal environment means creating a daily schedule that includes routines and transitions as well as activity periods. The interpersonal environment focuses on defining a positive social tone and atmosphere for children and families.

web resources

Environment Ratings Scales **http://ers.fpg.unc.edu**
LD Online **http://www.ldonline.org**
Teaching Strategies **http://teachingstrategies.com**

Teaching Tolerance **http://www.tolerance.org**
Teachers Resisting Unhealthy Children's Entertainment **http://www.truceteachers.org**

references

Allen, K. E., & Cowdery, G. E. (2015). *The exceptional child: Inclusion in early childhood* (8e). Cengage Learning.

California Department of Education (2008). *CA Preschool Learning Foundations, Volume 1: Social-Emotional Development, Language and Literacy, English-Language Development, and Mathematics*. Sacramento, CA: Authors.

Centers for Disease Control and Prevention. (2014). *The ABCs of safe and healthy child care*. http://www.cdc.gov/family/parentabc/

Chang, F., et al. (2007). "Spanish-speaking children's social and language development in pre-kindergarten classrooms," *Journal of Early Education & Development, 18*(2), 243–269.

Copple, C., & Bredekamp, S. (2010). *Developmentally appropriate practices in early childhood programs serving children from birth through age 8* (3e). Washington, DC: National Association for the Education of Young Children.

Cryer, D., Harms, T., & Riley, C. (2003). *All about the ECERS-R*. New York: Teachers College Press.

Derman-Sparks, L., & Olsen Edwards, J. (2010). *Anti-bias education for young children and ourselves*. Washington, DC: National Association for the Education of Young Children.

Dodge, D. T., Rudish, S., & Berke, K. L. (2010). *The creative curriculum for infants, toddlers, and twos* (2nd ed.). Washington, DC: Teaching Strategies.

Greenman, J. (2004). What is the setting? Places for childhood. In A. M. Gordon & K. Williams Browne. *Beginnings and beyond* (6th ed.). Clifton Park, NY: Thomson Delmar Learning.

Harms, T., Cryer, D., & Clifford, R. M.. *The early childhood rating scale-revised(2003), family day care (2007), infant/toddler (2006), and school age (1995)*

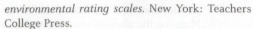

environmental rating scales. New York: Teachers College Press.

Haugen, K. (1997, March). Using your senses to adapt environments: Checklist for an accessible environment. Beginnings workshop. *Child Care Information Exchange.*

Heroman, C., Trister Dodge, D., Berke, K-L., & Bickart, T. (2010). *Creative curriculum for preschools* (5e). Teaching Strategies, Inc.

Marotz, L. R. (2015). *Health, safety, and nutrition for the young child* (9e). Cengage Learning.

NAEYC [National Association for the Education of Young Children]. (2007). *Early childhood program standards and accreditation criteria, revised edition.* Washington, DC: Author.

Needlman, R., & Needlman, G. (1995, November/December). Ten most common health problems in school. *Scholastic Early Childhood Today.*

Prescott, E. (1994, November). The physical environment—a powerful regulator of experience. *Exchange.*

Rivkin, M. S. & Schein, D. (2013). *The great outdoors: Advocating for natural spaces for young children (Revised edition)* Washington, DC: National Association for the Education of Young Children.

Zeavin, C. (1997, March). Toddlers at play: Environments at work. *Young Children,* 52.

10 curriculum essentials

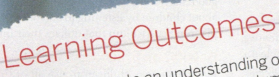

Learning Outcomes

10-1 Demonstrate an understanding of the relationship between a play-based curriculum and the development of skills, knowledge, and learning.

10-2 Define the framework for creating curriculum that is relevant and based on principles of child development and learning.

10-3 Identify the essential elements for assessing the effectiveness of the curriculum that addresses the ability to learn on many levels.

10-4 Describe how to plan curriculum that includes all developmental domains, engages children of all ages and abilities, and supports positive attitudes toward learning.

NAEYC Standards

The following NAEYC Standards for Early Childhood Professional Preparation are addressed in this chapter:

Standard 1: Promoting Child Development and Learning

Standard 2: Building Family and Community Relationships

Standard 4: Using Developmentally Effective Approaches to Connect with Children and Families

Standard 5: Using Content Knowledge to Build Meaningful Curriculum

Standard 6: Becoming a Professional

truth or fiction

T F Curriculum and play have little relevance to one another.

T F Curriculum includes all of the planned and unplanned activities in a child's day.

T F Curriculum assessment is an ongoing process.

T F Written curriculum plans are used to schedule the school year curriculum and activities.

10-1 Play-Based Curriculum

In Chapter 4, you learned about the value and process of children's play and why play-based curriculum enhances children's potential for learning. Children need active and meaningful materials and activities to learn. They need to be physically as well as mentally and emotionally involved in what and how they learn, and they experience this through play.

10-1a Learning How to Learn

Observe children at play: they are active, curious, creative, and eager to learn. Play is how children learn how to learn. They question, explore, and experiment with ideas, language,

play-based curriculum. Curriculum that is based on observation and interactions with children as they play.

and imagination. At play, children collaborate, negotiate, and learn from one another. They are learning how to learn. Figure 10-1 demonstrates how each developmental domain is used in children's play and transformed into knowledge.

10-1b The Teacher's Role in Play

Play is a basic need for all children and is at the heart of a good early childhood program. Classroom teachers learn about children by listening to and observing them at play and planning curriculum that utilizes their interests and needs.

Developmentally Appropriate Play

Play challenges children to use all of their abilities, and in doing so, the *whole* child is affected when play is developmentally appropriate.

Play Is the cornerstone of learning

Cognitive/Language
Distinguishes between reality and fantasy
Encourages creative thought and curiosity
Allows for problem solving
Encourages thinking, planning
Develops memory, perceptual skills, and concept formation
Learns to try on other roles
Acquires knowledge and integrates learning
Learns communication skills
Develops listening and oral language skills

Creative
Fosters use of imagination and make-believe
Encourages flexible thinking and problem solving
Provides opportunity to act upon original ideas
Supports taking risks
Learns to use senses to explore
Re-creates images in buildings and art media
Sharpens observational skills
Provides variety of experiences
Learns to express self in art, music, and dance
Develops abilities to create images and use symbols
Acquires other perspectives

Social
Tries on other personalities, roles
Learns cooperation and taking turns
Learns to lead, follow
Builds a repertoire of social language
Learns to verbalize needs
Reflects own culture, heritage, values
Learns society's rules and group responsibility
Shows respect for other's property, rights
Teaches an awareness of others
Learns how to join a group
Builds awareness of self as member of a group
Gives sense of identification
Promotes self-image, self-esteem
Experiences, joy, fun

Physical
Releases energy
Builds fine and gross motor skills
Grains control over body
Provides challenges
Requires active use of body
Allows for repetition and practice
Refines eye–hand coordination
Develops self-awareness
Encourages health and fitness

© Cengage Learning®

Emotional
Develops self-confidence and self-esteem
Learns to take a different viewpoint
Resolves inner fears, conflicts
Builds trust in self and others
Reveals child's personality
Encourages autonomy
Learns to take risks
Acts out anger, hostility, frustration, joy
Gains self-control
Becomes competent in several areas
Takes initiative

Figure 10-1

© Cengage Learning®

Hands-on Learning

Play-based curriculum is most effective when young children physically manipulate materials. Hands-on learning allows children to make sense of their environment. As active learners, children have to explore and manipulate. They push, pull, stack, build up, take down, sort, count, measure, dig, take apart, put together, pour, climb, and move about. The value of discovery cannot be underestimated as children find out for themselves how things work. The concept of creating the color green, for instance, is meaningless until children mix paints, have it turn into brown, start over with other colors, and eventually make green. This is a tangible, physical experience necessary for learning abstract concepts.

Children respond to curriculum materials that are inviting and accessible. ◄

T Ⓕ Curriculum and play have little relevance to one another.

Play is the avenue through which children explore curriculum activities and learning experiences. Play provides the context for exploring the world and finding meaning in a variety of experiences.

Planning for developmentally appropriate play brings to bear a teacher's knowledge about how children grow and learn, as well as an understanding of the cultural context in which children live. From that base, play experiences are woven into the curriculum to meet those three standards. Two key concepts in developmentally appropriate planning are to (1) set reasonable goals; and (2) meet children where they are (Copple & Bredekamp, 2009).

In the following discussion on curriculum, the issues of culturally appropriate play and play materials will be explored.

Supporting Play

Practicing for life through play is an important job for children, and they need teachers who appreciate and value the role of play in the early childhood setting. (See Chapter 4 for a discussion on the value the types of play.) Figure 10-2 highlights the teacher's role in supporting play.

Some parents and teachers do not recognize the importance of play in the early years and need help in understanding what learning takes place as children play. Learning takes place in every interaction, and you can share examples with families as illustrations of their child's imagination, abilities, and creativity.

Setting the Stage for Play

To set the stage for learning, the environment, schedule, and curriculum unite to create a program that fosters constructive play and hands-on learning through:

> Open-ended materials that expand the children's learning opportunities because they can be used in more than one way

A Dozen Ways to Facilitate Play

1. Guide the play, but do not direct or dominate.

2. Participate in the play, but do not overwhelm the children.

3. Start with the children's thoughts and ideas, but do not enforce a point of view on them.

4. Model play when necessary. Show children how a specific character might act, or how to ask for a turn, or how to hold a hammer when hammering.

5. Model ways to solve problems that involve children interacting on their own behalf.

6. Ask questions; clarify to children what is happening.

7. Help children start, end, and begin again.

8. Give them verbal cues to enable them to follow through on an idea.

9. Focus the children's attention on one another and encourage them to interact with each other.

10. Interpret children's behavior aloud, when necessary, and help them verbalize their thoughts and ideas.

11. Assist in verbalizing feelings as children work through conflict.

12. Expand the play potential by making statements and asking questions that lead to discovery and exploration.

Figure 10-2

Watch the TeachSource Video Case entitled, "Curriculum Planning: Implementing Developmentally Appropriate Practice in an Early Childhood Setting." After you study the video clip, view the artifacts, and read the teacher interviews and text, reflect on the following questions:

1. "Play is the child's work," according to one teacher in this case. How is that ideal implemented throughout the program?

2 How did the teaching staff at this preschool center demonstrate that they value meeting the needs of individual children?

© 2016 Cengage Learning®

> A variety of activity areas and learning centers set up with specific play and learning materials that provide children with choices for play, such as art, music, reading/literacy, science and discovery, music and movement, manipulatives and table toys, blocks, and dramatic play. These centers are explained in setting up environments in Chapter 9.

> Activities that are self-initiated and child-directed to foster children's independent use of materials.

> Photographs, pictures, bi-lingual books, and CDs are placed in the various centers to support dual-language learners.

> Use space, room arrangement, outdoor play area, materials, and daily schedule as a scaffold on which to build learning experiences to meet the varied interests and abilities of each child.

The teacher sets the tone and the emotional framework in which children work and play. A positive atmosphere supports the child's need for a safe and nurturing place to learn.

Many of these suggestions are covered in Chapter 9.

curriculum. Written plan that states the goals, learning experiences, and methods for children over a period of time.

10-2 Creating the Framework for Learning

In an early childhood education setting, the curriculum consists of the art activity and language game, the impulsive investigation of a bug crawling up the window, the song that accompanies digging in the sand, and the teacher's explanation of why the hamster died.

10-2a What Is Curriculum?

Curriculum includes all of the planned and unplanned activities as well as the subject matter, the interactions with people, and all of the experiences of the children's day. **Curriculum** is the sum of a teacher's knowledge and understanding of the process of how children interact with people and materials to learn.

truth or *fiction?*

Ⓣ F Curriculum includes all of the planned and unplanned activities in a child's day.

Curriculum is all of the experiences in the program that make up a child's day. It is the planned and unplanned learning that takes place as children and materials meet.

Bredekamp and Rosegrant (1995) define curriculum as an "organized framework" with four areas of focus:

1. The *content* consists of *what* children should learn and how it reflects their interests, needs, and experiences.
2. The *process* includes *how* and *when* learning takes place, the choice of activities, how they are integrated with one another, and the time frame within the daily schedule.
3. *Teachers* are the people who *use* their knowledge of child development theory to individualize the activities to meet the needs of all children in the class.
4. The *context* is *why* certain projects and activities are chosen and is based on the program's philosophy and goals, in conjunction with the children's family and community.

Developing curriculum is a decision-making process whose goal is to translate theories of education and development into practice. There are curriculum models that promote good practices in developmentally appropriate learning and that have their own philosophical thrust. These include HighScope, Bank Street, the Schools of Reggio Emilia, Montessori, Waldorf, and the Creative Curriculum, which are summarized in Figure 10-10. Many schools adopt a particular model or integrate elements from several models into their planning.

© Cengage Learning®

Curriculum begins when children and materials meet. What can this toddler learn from his play? ◄

Developmentally Appropriate Curriculum

As noted in Chapter 2, developmentally appropriate programs, curricula, and practices are defined by the NAEYC (Copple & Bredekamp, 2009) as having the following core considerations:

> *Age-appropriateness.* What is known about child development and learning of a specific age group in order to provide appropriate experiences and learning activities to challenge children and help them achieve success.

> *Individual appropriateness.* What is known about each individual child, the individual rate of growth, and the unique learning style so that curriculum reflects their needs, interests, abilities, and preferences.

> *Social and cultural appropriateness.* What is known about the social and cultural context of each child so that the curriculum provides meaningful and relevant learning experiences that are respectful of the backgrounds of the children and families in the group. This includes awareness of dual-language learners and their families.

The foundation for developmentally appropriate practices and curriculum content is historically rooted in John Dewey's

vision that schools prepare students to think and reason to participate in a democratic society (see Chapter 1). Figure 10-3 lists 20 guidelines jointly endorsed by the NAEYC and the National Association of Early Childhood Specialists in state departments of education to ensure developmentally appropriate curriculum.

10-2b Culturally Appropriate Curriculum

If meaningful learning is derived from a social and cultural context, a multicultural atmosphere must be created in which awareness and concern for true diversity—including ethnicity, gender, abilities, and dual-language learning—permeate the program.

Diversity

Transformative Curriculum

Creating a truly multicultural classroom calls into question the familiar way of doing things and provides new insights and ways of thinking about culture. Banks (2006) describes this approach as **transformative curriculum.**

Transformative curriculum helps teachers develop critical thinking skills so that they question some of the opinions and images of people and cultures that are represented in the Eurocentric curriculum that dominates American schools. For instance, this approach encourages teachers to look at Christopher Columbus from the perspective of a Native American before creating curriculum about Thanksgiving, the Pilgrims, or Native Americans. Transformative curriculum is a way to help develop more positive attitudes toward all racial, ethnic, and cultural groups.

The common practice in many early childhood programs of cooking ethnic foods or celebrating ethnic or cultural holidays as isolated experiences often trivializes or stereotypes groups of people. Folk tales, songs, food, and dress are symbols and expressions of a culture, not the culture itself. For children to gain any meaningful knowledge, the content must contribute to a fuller understanding of human diversity, not just a special-occasion topic. Including diverse food, music, and clothing are important artifacts in the curriculum only when they expand on a concept of diversity and serve as a link to discuss other aspects of a culture. Songs and dances of one culture could lead to a discussion of what games children play in different parts of the world.

---

developmentally appropriate practices. That which is suitable or fitting to the development of the child; refers to those teaching practices that are based on the observation and responsiveness to children as learners with developing abilities who differ from one another by rate of growth and individual differences, rather than of differing amounts of abilities. It also refers to learning experiences that are relevant to and respectful of the social and cultural aspects of the children and their families.

transformative curriculum. The process of viewing events and situations from diverse perspectives to gain new insights and ways of thinking in order to create more culturally appropriate curriculum.

NAEYC and the National Association of Early Childhood Specialists in State Departments of Education recommend implementing curriculum that is thoughtfully planned, challenging, engaging, developmentally appropriate, culturally and linguistically responsive, comprehensive, and likely to promote positive outcomes for all young children. The indicators of effectiveness for developing curriculum are:

> *Children are active and engaged.* Children of all ages and abilities can become interested and engaged, develop positive attitudes toward learning, and be supported in their feelings of security, emotional competence, and links to family and community.

> *Goals are clear and shared by all.* Curriculum goals are clearly defined, shared, and understood by program administrators, teachers, and families. The curriculum, activities, and teaching strategies are designed to help achieve the goals in a unified, coherent way.

> *Curriculum is evidence-based.* The curriculum is based on evidence that is developmentally, culturally, and linguistically relevant for each group of children and is organized around principles of child development and learning.

> *Valued content is learned through investigation, play, and focused, intentional teaching.* Children learn by exploring, thinking about, and inquiring about all sorts of things that are connected to later learning. Teaching strategies are tailored to children's ages, developmental capabilities, language and culture, and abilities or disabilities.

> *Curriculum builds on prior learning and experience.* The content and implementation builds on children's prior individual, age-related, and cultural learning, is inclusive of all children, and is supportive of the knowledge learned at home and in the community. The curriculum supports children whose home language is not English by building a base for later learning.

> *Curriculum is comprehensive.* All developmental domains are included in the curriculum, such as physical well-being and motor development, social and emotional development, language development, and cognition and general knowledge. Subject matter areas are included, such as science, mathematics, language, literacy, social studies, and the arts.

> *Professional standards validate the curriculum's subject-matter content.* Curriculum meets the standards of relevant professional organizations. (For instance, The American Alliance for Health, Physical Education, Recreation and Dance, The National Council of Teachers of English, The National Science Teachers Association) and are reviewed so they fit together coherently.)

> *Curriculum is likely to benefit children.* Research indicates that the curriculum, if implemented as intended, will likely have beneficial effects. These benefits include a wide range of outcomes.

Figure 10-3 Developmentally appropriate practices are based on knowledge of how children develop, which is based on research, theory, and observation (Bredekamp & Copple, 2009.) (© Cengage Learning®)

Culturally appropriate curriculum is also developmentally appropriate curriculum. The challenge is to develop a curriculum that reflects the plurality of contemporary American society in general and in the individual classroom, in particular, and present them in sensitive, relevant ways.

10-3 Elements for Assessing Effective Curriculum

To meet the needs, interests, experiences, and abilities of each child, curriculum needs to be evaluated on an ongoing basis. At the end of the day, teachers informally assess an activity; in planning sessions, curriculum is evaluated for future planning or as part of staff development and accreditation processes. Many of the following factors are considered when assessing effective curriculum.

truth or *fiction?*

T F Curriculum assessment is an ongoing process.

Assessing curriculum is an ongoing process as children change, grow, and develop new interests and abilities and teacher implement the appropriate changes.

10-3a Integrated Curriculum

The *whole* child approach, which you learned about in Chapters 3 and 4, stresses the interaction and relationship among the physical, social, intellectual, language,

---

culturally appropriate curriculum. Curriculum that helps children understand the way individual histories, families of origins, and ethnic family cultures make us similar to and yet different from others.

and cognitive areas of the developing child. Think of integrated curriculum in the same way because it weaves across many subject areas throughout the school day so that skills are developed in the context of other learning. Subject such as math, science, art, and language are all planned components of an integrated curriculum. The subject areas cut across the learning activity and reinforce concepts in meaningful ways as children engage in their work and play.

10-3b Emergent Curriculum

Emergent curriculum is just what it says: curriculum that comes out of the child's experiences and interests. The teacher observes what children do, how they play, what they talk about, and what captures their interests and imagination. The point of emergent curriculum is to deepen and extend children's learning as they discover meaning and understanding in their own play.

Taking cues from children—noting what they play with, what they avoid, what they change—stems from the belief that to be a meaningful learning experience, the curriculum should come out of the daily life in the classroom. Based on the principles of Erikson, Piaget, and Vygotsky, emergent curriculum assumes that children are active, curious, powerful learners, capable of taking the initiative and constructing their knowledge through experience.

Emergent curriculum calls for collaboration and mutual learning between and among children and adults. Teachers and children both offer suggestions and ideas. It begins with an idea or activity that expands as children explore the learning potential. This type of activity may continue for days and weeks. Emergent curriculum in one kindergarten class started when the children were learning their addresses. This led to further discussion of neighborhoods and where children lived. This activity led to a map project as the learning expanded into the community in which they live.

10-3c Inclusive Curriculum

An inclusive curriculum goes beyond creating curriculum that meets the needs of the individual child. An inclusive curriculum:

> Is broader in scope and challenges the teacher to provide opportunities for all children, regardless of gender, abilities, disabilities, language, culture, ethnicity, and religion
> Has activities and materials that are chosen to enhance the potential of each child and are reflective of the diversity of abilities within the classroom
> Includes activities that adjust to a wide range of skills and abilities
> Is flexible enough to accommodate the needs of each child
> Challenges children's learning

"Integrated Learning Through Block Play"

Every child loves to play with blocks. Unit blocks are a staple in most early childhood programs and demonstrate the concept of integrated learning as it provides for learning to take place within the context of meaningful activity. Here is what children learn in the block corner:

> *Science:* weight, gravity, balance, stability, height, inclines, ramps, interaction of forces
> *Mathematics:* classification, order, number, fractions, depth, width, height, length, fractions, size relationships, volume, area, measurement, shape, size, space, mapping
> *Social Studies:* symbolic representation, mapping, grids, patterns, people and their work
> *Art:* patterns, symmetry, balance, design, texture, creativity, and drawing
> *Language:* making comparisons, recognizing shapes and sizes, labeling, giving directions, communicating ideas and needs, writing and drawing plans, using books as resources
> *Physical Development:* eye–hand coordination, clean up, hand manipulation, fine motor skills, and visual perception
> *Social Development:* cooperation, sharing, clean up, conflict resolution, negotiation, respect for the work of others
> *Cognitive Development:* planning, naming, differentiation of sizes and shapes, inductive thinking, discovery, creativity

Integrated curriculum is teaching "across the curriculum" as children experience the materials in the natural context of playing with blocks.

Ann Gordon

How is this block structure an example of integrated curriculum? ◄

---

integrated curriculum. A set of courses designed to form a whole; coordination of the various areas of study, making for continuous and harmonious learning.

emergent curriculum. A process for curriculum planning that draws on teachers' observations and children's interests. Plans emerge from daily life interests and issues. This approach takes advantage of children's spontaneity and teachers' planning.

inclusive curriculum. A curriculum that reflects awareness of and sensitivity to a person's culture, language, religion, gender, and abilities.

Adapting Art Activities for Children with Special Needs

____Visual:

Verbally describe materials and how they might be used.

Provide a tray that outlines the visual boundaries.

Offer bright paint to contrast with paper.

Go slowly and encourage children to manipulate the items as you talk.

____Auditory:

Model the process, facing the child and using gestures for emphasis.

Use sign language as needed.

____Physical:

Make sure there is a clear path to the art center.

Provide adaptive art tools such as chunky crayons, large markers.

Provide double ambidextrous scissors so you can help, or a cutting wheel.

Velcro can be attached to marking instruments or paintbrushes.

Use contact paper for collage, or glue sticks instead of bottles.

____Attention-deficit and/or behavioral:

Provide children with their own materials and workspace, minimizing waiting and crowding.

Offer materials like Play-Doh® to express feelings and energy.

Limit children to a few choices rather than overwhelming them with everything in the art center.

© Cengage Learning®

Figure 10-4

Look back at Chapter 9, Figure 9-4, for a checklist that measures the inclusive nature of a classroom. Figure 10-4 shows an example of how an art activity can be adapted to meet the needs of children who have disabilities.

10-3d Individualized Curriculum

Children have varying multiple intelligences and learning and sensory styles that are important considerations when planning and implementing an individualized curriculum. When assessing the effectiveness of a curriculum, these factors must be taken into consideration.

---

multiple intelligences. A theory of intelligence, proposed by Howard Gardner, that outlines several different kinds of intelligence, rather than the notion of intelligence as measured by standardized testing, such as the IQ test.

individualized curriculum. A course of study developed and tailored to meet the needs and interests of an individual, rather than those of a group without regard for the individual child.

Multiple Intelligences

In Chapter 4, you read about Gardner's theory of multiple intelligences (MI) that holds that children possess different kinds of minds, and therefore, understand, learn, remember and perform in different ways. Most experts agree that intelligence is complex and that traditional tests do not measure the entire host of skills or abilities involved.

Gardner's theory is that we have at least nine ways of knowing or of being "smart." They are:

1. Linguistic: word games, storytelling
2. Logical-Mathematical: numbers, patterns, shapes, puzzles
3. Spatial: build, draw, design, videos
4. Body-Kinesthetic: touch, run, coordinated,
5. Musical: sing, dance, play instruments
6. Interpersonal: social, talkative,
7. Intrapersonal: label feelings, reflective, set goals
8. Naturalist: science, discovery of natural outdoor world
9. Existential: asks questions about deeper aspects of life, questios ethics

Refresh your memory by reviewing Chapter 4, Figure 4-8.

It is easy to see these intelligences in any preschool classroom. Some children excel at puzzles and manipulative games, whereas others are busy dictating stories, building a boatyard with blocks, or holding the guinea pig. All children have the capacity for the nine categories of MI, but are not equally proficient in all of them.

The relationship of MI-based curriculum to integrated curriculum is fairly clear. If children have different ways of knowing, they should experience a concept, lesson, or subject matter in a variety of ways. Teachers can vary what and how they teach to many intelligences instead of just one, just as they teach to many developmental areas, not just one.

Learning Styles

Some people like to learn by reading books or having someone teach them. Others prefer to experiment and learn by trial and error. Each of these is a legitimate method of learning and processing information, and each indicates the preferred style of that particular person.

There are three basic sensory styles young children use to learn: visual, auditory, and tactile-kinesthetic. Each child has a preferred mode, although it is not the only way a child integrates knowledge.

1. *Visual learners* like to represent knowledge by reading, writing and drawing. After a field trip to the aquarium, Inez writes and illustrates a story about sharks.
2. *Auditory learners* listen to others and like to talk to others about what they learn. On the way home from the aquarium, Darius makes up a song about a starfish. The teacher asks him to teach it to the rest of the class.

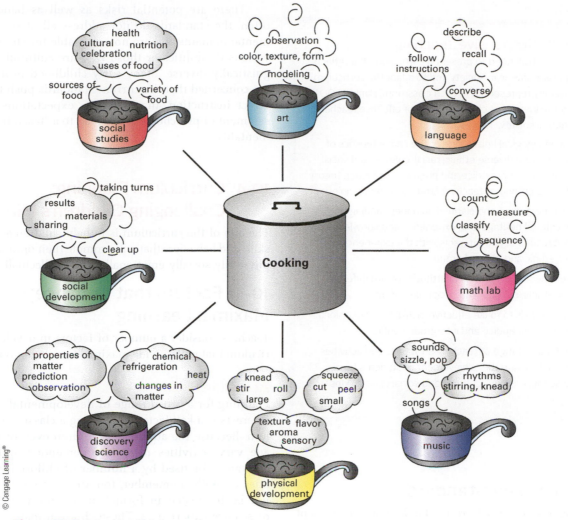

Figure 10-5 A Cooking Web.

3. *Tactile-kinesthetic learners* are physically active and learn by doing rather than listening. Back in the classroom, Joel and Martha go straight to the block corner to build an aquarium.

Effective curriculum must be judged on how the teaching strategies involve many intelligences and learning styles in a wide range of activities to enable children to succeed by drawing on their own capacities to learn.

10-3e Developmental Domains

Child development theory tells us that all developmental domains—social-emotional, language, physical, and cognitive—are related to and interact with one another. Effective curriculum is a "whole child" curriculum, with equal attention to all areas of the child's development. Critics of early learning standards in some states note that greater emphasis is too often placed on language, math, and cognition, and less attention is given to social-emotional and physical

development. Figure 10-5 demonstrates how one activity can enhance all developmental domains.

Children learn best when the school environment is welcoming and says we care about you and your family. This is especially true for children and families whose culture and background differ from that of the teaching staff. Positive relationships with children's home and community begin with honoring the family's cultural values and creating avenues for working together in the child's best interests. This is especially true for families whose children are dual-language learners.

learning styles. A child's preferred method of integrating knowledge and experiences.

developmental domains. An area of growth such as social, cognitive, or physical development.

learning standards. The level of attainment mandated by local or national government agencies that describe learning outcomes for various age groups.

Ethics

10-3f Learning Standards

Across the country, early learning standards are being adopted to create a set of expectations for children and to measure the kinds of development and learning that are taking place. Most states have adopted some form of standards for children aged 3 to 5 years and for children in the primary grades. Gronlund (2006) identified how early learning standards can benefit children:

> When they are linked to primary grade standards, they ensure school readiness.
> Standards can define the foundational skills for learning.
> They help teachers identify the next steps and have appropriate expectations for children.
> They professionalize the field of early childhood education.

There are potential risks as well as benefits. Too often, the standards do not address all of the developmental domains and are not adaptable for children with various disabilities or those who are culturally and linguistically diverse. Many early childhood professionals are concerned that the current standards push too much direct instruction, inappropriate expectations, and assessment of preschoolers and lead to a "teach to the test" mentality.

10-4 Curriculum Planning: Challenging Children's Minds

The aim of the curriculum is to help children acquire the skills and behaviors that will promote their optimal growth physically, socially, emotionally, and intellectually.

10-4a Factors that Enhance Maximal Learning

Teachers consider a number of factors in developing curriculum that will provide maximal learning opportunities.

Acquiring Skills

Planning for a broad range of developmental skills and interests is a key factor in creating a classroom curriculum. Because the abilities of children even of the same age vary, activities must be open-ended and flexible enough to be used by a number of children with varieties of skills. Remember, too, that some children may not be interested in formal or organized art projects or science experiences. These children may learn more easily through self-selected play: by wearing a space helmet and fantasizing a trip to the moon, by building

Brain Research Findings

The brain is strongly run by patterns rather than facts. Children learn best with curriculum developed around themes, integrated learning, and whole experiences. The key to our intelligence is the recognition of patterns and relationships.

Stress and threat affect the brain in many ways. Emotions run the brain, and bad emotions reduce the capacity for memory and understanding, as well as reducing higher-order thinking skills. Good emotions create excitement and love of learning.

The brain runs better when food intake is steady. Insulin levels stay more even, cortisol levels are lower, and glucose tolerance is better. Diet activates memory; children need diets rich in proteins (meats, nuts, cheese), omega-3 fatty acids, and selenium and boron (leafy green vegetables), as well as enough restful sleep so the brain can reorganize itself.

All learning is mind–body. A child's physical state, posture, and breathing affect learning. Our brain is designed for cycles and rhythms. Practice makes permanent, and memory is kept more accurate when information is revisited.

Curriculum Implications

Conclusion: Develop meaningful themes for activity planning. Uninteresting or abstract pieces of information (e.g., drilling young children on alphabet letters) will not provide understanding. Plan some kinds of "immersion experiences" that encourage children to go deeply into their play and work.

Conclusion: Make a positive, personal connection with each child, and avoid threats by loss of approval, hurried schedules, or implying children are helpless or bad. A secure environment counteracts the problems that may occur when the stress regulation mechanisms are triggered too often. Good emotions enhance memory.

Conclusion: Snacks are good! Regular snack times may lead to better cognitive functioning, fewer discipline problems, and an enhanced sense of wellbeing.

Conclusion: Keep track of and teach to children's bodily functions and body states and how long they are expected to sit or nap. Plan a daily schedule with both variety and balance, and work in regular routines and productive rituals.

Effective curriculum engages children's minds and promotes problem solving. <

with blocks for long periods, or by running and climbing outdoors.

The developmental Word Pictures of children from birth through age 8 found in Chapter 3 can be useful in planning for the development of age-appropriate skills.

Teacher-Directed Learning

This text promotes teaching through active learning by children who have an active part in creating the curriculum. That does not exclude, however, the need for teacher-planned experiences in order to further the educational goals of the program.

When materials and information are complex or the concept is unknown to the children, teachers provide specific directions and knowledge to illustrate the behavior or concept. Teaching certain skills, such as cleaning off the paintbrush before dipping into another color, requires teacher guidance, as done learning to print lower and upper case letters.

10-4b Creating Written Plans

A written lesson plan provides a map that may outline a single activity, a daily plan, or a long-term project. The plan provides a format to follow and a tool for evaluation and assessment.

Planning for Groups

There are times within the daily routine when teachers gather children together in large and small groups. Various types of learning experiences best lend themselves to small- or large-group discussions. A visit from a firefighter would work well with a large group where all could see and hear. Small groups could then form to discuss the presentation in greater detail.

Large group times are used to:

> Provide transitions in the daily schedule
> Bring in a special guest
> Introduce new ideas and materials
> Sing, dance, do fingerplays
> Read stories
> Plan activities with children
> Review the day's events
> Initiate group problem solving

Group times are more meaningful when children's home language is used for story time. One teacher reads the book in English; the other reads it in Spanish. <

Small groups:

> Provide a closer and more personal experience and supervision for children
> Help children practice a specific skill, such as listening and taking turns to talk
> Encourage children in their social action with one another and with the teacher
> Allow for individualized teaching and give teachers an opportunity to observe each child's growth and development
> Become the arena for discussions and problem solving about projects, behavior, and other classroom issues
> Give time for exploring topics in depth
> Eat a meal or have a snack together

What is common to all group times is the occasion for teachers to encourage listening and speaking skills, to provide an arena in which children share thoughts and ideas with one another, and to introduce any number of cognitive and social activities.

Setting Goals

The process of developing curriculum begins with setting goals for learning. These goals are based on the teacher's knowledge of child development, of the individual child, and of the educational philosophy of the program. Goals may be short- or long-range and may focus on skill development, themes, or projects. Setting goals includes:

> State clearly what it is you want children to learn. List three to five objectives that you want children to achieve
> State the reasons for your choices based on your own values and educational priorities
> Gather the resources needed to achieve the goals you set, collecting materials, props, information, and ideas for what you need
> Set regular times to meet for curriculum planning—on a weekly, monthly, or seasonal basis
> Reflect and evaluate the outcomes; consider what worked well and what was not successful, and use the feedback to adopt further goals

Lesson Plans

A **lesson plan** is a written outline that helps teachers articulate and implement goals they have set yet is flexible enough to be changed as needed. The plan may include a list of activities, goals for children's learning experiences, the process or method of instruction, the teacher's responsibilities, the time of day, and other notations. A written plan may or may not include all of the other activities normally available in the interest centers. Blocks, manipulatives, dramatic play, science, math, and language materials remain available to children, but some teachers only include the planned learning experience and teacher-directed activities in their plans. Figure 10-6 is a sample of a weekly lesson plan, and Figure 10-7 is sample lesson plan for a single activity that includes space for evaluation.

Webbing

Another way that teachers create written plans is the process known as **webbing**. Webbing is a planning tool that provides depth to a topic and creates a map of possible activities and projects. The web integrates the activities and content in a visual way that is flexible and expands with children's interest and input. A web may be organized around a theme (cooking), into curriculum areas (language, arts, music), or around program goals such as cooperation, as illustrated in Figure 10-8. Other webbing examples are Figure 9-3 in Chapter 9 and 10-5 in this chapter.

To begin a web, identify a key theme or topic that becomes the center of the web. Radiating from the center

lesson plan. A written outline that states the activity, time, materials, and resources needed to implement a learning experience.

webbing. A process through which teachers create a diagram based on a topic or a theme. It is a planning tool for curriculum and includes many resources.

are other aspects of the theme, such as concepts and activities. Often the activities, experiences, and materials that may be needed are woven into the web. This type of planning is fluid and continues to change. Starting with what children already know about the theme or with what the teacher wants children to learn, the web grows with new ideas.

10-4c Themes

A traditional method of developing curriculum is to focus on a broad, general topic or theme, such as the five senses, home and family, or sea life. Classroom themes should reflect the children's interests and abilities. An urban child will relate to themes about subways, taxis, and tall buildings. A child living in Houston or central Florida may have more of an interest in space exploration. By choosing themes that coincide with children's daily lives, teachers promote connected and relevant learning.

A thematic approach uses many of the attributes of an inclusive, integrated, and developmentally appropriate curriculum:

1. Children can help choose and plan themes, thereby constructing their own learning.
2. Activities can be chosen to reflect the curriculum goal.
3. The emphasis is on active learning.
4. Many subject areas can be integrated in the different activities.
5. A variety of learning styles can be accommodated through different media and teaching techniques.
6. It has the potential for multicultural emphasis.

Holidays could offer an opportunity to use a thematic approach to creating curriculum. What is critical is to remember that if holidays are celebrated, celebrations beyond the dominant culture should be included.

The theme of "Magnificent Me!" is found in Figure 10-6. "Cooking" as a theme is visualized in the web in Figure 10-5, and "Cooperation" is the focus in Figure 10-8.

Professionalism

A Balancing Act: Child-Directed and Teacher-Directed Experiences

Intentional teaching involves deciding if a child-directed or adult-directed experience is best under particular circumstances. One researcher (Epstein, 2007) explored the similarities between both approaches to teaching and learning. It turns out that neither way is controlled exclusively by the teacher or by the child; both are actively involved in the activity and process. When the experience is teacher-directed, children are encouraged to make suggestions, ask questions, and otherwise actively participate. The teacher deliberately keeps the focus on the purpose of the lesson while responding to the children's involvement. For a child-directed experience, teachers are similarly intentional in their involvement. As children investigate and explore, the teacher is primed to observe and get involved when it seems appropriate. Neither teaching strategy is a passive approach, but in both, the teacher times suggestions and interactions with the children and the activity. The teacher's role is to help advance the experience and guide their learning to greater depths.

> As we think about the learning experience, we ask ourselves:
> Which method best suits the goals for learning?
> Which method is best for this particular group?
> Which method extends children's knowledge and deepens their understanding of this particular lesson or information?
> Which method am I most comfortable with for this experience?

There is no right or wrong answer to these questions. Both methods are developmentally appropriate and children learn through both ways. Whether child- or adult-directed, teaching with intention fosters children's initiative and learning.

Think About This

1. Describe a teaching situation where you would use teacher-directed methods. How would you get the class involved and keep interest high?

2. Describe a situation where you would interact with a child-directed activity. How would you establish your involvement and keep children focused without dominating the activity?

truth or fiction?

T F Written curriculum plans are used to schedule the school year curriculum content and activities.

Written plans are flexible outlines for an individual activity, a project, a day, or a week. Plans are usually short-term so that they may be readily changed to meet children's needs, interests, and abilities.

10-4d The Project Approach

The word "project" implies a long-term activity that requires planning, questioning, making choices, and gathering resources. That is just what **project approach** consists

project approach. An in-depth study of a particular subject or theme by one or more children. Exploration of themes and topics over a period of days or weeks. Working in small groups, children are able to accommodate various levels of complexity and understanding to meet the needs of all the children working on the project.

Sample Preschool-Kindergarten Lesson Plan

TEACHER(S):   **DATES:**   **THEME:** Magnificent Me!

CONCEPTS: I am unique, special, and part of a family

SKILLS: Prewriting, writing, measuring, graphing, problem solving, and awareness of similarities/differences

CENTERS & ACTIVITIES	MONDAY	TUESDAY	WEDNESDAY	THURSDAY	FRIDAY
MORNING GROUP ACTIVITY	Sing "Good Morning." Introduce "My Body."	Take individual instant photos. Introduce "My ends"	Read On the Day You Were Born. Introduce "My Family."	Make breadsticks formed in initials. Introduce "My Home."	Healthy snack chart: finish & discuss.
AFTERNOON GROUP ACTIVITY	Identify body parts and what they do.	Animal friends: share stuffed animals and/or pets	Chart birthdays of the children and family members.	Read How My Parents Learned to Eat.	Bring and share something about yourself.
LANGUAGE & LITERACY	Begin "All About Me" books.	Write about photo and put into "Me" book with photo.	Add family photo to book. Write or draw about photo.	Write class story about field trip experience.	Finish "All About Me" books and share. Finish class story.
ART	Make life-sized self-portraits.	Make thumbprint and footprint pictures.	Make puppet papercup family pop-ups.	Make kitchen gadget puppets.	Mix playdough to match skin color.
MUSIC & MOVEMENT	"Name Song" Body parts move to music.	Sing "I'm A Special Person and So Are You" and "Friends Go Marching"	Beanbag toss and Kitchen marching band	Sing "So Many Ways to Say Good Morning" and dance.	Dance in hats with streamers to music.
DRAMATIC PLAY HOME LIVING	Home living center with a full mirror and baby pictures of children.	Add phones, paper, and pencils for message-taking.	Bathe baby dolls in warm sudsy water. Add stuffed animals to area.	Add a Wok and other cookware to center.	Add hats to dress-up clothes.
MATH MANIPULATIVE	Measure and record height of each child.	Graph the children's heights.	Use puzzles of family celebrations.	Gather items from home and play "What's missing?"	Estimate number of pennies in a jar, then count them.
SCIENCE & DISCOVERY	Listen to heart with stethoscope. Examine pictures or model of skeleton.	Magnifying glasses to see thumbprints. Exploring shadows.	Food colors, eye droppers, and ice trays	Weigh on scales for "Me" book. "What's That Sound?"	Magnets and what sinks, what floats?

OUTDOOR/LARGE MUSCLE

BLOCKS

Add: People figures, animal figures, boxes, houses, cars

Nature walk: obstacle course on playground
Hop, run, skip, jump

TRANSITIONS

Puppet helper of the day
Variations of "Name Song"

SENSORY CENTERS

SOCIAL STUDIES

Water table with warm, soapy water
Multicultural skin colored playdough
Healthy snacks "Tasting Tray"

Invite family members to visit.
Field Trip to grocery store.
We are all alike. We are all different.

BOOKS OF THE WEEK

My Five Senses, Big Friend Little Friend
Mommy's Office, William's Doll

SPECIAL ACTIVITIES & NOTES

Field trip to grocery store. Children decide which healthy snacks to buy. Explain decisions.
Week-long project: Make chart or diagram re: food groups. Prepare and eat snacks. Write class story.

Figure 10-6 Sample Weekly Lesson Plan. Source: From Jackman H. L. Early education curriculum: A child's connection to the world (5th ed.). Wadsworth, a part of Cengage Learning, Inc. 2012, p. 66.

Sample Single-Activity Lesson Plan

Activity Name: _____

Purpose/Goal: _____

Context: _____

Location (indoors/outdoors, in what section of yard or room): _____

Time of day: _____

Type and size of group: _____

Materials needed and how children will use them: _____

How to introduce activity and what antecedents are necessary for this group: _____

Clean-up provisions: _____

How will children be involved? _____

Results: _____

What were the children's responses? _____

Were the goals achieved? _____

Problems? _____

Solutions for next time: _____

Implications for other activities: _____

Next steps/other activities: _____

Title: Planning an Activity _____

Figure 10-7 Good planning takes time and thought. (From A. M. Gordon & K. W. Browne, Guiding young children in a diverse society. Published by Allyn and Bacon, Boston, MA. © 1996 by Pearson Education. Reprinted by permission of the publisher.)

Language
Plan and perform a favorite story.
Choose a story at the listening post together.
Learn "I love you" in sign language.
Copy someone's motions, dance, block patterns.
Put on a puppet show.
Develop a "What Can I Share?" chart.
Discuss how new toys, equipment will
   be shared so everyone gets a turn.

Social Studies
Make a group gift for hospital, rest home.
Create an art display for the local library.
Make cookies to sell at the school fair.
Run errands for teachers, each other.
Develop dramatic play themes of:
   shoe stores, hospital, doctors, ecology.
Collect and sort recycling materials.
Take a field trip to the town dump for
   recycling.
Write a "protest letter" about
   an inferior product.

Music
Sing together each day.
Have a rhythm band.
Dance in groups of two or three.
Dance with a parachute.

Science
Care for classroom pets.
Have group cooking projects.
Plan and plant a garden.

Environment
Schedule cleanup daily.
Have two children share cubbies.
Bring snacks from home to share.
Set tables for two or more children.
Use large bins to store some materials;
   children will need to share contents.

COOPERATION

Games
Play Simon Says.
Play board games:
Winnie-The-Pooh and
   Candy Land.
Play Lotto.
Play Bingo.

Art
Trace each other's bodies on paper.
Share paste and collage materials.
Share paints.
Make a mural.
Make litter bags.
Create a wall hanging: fabric, crayons
   and sheets; each child draws part.
Create a class quilt: each child sews a
   square; teacher puts it together.

Outdoors
Push someone on a swing.
Pull a friend in a wagon.
Make bird feeders.
Set up bowling alley, with bowler
   and pin setters.
Make an obstacle course.
Use seesaws.
Play group jump rope.
Play Follow the Leader.

Figure 10-8 The social skill of cooperation can be fostered throughout the curriculum as illustrated by webbing. (© Cengage Learning 2013)

of: exploring a theme or topic (such as building a table for the science area) over a period of days or weeks. The first step is for the children and teachers to investigate what they need to know. They observe, question, estimate, experiment, and research items and events related to the table size and construction. They may take a field trip to a cabinet shop to find out about different types of wood they could use. They may make models of the table they want, using paper, cardboard, wood, and plastic. Children work in small groups throughout the process and have the opportunity to make many choices about their level of participation ("I want to help measure the table.") "I want to paint it." "My grandpa says he will build it and we can all help." The teacher often records their activities with photographs. Project work has different levels of complexity so that it meets the needs of children of different ages and abilities "What does it mean to measure in feet? Whose feet?" "I'm making a picture of me sitting at the table when it is finished." "I know how to hammer! Let me do it."

The underlying philosophy of the project approach is that children can be co-constructors of their own learning. The teacher helps the children explore what they already know about the topic, what they might need to know, and how they can represent that knowledge through various media (dramatic play, art, music). Teachers pose questions for children—(What might happen if you do that? How do you think you could make that work?)—which led them to suggest a hypothesis. This reinforces Vygotsky's theory that interaction and direct teaching are important aspects of intellectual development.

10-4e Technology in the Classroom

Many children come to early childhood settings having some knowledge and competency with today's technology tools. The digital age is part of their home setting as they see parents with cellphones, computers, cameras, DVD players, and a host of interactive tablets, games, and music devices. Many of these tools have found their way into the early childhood classrooms and challenge the early childhood professional to assess their usefulness and potential for learning. As with any other aspect of curriculum, teachers need to use their knowledge of child development principles and awareness of how children learn as guidelines for integrating technology and media into the curriculum.

The National Association for the Education of Young Children and the Fred Rogers Center for Early Learning and Children's Media position statement, (2012), *Technology and Interactive Media as Tools in Early Childhood Programs Serving Children from Birth through Age 8,* sets out guidelines that help inform a teacher's decision of how and when to use technology and interactive media with children, noting that these activities should never replace

"creative play, real-life exploration, physical activity, outdoor experiences, conversation, and social interactions.":

1. Choose and evaluate interactive media tools intentionally, keeping in mind their developmental appropriateness and their potential for an interactive experience.
2. Use interactive media as a way to intentionally extend and support hands-on activities to enhance children's engagement with their real world and expands their ability to gain to new information.
3. Avoid the passive use of television, videos, DVD's and other non-interactive media in early childhood programs for children under age 2. Among 2- to 5-year-olds, discourage use of media in which children do not take an active part.
4. In programs for children under age 2, only use technology and interactive media that support responsive and positive interactions between children and caregivers.
5. Follow screen time recommendations from public health organizations that limit how much time children should spend in front of media screens.
6. Help ensure equitable access to technology and interactive media for children and their families.

10-4f Developmentally Appropriate Curriculum Models

There are many choices available for curriculum that is child-centered, where "work" or play is the foundation for learning, and where the developmentally appropriate principles set out by NAEYC are respected. The models that are outlined in Figure 10-9 encourage teaching to enhance development and learning, planning curriculum that is based on setting goals for children's progress, assessing children's development, and creating caring communities, and promoting strong relationships with families.The models in the Figure have many characteristics in common; they also have distinct and unique features that set them apart from one another.

Developmentally Appropriate Curriculum

Program	Founder	Philosophy	Environment [physical, temporal, interpersonal]	Teacher Role	Key Characteristics
Montessori A Prepared Environment Approach	Dr. Maria Montessori [early 1900s, Italy]	> Learning is an individual experience; > Group instruction is to introduce proper use of materials and new tasks; > Curriculum is to be adapted to the individual rather than molding the child to the curriculum; > Child is free to select own materials & learns at own pace; > "Work," not play, is used to describe children's activity; > Children learn through the use of their senses.	[P]The "prepared environment" has child-sized furniture and carefully arranged work areas. Teachers organize areas and select deliberate materials. [T]Schedule has work period of long duration to encourage child choice, task persistence, concentration, and accomplishment. [I]Tone is quiet, focused, and harmonious; social interaction is allowed but not primary focus of schooling.	Must be Montessori certified; Guide and observer of children; Teach the precise way to use the materials; Redirect child to focus on correct use of materials to complete task for concept mastery.	Materials that are self-correcting, sensory, sequential and didactic: > Training of the senses with sensory, practical life, grace & courtesy tasks; > Mixed age groups; > Focused curriculum for infants & toddlers (1-3), preschool (3-5), elementary (K-5th) & high school students.
Bank Street: A Developmental-Interactive Approach	Lucy Sprague Mitchell [early 1900s, USA]	> Influenced by Dewey's Progressive Education Movement of "learning by doing"; > Priority on social and emotional growth and holds to Erikson's psychosocial development views: > The "whole child" and developmental principles influence curriculum planning;	[P]Classroom organized into learning centers; Children work individually or in groups; [T] Activities are given priority with large blocks of free-play to provide concrete, first-hand experiences; [I]Emphasizes the interaction between the child and the environment; [I] Community and neighborhood connections are stressed.	Knowledge and preparation of the teacher is emphasized; Teacher's knowledge of child development principles is imperative to emphasize individual children and how they learn; Teacher is guide and facilitator of experiential learning; Teacher responds to activities initiated by children with questions, and plans curriculum from assessing via observation.	Originated the play-based approach and the beginning of child-centered learning; Interactive between children & adults as well as the community; Mixed age groups are common; Field trips are emphasized with curriculum units to follow up; Blocks are the primary material in the classroom; Social studies is at the core of the curriculum; All forms of literacy are emphasized;

Figure 10-9 An overview of curriculum models. Each is unique with its own strengths and characteristics.

(Continued)

Program	Founder	Philosophy	Environment [physical, temporal, interpersonal]	Teacher Role	Key Characteristics
		> Goals for children are based on developmental sequence and learning processes; > Play is used to enhance children's cognitive and language skills through frequent conversations and interactions.			Support for the social-emotional & cognitive relationships as well as a sense of autonomy with children as active learners, explorers and experimenters.
Waldorf Schools: Protected Play for the Spirit	Rudolf Steiner [early 1900s, Germany]	Emphasis on development of the whole child through sequential focus on "head, heart, and hands"; Based on belief that young children learn primarily through observation, imitation, and experience; Cultivates social and emotional intelligence; Connects children to nature; Emphasis on community building within the classroom.	[P] The environment is protective of children, keeping them shielded from negative influences of larger society; [P] Environments that nourish the senses through using natural materials; [T] Large blocks of time for creative play; [I]Relationships are primary, particularly between teacher and child; teacher and group stay together for several years.	Must be Waldorf -certified; Provides structure and routine in a home-like atmosphere; Fosters an enthusiasm for learning and nourishes the power of imagination through legends, myths, and storytelling; Models domestic, practical, and artistic activities.	Play as an imitation of life; The rhythm of the day/week is based on the cycles of life and nature; Extensive use of natural materials in furnishings and play materials; Mixed age groups; Looping, sometimes up to 8 years; Encourages skill development that imitates the work of the adult; A sense of reverence and wonder throughout the changing seasons; Imagination is stressed; Storytelling is emphasized for children and adults; Children are protected from harmful elements of common societal influences.

Program	Founder	Philosophy	Environment [physical, temporal, interpersonal]	Teacher Role	Key Characteristics
Schools of Reggio Emilia: An Aesthetic Approach	Loris Malaguzzi [mid 1900s, Italy]	Influenced by Dewey, Piaget, Vygotsky, & Gardner; Reggio Emilia is a town that believes children are the collective responsibility of the community. The schools are financed by the town.	[P] The environment is the third teacher [after family and class teacher]; [P] All of the environment has identity and purpose, aiming to encourage encounters, communication and relationships; [P] Order and beauty is apparent in design, space, equipment, and materials; Classrooms and entryways have natural light, large windows, and courtyards; Mirrors are used on the floors, walls, and ceilings; [P] Children's artwork and projects are displayed throughout the school; [P] Each classroom has an atelier (studio space); [T] Flexible routines and large periods of free play, including time in atelier; [I] Atmosphere is engaged and active, with teacher involvement to encourage investigations and expressions.	Teacher is co-learner and collaborator with children, team teacher and atelerista; Two Co-teachers per class, rather than Lead & Assistant. Teachers serve as researchers who ask questions, listen, observe, and guide open-ended discovery; A pedigogista (early childhood professional) meets with teachers once a week; An atelierista (trained in the arts) teaches techniques and skills to children; The teacher documents children's learning through a variety of media to make learning visible.	Infant/toddler programs begin the process; Children are strong, capable and can construct their own learning and need endless ways and opportunities to express themselves; Children are natural researchers; The child is collaborator, learning through the project approach in small groups where debate and discussion prevail; The child is communicator who symbolizes learning through the "hundred languages," of music, dance, art, sculpting, building, and writing; Documentation through photos, recordings, and stories is used to communicate to children, parents, and other children what they are working on and learning; Groups of children stay with one teacher for a 3-year period; Parents are seen as partners who collaborate with teachers in every aspect of the curriculum; The community is seen as an extension of the school; many projects take place throughout the town.

(Continued)

Developmentally Appropriate Curriculum (Continued)

Program	Founder	Philosophy	Environment [physical, temporal, interpersonal]	Teacher Role	Key Characteristics
High/Scope: A Cognitively-Oriented Approach	David Weikart, [1960s, USA]	Influenced by Piaget, Dewey, & Vygostsky. Based on results of the Perry Preschool Project; Expanded to infants and toddlers	[P]Well-defined activity areas that reflect children's interests; [P] Print-rich and language-enriched environment; [T] Follow a consistent Daily Routine of Plan–Do–Review sequence; [I] The atmosphere is engagement in active learning.	Teachers are trained in the High/Scope methods to develop skills in asking questions, reflection, and communication; Teachers are considered partners rather than managers in supporting children's play ideas and forming authentic relationships; Teachers focus on children's strengths and positive interaction strategies. Observation is a major role of the teacher, and each day they write anecdotal notes that influence the curriculum and individual children's growth through their own Child Observation Record (COR); Teachers help children deal with social conflict through a problem-solving approach.	Children construct their own knowledge through self-selected learning activities; Plan–Do–Review sequence leads children to make a plan, act on it, then reflect on the results; The "Do" part of Plan-Do-Review is called work time, not play; Shared control between children and teachers; Eight content areas with 58 key developmental indicators of observable behavior; Assessments based on teacher's anecdotes and ratings of children in 6 areas of development; Conflict resolution is a six-step process systematically taught, modelled and followed-through during the day.

Program	Founder	Philosophy	Environment [physical, temporal, interpersonal]	Teacher Role	Key Characteristics
The Creative Curriculum: A Comprehensive Approach	Diane Trister Dodge and others at Teaching Strategies [1970s, USA]	Influenced by Dewey, Erikson, Piaget, Maslow, Vygotsky, Smilansky, and Gardner	[P] The learning environment is the basic framework used to support children's play and self-selected activities; [P] The focus is on the various interest areas in the classroom; [T] Large blocks of free play are dedicated for individual and small group play in all interest areas; [T] Tone is active, social, and creative.	Teachers are trained in the approach; Teachers observe children as part of a systematic assessment process; Teachers take an active role in children's learning; Teachers integrate learning standards into daily experiences; Creating positive relationships and a caring community are emphasized, as are strong partnerships with families; Teachers are accountable for achieving positive results.	Curriculum incorporates latest research and includes curriculum for infants and toddlers as well as family child care, preschool, and children with special needs; Fully bi-lingual; Includes a complete assessment system; Assessments are aligned with Common Core standards, various state standards, and the standards of Head Start and the Office of Special Education Programs; Some publications are designed for parents; Uses in-depth studies (projects) to promote investigation.

I am a teacher who has been working in a Reggio-inspired program for more than 10 years. Our program has continued to grow over the years and is ever evolving in our work with young children. The foundation of the Reggio philosophy is that children are very competent learners. With the proper support from adults, children can reach amazing heights in their understanding of the world around them.

The children's ideas and thoughts provide the basis to our approach to curriculum. Children learn by doing. As teachers we provide the opportunity for children to express their ideas by any means available. Their experimentation in different media will often provide blueprints to their ideas, which in turn help them further their studies. We often encourage children to draw, paint, or sculpt their ideas and invite them to revisit these works. By introducing further provocations, such as questioning their thought process, children will continue researching their ideas, thus expanding their understanding of the world around them.

Another aspect to our curriculum-building is making the children's learning visible buy documenting their work. We will photograph, take dictations and record the work the children are doing. Documentation gives the children ways to revisit their work and provide a foundation to further their investigations. It also makes the children's learning more transparent to teachers and parents alike allowing us to help support and expand on their ideas.

An example of helping children further their thought process can be seen in an investigation into superheroes we did one summer. I had a class of 15 children, 4 and 5 years of age, many of whom spent large amounts of time flying and fighting "bad guys" in the play yard. We wanted to help them expand beyond their traditional superhero play and get them thinking more about the daily life of a superhero. We read a book entitled "Ordinary Boy" by William Boniface which was about an entire city of people with superhero traits. We encouraged the children to pick one trait that they would like to have if they were a superhero. We worked together to develop their ideas for costumes, where they would live, what their homes would look like, where they would eat and play, creating our own city of superheroes. The project culminated in a giant hand-drawn wall map depicting everything the children felt was important to their city.

There is no cookie-cutter formula to creating a curriculum in an ECE program. Curriculum must be continually emergent, evolving, flexible, and fluid. Learning is never-ending for children and adults alike. That is why the Reggio Emilia approach works well in so many early childhood programs.

—Tracy

summary

10.1 Early childhood educators are aware that play is the foundation for learning and provide and an atmosphere that supports the play process. Play is recognized as the curriculum of the child through hands-on activities where discovery and experiment are the basis for learning.

10.2 Through developmentally appropriate curriculum, children are challenged in all areas of development when the curriculum is age-appropriate, individually appropriate, and framed in the context of their culture. Culturally appropriate curriculum reflects the children, their families, and their community and supports efforts to view events and situations from a different cultural perspective.

10.3 Integrated, individualized, and inclusive curriculum provides opportunities for children of diverse skills and abilities to learn through the same experiences. Emergent curriculum takes its cues from the children's interests as teachers help them explore their ideas in greater depth and involvement. There are many ways of learning, and the multiple intelligences theory and learning styles help teachers create curriculum that covers a broad range of methods, abilities, and interests. State-mandated learning standards could be successfully integrated into a developmentally appropriate curriculum.

10.4 Developing curriculum includes setting goals, establishing priorities, knowing what resources are available and then evaluating the process. Teacher-directed learning is effective when new information or concepts are introduced. The project approach offers an in-depth exploration of a topic that call for teachers and children to collaborate in planning and developing materials and resources.

web resources

Bank Street School **www.bankstreet.edu**
Creative Curriculum
 http://teachingstrategies.com/curriculum/
HighScope **http://www.highscope.org**

NAEYC **http://www.naeyc.org**
The Schools of Reggio Emilia **http://reggioalliance.org**
Waldorf Schools **http:// www.whywaldorf.org**
Montessori Schools **http://ami-global.org/**

references

Banks, J. A. (2001). *Cultural diversity and education: Foundations, curriculum and teaching.* Boston: Allyn & Bacon.

Banks, J. A. (2006). *Cultural diversity and education: Foundations, curriculum, and teaching* (5th ed). Boston: Allyn & Bacon.

Bredekamp, S., & Rosegrant, T. (Eds.). (1995). *Reaching potentials: Transforming early childhood curriculum and assessment* (Vol. 2). Washington, DC: National Association for the Education of Young Children.

Copple, C., & Bredekamp, S. (Eds.). (2009). *Developmentally appropriate practice in early childhood programs serving children from birth through age 8.* Washington, DC: National Association for the Education of Young Children.

Gronlund, G. (2006). *Making early learning standards come alive: Connecting your practice and curriculum to state guidelines.* St. Paul, MN: Redleaf Press.

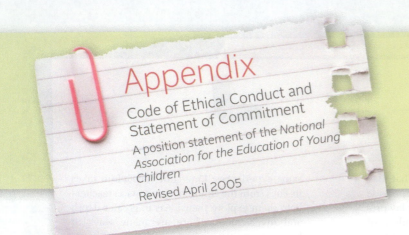

Appendix

Code of Ethical Conduct and
Statement of Commitment

A position statement of the National
Association for the Education of Young
Children

Revised April 2005

Preamble

NAEYC recognizes that those who work with young children face many daily decisions that have moral and ethical implications. The NAEYC Code of Ethical Conduct offers guidelines for responsible behavior and sets forth a common basis for resolving the principal ethical dilemmas encountered in early childhood care and education. The Statement of Commitment is not part of the Code but is a personal acknowledgement of an individual's willingness to embrace the distinctive values and moral obligations of the field of early childhood care and education. The primary focus of the Code is on daily practice with children and their families in programs for children from birth through 8 years of age, such as infant/toddler programs, preschool and prekindergarten programs, child care centers, hospital and child life settings, family child care homes, kindergartens, and primary classrooms. When the issues involve young children, then these provisions also apply to specialists who do not work directly with children, including program administrators, parent educators, early childhood adult educators, and officials with responsibility for program monitoring and licensing. (Note: See also the "Code of Ethical Conduct: Supplement for Early Childhood Adult Educators.")

Core Values

Standards of ethical behavior in early childhood care and education are based on commitment to the following core values that are deeply rooted in the history of the field of early childhood care and education. We have made a commitment to:

> Appreciate childhood as a unique and valuable stage of the human life cycle.
> Base our work on knowledge of how children develop and learn.
> Appreciate and support the bond between the child and family.
> Recognize that children are best understood and supported in the context of family, culture,* community, and society.

*There is not necessarily a corresponding principle for each ideal.

> Respect the dignity, worth, and uniqueness of each individual (child, family member, and colleague).
> Respect diversity in children, families, and colleagues.
> Recognize that children and adults achieve their full potential in the context of relationships that are based on trust and respect.

Conceptual Framework

The Code sets forth a framework of professional responsibilities in four sections. Each section addresses an area of professional relationships: (1) with children, (2) with families, (3) among colleagues, and (4) with the community and society. Each section includes an introduction to the primary responsibilities of the early childhood practitioner in that context. The introduction is followed by (1) a set of ideals that reflect exemplary professional practice and (2) a set of principles describing practices that are required, prohibited, or permitted.

*Culture includes ethnicity, racial identity, economic level, family structure, language, and religious and political beliefs, which profoundly influence each child's development and relationship to the world.

The **ideals** reflect the aspirations of practitioners. The **principles** guide conduct and assist practitioners in resolving ethical dilemmas.* Both ideals and principles are intended to direct practitioners to those questions which, when responsibly answered, can provide the basis for conscientious decision making. While the Code provides specific direction for addressing some ethical dilemmas, many others will require the practitioner to combine the guidance of the Code with professional judgment.

The ideals and principles in this Code present a shared framework of professional responsibility that affirms our commitment to the core values of our field. The Code publicly acknowledges the responsibilities that we in the field have assumed and in so doing supports ethical behavior in our work. Practitioners who face situations with ethical dimensions are urged to seek guidance in the applicable parts of this Code and in the spirit that informs the whole.

Often, "the right answer"—the best ethical course of action to take—is not obvious. There may be no readily apparent, positive way to handle a situation. When one important value contradicts another, we face an ethical dilemma. When we face a dilemma, it is our professional responsibility to consult the Code and all relevant parties to find the most ethical resolution.

Section I: Ethical Responsibilities to Children

Childhood is a unique and valuable stage in the human life cycle. Our paramount responsibility is to provide care and education in settings that are safe, healthy, nurturing, and responsive for each child. We are committed to supporting children's development and learning; respecting individual differences; and helping children learn to live, play, and work cooperatively. We are also committed to promoting children's self-awareness, competence, self-worth, resiliency, and physical well-being.

Ideals

I-1.1—To be familiar with the knowledge base of early childhood care and education and to stay informed through continuing education and training.

I-1.2—To base program practices upon current knowledge and research in the field of early childhood education, child development, and related disciplines, as well as on particular knowledge of each child.

I-1.3—To recognize and respect the unique qualities, abilities, and potential of each child.

I-1.4—To appreciate the vulnerability of children and their dependence on adults.

I-1.5—To create and maintain safe and healthy settings that foster children's social, emotional, cognitive, and physical development and that respect their dignity and their contributions.

I-1.6—To use assessment instruments and strategies that are appropriate for the children to be assessed, that are used only for the purposes for which they were designed, and that have the potential to benefit children.

I-1.7—To use assessment information to understand and support children's development and learning, to support instruction, and to identify children who may need additional services.

I-1.8—To support the right of each child to play and learn in an inclusive environment that meets the needs of children with and without disabilities.

I-1.9—To advocate for and ensure that all children, including those with special needs, have access to the support services needed to be successful.

I-1.10—To ensure that each child's culture, language, ethnicity, and family structure are recognized and valued in the program.

I-1.11—To provide all children with experiences in a language that they know, as well as support children in maintaining the use of their home language and in learning English.

I-1.12—To work with families to provide a safe and smooth transition as children and families move from one program to the next.

Principles

P-1.1—**Above all, we shall not harm children. We shall not participate in practices that are emotionally damaging, physically harmful, disrespectful, degrading, dangerous, exploitative, or intimidating to children.** *This principle has precedence over all others in this Code.*

P-1.2—We shall care for and educate children in positive emotional and social environments that are cognitively stimulating and that support each child's culture, language, ethnicity, and family structure.

P-1.3—We shall not participate in practices that discriminate against children by denying benefits, giving special advantages, or excluding them from programs or activities on the basis of their sex, race, national origin, religious beliefs, medical condition, disability, or the marital status/family structure, sexual orientation, or religious beliefs or other affiliations of their families. (Aspects of this principle do not apply in programs that have a lawful mandate to provide services to a particular population of children.)

P-1.4—We shall involve all those with relevant knowledge (including families and staff) in decisions concerning a child, as appropriate, ensuring confidentiality of sensitive information.

P-1.5—We shall use appropriate assessment systems, which include multiple sources of information, to provide information on children's learning and development.

P-1.6—We shall strive to ensure that decisions such as those related to enrollment, retention, or assignment to special education services, will be based on multiple sources of information and will never be based on a single assessment, such as a test score or a single observation.

P-1.7—We shall strive to build individual relationships with each child; make individualized adaptations in teaching strategies, learning environments, and curricula; and consult with the family so that each child benefits from the program. If after such efforts have been exhausted, the current placement does not meet a child's needs, or the child is seriously jeopardizing the ability of other children to benefit from the program, we shall collaborate with the child's family and appropriate specialists to determine the additional services needed and/or the placement option(s) most likely to ensure the child's success. (Aspects of this principle may not apply in programs that have a lawful mandate to provide services to a particular population of children.)

P-1.8—We shall be familiar with the risk factors for and symptoms of child abuse and neglect, including physical, sexual, verbal, and emotional abuse and physical, emotional, educational, and medical neglect. We shall know and follow state laws and community procedures that protect children against abuse and neglect.

P-1.9—When we have reasonable cause to suspect child abuse or neglect, we shall report it to the appropriate community agency and follow up to ensure that appropriate action has been taken. When appropriate, parents or guardians will be informed that the referral will be or has been made.

P-1.10—When another person tells us of his or her suspicion that a child is being abused or neglected, we shall assist that person in taking appropriate action in order to protect the child.

P-1.11—When we become aware of a practice or situation that endangers the health, safety, or well-being of children, we have an ethical responsibility to protect children or inform parents and/or others who can.

Section II: Ethical Responsibilities to Families

Families* are of primary importance in children's development. Because the family and the early childhood practitioner have a common interest in the child's well-being, we acknowledge a primary responsibility to bring about communication, cooperation, and collaboration between the home and early childhood program in ways that enhance the child's development.

Ideals

I-2.1—To be familiar with the knowledge base related to working effectively with families and to stay informed through continuing education and training.

I-2.2—To develop relationships of mutual trust and create partnerships with the families we serve.

I-2.3—To welcome all family members and encourage them to participate in the program.

I-2.4—To listen to families, acknowledge and build upon their strengths and competencies, and learn from families as we support them in their task of nurturing children.

I-2.5—To respect the dignity and preferences of each family and to make an effort to learn about its structure, culture, language, customs, and beliefs.

*The term *family* may include those adults, besides parents, with the responsibility of being involved in educating, nurturing, and advocating for a child.

I-2.6—To acknowledge families' childrearing values and their right to make decisions for their children.

I-2.7—To share information about each child's education and development with families and to help them understand and appreciate the current knowledge base of the early childhood profession.

I-2.8—To help family members enhance their understanding of their children and support the continuing development of their skills as parents.

I-2.9—To participate in building support networks for families by providing them with opportunities to interact with program staff, other families, community resources, and professional services.

Principles

P-2.1—We shall not deny family members access to their child's classroom or program setting unless access is denied by court order or other legal restriction.

P-2.2—We shall inform families of program philosophy, policies, curriculum, assessment system, and personnel qualifications, and explain why we teach as we do—which should be in accordance with our ethical responsibilities to children (see Section I).

P-2.3—We shall inform families of and, when appropriate, involve them in policy decisions.

P-2.4—We shall involve the family in significant decisions affecting their child.

P-2.5—We shall make every effort to communicate effectively with all families in a language that they understand. We shall use community resources for translation and interpretation when we do not have sufficient resources in our own programs.

P-2.6—As families share information with us about their children and families, we shall consider this information to plan and implement the program.

P-2.7—We shall inform families about the nature and purpose of the program's child assessments and how data about their child will be used.

P-2.8—We shall treat child assessment information confidentially and share this information only when there is a legitimate need for it.

P-2.9—We shall inform the family of injuries and incidents involving their child, of risks such as exposures to communicable diseases that might result in infection, and of occurrences that might result in emotional stress.

P-2.10—Families shall be fully informed of any proposed research projects involving their children and shall have the opportunity to give or withhold consent without penalty. We shall not permit or participate in research that could in any way hinder the education, development, or well-being of children.

P-2.11—We shall not engage in or support exploitation of families. We shall not use our relationship with a family for private advantage or personal gain or enter into relationships with family members that might impair our effectiveness working with their children.

P-2.12—We shall develop written policies for the protection of confidentiality and the disclosure of children's records. These policy documents shall be made available to all program personnel and families. Disclosure of children's records beyond family members, program personnel, and consultants having an obligation of confidentiality shall require familial consent (except in cases of abuse or neglect).

P-2.13—We shall maintain confidentiality and shall respect the family's right to privacy, refraining from disclosure of confidential information and intrusion into family life. However, when we have reason to believe that a child's welfare is at risk, it is permissible to share confidential information with agencies, as well as with individuals who have legal responsibility for intervening in the child's interest.

P-2.14—In cases where family members are in conflict with one another, we shall work openly, sharing our observations of the child, to help all parties involved make informed decisions. We shall refrain from becoming an advocate for one party.

P-2.15—We shall be familiar with and appropriately refer families to community resources and professional support services. After a referral has been made, we shall follow up to ensure that services have been appropriately provided.

Section III: Ethical Responsibilities to Colleagues

In a caring, cooperative workplace, human dignity is respected, professional satisfaction is promoted, and positive relationships are developed and sustained. Based upon our core values, our primary responsibility to colleagues is to establish and maintain settings and relationships that support productive work and meet professional needs. The same ideals that apply to children also apply as we interact with adults in the workplace.

A—Responsibilities to Co-workers

Ideals

I-3A.1—To establish and maintain relationships of respect, trust, confidentiality, collaboration, and cooperation with co-workers.

I-3A.2—To share resources with co-workers, collaborating to ensure that the best possible early childhood care and education program is provided.

I-3A.3—To support co-workers in meeting their professional needs and in their professional development.

I-3A.4—To accord co-workers due recognition of professional achievement.

Principles

P-3A.1—We shall recognize the contributions of colleagues to our program and not participate in practices that diminish their reputations or impair their effectiveness in working with children and families.

P-3A.2—When we have concerns about the professional behavior of a co-worker, we shall first let that person know of our concern in a way that shows respect for personal dignity and for the diversity to be found among staff members and then attempt to resolve the matter collegially and in a confidential manner.

P-3A.3—We shall exercise care in expressing views regarding the personal attributes or professional conduct of co-workers. Statements should be based on firsthand knowledge, not hearsay, and relevant to the interests of children and programs.

P-3A.4—We shall not participate in practices that discriminate against a co-worker because of sex, race, national origin, religious beliefs or other affiliations, age, marital status/family structure, disability, or sexual orientation.

B—Responsibilities to Employers

Ideals

I-3B.1—To assist the program in providing the highest quality of service.

I-3B.2—To do nothing that diminishes the reputation of the program in which we work unless it is violating laws and regulations designed to protect children or is violating the provisions of this Code.

Principles

P-3B.1—We shall follow all program policies. When we do not agree with program policies, we shall attempt to effect change through constructive action within the organization.

P-3B.2—We shall speak or act on behalf of an organization only when authorized. We shall take care to acknowledge when we are speaking for the organization and when we are expressing a personal judgment.

P-3B.3—We shall not violate laws or regulations designed to protect children and shall take appropriate action consistent with this Code when aware of such violations.

P-3B.4—If we have concerns about a colleague's behavior, and children's well-being is not at risk, we may address the concern with that individual. If children are at risk or the situation does not improve after it has been brought to the colleague's attention, we shall report the colleague's unethical or incompetent behavior to an appropriate authority.

P-3B.5—When we have a concern about circumstances or conditions that impact the quality of care and education within the program, we shall inform the program's administration or, when necessary, other appropriate authorities.

C—Responsibilities to Employees

Ideals

I-3C.1—To promote safe and healthy working conditions and policies that foster mutual respect, cooperation, collaboration, competence, well-being, confidentiality, and self-esteem in staff members.

I-3C.2—To create and maintain a climate of trust and candor that will enable staff to speak and act in the best interests of children, families, and the field of early childhood care and education.

I-3C.3—To strive to secure adequate and equitable compensation (salary and benefits) for those who work with or on behalf of young children.

I-3C.4—To encourage and support continual development of employees in becoming more skilled and knowledgeable practitioners.

Principles

P-3C.1—In decisions concerning children and programs, we shall draw upon the education, training, experience, and expertise of staff members.

P-3C.2—We shall provide staff members with safe and supportive working conditions that honor confidences and permit them to carry out their responsibilities through fair performance evaluation, written grievance procedures, constructive feedback, and opportunities for continuing professional development and advancement.

P-3C.3—We shall develop and maintain comprehensive written personnel policies that define program standards. These policies shall be given to new staff members and shall be available and easily accessible for review by all staff members.

P-3C.4—We shall inform employees whose performance does not meet program expectations of areas of concern and, when possible, assist in improving their performance.

P-3C.5—We shall conduct employee dismissals for just cause, in accordance with all applicable laws and regulations. We shall inform employees who are dismissed of the reasons for their termination. When a dismissal is for cause, justification must be based on

evidence of inadequate or inappropriate behavior that is accurately documented, current, and available for the employee to review.

P-3C.6—In making evaluations and recommendations, we shall make judgments based on fact and relevant to the interests of children and programs.

P-3C.7—We shall make hiring, retention, termination, and promotion decisions based solely on a person's competence, record of accomplishment, ability to carry out the responsibilities of the position, and professional preparation specific to the developmental levels of children in his/her care.

P-3.C.8—We shall not make hiring, retention, termination, and promotion decisions based on an individual's sex, race, national origin, religious beliefs or other affiliations, age, marital status/family structure, disability, or sexual orientation. We shall be familiar with and observe laws and regulations that pertain to employment discrimination. (Aspects of this principle do not apply to programs that have a lawful mandate to determine eligibility based on one or more of the criteria identified above.)

P-3C-9—We shall maintain confidentiality in dealing with issues related to an employee's job performance and shall respect an employee's right to privacy regarding personal issues.

Section IV: Ethical Responsibilities to Community and Society

Early childhood programs operate within the context of their immediate community made up of families and other institutions concerned with children's welfare. Our responsibilities to the community are to provide programs that meet the diverse needs of families, to cooperate with agencies and professions that share the responsibility for children, to assist families in gaining access to those agencies and allied professionals, and to assist in the development of community programs that are needed but not currently available.

As individuals, we acknowledge our responsibility to provide the best possible programs of care and education for children and to conduct ourselves with honesty and integrity. Because of our specialized expertise in early childhood development and education and because the larger society shares responsibility for the welfare and protection of young children, we acknowledge a collective obligation to advocate for the best interests of children within early childhood programs and in the larger community and to serve as a voice for young children everywhere.

The ideals and principles in this section are presented to distinguish between those that pertain to the work of the individual early childhood educator and those that more typically are engaged in collectively on behalf of the best interests of children—with the understanding that individual early childhood educators have a shared responsibility for addressing the ideals and principles that are identified as "collective."

Ideal (Individual)

1-4.1—[NL_first and last]To provide the community with high-quality early childhood care and education programs and services.

Ideals (Collective)

I-4.2—To promote cooperation among professionals and agencies and interdisciplinary collaboration among professions concerned with addressing issues in the health, education, and well-being of young children, their families, and their early childhood educators.

I-4.3—To work through education, research, and advocacy toward an environmentally safe world in which all children receive health care, food, and shelter; are nurtured; and live free from violence in their homes and their communities.

I-4.4—To work through education, research, and advocacy toward a society in which all young children have access to high-quality early care and education programs.

I-4.5—To work to ensure that appropriate assessment systems, which include multiple sources of information, are used for purposes that benefit children.

I-4.6—To promote knowledge and understanding of young children and their needs. To work toward greater societal acknowledgment of children's rights and greater social acceptance of responsibility for the well-being of all children.

I-4.7—To support policies and laws that promote the well-being of children and families, and to work to change those that impair their well-being. To participate in developing policies and laws that are needed and to cooperate with other individuals and groups in these efforts.

I-4.8—To further the professional development of the field of early childhood care and education and to strengthen its commitment to realizing its core values as reflected in this Code.

Principles (Individual)

P-4.1—We shall communicate openly and truthfully about the nature and extent of services that we provide.

P-4.2—We shall apply for, accept, and work in positions for which we are personally well-suited and professionally qualified. We shall not offer services that we do not have the competence, qualifications, or resources to provide.

P-4.3—We shall carefully check references and shall not hire or recommend for employment any person whose competence, qualifications, or character makes him or her unsuited for the position.

P-4.4—We shall be objective and accurate in reporting the knowledge upon which we base our program practices.

P-4.5—We shall be knowledgeable about the appropriate use of assessment strategies and instruments and interpret results accurately to families.

P-4.6—We shall be familiar with laws and regulations that serve to protect the children in our programs and be vigilant in ensuring that these laws and regulations are followed.

P-4.7—When we become aware of a practice or situation that endangers the health, safety, or well-being of children, we have an ethical responsibility to protect children or inform parents and/or others who can.

P-4.8—We shall not participate in practices that are in violation of laws and regulations that protect the children in our programs.

P-4.9—When we have evidence that an early childhood program is violating laws or regulations protecting children, we shall report the violation to appropriate authorities who can be expected to remedy the situation.

P-4.10—When a program violates or requires its employees to violate this Code, it is permissible, after fair assessment of the evidence, to disclose the identity of that program.

Principles (Collective)

P-4.11—When policies are enacted for purposes that do not benefit children, we have a collective responsibility to work to change these practices.

P-4.12—When we have evidence that an agency that provides services intended to ensure children's well-being is failing to meet its obligations, we acknowledge a collective ethical responsibility to report the problem to appropriate authorities or to the public. We shall be vigilant in our follow-up until the situation is resolved.

P-4.13—When a child protection agency fails to provide adequate protection for abused or neglected children, we acknowledge a collective ethical responsibility to work toward the improvement of these services.

Statement of Commitment *

As an individual who works with young children, I commit myself to furthering the values of early childhood education as they are reflected in the ideals and principles of the NAEYC Code of Ethical Conduct. To the best of my ability, I will:

> Never harm children.
> Ensure that programs for young children are based on current knowledge and research of child development and early childhood education.
> Respect and support families in their task of nurturing children.
> Respect colleagues in early childhood care and education and support them in maintaining the NAEYC Code of Ethical Conduct.

> Serve as an advocate for children, their families, and their teachers in community and society.
> Stay informed of and maintain high standards of professional conduct.
> Engage in an ongoing process of self-reflection, realizing that personal characteristics, biases, and beliefs have an impact on children and families.
> Be open to new ideas and be willing to learn from the suggestions of others.
> Continue to learn, grow, and contribute as a professional.
> Honor the ideals and principles of the NAEYC Code of Ethical Conduct.

*This Statement of Commitment is not part of the Code but is a personal acknowledgement of the individual's willingness to embrace the distinctive values and moral obligations of the field of early childhood care and education. It is recognition of the moral obligations that lead to an individual becoming part of the profession.

Reprinted by permission of the National Association for the Education of Young Children. Copyright ©2008. National Association for the Education of Young Children.

Glossary

Accommodation A concept in Piaget's cognitive theory as one of two processes people use to learn and incorporate new information.

Accommodations Alterations in the way tasks are presented or activities experienced that allow children with learning disabilities to compete the same as other children.

Active listening A child guidance technique of reflecting back to the speaker what the listener thinks has been said.

Active problem solving A principle in which adults actively engage children in confronting their differences and working together to solve their problems. The adult guides children toward solutions but does not solve problems for them. Posing open-ended questions, the adult helps children keep focused so that they can suggest alternative solutions.

Advocacy The act of supporting, pleading for, or recommending and espousing a particular action or set of ideas on behalf of early education.

Advocate Someone who furthers the principles and issues of the early childhood field by speaking to others about such issues.

Alignment Coordinated curriculum between various levels of education as well as between curriculum and learning standards.

Anti-bias A phrase describing the development of curriculum that emphasizes an inclusive look at people and problems, extending the tenets of multicultural education and pluralism.

Anti-bias A phrase describing the development of curriculum that emphasizes an inclusive look at people and problems, extending the tenets of multicultural education and pluralism.

Asperger syndrome (AS) A developmental disorder linked to autism and characterized by a lack of social skills, poor concentration, self-absorption, and limited interests.

Assessment An evaluation or determination of the importance, disposition, or state of something or someone, such as in evaluating a child's skills, a classroom environment, or a teacher's effectiveness.

Assimilation A concept in Piaget's cognitive theory as one of two processes people use to learn and incorporate new information; the person takes new information and puts it together with what is already known in order to "assimilate" the new information intellectually, such as when a toddler shakes a toy magnet first, as with all other toys, in order to get to know this new object. Children usually first try to put new experiences into the "schema," or categories, they already know and use.

Attachment The relational bond that connects a child to another important person; feelings and behaviors of devotion or positive connection.

Attention-deficit hyperactivity disorder (ADHD) A medical condition also known as attention-deficit hyperactivity disorder. It affects up to 3% to 5% of all school-age children. Children with ADHD can be difficult to manage, both at home and in the classroom. They are prone to restlessness, anxiety, short attention spans, and impulsiveness. Medication with a drug (Ritalin®) is a common treatment, but the most effective treatment appears to be a combination of medication and individual behavior management strategies.

Authoritarian Parents whose child-rearing patterns reflect high control and strict maturity demands combined with relatively low communication and nurturance. Authoritarian parents are dictatorial; they expect and demand obedience, yet lack warmth and affection.

Authoritative Parents whose child-rearing patterns are associated with the highest levels of self esteem, self reliance, independence, and curiosity in children. They provide a warm, loving atmosphere with clear limits and high expectations.

Autonomy The state of being able to exist and operate independently, of being self-sufficient rather than dependent on others.

Baby biographies One of the first methods of child study, these narratives were written accounts by parents of what their babies did and said, usually in the form of a diary or log.

Bias A personal and sometimes unreasoned judgment inherent in all our perceptions.

Bicognitive A term coined by Ramirez and Casteneda (see Chapter 4) to describe a set of experiences and environments that promote children's ability to use more than one mode of thinking or linguistic system. Each of us grows up with a preferred cognitive style, such as global or analytic, field dependent or field independent, seeing the parts vs. seeing the whole, as well as a linguistic style. For true cultural democracy to take place, we need to develop a flexibility to switch learning styles or cognitive modes (i.e., develop bicognitive abilities) and have an awareness of and respect for differing cognitive styles.

Bilingual education Varied and difficult to assess, it is a system of teaching and learning in which children who speak limited English are taught in English-speaking classrooms.

Biracial Having parents of two different races.

Checklist A modified child study technique that uses a list of items for comparison, such as a "yes/no" checklist for the demonstration of a task.

Child-centered approach The manner of establishing educational experiences that takes into consideration children's ways of perceiving and learning; manner of organizing a classroom, schedule, and teaching methods with an eye toward the child's viewpoint.

Child abuse Violence in the form of physical maltreatment, abusive language, and sexual harassment or misuse of children.

Child care The care, education, and supervision of another's child, especially in an organized center or home dedicated to the enterprise; usually denotes full-day services.

Child care centers A place for care of children for a large portion of their waking day; includes basic caretaking activities of eating, dressing, resting, and toileting, as well as playing and learning time.

Child neglect The act or situation of parents' or other adults' inattention to a child's basic health needs of adequate food, clothing, shelter, and health care; child neglect may also include not noticing a child or not paying enough attention in general.

Children with special needs Children whose development and/or behavior require help or intervention beyond the scope of the ordinary classroom or adult interactions.

Classical conditioning A form of learning in which one stimulus is repeatedly paired with another so that the second one brings forth a response.

Clinical method (*la méthode clinique*) An information-gathering technique, derived from therapy and used by Piaget, in which the adult observes and then interacts with the child[ren] by asking questions and posing ideas to see the reaction and thinking.

Compensatory education Education designed to supply what is thought to be lacking or missing in children's experiences or ordinary environments.

Confidentiality Spoken, written, or acted on in strict privacy, such as keeping the names of children or schools in confidence when discussing observations.

Conflict resolution Helping children solve disagreements nonviolently and explore alternative ways to reach their goals. By following such a process, children learn to respect others' opinions, to express their own feelings in appropriate ways, and to learn tolerance for doing things in a different way.

Constructivist A model of learning developed from the principles of children's thinking by Piaget and implemented in programs as those in Reggio Emilia, Italy, which states that individuals learn through adaptation. This model of learning posits that children are not passive receptacles into which knowledge is poured but rather are active at making meaning, testing out theories, and trying to make sense of the world and themselves. Knowledge is subjective as each person creates personal meaning out of experiences and integrates new ideas into existing knowledge structures.

Culturally appropriate curriculum Curriculum that helps children understand the way individual histories, families of origins, and ethnic family cultures make us similar to and yet different from others.

Culturally appropriate practice Curriculum that helps children understand the way individual histories, families of origins, and ethnic family cultures make us similar to and yet different from others.

Curriculum Written plan that states the goals, learning experiences, and methods for children over a period of time.

Development. The orderly set of changes in the life span that occurs as individuals move from conception to death.

Developmental domains An area of growth such as social, cognitive, or physical development.

Developmental domains The classifications of development that broadly define the three major growth areas of body, mind, and spirit that roughly correspond to biology, psychology, and sociology.

Developmentally appropriate practices (DAP) Practices that are suitable or fitting to the development of the child and are relevant and respectful to the social and cultural aspects of children and families.

Developmentally appropriate practices (DAP) That which is suitable or fitting to the development of the child; refers to those teaching practices that are based on the observation and responsiveness to children as learners with developing abilities who differ from one another by rate of growth and individual differences, rather than of differing amounts of abilities. It also refers to learning experiences that are relevant to and respectful of the social and cultural aspects of the children and their families.

Developmentally appropriate practices That which is suitable or fitting to the development of the child; refers to those teaching practices that are based on the observation and responsiveness to children as learners with developing abilities who differ from one another by rate of growth and individual differences, rather than of differing amounts of abilities. It also refers to learning experiences that are relevant to and respectful of the social and cultural aspects of the children and their families.

Diary descriptions A form of observation technique that involves making a comprehensive narrative record of behavior, in diary form.

Differentiated instruction Using different methods to teach the same concept, used to accommodate the different learning styles of individual children.

Direct guidance Methods used while interacting with children.

Discipline Ability to follow an example or to follow rules; the development of self-control or control in general, such as by imposing order on a group. In early childhood terms, discipline means everything adults do and say to influence children's behavior.

Distraction A guidance method that helps a child focus on another activity.

Documentation The furnishing and use of documentary evidence; the written comments, graphical illustrations, photos, dictation, and other work samples.

Downshifting A process by which the brain reacts to perceived threat. The brain/mind learns optimally when appropriately challenged; however, should the person sense a threat or danger (either physical or emotional), the brain will become less flexible and revert to primitive attitudes and procedures (downshift).

Dyslexia An impaired ability to read and understand written language.

Early childhood The period of life from infancy through 8 years of age.

Early childhood education Education in the early years of life; the field of study that deals mainly with the learning and experiences of children from infancy through the primary years (up to approximately 8 *years* of age).

Early Head Start Federally funded comprehensive program for low-income infants, toddlers, and pregnant women.

Ecological Having to do with the relationships between people and their environment; Bronfenbrenner's theory is explained in terms of the balance and interplay of the child and the people and settings that influence development.

Educaring A concept of teaching as both educating and care giving; coined by Magda Gerber in referring to people working with infants and toddlers.

Egocentric Self-centered; regarding the self as the center of all things; in Piaget's theory, young children think using themselves as the center of the universe or as the entire universe.

Emergent curriculum A process for curriculum planning that draws on teachers' observations and children's interests. Plans emerge from daily life interests and issues. This approach takes advantage of children's spontaneity and teachers' planning.

Emotional framework The basic "feeling" of a classroom that determines the tone and underlying sensibilities that affect how people feel and behave while in the classroom.

Environment All those conditions that affect children's surroundings and the people in them; the physical, interpersonal, and temporal aspects of an early childhood setting.

Equilibration To balance equally; in Piaget's theory, the thinking process by which a person "makes sense" and puts into balance new information with what is already known.

Ethics A series or system of oral principles and standards; what is "right" and "wrong"; one's values; the principles of conduct governing both an individual teacher and the teaching profession.

Evaluation A study to determine or set significance or quality.

Event sampling An observation technique that involves defining the event to be observed and coding the event to record what is important to remember about it.

Experimental procedure Observation technique that gathers information by establishing a hypothesis, controlling the variables that might influence behavior, and testing the hypothesis.

Faith-based school A school that teaches religious dogma.

Family-centered approach An approach to parent–school relationships that supports the growth of the family as well as the child.

Family. A family unit [15]may consist of parents who may or may not be married to each other, or who may be adoptive or foster parents, as well as grandparents, aunts, uncles, and step- or half-siblings. Two people can be considered a family, as can a collective or commune.

Family child care Care for children in a small, homelike setting; usually six or fewer children in a family residence.

Frequency count A modified child study technique that records how often a behavior occurs within a certain time frame.

Full-day child care Child care that begins in the morning and goes through the day, often arranged for the hours that parents work.

Full inclusion Providing the "least restrictive environment" for children with physical limitations.

Gender The sociocultural dimension of being female or male that includes identity and appropriate roles.

Gifted and talented Children who have unusually high intelligence, as characterized by: learning to read spontaneously; being able to solve problems and communicate at a level far advanced from their chronological age; excellent memory; extensive vocabulary; and unusual approaches to ideas, tasks, people.

Guidance Ongoing system by which adults help children learn to manage their impulses, express feelings, channel frustrations, solve problems, and learn the difference between acceptable and unacceptable behavior.

Guidance continuum A range of guidance techniques starting with the least intrusive and moving to the most intervening strategies.

Head Start Federally funded comprehensive program for low-income children who are 3, 4, and 5 years old.

Humanism Maslow's theory that describes the conditions for health and well-being in a pyramid of human needs.

Hypotheses A tentative theory or assumption made to draw inferences or test conclusions; an interpretation of a practical situation that is then taken as the ground for action.

Identity The sense of self that develops and grows more complex over a lifetime.

Inclusion When a child with a disability is a full-time member of a regular classroom with children who are developing normally as well as with children with special needs.

Inclusion When a child with a disability is a full-time member of a regular classroom with children who are developing normally as well as with children with special needs.

Inclusive curriculum A curriculum that reflects awareness of and sensitivity to a person's culture, language, religion, gender, and abilities.

Indirect guidance Creating conditions that promote optimal behavior through the intentional use of the environment and overall classroom climate.

Individualized curriculum A course of study developed and tailored to meet the needs and interests of an individual, rather than those of a group without regard for the individual child.

Individualized Education Plan (IEP) A written plan designed to meet the individual, unique needs of a child, usually 3 years and older, with identified special needs; this is done in accordance with federal IDEA act and is developed and revised by an IEP team that identifies the child's learning needs, goals, accommodations, and services that will be provided.

Inductive guidance A guidance process in which children are held accountable for their actions and are called on to think about the impact of their behavior on others. Reasoning and problem-solving skills are stressed.

Integrated curriculum A set of courses designed to form a whole; coordination of the various areas of study, making for continuous and harmonious learning.

Integrated curriculum A set of courses designed to form a whole; coordination of the various areas of study, making for continuous and harmonious learning.

Intentional teaching The ability to plan with purpose and intent and articulate the rationale for your decisions.

Interest areas Centers in a classroom or yard that are organized for learning or experiences that will interest children.

Interpersonal Relating to, or involving relationships with, other people; those parts of the environment that have to do with the people in a school setting.

Interracial Relating to, involving, or representing different races.

Kindergarten A school or class for children 4-to 6-years-old; in the United States, kindergarten is either the first year of formal, public school or the year of schooling before first grade.

Kinship networks Groups formed when people bond together and pool resources for the common good.

Laboratory schools Educational settings whose purposes include experimental study; schools for testing and analysis of educational and/or psychological theory and practice, with an opportunity for experimentation, observation, and practice.

Learning centers Areas of a classroom or yard that are organized to draw attention to specific objects or an activity.

Learning standards The level of attainment mandated by local or national government agencies that describe learning outcomes for various age groups.

Learning styles A child's preferred method of integrating knowledge and experiences.

Least restrictive environment The IDEA (Individuals with Disabilities Education Act) requirement for placing students with disabilities such that children with disabilities are educated with those who are not disabled.

Least restrictive environment The least restrictive environment (LRE) is a special education term meaning that the child should be educated in the environment that is the least different from the regular classroom as long as the child can learn in that environment.

Lesson plan A written outline that states the activity, time, materials, and resources needed to implement a learning experience.

Limits The boundaries of acceptable behavior beyond which actions are considered misbehavior and unacceptable conduct; the absolute controls an adult puts on children's behavior.

Literacy The quality or state of being able to read and write.

Log/journal A form of observation technique that involves making a page of notes about children's behavior in a cumulative journal.

Logical consequences Consequences that adults impose upon a child's actions.

Looping The practice of keeping a teacher and a group of children in a class together for two or more years.

Maturation The process of growth whereby a body matures regardless of, and relatively independent of, intervention such as exercise, experience, or environment.

Media culture The term used to describe the behaviors and beliefs characteristic of those who engage regularly with various media such as television, computers, and video games.

Mixed-age group The practice of placing children of several levels, generally one year apart, into the same classroom. Also referred to as family grouping, heterogeneous grouping, multiage grouping, vertical grouping, and ungraded classes.

Modeling The part of behaviorist theory, first coined by Bandura, that describes learning through observing and imitating an example. The model observed can be real, filmed, or animated; and the child mimics in order to acquire the behavior.

Multicultural education The system of teaching and learning that includes the contributions of all ethnic and racial groups.

Multiple intelligences A theory of intelligence, proposed by Howard Gardner, that outlines several different kinds of intelligence, rather than the notion of intelligence as measured by standardized testing, such as the IQ.

Multiple intelligences A theory of intelligence, proposed by Howard Gardner, that outlines several different kinds of intelligence, rather than the notion of intelligence as measured by standardized testing, such as the IQ test.

Narratives A major observation technique that involves attempting to record nearly everything that happens, in as much detail as possible, as it happens. Narratives include several subtypes such as baby biographies, specimen descriptions, diary descriptions, and logs or journals.

Natural consequences The real-life outcomes of a child's own actions.

Nature/nurture The argument regarding human development that centers around two opposing viewpoints; *nature* refers to the belief that it is a person's genetic, inherent character that determines development; nurture applies to the notion that it is the sum total of experiences and the environment that determine development.

Negative reinforcement Response to a behavior that decreases the likelihood that the behavior will recur; for instance, a teacher's glare might stop a child from whispering at group time, and from then on, the anticipation of such an angry look could reinforce not whispering in the future.

Neuro-education The discipline that blends neuroscience, psychology, cognitive science, and education to apply knowledge of brain function with new ways of learning and teaching.

Neuroscience The field of cognitive study that involves the brain, neural anatomy of the body, and the functions of the brain that affect development.

Norms An average or general standard of development or achievement, usually derived from the average or median of a large group; a pattern or trait taken to be typical of the behavior, skills, or interests of a group.

Objectivity The quality or state of being able to see what is real and realistic, as distinguished from subjective and personal opinion or bias.

Observational learning The acquisition of skills and behaviors by observing others.

Operant conditioning A form of learning in which an organism's behavior *is shaped by what* is reinforced.

Parent cooperative schools An educational setting organized by parents for their young children, often with parental control and/or support in the operation of the program itself.

Parents Those individuals who are raising their own biological children as well as those who are raising foster children, adopted children, or children of other family members or friends.

Permissive A child-rearing pattern that is essentially the reverse of authoritarian parents. There is a high level of warmth and affection but little control. Clear standards and rules are not set, nor are they reinforced consistently.

Play-based curriculum Curriculum that is based on observation and interactions with children as they play.

Play Human activities and behaviors that are characterized by being relatively free of rules except for what participants will impose themselves, that focuses on the activity—the doing—rather than on the end result or product, that is controlled by the participants, and that requires interaction and involvement.

Portfolio-based assessment An evaluation of a teacher's work using materials, journals, and other resources compiled over a period of time.

Portfolio An assessment method that tracks children's growth and development.

Positive guidance Method based on caring, respectful, and supportive relationships.

Positive reinforcement A response to a behavior that increases the likelihood that the behavior will be repeated or increased; for instance, if a child gets attention and praise for crawling, it is likely that the crawling will increase—thus, the attention and praise were positive reinforcers for crawling.

Power assertive methods Harsh, punitive discipline methods that rely on children's fear of punishment rather than on the use of reason and understanding. Hitting and spanking are examples of power assertion.

Professional development The process of gaining the body of knowledge and educational foundation that will help in career progression and acquiring further skills on the job.

Professionalism The competence or skill expected of a professional; in early childhood education, this includes a sense of identity, purpose to engage in developmentally appropriate practices, a commitment to ethical teaching and to child advocacy, and participation in the work as a legitimate livelihood.

Project approach An in-depth study of a particular subject or theme by one or more children. Exploration of themes and topics over a period of days or weeks. Working in small groups, children are able to accommodate various levels of complexity and understanding to meet the needs of all the children working on the project.

Psychosexual Freud's theory of development that outlines the process by which energy is expressed through different erogenous parts of the body during different stages of development.

Psychosocial Those psychological issues that deal with how people relate to others and the problems that arise on a social level; a modification by Erikson of the psychodynamic theories of Freud with attention to social and environmental problems of life.

Public Law 94-142 The Education for All Handicapped Children Act. This so-called Bill of Rights for the Handicapped guarantees free public education to disabled persons from 3 to 21 years of age "in the least restrictive" environment. In 1990 Congress reauthorized PL 94-142 and renamed it the Individuals with Disabilities Education Act (IDEA) (PL 101-576). Two new categories, autism and traumatic brain injury, were included, and children from birth to age 5 years were now eligible to receive services.

Public Law 99-457 The Education of the Handicapped Amendments Act of 1986. Sections of this law provide funding for children who were not included in the previous law: infants, toddlers, and 3- to 5-year-olds. This law also allows for the inclusion of "developmentally delayed" youngsters and leaves local agencies the opportunity to include the "at-risk" child in that definition.

Punishment The act of inflicting a penalty for an offense or behavior.

Quality A function of group size, low teacher-child ratios, trained and experienced staff, adequate compensation, and safe and stimulating environments.

Racist Attitudes, behavior, or policies that imply either a hatred or intolerance of other race(s) or involving the idea that one's own race is superior and has the right to rule or dominate others.

Rating scales A modified child study technique similar to a checklist that classifies behavior according to grade or rank, such as using the descriptors "always, sometimes, never" to describe the frequency of a certain behavior.

Readiness The condition of being ready, such as being in the state or stage of development so that the child has the capacity to understand, be taught, or engage, and thus be successful.

Redirecting Calls for the adult to make an accurate assessment of what the children really want to do, then consider alternatives that permit the desired activity while changing the expression or form it takes.

Reflective teaching Thinking about the broader meaning of teaching through reflection about your role, your attitude, and your behavior.

Reinforcement A procedure, such as reward or punishment, that changes a response to a stimulus; the act of encouraging a behavior to increase in frequency.

Reinforcers Rewards in response to a specific behavior, thus increasing the likelihood that

behavior will recur; reinforcers may be either social (praise) or nonsocial (food) in nature and may or may not be deliberately controlled.

Routines Regular procedures; habitual, repeated or regular parts of the school day; in early childhood programs, routines are those parts of the program schedule that remain constant, such as indoor time followed by cleanup and snack, regardless of what activities are being offered within those time slots.

Running record The narrative form of recording behavior that involves writing all behavior as it occurs.

Scaffolding Vygotsky's term for guidance, assistance, or cognitive structures that help a child learn.

Schemas A plan, scheme, or framework that helps make an organizational pattern from which to operate; in Piaget's theory, cognitive schemas are used for thinking.

Self-actualization The set of principles set forth by Abraham Maslow for a person's wellness or ability to be the most that a person can be; the state of being that results from having met all the basic and growth needs.

Self-assessment A teacher's own evaluation of his or her performance, strengths, and challenges for personal and professional growth.

Self-discipline Gaining control over one's own behavior.

Self-help The act of helping or providing for oneself without dependence on others; in early childhood terms, activities that a child can do alone, without adult assistance.

Sexist Attitudes or behavior based on the traditional stereotype of sexual roles that includes a devaluation or discrimination based on a person's sex.

Shadow study A modified child study technique that profiles an individual at a given moment in time; similar to diary description, the shadow study is a narrative recorded as the behavior happens.

Social cognition Bandura's theory about learning that emphasizes the cognitive processes of observational learning.

Socialization. The process of learning the rules and behaviors expected when in situations with others.

Sociocultural Aspects of theory or development that refer to the social and cultural issues; key descriptor of Vygotsky's theory of development.

Sociodramatic A type of symbolic play with at least two children cooperating in dramatic play that involves imitation and make-believe.

Specimen description A form of narrative technique that involves taking on-the-spot notes about a child or behavior (the "specimen").

Staff-to-child ratio A numerical description of the number of staff to children, which will vary depending on the age of the children and the type of program activity and is established to provide for adult supervision of children at all times.

Standards The degree or level of requirement, excellence, or attainment, mandated by local or national government or private agencies that articulate the objectives necessary for teacher preparation.

Standards The rules and principles used as a basis for judgment of quality and positive models for professional preparation, children's programs, and educational practices.

Stimulus–response The kind of psychological learning, first characterized in the behaviorist theory of Pavlov, that takes place when pairing something that rousts or incites an activity with the activity itself in a way that the stimulus (such as a bell) will trigger a response (such as salivating in anticipation of food that usually arrives after the bell is sounded).

Tabula rasa A mind not affected yet by experiences, sensations, and the like. In John Locke's theory, a child was born with this "clean slate" upon which all experiences were written.

Team teaching Group-based model of teaching, whereby a group composed of people with varying skills, experience, and training teach jointly.

Temporal Having to do with time and time sequence; in the early childhood setting, refers to scheduling and how time is sequenced and spent, both at home and in school.

Theory A group of general principles, ideas, or proposed explanations for explaining some kind of phenomenon; in this case, child development.

Time out Removing a child from the play area when, owing to anger, hurt, or frustration, the child is out of control. It is a brief respite and a chance to stop all activity and regroup.

Time sampling An observation technique that involves observing certain behavior and settings within a prescribed time frame.

Traditional nursery school/preschool The core of early childhood educational theory and practice; program designed for children aged two-and-a-half to five years of age, which may be a part- or an all-day program.

Transformative curriculum The process of viewing events and situations from diverse perspectives to gain new insights and ways of thinking in order to create more culturally appropriate curriculum.

Transition A change from one state or activity to another; in early childhood terms, transitions are those times of change in the daily schedule (whether planned or not), such as from being with a parent to being alone in school, from playing with one toy to choosing another, from being outside to being inside, etc.

Trilemma A child care issue involving quality for children, affordability for parents, and adequate compensation for staff.

Unconscious. Not conscious, without awareness, occurring below the level of conscious thought.

Universal education Education for all, regardless of race/ethnicity, culture, gender, status, sexual orientation, or religion.

Unobtrusive Not noticeable or conspicuous, in the background.

Webbing A process through which teachers create a diagram based on a topic or a theme. It is a planning tool for curriculum and includes many resources.

Whole child Based on the accepted principle that all areas of human growth and development are interrelated. The concept of the whole child suggests the uniqueness of the person. Although they are often discussed separately, the areas of development (social-emotional, physical, language, cultural awareness, intellectual, and creativity) cannot be isolated from one another.

Word Pictures Descriptions of children that depict, in words, norms of development; in this text, these are age-level charts that describe common behaviors and characteristics, particularly those that have implications for teaching children (in groups, for curriculum planning, with discipline and guidance).

Zone of proximal development The term in Vygotsky's sociocultural theory that defines which children can learn. Interpersonal and dynamic, the zone refers to the area a child can master (skill, information, etc.) with the assistance of another skilled person; below that, children can learn on their own; above the limit are areas beyond the child's capacity to learn, even with help.

Index

STANDARD 2: Building Family and Community Relationships

2a. Knowing about and understanding diverse family and community characteristics.

2b. Supporting and engaging families and communities through respectful, reciprocal relationships.

2c. Involving families and communities in their children's development and learning.

**STANDARD 3: Observing, Documenting, and Assessing
              to Support Young Children and Families**
3a. **Understanding the goals, benefits, and uses of assessment.**
3b. **Knowing about assessment partnerships with families and with professional
colleagues.**
3c. **Knowing about and using observation, documentation, and other appropriate
assessment tools and approaches.**
3d. **Understanding and practicing responsible assessment to promote positive outcomes for
each child.**

**STANDARD 4: Using Developmentally Effective Approaches to Connect with Children
              and Families**
4a. **Understanding positive relationships and supportive interactions as the foundation
of their work with children.**
4b. **Knowing and understanding effective strategies and tools for early education.**
4c. **Using a broad repertoire of developmentally appropriate teaching/learning approaches.**
4d. **Reflecting on their own practice to promote positive outcomes for each child.**

STANDARD 5: Using Content Knowledge to Build Meaningful Curriculum
5a. **Understanding content knowledge and resources in academic disciplines.**
5b. **Knowing and using the central concepts, inquiry tools, and structures of content areas or academic disciplines.**
5c. **Using their own knowledge, appropriate early learning standards, and other resources to design, implement, and evaluate meaningful, challenging curricula for each child.**

STANDARD 6: Becoming a Professional
6a. **Identifying and involving oneself with the early childhood field.**
6b. **Knowing about and upholding ethical standards and other professional guidelines.**
6c. **Engaging in continuous, collaborative learning to inform practice.**
6d. **Integrating knowledgeable, reflective, and critical perspectives on early education.**
6e. **Engaging in informed advocacy for children and the profession.**